Teach Yourself
DATABASE
PROGRAMMING
WITH JDBC
in 21 days

Peter Michaler

Teach Yourself
DATABASE
PROGRAMMING
WITH JDBC
in 21 days

Ashton Hobbs

201 West 103rd Street
Indianapolis, Indiana 46290

Publisher and President   Richard K. Swadley
Publishing Manager   Rosemarie Graham
Director of Editorial Services   Cindy Morrow
Managing Editor   Jodi Jensen
Director of Marketing   Kelli S. Spenser
Assistant Marketing Managers   Kristina Perry, Rachel Wolfe

Acquisitions Editor
Steve Straiger

Development Editor
Kristi Asher

Software Development Specialist
John Warriner

Production Editor
Tonya R. Simpson

Copy Editors
Mitzi Foster
Bart Reed

Indexer
Cheryl Dietsch

Technical Reviewer
Karen Clere

Editorial Coordinator
Katie Wise

Technical Edit Coordinator
Lorraine Schaffer

Resource Coordinator
Deborah Frisby

Editorial Assistants
Carol Ackerman
Andi Richter
Rhonda Tinch-Mize

Cover Designer
Tim Amrhein

Book Designer
Gary Adair

Copy Writer
Peter Fuller

Production Team Supervisors
Brad Chinn
Charlotte Clapp

Production
Georgiana Briggs
Cynthia Davis
Gene Redding
Ian A. Smith

Overview

Contents

Acknowledgments

My thanks go to all of the people at Sams and Sams.net Publishing who helped bring this book to completion. I also want to thank all of my employees at STEP Consulting for their constant encouragement and rattling. I also want to thank my wife for putting up with me while I wrote the book. I hope this book is informative and encourages you to learn more about developing applications in Java and JDBC.

—Ashton Hobbs

About the Author

Ashton Hobbs

Ashton Hobbs is a Consultant at STEP Consulting in Greensboro, NC. He is a Certified PowerBuilder Developer as well as a Microsoft Certified Professional. He has written several articles on both PowerBuilder and Java for various developer magazines. He is currently working on training material for a Java/JDBC course that STEP Consulting will be offering. He is also working on SchemaSQL with Dr. Sadri at the University of North Carolina at Greensboro and doing research with the Emerging Technology Group at STEP Consulting.

Tell Us What You Think!

As a reader, you are the most important critic and commentator of our books. We value your opinion and want to know what we're doing right, what we could do better, what areas you'd like to see us publish in, and any other words of wisdom you're willing to pass our way. You can help us make strong books that meet your needs and give you the computer guidance you require.

Do you have access to CompuServe or the World Wide Web? Then check out our CompuServe forum by typing GO SAMS at any prompt. If you prefer the World Wide Web, check out our site at http://www.mcp.com.

NOTE

> If you have a technical question about this book, call the technical support line at 317-581-3833.

As the publishing manager of the group that created this book, I welcome your comments. You can fax, e-mail, or write me directly to let me know what you did or didn't like about this book—as well as what we can do to make our books stronger. Here's the information:

FAX: 317-581-4669

E-mail: enterprise_mgr@sams.samspublishing.com

Mail: Rosemarie Graham
           Sams.net Publishing
           201 W. 103rd Street
           Indianapolis, IN 46290

Introduction

Who Should Read This Book?

Anyone who has some programming skill, preferably in Java, should read this book. This book is not meant to be a beginner programming book, but more of an introduction to programming using database concepts.

Software Needed

Using the code examples in the book will require several pieces of software. You can use different software products than the ones listed here, but I used the following products in writing the book:

- ☐ Symantec's dbAnywhere: Used to provide JDBC Access (http://www.symantec.com).
- ☐ Sybase's SQL Anywhere: Used as a back-end database (http://www.sybase.com).
- ☐ JavaSoft's JDBC-ODBC Bridge: Also used to provide JDBC Access (http://www.javasoft.com).
- ☐ JavaSoft's Java 1.02 and 1.1 JDK: The Java language API (http://www.javasoft.com).

How To Use This Book

This book is set up so that you can finish all of the material within three full weeks. Each day, you should spend a fair amount of time reading through the material covered in each lesson as well as looking at the examples provided in each lesson. The examples are sometimes the most important part of learning because they give instructions on how to perform certain actions.

Along with looking at the examples, taking the Quiz at the end of most lessons and performing the exercises that accompany the lesson will boost your skills in the material covered. However, this book should not be used as an end all for learning Java/JDBC. There are many topics that are not covered in this book and should be explored individually. This book is a starting point for further exploration.

Week 1

The first week, which encompasses Days 1 through 7, covers some basic database topics and introduces most of the objects available in the JDBC API. These lessons are for people who are new to database concepts and JDBC. If you are already familiar with creating and using database objects, such as stored procedures, DDL, and DML, you can skip Day 2, which covers these database basics.

Days 3 through 7 introduce some of the basic functionality provided by JDBC and describe how to use most of the objects and their methods in your own applications.

Week 2

The second week, which encompasses Days 8 through 14, teaches you how to create and use components that use JDBC. These components enable you to provide built-in database functionality to your applications. These components work, but they offer limited functionality compared to some of the commercial data components. These components should be used as examples of how to build your own components, or the components can be used as ancestors for your own components. Either way, these lessons explain some of the details of using JDBC to create usable Java objects.

Week 3

The final week of the book, which encompasses Days 15 through 21, teaches you how to create applications that use JDBC. The first applications that you will create use the Java 1.02 APIs and use standard client/server techniques for creating an application. The second application uses the Java 1.1 APIs and serialization along with the JDBC to create an object server application. These are just two of many different methods for creating applications. You can use either method or a combination of methods to create sophisticated business applications.

Conventions Used in This Book

This book contains some special elements that help you understand JDBC and concepts as they are introduced:

- ☐ Notes
- ☐ Tips
- ☐ Warnings

NOTE Notes explain interesting or important points that can make you better understand programming with JDBC.

TIP Read these boxes for useful shortcuts and techniques for effective programming.

WARNING These boxes focus your attention on pitfalls or problems that can occur in specific situations.

In addition, sometimes you will see a small arrow at the beginning of some code lines that looks like this:

➥

When you see this code continuation character, it means that a line of code is just too long to fit on a printed page, and must continue on to another line. You should type in the full line of code as if it doesn't break.

WEEK 1

At a Glance

The first seven days cover some of the basic concepts of JDBC and databases. You will be introduced to the major topics and objects available in JDBC. You will connect to a database and execute SQL statements that retrieve results and update data within the database. You also will execute and create stored procedures and dynamic SQL statements.

On Day 1, "Introduction to JDBC," you are introduced to Java and Java Database Connectivity (JDBC).

On Day 2, "Database Concepts," you learn about some basic database concepts and how to use the SQL language.

On Day 3, "Connecting to a Database," you learn how to connect Java to a database.

On Day 4, "Database Transactions," you learn some of the basics of database transactions and how to use the Sybase SQL Anywhere database.

On Day 5, "JDBC Interfaces," you are introduced to some of the basic interfaces and methods provided by the JDBC API.

On Day 6, "Prepared Statements and Callable Statements," you learn how to use dynamic SQL statements and stored procedures in Java.

On Day 7, "Result Sets and Metadata," you learn how to execute SQL statements and retrieve and access results.

Day 1

Introduction to JDBC

Java. That word has been the focus of a lot of attention and discussion among computing individuals for the past 18 months. In case you have been on Mars for the last year or so, Java is the new development language from Sun Microsystems that lets you write applications or applets that can be executed on almost any platform. Java not only enables you to develop for multiple platforms, it also enables you to develop more easily.

Along with having the capability to be executed on multiple platforms, Java applets can be executed through the use of a Web browser. This enables Java applets to be developed and used by the millions of people using the World Wide Web.

Java introduces some new constructs to developers. The language syntactically resembles C or C++, but Java is a much easier language to learn and use than either of the C languages. Java doesn't contain pointers or multiple inheritance, but C++ contains both. Both pointers and multiple inheritance cause problems to both new and advanced developers.

Java also introduces what is called *garbage collection*. This new feature in Java is a thread that runs automatically in the background of every Java program. The thread runs when processor time is available so that it does not interfere with the execution of the program. Garbage collection will search through memory and free any variables or objects that are no longer being used. An object that is out of scope is one that is no longer used and therefore has its resources freed by the thread. This lets the developer concentrate on programming instead of cleaning.

TIP

> Although Java provides garbage collection, you should always try to keep your code as clean as possible. It makes for easier maintenance and it lets others understand what you were trying to do.

Java also removes pointers from the language. A *pointer* is an address that identifies where a certain object is stored in memory. In newer programming languages, pointers are hidden from the user. In languages such as C and C++, the developer has to code for handling pointers manually. Pointers have long been a nuisance for many developers. Pointers are difficult to understand and even more difficult to debug and maintain. Java removes all pointer references from the language so that the developer can worry about what his code is doing and not where it's doing it.

Applets Versus Applications

In the previous section, I mentioned that you can develop Java applications and applets. You know what an application is, but you might be wondering what an applet is. An *applet* is simply a Java program that has been written to be used within a Web browser. A Java applet can use most of the native objects within Java, so there are limitless opportunities for the creation of applets.

Java applets do have some limitations that applications do not have. Java applets cannot access the local directory for reading or writing. This is to prevent the applet from accessing the user's local data for harmful reasons.

Java applets also have limited connections they can make on the network. Applets can only connect back to the site from which they originated. This is to prevent an applet from being used to transmit unwanted material from sites other than the current site.

Java Interfaces, Objects, and Exceptions

Java provides a variety of interfaces and objects for manipulating data and executing SQL statements against the database. Most of the interfaces in the JDBC API are used to connect to the database and execute all forms of SQL statements.

Java Interfaces

Java provides various interfaces for connecting to the database and executing SQL statements. Using the JDBC API interfaces, you can execute normal SQL statements, dynamic SQL statements, and stored procedures that take both IN and OUT parameters. Table 1.1 displays the interfaces provided in the JDBC API.

Table 1.1. JDBC API interfaces.

Interface	Description
CallableStatement	Enables you to execute stored procedures that have OUT parameters.
Connection	The interface that connects your Java application to the database.
DatabaseMetaData	Provides Java with information concerning the database.
Driver	The interface that is built specifically for each individual vendor database.
PreparedStatement	An interface used to execute dynamic SQL statements and stored procedures.
ResultSet	An interface that accepts results from a SQL Select statement.
ResultSetMetaData	An interface that provides information on a result set returned from the database.
Statement	An interface for executing normal SQL statements and stored procedures.

The CallableStatement Interface

The CallableStatement interface provides methods for executing stored procedures that return OUT parameter values. The CallableStatement object inherits the PreparedStatement object, but also adds various methods for registering parameters to be OUT parameters and also provides methods to get the parameters passed back from the stored procedure.

The `Connection` Interface

The `Connection` interface is the object that provides your Java applications with a connection to the database. This object can be used to create all of the various `Statement` objects for executing SQL statements and stored procedures. It also enables you to set the transaction properties for the connection.

The `DatabaseMetaData` Interface

The `DatabaseMetaData` interface provides various methods for getting information about the database. The interface provides methods to get the listing of tables for a specific database as well as the primary keys, columns, and various other information for specified tables.

The `Driver` Interface

The `Driver` interface object is a database-specific `Driver` object provided by the JDBC vendor. It contains specific information about connecting your Java application. It also provides information about the database (for example, the version information).

The `PreparedStatement` Interface

The `PreparedStatement` interface enables you to execute dynamic SQL statements and stored procedures. Dynamic SQL statements differ from normal SQL statements in that values in dynamic statements are not known at the time of creation. The interface lets you set the various parameters in dynamic statements with specified data values.

The `ResultSet` Interface

The `ResultSet` interface is the object that is created and used to get information from a SQL `Select` statement. A SQL `Select` statement returns a cursor that is used by the `ResultSet` interface to navigate through the results returned by the `Select` statement. It provides various methods for getting information from the different columns contained in the cursor.

The `ResultSetMetaData` Interface

The `ResultSetMetaData` interface enables you to get information about a returned result set. The `ResultSetMetaData` object is created from a `ResultSet` object and provides information specific to that object. It enables you to get the number of columns in the result set, the names and types of the columns, as well as other information pertaining to the returned `ResultSet` object.

The `Statement` Interface

The `Statement` interface is created from the `Connection` object and can be used to execute standard SQL statements and stored procedures. The object provides two main methods: `executeQuery()` and `executeUpdate()`. These methods let you execute SQL queries and SQL updates. The `executeQuery()` method will return a `ResultSet` object. This object is the ancestor for both the `PreparedStatement` and `CallableStatement` interfaces.

Java Objects

Java also provides a handful of objects that you can use in your Java applications. Most of the objects are used to provide Java with some of the database-specific data types available in most databases. Table 1.2 lists the objects in the JDBC API.

Table 1.2. JDBC API objects.

Object	Description
Date	Provides an object that can accept database `Date` values.
DriverManager	Provides another way to make a connection to the database.
DriverPropertyInfo	Used to manage `Driver` objects.
Time	Provides an object that can accept database `Time` values.
Timestamp	Provides an object that can accept database `Timestamp` values.
Types	Provides a list of predefined integer values that identify the various data types that can be used in JDBC.

The `Date` Object

The `Date` object is inherited from the normal Java `Date` object, but provides methods for accessing the various values within the `Data` object.

The `DriverManager` Object

The `DriverManager` object provides another way to make a connection to the database. The object is mainly used to manage JDBC `Driver` objects and can be used to create a connection to the database. It provides various methods for registering drivers, getting connections, and sending information to the database output stream.

The DriverPropertyInfo Object

The DriverPropertyInfo object is used mainly by advanced programmers to manage specific properties of a Driver object. It should be used only by developers who are familiar with the workings of database drivers.

The Time Object

The Time object is inherited from the Java Date object. It provides various methods for getting and setting the values from the object. It can be used to get Time data values from the database.

The Timestamp Object

The Timestamp object can be used to get data values from the database that are of the timestamp data type. The object provides various methods for comparing the values of two different Timestamp objects.

The Types Object

The Types object contains a listing of predefined integer values that identify each of the different data types available for use in JDBC applications. The values are used in different methods of the JDBC API to specify or identify the data type of particular data values.

JDBC Exceptions

When an error occurs in Java, an exception is thrown. Any Java methods that "throw" an exception must be "caught" by the user. The JDBC API contains three new exceptions that can be caught identifying various errors in executing the JDBC methods. The three JDBC exceptions are listed next.

The DataTruncation Exception

The DataTruncation exception is thrown whenever JDBC unexpectedly truncates a data value. The exception provides methods for getting information about the data value that was truncated as well as to get information about the truncation error.

The SQLException Exception

The SQLException exception is thrown by almost all methods in the JDBC API. This exception provides various methods for getting information about the error and the current state of the SQL transaction.

The `SQLWarning` Exception

The `SQLWarning` exception is generated when the database issues a warning. The warning is sent silently to the object that caused the warning to be encountered.

Problems with Java

Java gives the developer some huge benefits for developing applications, but it also has some serious drawbacks. One of the drawbacks of Java is that it does not make developing Graphical User Interface (GUI) applications easy. Java limits the user to predefined managers for laying components on the screen. It does enable developers to place components on exact positions within the window, but this defeats the purpose of programming for multiple platforms.

Java also does not provide any printing support or any of the normal functionality that users of all platforms are accustomed to. For example, Java does not provide any way to implement menu shortcuts for the user to select menu items, and it does not provide pop-up menus that can be displayed when the user right-clicks on various areas of the application. Java also does not provide cut and paste operations, which are often used by users of all platforms.

One of the main disadvantages of the Java 1.02 release was that it did not contain any support for accessing databases. This drawback limited the usefulness of Java in the business arena. However, the new release of Java, Java 1.1, provides full support for databases through JDBC.

To solve this problem of database access in Java, Sun has introduced Java Database Connectivity (JDBC). JDBC enables Java applications to connect to any database using various drivers and a new set of Java API objects and methods.

The JDBC provides various objects for connecting to a database, executing SQL statements, and executing stored procedures. JDBC also provides various objects and methods for getting information about objects within the database.

Using JDBC Instead of CGI

Until now, the only way to access a database through Java has been to use streams in Java to call and access Common Gateway Interface (CGI) programs. Calling a CGI script from Java lets you call a separate program that accesses the database and returns results.

Using this approach is slow and also lets more bugs creep into your applications. Developing in two different development languages requires the knowledge of two technologies. When you use JDBC you need to know only the Java language, whereas when you use CGI you must use Java and another language.

Another reason to use JDBC is that it is noticeably faster than the CGI approach. Using CGI usually requires that you call another program that must be executed by the computer. This separate program then accesses the database and processes the data, returning it back to the calling program in a stream. This requires multiple levels of processing, which in turn increases wait time as well as enables more bugs to appear. Figure 1.1 displays how a CGI program is executed.

Figure 1.1.
Calling a CGI script.

Whereas calling a CGI script involves actually executing a new script, usually through a Web server, executing a JDBC statement against the database requires only some sort of server that passes the SQL commands through to the database. This speeds up dramatically the time it takes to execute SQL statements. Whereas the CGI script must actually connect to the database and process the results, the JDBC solution lets your Java application have the connection to the database so that the application can perform all of the processing. Figure 1.2 displays how a JDBC statement is executed.

Figure 1.2.
Executing a JDBC statement.

Summary

Today's lesson covered some of the basics of Java and introduced you to database access with Java using JDBC. I have listed and described all of the objects within the JDBC API and have also listed some of the problems with the current release of Java.

You might currently be using CGI to provide data to your Java applications. This approach can be slow and limiting to your applications. You can develop more robust applications in Java by using Sun's JDBC API for Java.

Workshop

The Workshop provides quiz questions to help you solidify your understanding of the material covered in the lesson. You can find the answers in Appendix A, "Quiz and Exercise Answers." Try to understand the quiz answers before you go on to tomorrow's lesson.

Quiz

1. What are some of the advantages of using Java?
2. What are some of the disadvantages of using Java?
3. What language(s) does Java resemble?
4. What is garbage collection in Java?
5. What is the difference between an application and an applet?
6. What does the `Statement` interface enable you to do?
7. What does the `executeQuery()` method do?
8. What is stored in a `ResultSet` object?
9. What three exceptions can be thrown in JDBC applications?
10. What methods usually throw the `SQLException` exception?

Day 2

Database Concepts

In today's lesson, you will learn some basics about database structure and SQL concepts. Before you can learn how to use JDBC to access the database, you'll need to know how to access the database. If you already are familiar with the concepts covered today, feel free to skip to tomorrow's lesson. If you are new to databases, then this is one of the more important lessons for you to read. The topics that will be covered in today's lesson include the following:

- ☐ Database tables
- ☐ Keys
- ☐ Indexes
- ☐ Column types
- ☐ Stored procedures
- ☐ Triggers
- ☐ Catalog tables
- ☐ SQL basics (data manipulation language)
- ☐ SQL basics (data definition language)

NOTE

 This lesson uses Sybase SQL Anywhere, included on this book's CD-ROM, for all database examples. Please refer to the manual for the database you are using for the proper syntax for the SQL examples.

Database Tables

A database contains objects known as tables, which usually contain similar information on a variety of items. A table can contain information on an employee, or it can contain pictures to be displayed in a window. A table is best illustrated by a structure created in any of the various programming languages. If you have ever used C or Pascal, then you have used structures to store information. Well, a table in a database is very similar to the structure you use in programming, except that a table is an array of structures.

Tables can be one of two different types. They can be either independent or dependent tables. An *independent* table is a table that does not have any foreign key columns in its primary key. Another way to say this is that the data contained in the table is not identified using information from another table.

A *dependent* table is a table that has a foreign key column in its primary key, or is a table that depends on information from other tables to define each record in it. For example, suppose you have two tables in which to store information about employees. You have a basic table that stores the employees' names and Social Security numbers. Call this table tEmployee. The second table will store the addresses of the employees in the first table, and you call it tEmployeeAddress. The tEmployee table needs to know only the Social Security number to identify a unique employee. However, the tEmployeeAddress table needs to know the Social Security number of the employee for which it is storing an address.

You could have just put all of the employee information in one table instead of breaking it into two tables. However, it is sometimes better to split information into different tables for efficiency and maintainability reasons. There are many different forms your database can be in. Each of the forms has standard rules and requirements; the most common forms are *third normal form* and *fourth normal form*. The various database normalization forms can be found in most books on database theory.

Primary Keys

Within each table of a well-designed database, there is a column or a group of columns that forms the *primary key* for the table. The *primary key* for a table is what makes each individual record within the table unique. The primary key is usually a column that uniquely identifies the record (for example, a Social Security number for an employee or a product identification number for a particular product). The primary key can be one column, or it can be all the columns within the table.

For example, look at the information in Table 2.1. The Social Security number column, SSN, is the primary key for the table. It uniquely identifies every record contained in the table.

Table 2.1. A sample table.

SSN	FirstName	LastName
123456789	Ashton	Hobbs
234567890	Michelle	Hobbs
345678901	Cheryl	Martin
456789012	Mike	Martin

Every record contained in the table can be identified with a Social Security number. This enables you to ensure that correct information is stored, but also lets you increase the speed of database queries.

When you are creating tables, it is best to use a small primary key. Avoid using data types that can take up large amounts of space, such as LongVarChar. This is because an index is created for the primary key. Indexes are discussed in the "Indexes" section of this chapter, but having a large primary key will cause the index created for the primary key to become large as well. It is sometimes better to create a separate integer column to use as the primary key. This column is sometimes referred to as an *internal ID* column. The column does not contain any data that would be used in your application, but is used strictly as the primary key for the table. Because the column is an integer, the index for the primary key would not be as large as an index for other types of primary keys. For example, using an integer key column instead of a character column to hold a Social Security number would create an index about half as large.

 TIP

It is a good idea to spend time designing a good database model so that it will be efficient and maintainable. Time spent on a good design will save time during development and maintenance.

Figure 2.1 displays how you can create a primary key column using SQL Anywhere's SQLCentral utility. To create a primary key, select all of the columns that you want to add to the primary key and click the Add To Key button. Here, select the column EmpId and add it to the primary key. After you have clicked the button to add the column to the primary key, click the Apply button. You will notice that there is now a graphical key displayed beside the column, indicating that it is part of the primary key.

Figure 2.1.

Adding a primary key.

Foreign Keys

Along with primary keys, tables can also contain foreign keys. A foreign key can be part of the primary key in a table or a column in the non-identifying columns of the table. This relationship enables you to link information between tables. The information from one table can be used to identify information in other tables. An example of this is the employee name and address tables. The Social Security number from the employee table can be used to identify an address from the employee address table.

Foreign keys also provide a way for you to ensure that your data remains complete. Without a foreign key, you could delete an employee from the main employee table without deleting the employee's address from the employee address table. This can cause problems in your application, because you will have data that is not valid. This will cause any statistics performed on your data to be incorrect.

When you create a foreign key relationship, you must copy the entire primary key from one table to another table. Because primary keys can be one or many columns, the foreign key for a table will be at least one column.

You can create a foreign key between tables either by using the Data Definition Language or by using the SQL Central utility included with Sybase SQL Anywhere. To create a foreign key, you will first need to select the table that will contain the foreign key. After you have selected the table that will contain the foreign key, you will need to select the foreign key Properties page for the table. You will see an option for Add Foreign Key. After you select this option, a wizard will guide you through the creation of the foreign key. You will have to specify the table that will be used to get the foreign key.

After you have selected the table that will be used for the foreign key, you will need to select the columns that will match up. Figure 2.2 shows how the wizard page will look when you create a foreign key for the tEmpAddress table. Notice that EmpId is in both the primary key for the referencing table and in the foreign key for the current table. After you match the columns in the appropriate order, give the foreign key a name. The name can be almost anything, but should be representative of what the foreign key's purpose is.

Figure 2.2.

Creating a foreign key.

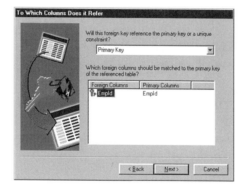

Indexes

Along with primary keys and foreign keys, a table can have multiple indexes. An *index* is basically what its name implies. It is a way to look up information arranged in a certain order. When you look up information for a business in the phone book, you can look up the information in two different indexes. You can look up the business listed alphabetically by its name, or you can look up the information by category groups in the Yellow Pages section of the phone book. The phone book, therefore, has the information listed in two different indexes: alphabetically and categorically.

The same distinction can be made for indexes used on a table. The table can have many different indexes that list data in different ways or forms. This enables your application to look up data in many different ways. Parts of your application might allow the user to look up employees by last name, while another might allow the user to look up all employees that have a Social Security number within a particular range. In the same way that you would not try to look up businesses alphabetically in the Yellow Pages of the phone book, you would not try to perform data lookup using an index that does not order the table in the required format.

One of the main advantages that indexes provide is speed. Your database queries can be sped up with multiple indexes. Most databases don't enable you to specifically choose the index to use for each query, but the database does perform a plan for the query and pick the best index available to use for the query, provided that an index exists. An index can make looking up data extremely fast. Suppose you have a table that contains one million records (not uncommon in real-world applications). Searching the table without using an index would possibly require the database to search through all of the records to find the information. Adding an index would reduce the worst-case search from searching one million rows to searching at most a couple of hundred rows, depending on the size of the index and the power of the database. Therefore, an index can dramatically speed up searching the data.

You might be wondering why you don't just add every possible index to the table that exists. The main drawback to indexes is that they require vast amounts of storage space. Indexes can be almost as large as the tables themselves. These large indexes present several problems when you are dealing with large databases. A table with one million records would have indexes that take up megabytes of space. Having every index for the table could make the table larger than most drives available today.

Another problem to look at when you are deciding if you need an index is to decide if the index will actually speed up searches. Poorly designed table indexes can actually cause the database to slow down. Whenever new items are added to a table that has an index, the index has to be updated so that it is up-to-date, with the current data stored in the table. By adding data, you possibly force the database to sort the new data item, which can be time-consuming. This slows down the database and uses resources. If you don't perform many queries on this table, then the time saved on the queries by having the index is offset by the space of the index and the time needed to re-create the index when new items are added to the table.

You can also selectively add indexes that you know will increase the speed of your queries. Instead of adding indexes to tables blindly, examine the SQL statements that you're sending to the database. If you find that you are using one particular query many times throughout your application, add an index that will cover that particular query. An index is said to *cover* a query when it contains all of the columns contained in the Where clause of the query. For example, suppose you had a query that you have run many times that retrieves information based on the Social Security number and last name of an employee. You could create an index on these two columns that would speed up the execution of all similar queries throughout the application that use these columns.

 TIP

> If you have a table that is used mainly for updates, don't add an index to it. Add indexes to tables that are used mainly for querying. Also, adding an index to a table after all or most updates have been completed can reduce the number of times the index will be re-created.

2

You can also use an index to ensure that data contained in one or more columns is unique. For example, suppose that you have the Social Security column in your table, but not as a primary key. You could add a unique index on the column to ensure that no duplicate Social Security numbers are entered. If a duplicate Social Security number is entered, the database would return an error and disallow the insertion of the record.

To create an index for a table, you can use the SQL Central utility for Sybase SQL Anywhere. Select Add Index from the Table properties. The Index Wizard initially will ask you for the name of the new index. You can name the index almost anything, but you should give it a descriptive name. The next page in the wizard will ask you for the columns that the index should contain. You can select any of the columns available within the table. You can also select whether you want those columns to be sorted in ascending or descending order. Which order you choose depends on the requirements needed within your application. After you have chosen the columns that you want to have in the index, you can specify where the index should be stored, as well as whether the index should be unique. Figure 2.3 contains the column selection page of the Index Wizard.

Figure 2.3.

The create index column selection.

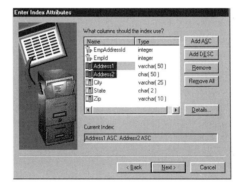

Column Types

Most databases provide a variety of column types. Different databases provide different column data types to differentiate their database from other databases currently on the market. Most databases support a standard set of column types that are covered in this section. These data types provide most of the functionality that you would need to store any form of information that your application might have. Table 2.2 contains a listing of the more common column data types used by the databases available today.

Table 2.2. Common database column data types.

Type	Description
Char	A simple character column. It can contain multiple characters.
VarChar	A column that expands to different lengths based on the size of the data.
Date	A column used to store a data value in a date format.
Time	A column used to store a data value in a time format.
DateTime	A column used to store a data value in both a date and time format.
Binary	A column used to store data values in binary format.
Decimal	A column used to store real numbers.
Integer	A column used to store integer numbers.
Numeric	A column also used to store real and integer numbers.
Timestamp	A special type of column that stores the time of any update on the record.

Char

The character column data type is used to store alphanumeric information. This column usually can vary in size from 1 to 32,000 bytes and can contain any type of alphanumeric column. The byte size of the column limits the number of characters that can be stored within the column. This column is usually used to store various string data values.

VarChar

Similar to the Char column data type, the VarChar column data type enables you to store alphanumeric data values. The main difference between the Char and VarChar data types is that the VarChar data type will reserve only as much space as is needed to hold the data. A character column that is declared to hold 100 characters will take up 100 bytes of information for every column, regardless of the size of the actual data contained within the column. The VarChar column, however, will use only as many bytes as is required to store the actual data value. This can significantly reduce the amount of space needed to store the database.

Along with the VarChar column data type, some databases offer what is known as a LongVarChar. This data type can store large amounts of alphanumeric data; usually, up to 2 to 4GB of data can be stored in a LongVarChar column. With this limit, you should be able to include any type of data within one of the columns.

2

Some databases have what is known as a Text data type. This data type is similar in functionality to the LongVarChar data types, with the exception that the Text data type requires a minimum amount of storage for every column. The Text data type generally requires a 2KB minimum amount of storage for every data value. This greatly restricts the usefulness of this data type, because the space requirements can increase the size of a database significantly.

TIP

Try to avoid using a VarChar or LongVarChar column within a primary key or index. Because these columns can require large amounts of space for data values, an index using these columns would greatly increase the size of the database.

Date

The Date column data type enables you to store data values as dates. These data values usually contain a date value in some format. The format of the data can generally be specified by the user when inserting dates. This column is useful for storing any form of date information, such as date of birth or hire date.

Some databases provide various methods or procedures for performing actions on date values. These methods enable you to get various information on date values, such as the difference between two dates in days, months, or years. They also provide you with methods for determining the literal day of a specified date value.

Time

Most databases provide a Time column data type. This data type enables you to store time values for use in your application. This column is not used as much as the DateTime column type, because when you are saving events, you will usually save the date and the time that it happened. However, using the Time data type would be useful if you want to store the times of activities that happen on a regular basis.

DateTime

The DateTime column data type enables you to store both a date and a time within a single column. The benefit of this column is that you can determine an exact time that something in the database occurred. For example, you could have a column that identifies the exact date and time that an employee was hired. This would make it easier to determine the length of service for your employees, because it would be almost impossible for two employees to be entered into the database at the exact same date and time.

Binary

The Binary column data type lets you store data values as binary streams. These binary streams can be used to hold any type of information that your application requires. The main use and advantage of the Binary column type is that it lets you store binary data such as images and sounds. This enables you to store almost all data related to items in your application within the database.

There are some databases that limit the number of bytes that is allocated for the Binary data type. However, these databases provide a column usually called Long Binary. This column type acts the same as the Binary column type, but enables you to store more binary data in the column.

Decimal

The Decimal column type enables you to store real numbers in the database. This column is very similar to the Float data type used in your applications. The size and precision offered by the Decimal column type depend on the particular database. Use this column to store any numbers that are not whole integers.

You might be thinking that you would use this column to store monetary data values. However, most databases offer either a Money or Currency column data type that is used specifically to handle monetary data values. Use either the Money or Currency column type to store your monetary entries before you use the Decimal column type.

Integer

The Integer column data type is used to store whole integer data values. An *integer value* is a value that is a whole number and that does not contain any fractional part. Most databases assign four bytes to the Integer column type, meaning that you can store up to four billion different values within the column.

Some databases also provide other integer column types that require less space. Some databases offer a SmallInt and a TinyInt. Both of these column types usually require less space than the normal Integer type. The SmallInt type usually uses two bytes of space, and the TinyInt usually uses only a single byte of space.

Numeric

Numeric column types are columns that are similar to Decimal columns, but let you specify the precision to use for the column. This data type can be useful in scientific applications where data values need to contain the same number of significant digits. Using a Decimal type would skew all data values to the maximum precision, whereas the Numeric type lets you specify how many precision digits to use.

Numeric columns are also used by most databases to create auto-incrementing columns. These columns are used to provide primary key information for the table. The database automatically increments these columns by one whenever a new record is added. This eliminates the coding you have to do to determine a new primary key for the table using this form of key.

TimeStamp

The TimeStamp column data type provided by most databases is simply a column that stores the date and time of the last update on the row. The user usually cannot edit this column, but it is changed whenever an update occurs on the record. When a record is updated or inserted, a new value is stored in the TimeStamp column. This column is useful for tracking transactions in your database, because you can determine when data was updated and inserted.

NOTE

Along with TimeStamp, most databases enable you to create a column and assign the user ID of the user who edited the data. This can make discovering data problems easier, because you can determine the time, date, and user who changed records in the database.

NULL **Data Values**

All of the column types that you just learned allow NULL values to be stored in them. NULL values sometimes present problems to beginning database users because they introduce a different type of data value. The NULL data value indicates that the current column does not apply to the current record.

A common example of a column that allows NULL values is the second address column of an address table. Most address tables provide for multiple lines of address information because some locations have multiple lines in their main address. However, most locations do not have a second line in their main address. Because they do not have this second line, the second address column will not apply to them.

A NULL value is different than an empty string. An empty string in a character column indicates that the value for the column is currently unknown, whereas a NULL value indicates that the value does not apply to the record.

When you are retrieving and updating data with SQL statements, you need to be aware of NULL values. If you perform a SQL Select statement that returns all records where a particular column is not equal to a data value, any records that have NULL as the data value will not be returned. NULL data values are used only in direct statements. You can use equality only to get records with NULL values, but inequality statements do not apply to NULL values. For example, the following statement will not return any records in which the LastName column is NULL:

```
Select *
From tEmployee
Where LastName <> "Hobbs"
```

This statement would return only records where the last name was not equal to the value "Hobbs". However, it would not return any records where the LastName was NULL, because NULL values do not apply in inequality statements. The following SQL Select statement will return all records where LastName is equal to a NULL value:

```
Select *
From tEmployee
Where LastName = NULL
```

Creating Columns and Assigning Data Types

The procedure for creating columns in each of the different databases varies from one to the other. This example describes how to create a column using Sybase SQL Anywhere, which is provided on the CD-ROM that accompanies this book. You first will create a table named tTest. This table will be used as your test table throughout the rest of the book.

After you have created the table tTest, choose the Add Column item from the right side of the SQL Central utility. The utility will then prompt you with a dialog box to enter the name and description of the column in one tab page, and the column type and any default or constraint information on the other tab page. Figure 2.4 shows the second tab page of the New Column Properties dialog box.

Figure 2.4.

*The New Column
Properties dialog box.*

Notice on the Data Type tab page that it lets you specify the data type of the column, as well as the Default and Check for the column. It provides information on whether the column is unique and also whether the column will accept NULL data values.

Most databases enable you to put a default on a column. A *default* is a value that will be inserted for you if you don't insert anything into the column. If you add a record to the database and don't specify anything for a column with a default, the default you specified for the column will be inserted into the column. This lets you provide basic information for a column. You can use the default property to assign 0 to columns that do not have an initial integer value, or an M or F to a column used for determining the sex of an employee.

The default for a column can also be AutoIncrement. AutoIncrement inserts a new value into the column for every record. This type of default is usually used on columns being used in the primary key to provide uniqueness. The database will automatically assign the next value in the column to a newly inserted record.

The Check property enables you to place certain constraints on the data that will be stored in a column. For the Sex column, for example, you want to limit the characters that can be stored in the column to M and F. Any other character stored in the column would be useless, because all employees will be either female or male. You could place a constraint on the column that requires either an M or F to be used in the column. Trying to assign any other data value to the column will result in a database error.

You can access the Advanced Column Properties dialog box by clicking the Edit button at the bottom of the Data Type tab page. The Advanced Column Properties dialog box enables you to specify the Default and Constraint properties for the column as well as specify whether the column should have NULL or unique values. Figure 2.5 displays the Advanced Column Properties dialog box used to edit the properties of the column.

Figure 2.5.

*The Advanced
Column Properties
dialog box.*

Stored Procedures

SQL provides you with a means to combine multiple SQL statements into an object that can be executed by a single command. Stored procedures are very similar to functions and procedures of common programming languages. Stored procedures enable you to combine multiple SQL statements into common functional groups and then compile these statements into procedures that are stored on the database.

Some of the main advantages of stored procedures include the capability to combine multiple SQL statements and improved speed provided by compiled procedures. When a procedure is created, the database determines the plan that it will use when executing the procedure. When you call the procedure, the database does not have to calculate how it will execute the procedure, because it has already stored the execution plan for the procedure.

Stored procedures can take multiple parameters that can be used within the stored procedure. These parameters can be IN, OUT, or INOUT parameters. IN parameters are parameters that are only allowed to be passed into the procedure. OUT parameters are parameters that are not initially specified, but can be used to pass back information to the calling object. OUT parameters enable the procedure to assign values to them and then have the user get the values assigned to them by the procedure. INOUT parameters allow you to send values and receive values from the procedure.

Figure 2.6 contains the basic stored procedure presented to you by the SQL Central utility. This utility gives you the basics needed to create a stored procedure and only forces you to provide the actual statements, parameters, and results for the procedure.

Figure 2.6.

The New Procedure window.

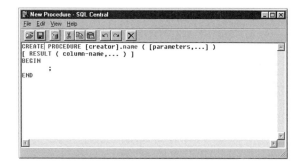

Triggers

Databases also provide what are known as *triggers*. Triggers enable you to perform specified actions when certain actions occur on data within tables. Triggers are executed whenever any update action—such as a delete, an insert, or an update—occurs on a table. Using triggers, you can have your own business logic applied to these update actions. You could use a trigger to ensure that only certain values are inserted into a table. You could also use it to prevent a delete or update from occurring if the data to be deleted or updated does not match specified criteria.

When you create triggers, you must specify the update actions for which they will be fired. You can have multiple triggers on a table that occur on different database actions. Along with specifying the action on which the trigger will be fired, most databases enable you to specify whether to fire the trigger before or after the action has occurred. A Before trigger allows actions to be performed on the data set before the update action occurs. After triggers occur after the data has been updated. If you specify that the trigger will fire before the action, then the trigger fires and, after the trigger finishes, the database action will be processed. Firing the trigger after the database action will cause the update to happen and then the trigger to be called. There are advantages to using each form of trigger, but the biggest advantage will be decided by the processing that you require from the trigger.

You can also specify whether the trigger will fire for each row updated or for each Update statement. Firing the trigger for each row enables you to control whether each individual row is updated. Using the statement-level trigger enables you to process all actions in one trigger. Updating 10 records would cause the row-level trigger to fire 10 successive times, whereas the statement-level trigger would be fired only once for the action.

Figure 2.7 displays the syntax generated by the Trigger Wizard provided by the SQL Central utility. It prompts you for information such as the name of the trigger, the action on which to fire the trigger, and other information, such as whether the trigger should fire before or after the execution of the action or whether the trigger is a row-level or statement-level trigger.

Figure 2.7.

The Create

Trigger *syntax.*

Catalog Tables

Most SQL databases contain what are known as *system catalogs.* The system catalog is a special set of tables that store information about the structure of the database and its associated objects. These system tables store information such as the names of all the tables in the database, as well as the columns associated with the tables. They also store the names of indexes and procedures. They usually store the syntax of the stored procedures as well. This is how most SQL utilities get the procedure syntax for display and editing.

Figure 2.8 displays a listing of some of the system catalog tables available within SQL Anywhere. You can access the system tables by selecting the Show System Objects property for the current database.

Figure 2.8.

*System catalog tables
in SQL Anywhere.*

SQL Basics (Data Manipulation Language)

Most databases provide two different parts of the SQL language. The first part of the language is the Data Manipulation Language. This is the part of SQL that enables you to manipulate the data contained in the database. The Select, Insert, Update, and Delete statements make up the core of the Data Manipulation Language (DML).

SQL Select

The SQL Select statement lets you query the database and get results that match the criteria you specified. There are many different options that you can use with the SQL Select statement to query the database and get results. The following list contains some of the main parts of the SQL Select statement, as well as some often-used options that you can use to limit the data more specifically:

- ☐ The Select clause
- ☐ The From clause
- ☐ The Where clause
- ☐ The Order By clause
- ☐ The Group By clause
- ☐ The Having clause

The Select Clause

The Select clause of the SQL Select statement specifies which column(s) you want returned in the result set from the database. You can return one column or all columns. The columns that are returned from the database are returned in the result set in the order they were specified in the Select statement. Therefore, the following Select clause returns FirstName and LastName in the result set (in that order). Notice that you separate columns by a comma.

```
Select FirstName, LastName
```

This example selects only two columns for the result set from the query. You can also tell the database that you want all columns returned in the result set for the query. To accomplish this, the database provides a special way to indicate that all columns from the query are to be returned into the result set. The database provides what is known affectionately as a *splat*. The splat is simply an asterisk that is specified in place of a column listing. Specifying a splat indicates that you want all columns returned in the result set. The following example indicates the use of the splat:

```
Select *
```

When you are performing queries that encompass more than one table, you will need to specify the table name before the column name. The two items will be separated by a period. This notation is used because two tables can have the same column name in them—not providing the name of the column for which to list data could pose problems for the database when it determines which column you are actually requesting. The following example uses the `FirstName` column from tEmployee and the `FirstName` column from tTempEmployee. These two columns will be returned in the result set in the order specified by the `Select` clause.

```
Select tEmployee.FirstName, tTempEmployee.FirstName
```

`Select` clauses can also return information other than data from column tables. `Select` clauses can return information such as computed column information and also various statistics that can be determined using aggregate functions provided by the database. Computed columns are simply columns that are computed by the database and returned in the result set specified. Computed columns let you return data that has been massaged to represent new data values. For example, you might have a `Price` column in a products table. When you are selecting information, you could have the sales tax added to the product and the entire price of the product displayed in the result set. This would free you from having to do the computations on the client machine. The following example will return the total price of an item, using the price of the item and a sales tax rate of 6 percent:

```
Select Price + Price * .06
```

Using computed columns can simplify the amount of processing that your local client machine has to do and also provides greater flexibility in what can be displayed to the user.

Along with computed columns, the `Select` clause can return aggregate information about the queried data. SQL provides five main aggregate functions for getting various information on queried data. The five functions provided are listed in Table 2.3.

Table 2.3. Aggregate functions.

Function	Description
AVG	A function that returns the average of a set of data values.
MIN	A function that returns the minimum of a set of data values.
MAX	A function that returns the maximum of a set of data values.
SUM	A function that returns the summation of a set of data values.
COUNT	A function that returns the number of items in the set of data values.

2

The AVG **Function**

The AVG function enables you to get an average for all of the data values contained in a specified column. The AVG function will sum all of the data values returned into the set and then divide by the number of items contained in the set. The following example returns the average price for the set returned in the Price column:

```
Select AVG(Price)
```

NOTE

> Unlike other Select statements, this Select statement will return only one value. It will only return a value that contains the average of the values in the Price column; it will not return the listing of data values in the Price column.

The MIN **Function**

The MIN function enables you to get the minimum data value returned in a set of data values. You specify the column to be checked for the minimum value just as you do for the AVG function. The MIN function returns one value for the entire set of values. The following example returns the minimum price from the set of prices returned in the result set:

```
Select MIN(Price)
```

The MAX **Function**

The MAX function enables you to get the maximum value contained in a set of data values. This function can be used to determine the maximum value that is contained within a column that is contained within a result set returned by the database. The following statement returns the maximum value contained in the Price column:

```
Select MAX(Price)
```

The SUM **Function**

The SUM function enables you to get the summation of all values contained in a column for a specified set. This function returns the value obtained by summing all of the values from the specified column. This function can be used to get the total expenditures spent on specific items, for example. The following example will return the summation of all prices for the specified set of records:

```
Select SUM(Price)
```

The COUNT **Function**

The COUNT function enables you to get the count of the items contained within a result set. It returns the number of items that were returned in the specified column. The following example will return the number of records that are contained in the specified result set:

```
Select COUNT(Price)
```

The From **Clause**

The From clause of the SQL Select statement enables you to specify which tables will be joined together to obtain data values. The clause's main function is to join the tables specified in the clause so that operations can be used on the combined tables. The tables are joined and a *Cartesian product* results. A Cartesian product contains a matrix of all the data values joined together. The following example lists the tables tEmployee and tEmpAddress. These two tables will be joined together so that limiting operations can be performed on the set of data.

```
From tEmployee, tEmpAddress
```

The Where **Clause**

The Where clause is the section of the SQL Select statement that determines which data values will be returned in the result set. The Where clause performs equality and inequality operations to limit the data that is returned in the result set. The Where clause can also perform operations to determine whether items are contained within sets of items.

The main use of the Where clause is to determine equality and inequality of items. To test for equality of items, you can use the equal sign to test the value of a column against a literal value or a data value contained in another column. The following example tests the LastName column against the literal value "Hobbs":

```
Where LastName = "Hobbs"
```

You could also have specified the equality test against a column such as the following example:

```
Where tEmployee.LastName = tTempEmployee.LastName
```

The Where clause is also used to remove items from the Cartesian product of two tables so that only matching values are displayed. For example, take the two tables tEmployee and tEmpAddress. The table tEmpAddress has the foreign key EmpId. When you join the two tables, you would get a result set containing many items that are not realistic in that they display records that have different EmpId values in the two different tables. To limit the result set to only values that match, you specify that you want only records that have matching EmpId values. This gives you a listing of only values that make sense. The following example displays how to limit the product of the Cartesian product to records that match linking columns:

```
Where tEmployee.EmpId = tEmpAddress.EmpId
```

The Where clause can also be used to test for items contained or not contained in a set of items. Using the IN keyword, you can test for data values that are within a specified range. The following example returns records that have a last name of either Hobbs or Martin:

```
Where LastName IN ("Hobbs", "Martin")
```

Along with the IN keyword, there is the NOT IN keyword, which lets you eliminate items that are contained with a particular set of data values. The following example will not display records with the last name equal to Hobbs or Martin:

```
Where LastName NOT IN ("Hobbs", "Martin")
```

In the Where clause, you can also have what are known as *outer joins*. These type of joins enable you to get information regardless of whether it matches the specified value. For example, suppose you had a table called tEmpPhone. You want to get a listing of all employees and their respective phone numbers. Some employees might not have a phone number, but you still want to display the employee. Using a regular join such as the following causes any employees who don't have a phone number to be excluded from the result set:

```
Where tEmployee.EmpId = tEmpPhone.EmpId
```

However, using an outer join enables you to get a listing of employees regardless of whether they have a phone number or not. The following example illustrates how to get all employees regardless of whether or not they have a phone number:

```
Where tEmployee.EmpId *= tEmpPhone.EmpId
```

Notice that an asterisk is used before the equal sign to indicate that this is an outer join. You can also have the outer join in the opposite direction to give a listing of phone numbers with employees.

Nested SQL Statements

Within the Where clause, you can also use nested SQL statements to provide criteria with which to limit the result set returned. Nested SQL statements enable you to provide dynamic data values with which to compare column data to. You can have multiple levels of nesting to give you as much flexibility as you need for your queries. The following example displays all employees who live in the state of North Carolina:

```
Select FirstName, LastName
From tEmployee
Where EmpId IN (Select EmpId
```

```
From tEmpAddress
Where State = "NC")
```

The Order By Clause

The Order By clause of the SQL Select statement lets you sort the items in the result set before returning them to the user. The result set can be sorted based on any number of the columns contained within the result set. The columns can be sorted in either ascending (ASC) or descending (DESC) order. You must specify which type of sorting will be used for each column in the Order By clause. The result set is sorted by the first column in the Order By clause, and then the second, and so on. The following example sorts each of the employee's names, first by last name and then by first name.

```
Select FirstName, LastName
From tEmployee
Order By LastName ASC, FirstName ASC
```

Figure 2.9 contains the display of the Interactive SQL (ISQL) utility provided with Sybase SQL Anywhere. At the bottom of the display you will see the preceding SQL statement. In the Data window of Interactive SQL, you will see the employees from the table tEmployee. Notice that the results are sorted first by last name and then by first name.

Figure 2.9.

Results from the
Order By *clause.*

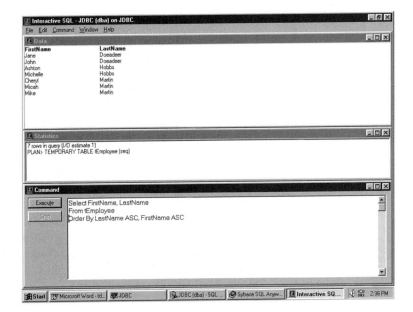

The Group By Clause

The Group By clause enables you to group employees based on a particular grouping. For example, you could have results returned so that all records are grouped with their respective state. You could also group employees by their department. The following example returns all employees from the tEmployee table grouped by their last name first and then the other columns.

```
Select *
From tEmployee
Group By LastName, FirstName, MiddleInitial, SSN, EmpId
```

The results will be returned with other results that match the specified grouping. Figure 2.10 displays the ISQL utility that contains the sample SQL statement as well as the returned results. Notice that the records are returned together with other results that match the grouping in the SQL statement.

Figure 2.10.

The Group By *results.*

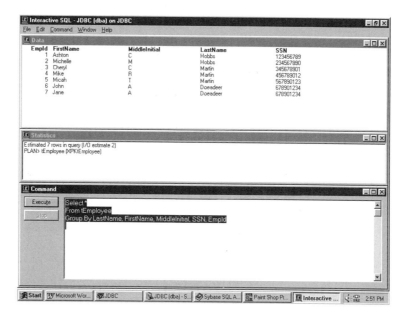

The Having Clause

The Having clause of the SQL Select statement enables you to return results that have values matching specified values. The aggregate functions mentioned earlier can be used in the Having clause. Therefore, you could return results that have a value greater than the average for all data values. The following example returns a listing of all grouped employee records that have an average for the group that is greater than 2:

```
Select EmpId
From tEmployee
Group By EmpId
Having AVG(EmpId) > 2
```

SQL Delete Statements

SQL provides a statement that enables you to delete records from database tables. You can use the SQL Delete statement to delete records from tables blindly or to delete records that match specified criteria. The statement is very simple to execute. It can use most of the clauses that are provided by the SQL Select statement, such as the From and Where clauses. The Delete clause of the statement can be either blank or contain one table name. If no table is specified, then the one table specified in the From clause will be used to delete items. If a table is specified in the Delete clause, then that table will have items deleted from it.

TIP   You need to specify only the table name in the Delete clause if you are using multiple tables to determine the records to delete.

The following example deletes all records from the tEmployee table:

```
Delete
From tEmployee
```

Notice that I did not specify a table in the Delete clause, and I did not specify any criteria for deleting. This would cause all records in the table to be deleted.

The following example deletes all employees that do not have a phone number listed in the tEmpPhone table:

```
Delete tEmployee
From tEmployee
Where tEmployee.EmpId NOT IN (Select EmpId
            From tEmpPhone)
```

This statement uses a nested SQL Select statement to provide the criteria to use for deleting items. You also use the NOT IN clause to tell the Delete statement that you want only records that are not in tEmpPhone, or employees who do not have phone numbers.

The SQL Update Statement

SQL provides an Update statement to let you update records currently in the database with new values. The Update statement contains three main clauses. The first clause enables you to specify the table that you will be updating. The second clause enables you to specify the columns that you will be updating as well as the new data values that you will be placing in these columns. The third clause of the Update statement enables you to specify criteria for the records that you want to update.

The first clause is where you specify which table you will be updating. The following syntax would update the tEmployee table:

```
Update tEmployee
```

The second clause of the Update statement enables you to specify which columns you will be updating as well as the new data values to place in these columns. You must use the SET keyword to indicate that you are setting the column to the new data values. You can update multiple columns in one Update statement by separating the columns with a comma. The following Set clause sets the values for the FirstName column and LastName column, respectively, to "Ashton" and "Hobbs":

```
SET FirstName = "Ashton",
    LastName = "Hobbs"
```

The final clause of the SQL Update statement is the Where clause. This is the clause that determines which records will be updated. The following Where clause updates any record that has an EmpId column with the data value 1:

```
Where EmpId = 1
```

So, the full Update statement to update any records that have EmpID = 1 for tEmployee would be as follows:

```
Update tEmployee
Set FirstName = "Ashton",
    LastName = "Hobbs"
Where EmpId = 1
```

The SQL Insert Statement

The SQL Insert statement lets you insert new records into database tables. You can insert records one at a time by specifying the data values directly, or you can insert multiple columns by using a Select statement to provide the data values. The Select statement must return columns that match the column listing provided by the Insert statement.

When you use the Insert statement, you can either leave the column listing off, or you can specify which columns you will be inserting data into. It is always best to specify the columns because this insulates you from database changes. If you leave off the column listing, then the Insert statement expects all columns to be specified in the proper order. The following is the Insert clause for an Insert statement that expects all column data to be provided for the table in the correct order:

```
Insert Into tEmployee
```

However, using the column names to identify which data values you will specify and also the order in which you will specify them gives you more flexibility in how you create SQL statements. The following example specifies the columns for which you will be providing data:

```
Insert Into tEmployee (LastName, FirstName, SSN)
```

The second part of the Insert statement is the section in which you specify the data that will be inserted into the database. You can either specify a single record's worth of data, or you can insert multiple records using a SQL statement. The following example inserts only a single record of data into the table:

```
Insert Into tEmployee (LastName, FirstName, SSN)
Values ("Doe", "John", "123456789")
```

The Values keyword was specified to indicate that the values are to be inserted manually. Using a Select statement, however, you can insert many records into the database using one Insert statement. The following example inserts all records from the imaginary table tTempEmployee into the table tEmployee using a Select statement:

```
Insert Into tEmployee (LastName, FirstName, SSN)
Select T.LastName, T.FirstName, T.SSN
From tTempEmployee T
```

SQL Basics (Data Definition Language)

Along with the Data Manipulation Language of SQL, there is also the Data Definition Language (DDL). The DDL enables you to create objects within the database such as tables, stored procedures, and indexes. It also enables you to destroy any objects that you created. Using Sybase SQL Anywhere, you will probably prefer to use the SQL Central utility to create all tables, but you could use ISQL to create tables within the database using DDL.

This section goes over some of the basics of the DDL. You will learn about the following DDL topics:

- [ ] CREATE TABLE
- [ ] DROP TABLE
- [ ] CREATE PROCEDURE
- [ ] DROP PROCEDURE
- [ ] CREATE INDEX
- [ ] DROP INDEX
- [ ] CREATE TRIGGER

CREATE TABLE

Not only can you use the SQL Central utility to create tables, but you can also create them directly using SQL Data Definition Language. The DDL lets you create tables and is usually used more than the graphical creation utilities because it allows for faster creation of large databases.

Most industrial databases are modeled with a data modeling tool such as S-Designer or ERWin. Both of these tools enable you to design the database graphically; then the utility generates the DDL for you to execute manually, or both of these programs enable you to have the program connect to the database and execute the DDL for you.

 TIP

I strongly suggest that you spend time designing your database. A good database will provide you with more speed and be easier to maintain. Having to make database changes during the design of your application can make for easier maintenance.

When you create a table, you specify the table name that you want to create. This table name can be almost anything that you want, provided that it uses characters allowed in table names by the database. You specify the table name directly after the CREATE TABLE command.

You also specify the columns that your table will contain. When you specify columns, you specify the column name along with the column data type. To add multiple columns, you can separate the column definitions by commas. The following example creates a table named tTest. It creates two columns for the table named TestId and TestName. The TestId column will be an integer, and the TestName column will be a VarChar column with a maximum length of 200 characters.

```
CREATE TABLE tTest (
    TestId     integer,
    TestName   varchar(200)
)
```

DROP TABLE

Along with creating a table, you can drop a table using the SQL DROP TABLE statement. This statement removes the table definition from the database. Using the DROP TABLE statement is different from deleting all of the records in the table. Deleting all of the records leaves the table but removes the records, whereas using the DROP TABLE command deletes all records and also removes the table so that it cannot be used any longer. Before you can drop a table, though, you will have to ensure that any columns in other tables that depend on this table have also been dropped or have had the constraints removed. The syntax for dropping a table is as follows:

```
DROP TABLE tTest
```

WARNING

After you drop a table, it is deleted along with all of the data contained in the table. Unlike the Delete statement, using the DROP TABLE command does not let you roll back changes to the database. After the table is dropped, it is gone for good. It is a good idea to use the Select Into statement to make a duplicate of the table before you drop it completely. You can always use the backup table to repopulate the table.

CREATE PROCEDURE

Along with creating tables using DDL, you can also create stored procedures for use in your applications. The basic syntax for creating a stored procedure is as follows:

```
CREATE PROCEDURE [creator].name ( [parameters,...] )
[ RESULT ( column-name,... ) ]
BEGIN
        ;
END
```

The DDL for creating a stored procedure uses the CREATE PROCEDURE SQL command to create the basic procedure. Within the DDL, you specify the parameters that the stored procedure takes as well as the result set that is returned. All SQL commands are placed between the BEGIN and END blocks of the procedure.

NOTE   The syntax for creating stored procedures for your particular database might differ. Consult your user's manual for the appropriate syntax.

2

DROP PROCEDURE

Along with creating stored procedures, you can also drop or delete stored procedures from the database. Dropping a stored procedure will remove both the procedure definition from the catalog tables and the compiled procedure object from the database. The syntax for dropping a procedure is as follows:

```
DROP PROCEDURE name
```

CREATE INDEX

To create indexes, you can either use the SQL Central utility, or you can create them directly using DDL. Using DDL enables you to create multiple indexes on multiple tables more quickly than by using the SQL Central utility. However, if you are new to creating indexes, you should use the SQL Central utility to create the index because it provides a wizard to walk you through the creation of an index.

To create an index in DDL, you must specify a name for the index as well as whether the index will be unique. A unique index specifies that all data values in the index will be unique. Along with the name for the index, you must provide the name of the table on which you will create the index. Indexes must be created for a table and cannot be created across multiple tables. After you have specified the index name and table name, you must identify the columns that make up the index and whether they should be sorted in ascending or descending order. The syntax for creating a stored procedure is as follows:

```
CREATE [UNIQUE] INDEX index-name
   . . . ON table-name
   . . . ( column-name [ ASC ¦ DESC ], ... )
```

DROP INDEX

Dropping an index is very similar to dropping a stored procedure or a table. You need to specify the DROP command and then the INDEX keyword to indicate that you are dropping an index rather than a table or procedure. You then need to specify the index that you will be dropping. After you drop the index, the index definition is removed from the system catalog and the actual index is removed from the database. The syntax for dropping an index is as follows:

```
DROP INDEX index_name
```

CREATE TRIGGER

Along with the Trigger Wizard provided by the SQL Central utility, you can also create triggers directly using DDL. The syntax for creating a trigger involves specifying the trigger name and the various options provided for triggers. Use the following syntax to create triggers:

```
CREATE  TRIGGER  trigger-name  trigger-time  trigger-event,...
    . . .    [ ORDER integer ]  ON  table-name
    . . .    [ FOR EACH { ROW ¦ STATEMENT } ]
    . . .    [ WHEN ( search-condition ) ]
    . . .    [ IF UPDATE (column-name)
    . . .    [ {AND ¦ OR} UPDATE (column-name) ] . . . ]
    . . .    compound-statement
    . . .    [ ELSE IF UPDATE (column-name)
    . . .    [ {AND ¦ OR} UPDATE (column-name) ] . . .
    . . .    compound-statement
    . . .    ENDIF ]   ]
```

Summary

In this lesson you have learned some of the basics of using databases and SQL. Now that you have a basic understanding of these concepts, you can begin to learn JDBC. Today's lesson has only touched on a portion of the power and functionality provided by databases. They are capable of many things that were not addressed in this lesson.

I urge you to look at the manual specific to your database to learn more about the power your database offers. By knowing what your database can do, you will be able to design and develop better applications using JDBC or any other connectivity.

Workshop

The Workshop provides quiz questions to help you solidify your understanding of the material covered and exercises to give you experience in using what you've learned. The answers are provided in Appendix A, "Quiz and Exercise Answers." Try to understand the quiz and exercise answers before you go on to tomorrow's lesson.

Quiz

1. What is a primary key?
2. What is a foreign key?
3. What is a `VarChar` column?
4. What is the difference between `Decimal` and `Numeric` columns?
5. What three types of parameters can you pass into a stored procedure?
6. When can triggers be executed?
7. What is the difference between row-level and statement-level triggers?
8. What is Data Definition Language?
9. What is the syntax for dropping a table using DDL?
10. What information does the system table contain?

Exercises

1. Create a stored procedure that takes in an `IN` parameter value and returns it in an `OUT` parameter value.
2. Create a table named tTempTable that contains two columns: `TempId` and `TempName`. Use DDL to create the table. After you have created the table, go into the SQL Central utility and make `TempId` an `AutoIncrement` column. When you have finished creating the table, drop the table using DDL.
3. Display the system tables for the current database. After the tables are displayed, look at the data contained in the SYSTABLE table.

Day 3

Connecting to a Database

Today's lesson introduces you to the JDBC objects and interfaces that enable you to connect to a database. The JDBC Driver interface and the DriverManager object can both be used to create a connection to the database.

For today and for most of the book, you will be using the dbAnywhere JDBC product from Symantec and the Sybase SQL Anywhere relational database from Sybase. However, these two products are not the only products that can be used for JDBC applications.

Today's lesson covers the following topics:

- [ ] JDBC solutions
- [ ] The Driver interface
- [ ] The DriverManager object
- [ ] The Connection object
- [ ] Native and ODBC data sources

JDBC Solutions

In the introduction to this lesson, I mentioned that you would be using the dbAnywhere JDBC product. This product from Symantec provides you with the needed database drivers to connect your Java applications to various databases. The product comes with a server application that enables the JDBC statements and commands to be passed from the Java application to the specified database product.

Along with dbAnywhere, there are several other JDBC drivers that you can use. Table 3.1 lists some of the vendors who provide JDBC drivers. This table also lists the vendors' products.

Table 3.1. JDBC driver products.

Vendor	Product
Agave Software Design	JDBC Net Server
Asgard Software	Open/A for Java
Borland	InterClient
Connect Software	Connect
DataRamp	Client for Java
IBM	DB2 Client Support
Imaginary	mSQL-JDBC Driver
InterSoft	Essentia-JDBC
Intersolv	DataDirect
JavaSoft	JDBC-ODBC Bridge
OpenLink	JDBC Drivers
SAS	SHARE*NET
SCO	SQL-Retriever
StormCloud Development	WebDBC 3.0 Enterprise
Symantec	dbAnywhere
Visigenic	VisiChannel for Java
WebLogic	jdbcKona, jdbcKonaT3

The dbAnywhere product includes the JDBC API and also includes a server application that acts as a passthrough for all the SQL statements. Your application uses the dbAnywhere product to send SQL statements from your application to the database specified by the URL.

The dbAnywhere product comes with the JDBC API classes. However, these classes are in a package different than the proposed package. JavaSoft has proposed that the JDBC API be included in the `java.sql` package. However, dbAnywhere includes all of the JDBC API in the `symjava.sql` package. This was done for security reasons because the current crop of browsers don't let packages that have the form `java.*` to be used.

NOTE

> In all of the applications throughout this book, the `symjava.sql` package will be imported. After Symantec changes the dbAnywhere product to use the appropriate package, you'll need to change all of the import statements for the examples to use the `java.sql` package in place of the `symjava.sql` package.

To use the dbAnywhere product, you first need to start the database you'll be using. After you start the database, you need to start the dbAnywhere application server, and after you start the dbAnywhere server, you can begin any application that will use the dbAnywhere driver.

The `Driver` Interface

JDBC provides you with two different objects for handling database drivers. A *database driver* is an object specific to a database that defines how statements are executed against that particular database. The first object JDBC provides is the `Driver` interface.

The `Driver` interface provides various methods for getting information about the current database driver as well as providing the `connect()` method, which creates a `Connection` object that can be used to access the database.

The `Driver` interface provides the methods shown in Table 3.2 for use in your Java applications. The table lists all of the methods for the `Driver` interface and their descriptions.

Table 3.2. The `Driver` interface methods.

Method	Description
acceptsURL	Returns a Boolean value indicating whether the driver can connect to the specified URL.
connect	Creates a connection to the database and returns a `Connection` object for the application to use.
getMajorVersion	Gets the major version of the driver.
getMinorVersion	Gets the minor version of the driver.

continues

Table 3.2. continued

Method	Description
getPropertyInfo	Determines the base properties required from the user to create a connection using the current driver.
jdbcCompliant	Returns a Boolean value indicating whether the current Driver object is JDBC-compliant.

acceptsURL()

The acceptsURL() method of the Driver object enables you to determine whether the current object can make a connection to the database at the specified URL. The method takes a String parameter that contains the URL of the database to which you want to connect. If the Driver object can successfully create a connection to the specified URL, then the method will return true; otherwise, it will return false. Listing 3.1 contains a sample application that lets you determine whether a specified URL is valid for a database connection.

TYPE   **Listing 3.1. The CheckURL example.**

```
import symjava.sql.*;

public class CheckURL {
    public CheckURL () {

        try {
            String driverName = "symantec.itools.db.jdbc.Driver";
            Driver driver =  (Driver)Class.forName(driverName).newInstance();
            String dbURL = "jdbc:dbaw://localhost:8889/WATCOM/JDBC/JDBC";
            // Check whether Driver can connect to URL
            if (driver.acceptsURL(dbURL)) {
                System.out.println("URL is valid");
            }
            else {
                System.out.println("URL is not valid");
            }
        }
        catch (Exception e) {}
    }

    public static void main (String args[]) {
        CheckURL app = new CheckURL();
    }
}
```

3

connect()

The connect() method of the Driver object enables you to create a physical connection to the database located by a specified String parameter. The method takes two parameters. The first parameter specifies the URL of the database to which a connection should be made. This URL is in the form of a String object and can be any valid database that the current Driver object supports. The second parameter is a Properties object that contains various items needed to connect to a specific database. These items normally include a username and password, but can include other items, as well.

Listing 3.2 demonstrates how to create a connection to a database using the connect() method of the Driver object.

Listing 3.2. connect() example.

```
import symjava.sql.*;
import java.util.*;

public class Connect {

    public Connect () {
        try {
            String driverName = "symantec.itools.db.jdbc.Driver";
            Driver driver = (Driver)Class.forName(driverName).newInstance();
            // Create a properties object and add username and password
            Properties p = new Properties();
            p.put("user", "dba");
            p.put("password", "sql");
            // Specify a Url for the database
            String dbURL = "jdbc:dbaw://localhost:8889/WATCOM/JDBC/JDBC";
            Connection c = driver.connect(dbURL, p);
        }
        catch (Exception e) {}
    }

    public static void main (String args[]) {
        Connect app = new Connect();
    }
}
```

getMajorVersion() **and** getMinorVersion()

The getMajorVersion() and getMinorVersion() methods enable you to determine the current version information for the Driver object. This enables you to determine whether you have the latest driver version from the manufacturer. Sometimes, problems arise due to incorrect version drivers; these methods can enable you to determine whether the current version is the correct version. Both of the methods return the version information as integer values. Listing 3.3 contains a sample application that outputs the current major and minor version of the Driver object.

TYPE **Listing 3.3. Version example.**

```
import symjava.sql.*;

public class Version {

    public Version () {
        try {
            String driverName = "symantec.itools.db.jdbc.Driver";
            Driver driver = (Driver)Class.forName(driverName).newInstance();
            System.out.println("Driver version is " +
                Integer.toString(driver.getMajorVersion()) +
                "." + Integer.toString(driver.getMinorVersion()));
        }
        catch (Exception e) {}
    }

    public static void main (String args[]) {
        Version app = new Version();
    }
}
```

getPropertyInfo()

The getPropertyInfo() method enables you to get the current property items, such as the username and password, for the Driver object. Using this method enables you to determine which items must be specified in order to make a connection to the database.

The getPropertyInfo() method returns an array of DriverPropertyInfo objects. These objects contain various object fields or variables that store information such as the name of the property, description, whether the property is required, and the current value of the property. Using this method enables you to prompt the user to enter the value required by the database.

Listing 3.4 outputs a listing of all the properties required for the current driver to create a connection to a database. It lists the names of all the properties that are needed by the system. Listing 3.4 contains the DBProperty example.

TYPE **Listing 3.4. The** `DBProperty` **example.**

```
import java.util.*;
import symjava.sql.*;

public class DBProperty {

    public DBProperty () {
        try {
            String driverName = "symantec.itools.db.jdbc.Driver";
            Driver driver = (Driver)Class.forName(driverName).newInstance();
            String dbURL = "jdbc:dbaw://localhost:8889/WATCOM/JDBC/JDBC";
            DriverPropertyInfo p[] =
            ➥driver.getPropertyInfo(dbURL, new Properties());
            for (int i = 0; i < p.length; i++) {
                System.out.println("Required - " + p[i].name);
            }
        }
        catch (Exception e) {}
    }

    public static void main (String args[]) {
        DBProperty app = new DBProperty();
    }
}
```

---

jdbcCompliant()

The `jdbcCompliant()` method enables you to determine whether the current driver being used is a JDBC-compliant database driver. A driver is fully JDBC-compliant if it supports all of the JDBC API objects and methods and also provides ANSI SQL 92–level functionality. ANSI SQL 92 is entry-level support for basic SQL operations. Most databases add their own extensions such as Transact-SQL and PSQL. The method returns a Boolean indicating whether the current driver is JDBC-compliant.

```
Boolean b = driver.jdbcCompliant();
```

The DriverManager Object

The `DriverManager` object provides services for managing `Driver` objects. The `DriverManager` object will look in the `jdbc.drivers` system property. This enables you to specify different JDBC drivers for different applications. You can access the system properties using the `getProperties()` method of the `System` object. After you have changed the value for the `jdbc.drivers` property, you can set the system properties using the `setProperties()` method.

Table 3.3 lists all of the methods in the `DriverManager` object and their descriptions.

Table 3.3. The `DriverManager` **methods.**

Method	Description
`deregisterDriver()`	Removes a `Driver` object from the list of drivers.
`getConnection()`	Creates a connection to the database.
`getDriver()`	Finds a `Driver` object that will connect to the specified URL.
`getDrivers()`	Returns an array containing all of the `Driver` objects currently registered with the manager.
`getLoginTimeout()`	Returns the number of seconds a driver will wait for a connection.
`getLogStream()`	Returns the logging/tracing stream that the manager will use for the `Driver` objects.
`println()`	Sends the specified string to the current log stream.
`registerDriver()`	Registers the specified `Driver` object with the manager.
`setLoginTimeout()`	Sets the maximum number of seconds that a driver will wait for a connection.
`setLogStream()`	Sets the logging/tracing stream that the `Driver` objects will use.

deregisterDriver()

The `deregisterDriver()` method of the `DriverManager` object enables you to remove a `Driver` object from the current list of objects maintained by the `DriverManager`. This method complements the `registerDriver()` method, which is used to add a `Driver` object to the list of objects maintained by the `DriverManager`. The following example illustrates how to deregister a `Driver` object:

```
DriverManager.deregisterDriver(symantec.itools.db.jdbc.Driver);
```

The getConnection() Methods

The `DriverManager` object provides three different methods for creating a connection to the database. Each of the three methods creates a connection and returns a `Connection` object, but each method takes a different set of parameters.

The first `getConnection()` method takes only the URL for a database. It will try to connect to the specified database using the current `Driver` object or an appropriate `Driver` object from the list of registered `Driver` objects. This method assumes that no username, password, or any other database property is required to form a connection to the database.

3

The second getConnection() method takes the URL of the database, but also takes a Properties object that contains various database properties needed to connect to the database. The second parameter must be a Properties object that contains the items needed to make a connection to the specified database.

The final getConnection() method takes the URL of the database like the other methods, but instead of taking a Properties object, this method takes two String objects. The first string identifies the username with which to connect to the database. The second string contains a password that should be used for the given username when the DriverManager makes a connection to the database.

The following example illustrates how to make a connection to a database using the third getConnection() method. The example specifies a username and password that will be used to create a connection to the database. Listing 3.5 contains the code for the ManagerConnect example.

TYPE **Listing 3.5. The ManagerConnect example.**

```
import java.util.*;
import symjava.sql.*;

public class ManagerConnect {

    public ManagerConnect () {
        try {
            String driverName = "symantec.itools.db.jdbc.Driver";

            // Set the log stream for the manager
            DriverManager.setLogStream(System.out);

            // Get the current system properties
            Properties system = System.getProperties();
            system.put("jdbc.drivers", driverName);
            System.setProperties(system);

            // Create the URL, username, and password strings
            String dbURL = "jdbc:dbaw://localhost:8889/WATCOM/JDBC/JDBC";
            String user = "dba";
            String pass = "sql";

            // create the connection
            Connection c = DriverManager.getConnection(dbURL, user, pass);
        }
        catch (Exception e) {}
    }

    public static void main (String args[]) {
        ManagerConnect app = new ManagerConnect();
    }
}
```

getDriver()

The getDriver() method of the DriverManager object enables you to get a Driver object from the registered drivers of the DriverManager that allows a connection to a specified database. The method takes a URL to a database as a parameter. The getDriver() method returns a Driver object currently registered with the DriverManager object that can create a connection to the specified URL. The following code shows how to use the getDriver() method:

```
String dbURL = "jdbc:dbaw://localhost:8889/WATCOM/JDBC/JDBC";
Driver driver = DriverManager.getDriver(dbURL);
```

getDrivers()

The getDrivers() method of the DriverManager object enables you to get an array of all the Driver objects currently registered with the DriverManager object. This enables you to manually get and manage all of the Driver objects known to the DriverManager. You can then use the Driver objects for any processing needed in your application. The following example gets an array of all Driver objects currently registered with the DriverManager object:

```
Driver driver[] = DriverManager.getDrivers();
```

getLoginTimeout()

The getLoginTimeout() method enables you to get the current timeout being used by all of the Driver objects in the DriverManager. The timeout is the time in seconds that the Driver object will wait while attempting to connect to a database. If it takes longer than the current timeout to make a connection to the database, then the Driver object will fail. The following code illustrates how to get the current timeout for the Driver objects:

```
int seconds = DriverManager.getLoginTimeout();
```

getLogStream()

The getLogStream() method for the DriverManager object enables you to get the current logging/tracing stream being used by the Driver objects in the DriverManager. The *log stream* is the stream in which all errors and information generated by the Driver object are sent. This stream could be the System.out stream, or it could be any other type of stream, such as a file stream, that outputs information to a file. The following example illustrates how to use the getLogStream() method:

```
OutputStream ostream = DriverManager.getLogStream();
```

println()

The println() method of the DriverManager performs the same functionality as the println() method for the stream objects. This method sends the specified string to the current log stream for the DriverManager. You can use this method to output information to the user concerning database activity. This method is especially helpful for developers because it can enable you to send output whenever certain conditions are encountered. The following code displays an example of using the println() method:

```
DriverManager.println("Error connecting to database");
```

registerDriver()

The registerDriver() method for the DriverManager enables you to register a specific Driver object with the DriverManager. Registering a Driver object enables it to be used by the DriverManager methods that attempt to determine whether certain database URL addresses can be reached using the available driver list. Listing 3.6 contains an example that registers a Driver object with the DriverManager.

TYPE | **Listing 3.6. Registering a driver.**

```
import symjava.sql.*;

public class Register {

    public Register () {
        try {
            String driverName = "symantec.itools.db.jdbc.Driver";
            Driver driver = (Driver)Class.forName(driverName).newInstance();
            DriverManager.registerDriver(driver);
        }
        catch (Exception e) {}
    }

    public static void main (String args[]) {
        Register app = new Register();
    }
}
```

setLoginTimeout()

The setLoginTimeout() method for the DriverManager object enables you to set the timeout that will be used by the Driver objects registered with the DriverManager when the DriverManager connects to a database. The timeout specifies how many seconds the Driver object will wait for a connection to the database. The following code sets the timeout used by the Driver objects in the DriverManager to 30 seconds:

```
DriverManager.setLoginTimeout(30);
```

setLogStream()

The setLogStream() method for the DriverManager object enables you to set the logging/ tracing stream that will be used by all Driver objects. The log stream is where all errors and information generated by the Driver objects are sent. The example in Listing 3.7 tells the DriverManager object to send all logging information to the file ERROR.DAT.

TYPE   Listing 3.7. Logging example.

```
import symjava.sql.*;
import java.io.*;

public class Logging {

    public Logging () {
        try {
            PrintStream p = new PrintStream(new FileOutputStream("ERROR.DAT"));
            DriverManager.setLogStream(p);
        }
        catch (Exception e) {}
    }

    public static void main (String args[]) {
        Logging app = new Logging();
    }
}
```

The Connection Object

The Connection object is the main object used to provide a link between the database and your Java applications. The Connection object enables you to create all of the Statement objects to use for executing SQL statements and getting results from the database.

You can use both the Driver object and the DriverManager object to create a Connection object. You can use the connect() method for the Driver object or the getConnection() method for the DriverManager object to create a Connection object to use in your applications.

The `Connection` object provides a static connection to the database. This means that until an explicit `close` is called or the `Connection` object is destroyed, the connection to the database will remain active. This can pose problems if you have a limited number of connections to your database. If you do have limited connections, you can connect and disconnect from the database as needed. This will cause delays in your application, because it will be forced to connect to the database (an expensive function) each time the user wants to execute a SQL statement.

The `Connection` object is covered more fully on Day 5, "JDBC Interfaces."

Native and ODBC Databases

You can use JDBC to write your applications without regard for the database you are using. This section introduces you to some of the more well-known database systems used in the industry. This section is not meant to recommend any database product, but rather to introduce you to some of the products available.

There are two different types of drivers available for JDBC: native drivers and ODBC drivers. *Native drivers* are usually used for large database systems, whereas *ODBC drivers* are used for smaller database systems. Large databases that usually run on UNIX or mainframe machines normally use a native database driver. These drivers are faster than their ODBC counterparts because they usually are specific to the database. ODBC drivers, on the other hand, are usually not as fast, but they are more flexible as to what databases they can support. Also, ODBC drivers are usually less expensive than native drivers. You can usually get native or ODBC drivers for most databases, depending on your needs and finances.

Database Products

There are many different database products that you can use to implement your development solutions. Each of these products provides various features that make them unique. You will need to decide which features are important to you and what price you are willing to pay for a good product solution.

DB2

DB2 is the relational database system from IBM and is one of the oldest relational databases on the market. It is used mainly on mainframe systems such as AS/400 and RS/6000. This database provides many advanced features and is used primarily for large-scale database solutions.

Informix

The Informix relational database from Informix Software, Inc. is available on both the UNIX and Windows NT platforms. This database is used more for small to midrange applications, but can be used for larger development projects. By the time you read this, Informix should have introduced its new Object Relational database product, which provides some support for objects in the database. This new breed of databases will greatly improve the solutions developers can offer their clients.

Oracle

The leader in the database market, Oracle, by Oracle Corporation, is the most widely used relational database. This database offers various features and provides users with many niceties. The database should be at version 8.0 by the time you read this book. Like the Informix database, Oracle v8.0 should be an object-relational database, providing some features of object-oriented databases.

Microsoft SQL Server

The version of SQL Server from Microsoft is becoming more of a contender for real database applications. Microsoft has improved the database product and includes it in its BackOffice suite. The database is somewhat less expensive than the other database products and is used more for smaller application development.

Sybase System 10/11

Sybase System 10 and 11 are used mainly in mid- to large-scale applications. Sybase System 11 addresses some of the problems with System 10, and is now being implemented.

Sybase SQL Anywhere

Although I've already listed Sybase System 11, I feel a need to list Sybase SQL Anywhere, as well. This database is an ODBC database that provides many features of the more advanced databases. It provides replication services that let field representatives replicate data on their local machines, and it also contains other features found in the larger database products. SQL Anywhere is one of the few database products that does not need to run on a server machine. SQL Anywhere can be run on a Windows 95 machine as well as Windows NT. The database can support connections from one user to hundreds of users. The database is the least expensive of the ones listed here and should strongly be considered for small-scale applications.

3

Summary

Today's lesson introduced you to JDBC drivers, which enable you to create connections to a database. Using either the `Driver` object or the `DriverManager` object, you can create a connection to a database that can then be used to send SQL statements and receive results.

Today's lesson also introduced you to the basics of using dbAnywhere. This JDBC product from Symantec enables you to create JDBC applications that can connect to a variety of database sources.

Workshop

The Workshop provides quiz questions to help you solidify your understanding of the material covered and exercises to give you experience in using what you've learned. The answers are provided in Appendix A, "Quiz and Exercise Answers." Try to understand the quiz and exercise answers before you go on to tomorrow's lesson.

3

Quiz

1. In what package does dbAnywhere store the JDBC API?
2. Why is the JDBC API stored in a different package than the proposed package?
3. What method of the `Driver` object will create a connection to the database?
4. What method will get the properties needed to connect to the database?
5. What is the login timeout?
6. What method can change the logging/tracing stream used by the `DriverManager`?
7. What does a driver need to support in order to be JDBC compliant?
8. In what system property does the `DriverManager` object look for `Driver` objects?
9. List the three different methods that the `DriverManager` can use to create a connection to the database.
10. For what type of applications should Sybase SQL Anywhere be used?

Exercises

1. Create a database Login window that prompts the user for all properties required to connect to the database. Use the `getPropertyInfo()` method.
2. Use both the `Driver` object and `DriverManager` object to create connections to the database.

Day **4**

Database Transactions

In today's lesson, you learn about some database-specific topics, including logical units of work, transaction logs, and managing the database transactions that are used to execute SQL statements. Logical units of work define a group of statements that are handled as one unit.

Today's lesson also covers transaction logs and handling transactions. It introduces you to the process of committing transactions and also rolling transactions back to a previous state. Transactions enable you to keep dependent data correct in the database. The following topics are covered today:

- ☐ Logical units of work
- ☐ Transaction logs
- ☐ `AutoCommit`
- ☐ Committing transactions
- ☐ Rolling back transactions
- ☐ Sybase SQL Anywhere functions

Logical Units of Work

When you interact with a database, the statements sent to the database are treated as logical units of work. When you write database applications, you should treat all transactions to the database as part of a logical unit.

A logical unit could include one SQL statement or many SQL statements. You can think of the unit as being a functional group of statements. You might be wondering why you should even think about logical units of work. They are important because they enable you to keep your database correct and precise.

You can best think of a logical unit of work as a transaction. One transaction to the database can include multiple SQL statements or just one statement. Transactions can be committed if all statements in the transaction succeed, or the entire transaction can be rolled back if any of the statements in the transaction fails.

Transaction Logs

Most of the relational databases that you will be using have some form of *transaction logging*. Transaction logging is where each transaction committed against the database is logged and the original data is stored. Whenever a SQL statement that makes changes to the data contained in the database is executed, the original data values are stored in the transaction log. They are stored so that they can be used to re-create the database exactly as it was before the SQL statement was executed. A transaction log will continue to store data until the transactions contained within the log are either committed or rolled back.

Another thing to be aware of with transaction processing is *locking*. Most databases perform some type of locking with certain data values. For example, if you started a transaction and performed an action that caused the database to lock some portion of the database, then no other user is allowed to access the locked data until the transaction is finished. This can cause deadlocks for people trying to gain access to certain data values.

TIP

You should never start a transaction and then display a message box in the middle of the open transaction. Displaying a message box in the middle gives the user a chance to walk away from his or her desk with an open transaction that might not be closed for a long period of time. If you need to interact with the user, display the message box and begin the transaction after the user has finished.

AutoCommit

In tomorrow's lesson you will learn about the methods offered by the Connection object. Two of these methods involve setting and getting the AutoCommit switch. The AutoCommit switch indicates to the database whether a commit should be issued after every SQL statement. If AutoCommit is turned on, then the database will perform an implicit commit after each SQL statement executed against the database for the current connection. If the AutoCommit switch is turned off, then the database will not automatically issue a commit after each SQL statement.

Sometimes, you will want to have AutoCommit turned on, but for most business applications, you will want to perform transaction management within your application. Manual transaction management enables you to specify when transactions should be committed.

As an example of when to use transaction processing and how important it is to your applications, imagine the following scenario. You are using a connection to the database that has AutoCommit turned on, and you want to update items that a customer has specified. The customer is changing his address and phone number. You first change the phone number for the customer, and the statement succeeds. You then change the customer's address, but the statement fails. You now have a correct phone number for the customer but an incorrect address. This can lead to false data in your system. To prevent this from happening, you can place the two statements in a transaction. When the second statement fails, you can roll back the transaction so that the data returns to its original state. This can give you the chance to fix the problem that caused the error and then retry the new data entry. Using this method, your database will not contain very many discrepancies.

4

Committing Transactions

When a transaction is committed, the statements that were part of that transaction are removed from the transaction log, and the changes become permanent. Committing a transaction tells the database that you want all of the statements executed within that transaction to be removed from the transaction log. The statements have already taken effect within the database, but clearing the transaction log ensures that they will not be changed back to their previous values.

It is very important that you commit or roll back changes after every transaction. If the transaction log continues to increase in size without being committed or rolled back and a rollback is finally executed for the entire transaction log, then all statements contained in the transaction log will revert to their original values.

Rolling Back Transactions

You can commit transactions, and you also can roll back transactions. Rolling back transactions to their original state takes the data stored in the transaction log and uses the values
to reconstruct the database. Rolling back transactions should usually be done after a
statement within a transaction fails. If one statement fails, then the entire transaction should
be declared null, because it would let incomplete data creep into the database.

Sybase SQL Anywhere Functions

Because you will use the Sybase SQL Anywhere database throughout most of this book, I'll
introduce you to some of the functions available from the SQL Anywhere database. These
functions provide a variety of functionality for use in database stored procedures. Although
these functions are for the Sybase SQL Anywhere database, many of the functions are
available in other SQL databases.

This lesson covers the following function groups:

☐ Aggregate functions
☐ Numeric functions
☐ String functions
☐ Date and time functions
☐ System functions

Aggregate Functions

The SQL Anywhere database offers several aggregate functions that you can use within any
of the SQL statements. You can use these aggregate functions to compare database values
with an aggregation of multiple data values. Table 4.1 lists the aggregate functions available
and their descriptions.

Table 4.1. Aggregate functions.

Function	Description
AVG	Returns the average for a range of numbers
COUNT	Returns the number of items within a range
MAX	Returns the maximum value within a range of numbers
MIN	Returns the minimum value within a range of numbers
SUM	Returns the sum of all data values within a range of numbers

Numeric Functions

SQL Anywhere also provides various numerical functions that you can use to determine numerical information. These functions enable you to get numerical information such as the sine, cosine, tangent, and so on. Table 4.2 lists some of the numerical functions available in SQL Anywhere.

Table 4.2. Numerical functions.

Function	Description
ABS	Returns the absolute value for a specified numerical value
ACOS	Returns the arc cosine of a specified data value
ASIN	Returns the arc sine of a specified data value
ATAN	Returns the arc tangent of a specified data value
CEILING	Returns the smallest integer that is greater than the specified data value
COS	Returns the cosine for a specified data value
COT	Returns the cotangent for a specified data value
DEGREES	Returns a specified data value in radians to a converted value in degrees
EXP	Returns the exponential value of a specified data value
FLOOR	Returns the largest integer that is smaller than the specified data value
LOG	Returns the logarithm of the specified data value
MOD	Returns the remainder that occurs when you divide a specified dividend by a specified divisor
PI	Returns the value of pi
RADIAN	Returns a radian data value that is converted from degrees of the specified value
RAND	Returns a random number
SIN	Returns the sine of the specified data value
SQRT	Returns the square root of the specified data value
TAN	Returns the tangent of the specified data value

The ABS Function

The ABS function enables you to get the absolute value for a specified value. The absolute value is a non-negative value that eliminates the sign for the value, whether it be positive or negative. For example; the absolute value for -1 is 1, and the absolute value for 1 is 1.

The CEILING Function

The CEILING function enables you to get the smallest integer value that is greater than the current value. For example, the CEILING function returns the integer value 4 for the data value 3.3.

The FLOOR Function

The FLOOR function enables you to get the largest integer value that is less than the current value. For example, the FLOOR function returns the integer 3 for the data value 3.3.

The COS, SIN, and TAN Functions

The COS, SIN, and TAN functions all enable you to use the various trigonometry functions to get data values. Each of these functions takes an integer value and returns the appropriate data value.

String Functions

SQL Anywhere provides functions that can be applied to string data values. These functions enable you to determine information concerning strings, and also enable you to get various substrings for string data. Table 4.3 displays a listing of most of the string functions and their descriptions.

Table 4.3. String functions.

Function	Description
ASCII	Returns the ASCII numerical value for the first character of the specified string.
BYTE_LENGTH	Returns the number of bytes contained in a specified string.
CHAR	Returns the character value for a specified numerical data value.
INSERTSTR	Inserts a specified string into another string at the specified position.
LCASE	Returns the specified string in all lowercase characters.
LEFT	Returns a substring consisting of the specified number of characters from the farthest left part of the string.
LENGTH	Returns the number of characters that are in the specified string.
LTRIM	Returns the specified string with all leading spaces removed.
RIGHT	Returns a substring consisting of the specified number of characters from the farthest right part of the specified string.

Function	Description
RTRIM	Returns the specified string with all trailing spaces removed.
SIMILAR	Returns a value between 0 and 100 that determines whether two specified data values match. A match of 100 indicates a perfect match.
SOUNDEX	Returns a numerical value that represents the value of the specified string.
STRING	Concatenates up to 99 string values into one string expression.
TRIM	Returns a string that has had all leading and trailing spaces removed.
UCASE	Returns a specified string in all uppercase characters.

The LCASE Function

The LCASE function enables you to take a string and convert all characters contained in the string to lowercase. This enables you to do comparisons without regard to the case of the strings.

The UCASE Function

The UCASE function enables you to take a string and convert all characters contained in the string to uppercase. This lets you do string comparisons without regard to the case of the string text.

The TRIM Function

The TRIM function enables you to trim all leading and trailing spaces contained in a string expression. This lets you remove any extra padding so as to use only the actual text in the string.

The SIMILAR Function

The SIMILAR function enables you to determine how similar two different string values are. This function makes it possible to find spelling and data entry errors within the database. By finding values that are very similar but not exactly alike, you can determine whether incorrect data values have been entered into the database.

The SOUNDEX Function

The SOUNDEX function enables you to determine if one string sounds like another. Each string is given a numerical representation, and by comparing the returned integer values, you can find values that sound like the value you are looking for. This function can be used for telephone operators trying to find customer information. By entering what a telephone operator hears, he or she can find a listing of customers who have last names that sound like what was entered.

Date and Time Functions

SQL Anywhere provides various date and time functions that enable you to get information about date and time data values. Table 4.4 lists many of these functions and their descriptions.

Table 4.4. Date and time functions.

Function	Description
DAY	Returns an integer value between 1 and 31 that indicates the day of the month for the specified date
DAYNAME	Returns a string expression that indicates the name of the day for a specified date expression
DAYS	Returns an integer value that indicates the number of days since the specified date expression
DOW	Returns an integer value that corresponds to the day of the week the specified data expression occurred on
HOUR	Returns an integer value between 0 and 23 that corresponds to the hour contained in a specified date/time expression
HOURS	Returns an integer value that indicates the number of hours that have passed since a specified date/time expression occurred
MINUTE	Returns an integer between 0 and 59 that corresponds to the minutes in the specified date/time expression
MINUTES	Returns an integer value that indicates the number of minutes that have passed since a specified date/time expression occurred
MONTH	Returns an integer value between 1 and 12 that indicates the month number for a specified date expression
MONTHNAME	Returns the name of the month contained in a specified date expression
MONTHS	Returns an integer value that indicates the number of months that have passed since a specified date expression
QUARTER	Returns an integer that indicates the quarter that a specified data occurred within

Function	Description
SECOND	Returns an integer value between 0 and 59 that indicates the number of seconds in a specified date/time expression
SECONDS	Returns an integer value that indicates the number of seconds that have passed since a specified date/time expression occurred
WEEKS	Returns an integer value that indicates the number of weeks that have occurred since a specified date/time expression occurred
YEAR	Returns an integer value that indicates the data contained within a specified date/time expression
YEARS	Returns an integer value that indicates the number of years that have passed since a specified date/time expression occurred
DATE	Converts a string expression into a date format
NOW	Returns the current system date and time
TODAY	Returns the current system date
YMD	Returns a date that contains the specified year, month, and day values

System Functions

SQL Anywhere also provides a set of system functions that lets you get information about the current system setup. Table 4.5 lists these system functions.

Table 4.5. SQL Anywhere system functions.

Function	Description
datalength	Returns an integer that contains the number of bytes contained in the given expression
db_id	Returns the current database ID number
db_name	Returns the current database name
db_property	Returns a string that contains the value of the specified property
next_connection	Returns an integer that contains the next connection number
next_database	Returns an integer that contains the next database number
property	Returns a string that contains the value of the specified property
property_name	Returns a string that contains the name of the specified property number
property_number	Returns an integer that contains the property number for the specified property name

Summary

Today's lesson introduced you to an important part of database applications. Transactions enable you to keep your database intact and synchronized. Without transactions, database systems would be of little value. Transactions enable the database to maintain information and also provide for recovery.

If a database crashes, transaction logs enable the database to be reconstructed to a somewhat reusable point. This chapter also discussed committing transactions and rolling back transactions. Committing transactions enables you to clear the contents of the transaction log and make the current changes permanent. Rolling back changes enables you to take the contents of the transaction log and reconstruct the database to its original state.

This chapter also introduced you to some of the many functions available in Sybase SQL Anywhere. These are not all of the functions available, nor are they all of the functions available in other database systems. They are meant to give you an idea of what types of logic can be used in your SQL statements and stored procedures.

Workshop

The Workshop provides quiz questions to help you solidify your understanding of the material covered and exercises to give you experience in using what you've learned. The answers are provided in Appendix A, "Quiz and Exercise Answers." Try to understand the quiz and exercise answers before you go on to tomorrow's lesson.

Quiz

1. What is a logical unit of work?
2. What is contained within a transaction log?
3. What setting of AutoCommit will force a commit after every SQL statement?
4. Describe the difference between a commit and rollback.
5. What does the CEILING function do?
6. What would the FLOOR function return if passed the value 7.4?
7. What does the SOUNDEX function do?
8. What does the TRIM function do?
9. What does the DATALENGTH function return?
10. What does the NOW function return?

Exercises

1. Write and execute a SQL statement that returns the current date and time.
2. Write and execute a SQL statement that displays the last names of all employees and the SOUNDEX value for each name.
3. Write and execute a SQL statement that displays the DATALENGTH value for the last name column.

4

Day 5

JDBC Interfaces

Today you learn about objects and interfaces that allow connections to the database and allow SQL statements to be executed and results to be returned. You also learn how to access and determine what features the current database offers. Finally, you will also be able to view special database information such as a list of tables and stored procedures. Today's main topics include the following:

☐ Creating and using the `Connection` interface

☐ Creating and using the `Statement` interface

☐ Creating and using the `DatabaseMetaData` interface

The `Connection` Interface

The JDBC `Connection` interface provides methods to handle transaction processing, create objects for executing SQL statements, and to create objects for executing stored procedures. It also provides some basic error-handling methods.

Because the `Connection` interface is an interface, it cannot directly be created in code; instead, the `Connection` interface is created by the `Driver.connect()` method. When the `connect()` method is called, it returns a `Connection` object that instantiates your `Connection` object as demonstrated in the following code:

```
Connection connection = driver.connect(dbURL, properties);
```

When you call the `connect()` method of the `Driver` object, you create a permanent connection to the database. This connection is a static connection to the database; it will remain open until the variable goes out of scope or until you explicitly close the connection. Unlike HTTP, which opens a connection to a Web server, retrieves a document, and then disconnects, the database connection opens and remains open until it is closed.

Creating a `Connection` Object

To create a `Connection` object, you must first import the Java class files that contain the JDBC objects and interfaces. The Java 1.02 release does not include the JDBC, so the current package that Symantec's dbAnywhere uses is the `symjava.sql.*` package. This will be changed to `java.sql.*` in subsequent versions as the Java 1.1 release becomes standard.

In this example, you will first import three packages to be used in the `ConnectionExample` class. The three packages, `java.awt.*`, `java.util.*`, and `symjava.sql.*`, all contain objects and interfaces that the application will use. The code to import the three packages is as follows:

```
import java.awt.*;
import java.util.*;
import symjava.sql.*;
```

After you import the required packages, perform some basic application processing to create and display the frame. Size the frame to be 300×300. After you create and display the frame, create a `Driver` object using the following syntax:

```
String driverName = "symantec.itools.db.jdbc.Driver";
Driver driver = (Driver)Class.forName(driverName).newInstance();
```

You might be wondering what the `driverName` string was used for. In JDBC, you must specify a driver to use when you connect to a database. In the preceding code, you specified that you are going to use the driver that is contained in the specified package—`symantec.itools.db.jdbc.Driver`. After you create the `Driver` object, create a `Properties`

object to hold the username and password with which you will connect to the database. You use a `Properties` object simply because the `Driver.connect()` method takes a `Properties` object as a parameter. The syntax for specifying the username and password is as follows:

```
Properties p = new Properties();
p.put("user", "dba");
p.put("password", "sql");
```

Now that you have specified the username and password for the database connection, you are almost finished. In JDBC, all database connections occur over a TCP/IP network. To make things easier to manage in Java, all database connections will be URLs. The dbAnywhere driver takes a special type of URL to connect to the database. The format for the URL is as follows:

```
jdbc:dbaw://<IPAddress>:<Port>/<ODBC Engine>/<DataSource>/<DataSource>
```

Table 5.1 gives a description of what each component of the URL means.

Table 5.1. JDBC URL components.

Component	Description
IPAddress	The TCP/IP address of the dbAnywhere application server.
Port	The port number on which the dbAnywhere application server is listening.
ODBC Engine	The ODBC interface being used. Possible values include ODBC_via_Intersolv, WATCOM, and MS_Access.
DataSource	The data source being used.

Now that you have all of the components, you can create your connection to the database.

NOTE These examples use the dbAnywhere JDBC interface and the JDBC database provided on the accompanying CD-ROM.

To create the connection to the database, simply specify the URL of the database to which you want to connect and the `Properties` object that contains your username and password, as follows:

```
String dbURL = "jdbc:dbaw://localhost:8889/WATCOM/JDBC/JDBC";
Connection connection = driver.connect(dbURL, p);
```

Almost all of the JDBC objects and interfaces throw the `SQLException` exception when they are created or their methods are called. You must catch this exception or throw it again to prevent the compiler from giving an error.

The full text for the `ConnectionExample` class is shown in Listing 5.1.

TYPE **Listing 5.1. The `ConnectionExample` class.**

```
import java.awt.*;
import java.util.*;
import symjava.sql.*;

public class ConnectionExample extends Frame {
    public ConnectionExample () {
        super();
        this.show();
        this.resize(300, 300);

        try {
            String driverName = "symantec.itools.db.jdbc.Driver";
            Driver driver = (Driver)Class.forName(driverName).newInstance();
            Properties p = new Properties();
            p.put("user", "dba");
            p.put("password", "sql");
            String dbURL = "jdbc:dbaw://localhost:8889/WATCOM/JDBC/JDBC";
            Connection connection = driver.connect(dbURL, p);
        }
        catch (SQLException e) {}
        catch (Exception e) {}
    }
    public static void main (String args[]) {
        ConnectionExample app = new ConnectionExample();
    }
}
```

`Connection` Interface Methods

The `Connection` interface provides many methods to handle transaction processing and the creation of SQL statements and SQL stored procedures. It also provides some basic error-handling methods. The list of methods is displayed in Table 5.2.

Table 5.2. `Connection` interface methods.

Method	Description
clearWarnings	Clears the current warning for the connection.
close	Closes the connection to the database.
commit	Issues a commit to the database. Useful only if `AutoCommit` = `FALSE`.
createStatement	Creates a `Statement` object that can be used to execute SQL statements to the database.

Method	Description
getAutoCommit	Returns the value of the current AutoCommit parameter.
getCatalog	Returns a string that contains the current catalog for the connection.
getMetaData	Returns a DatabaseMetaData object that can be used to determine database features.
getTransactionIsolation	Returns the current isolation mode of the transaction associated with the Connection object.
getWarnings	Returns a SQLWarning object that contains the current warning for the Connection object.
isClosed	Returns a Boolean true if the connection is closed or a Boolean false if the connection is open.
isReadOnly	Returns a Boolean true if the connection is read-only or cannot be updated and a Boolean false if the connection is not read-only or can be updated.
nativeSQL	Returns the SQL statement as the JDBC driver presents it to the database.
prepareCall	Returns a CallableStatement object that is initialized to call the passed stored procedure.
prepareStatement	Returns a PreparedStatement object that can be used to execute dynamic SQL statements.
rollback	Issues a rollback to the database. Useful only if AutoCommit = FALSE.
setAutoCommit	Sets AutoCommit to the Boolean variable passed.
setCatalog	Sets the current connection catalog to a different database catalog.
setReadOnly	Sets the connection to be read-only (no updates).
setTransactionIsolation	Sets the connection's transaction isolation value to the passed integer.

5

close()

The close() method of the Connection object explicitly closes the connection to the database. The connection will be closed automatically when the application is terminated. The close() method is useful if you have a limited number of available connections to the database. With a limited number of connections, some users might be unable to access the database if other users hold connections for long periods of time. Using the `close()` method, you can terminate a connection after an unspecified period of inactive time so that other users may use the waiting connection. The syntax for the `close()` method is as follows:

```
connection.close();
```

commit()

The `commit()` method issues a commit command to the database. The commit command tells the database to empty the transaction log, and, in effect, make permanent the changes to the database since the last commit or rollback. Whenever SQL statements are executed against the database, the changes are stored in the database's transaction log. Whenever a database commit or rollback is executed, the transaction log is emptied. A commit will empty the transaction log and apply the changes to the database. A rollback will empty the transaction log and convert the database back to its state before the changes in the transaction log were executed.

The `commit()` method applies to the database only when `AutoCommit` is set to Boolean `false`. If `AutoCommit` is set to Boolean `true`, then a commit is implicitly applied after the execution of every SQL statement. The syntax for committing a transaction is as follows:

```
connection.setAutoCommit(false)
..some successful database processing
connection.commit()
```

createStatement()

The `createStatement()` method of the `Connection` object creates a `Statement` object and returns it as the return value. The `Statement` object is used to execute SQL statements and to get results. The `Statement` object is used to execute only static SQL statements. To execute dynamic SQL statements or stored procedures, use the `PreparedStatement` and `CallableStatement` objects. The syntax for the `createStatement()` method is as follows:

```
Statement statement = connection.createStatement();
```

getCatalog() and setCatalog()

The `getCatalog()` method of the `Connection` object returns the current connection's catalog name. The catalog being used determines which tables are accessible. The syntax for the `getCatalog()` method is as follows:

```
String catalog = connection.getCatalog();
```

The `setCatalog()` method of the `Connection` object enables you to specify a database catalog to use other than the current catalog. Specifying a different database catalog will allow access to a subset of the full database table list. Use this function to give certain groups of users access to only the tables from which they need information. This prevents users from gaining access to private or protected data. The syntax for calling the setCatalog() method is as follows:

```
connection.setCatalog("UserCatalog");
```

getMetaData()

The getMetaData() method of the Connection object returns a DatabaseMetaData object that can be used to determine certain database features such as whether the database supports transaction processing and outer joins. The DatabaseMetaData object provides methods that return database-specific information such as the available tables and stored procedures currently in the database. The syntax for getting a DatabaseMetaData interface from the Connection object is as follows:

```
DatabaseMetaData metadata = connection.getMetaData();
```

isClosed()

The isClosed() method of the Connection object returns a Boolean true if the connection to the database is closed and a Boolean false if the database connection is currently open. If the connection to the database has been closed, then you must issue another connect using the Driver object to create a connection to the database. When the connection to the database has been closed, the only way to reconnect to the database is to specify the URL, username, and password. To determine whether the database connection has been closed and to reconnect back to the database, use the following code:

```
if (connection.isClosed()) {
    connection = driver.connect(dbURL, p);
}
```

The *dbURL* is the URL to the database to which you want to connect, and p is the Properties object that contains the username and password properties with which you want to connect to the database.

isReadOnly() **and** setReadOnly()

The isReadOnly() method returns a Boolean true if the database connection is read-only and a Boolean false if the database connection is not read-only. A read-only connection simply implies that no SQL update commands such as delete, insert, or update can be executed against the database. This type of connection can be useful for security measures when you don't want certain groups of users to have update capabilities to the database. For example, if you want a group of users to be able to view their own employee information, but you do not want them to be able to edit the information, then a read-only connection would ensure that the employees would not be able to update any information to the database. The syntax for the isReadOnly() method is as follows:

```
boolean readable = connection.isReadOnly();
```

The setReadOnly() method enables you to determine whether the connection to the database will be read-only. The method takes a Boolean parameter; true specifies that the connection will be read-only and false specifies that the connection will be updatable. To set the connection to read-only mode, use the following code:

```
connection.setReadOnly(true);
```

To turn the read-only feature off, use the following code:

```
connection.setReadOnly(false);
```

prepareCall()

The prepareCall() method returns a CallableStatement object that contains the precompiled SQL stored procedure statement. Calling a stored procedure in this way is necessary only if the stored procedure uses any INOUT or OUT parameters. All other stored procedures can be executed with the normal Statement object. To create a CallableStatement object that will execute the stored procedure pGetEmployees, use the following syntax:

```
try {
    String sql = "pGetEmployees";
    CallableStatement c = connection.prepareCall(sql);
}
catch (SQLexception e) {}
```

prepareStatement()

The prepareStatement() method creates a PreparedStatement object and returns it as a return value. The PreparedStatement object is used to execute dynamic SQL statements against the database. A *dynamic* SQL statement is a statement in which some of the parameters in the statement are unknown when the statement is created. The parameters are placed into the SQL statement as they are determined by the application. When all the parameters have been specified for the SQL statement, the dynamic SQL statement will be executed just as a static statement is executed. To create a dynamic SQL statement that takes a FirstName and LastName as parameters, use the following code:

```
try {
    String sql = "select * from tEmployee " +
            "where firstname = ? " +
            "and lastname = ?";
    PreparedStatement p = connection.prepareStatement(sql);
}
catch (SQLException e) {}
```

rollback()

The rollback() method of the Connection object issues a SQL rollback command to the database. When a rollback is issued to the database, the database transaction log is emptied and all changes made to the database revert back to their original values. A rollback is useful only if AutoCommit is set to false. If AutoCommit is true, then a commit will be implicitly issued after every SQL statement. This implicit commit will empty the transaction log and make permanent all changes to the database. The code to perform a rollback is as follows:

```
connection.setAutoCommit(false);
..some unsuccessful database processing
connection.rollback();
```

setAutoCommit()

The setAutoCommit() method enables you to determine whether transaction processing statements such as commit and rollback will be handled by you or handled automatically by the database. If AutoCommit is turned on (true), then after every SQL statement a commit command will be sent to the database. This will immediately empty the transaction log and apply the changes to the database. Using a rollback after a SQL statement has executed with AutoCommit turned on will not roll back the database because the changes have already been implicitly committed.

Using manual transaction processing also enables your business logic to be more complete and robust. If you are updating information with AutoCommit turned on and one SQL statement fails, then any previous information will remain in the database. This type of approach can create incomplete data. Using manual transaction processing, you could execute all SQL statements and, if all statements are successful, issue a commit to the database to make the changes permanent. This would ensure that all data in the database remains complete and accurate.

To turn AutoCommit on, which is also the default for the Connection object, use the following code:

```
connection.setAutoCommit(true);
```

To turn AutoCommit off and allow manual transaction processing control, use the following code:

```
connection.setAutoCommit(false);
```

The Statement Interface

In the previous section, you learned how to create a Connection object that lets you connect to the database. The Connection object does just that—it connects you to the database. To execute SQL statements and get results back from the database, you must use the Statement object.

The Statement object, much like the Connection object, cannot be directly created. As with the Connection object, you create a Statement object by assigning it the return value from a method of another object, in this case the Connection object. The createStatement() method returns a Statement object as a return value.

You can use a Statement object to execute static SQL statements and get results back from SQL queries. A *static* SQL statement does not take any arguments to be complete. A dynamic statement, for example, is not complete until a certain number of arguments are passed into the SQL statement. A static SQL statement can be a select statement, delete statement, an update statement, an insert statement, and even a stored procedure call. The update, delete, and insert statements do not return any results; these procedures simply update data in the database and do not return any new data from the database. A select statement will return data from the database, in most cases. A stored procedure can be executed in both ways. A stored procedure can carry out any of the update statements on data, and it can also return a selection of results from the database.

Creating a Statement Object

Creating a Statement object is a very simple procedure. The Connection.createStatement() method returns a Statement object as its return value. The return Statement object has all of the methods assigned to the Statement object.

To create a Statement object, you must first import all of the necessary classes that will be used. Import the java.util.* package, the java.awt.* package, and the symjava.sql.* package. The symjava.sql.* package is a dbAnywhere-specific package and will be changed to java.sql.* when the Java 1.1 SDK is released. The following is the code for importing the appropriate packages:

```
import java.awt.*;
import java.util.*;
import symjava.sql.*;
```

After you have imported all of the packages you need, you need to create a frame in which to display information. This frame should be a default frame with a size of 300×300 pixels. The code for this is as follows:

```
super();
this.resize(300, 300);
this.show();
```

After the window has been displayed, you will need to make a connection to the database. Using the same URL used in the previous section as well as the same properties object used, the code to connect to the database would be as follows:

```
Connection connection = driver.connect(dbURL, p);
```

After you have established the connection to the database, you can create a Statement object by calling the createStatement() method of the Connection object. The method returns a Statement object and takes no parameters. The code to create a Statement object is as follows:

```
Statement sqlStatement = connection.createStatement();
```

The code for the StatementExample class is shown in Listing 5.2.

TYPE **Listing 5.2. The StatementExample class.**

```
import java.awt.*;
import java.util.*;
import symjava.sql.*;

public class StatementExample extends Frame {
    public StatementExample () {
        super();
        this.resize(300, 300);
        this.show();

        try {
            String driverName = "symantec.itools.db.jdbc.Driver";
            Driver driver = (Driver)Class.forName(driverName).newInstance();
            Properties p = new Properties();
            p.put("user", "dba");
            p.put("password", "sql");

            String dbURL = "jdbc:dbaw://localhost:8889/WATCOM/JDBC/JDBC";
            Connection connection = driver.Connect(dbURL, p);
            Statement sqlStatement = connection.createStatement();
        }
        catch (SQLException e) {}
        catch (Exception e) {}
    }

    public static void main (String args[]) {
        StatementExample app = new StatementExample();
    }
}
```

Statement **Interface Methods**

The Statement interface provides many methods for handling the creation and execution of SQL statements. Table 5.3 shows a listing of these methods.

Table 5.3. `Statement` **methods.**

Method	Description
cancel()	Enables a thread outside of the thread executing the SQL statement to cancel the execution of the statement.
clearWarnings()	Clears the current warning for the `Statement` object.
close()	Closes the current `Statement` object.
execute()	Executes the `Statement` object. Used primarily when a SQL statement will return multiple result sets.
executeQuery()	Executes a SQL `Select` statement and returns a result set containing the records matching the criteria of the specified SQL statement.
executeUpdate()	Executes a SQL update statement, which could be a SQL `Update`, `Delete`, or `Insert`.
getMaxFieldSize()	Returns the current maximum size that a field returned in a result set can be.
getMaxRows()	Returns the current maximum number of rows that a returned result set can contain.
getMoreResults()	Moves to the next result in the `Statement` object. Used for SQL statements that return multiple results.
getQueryTimeout()	Returns the number of seconds that the JDBC driver will wait for the `Statement` object to execute a SQL statement.
getResultSet()	Returns the current result set.
getUpdateCount()	Returns the current result in multiple result statements.
getWarnings()	Returns a `SQLWarning` object that contains the current warning for the statement.
setCursorName()	Sets the `Statement` object to use the passed cursor.
setEscapeProcessing()	Turns on or off escape processing for the statement.
setMaxFieldSize()	Sets the maximum size of a field returned in a result set.
setMaxRows()	Sets the maximum number of rows that can be returned in a result set.
setQueryTimeout()	Sets the timeout a JDBC driver will wait for a `Statement` object to execute a SQL statement.

cancel()

The cancel() method of the Statement object enables you to cancel the execution of the statement after it has begun. The execution of the statement must occur in a thread running outside of the thread that executed the statement. The statement being executed will be stopped and will not continue. The syntax for the cancel() method is as follows:

```
connection.cancel();
```

close()

The close() method of the Statement object enables you to explicitly close the Statement object. This releases the resources being used by both the JDBC driver objects as well as the resources being used on the database server to handle the execution of the statement and the return of results. The close() method can also be used to ensure that any locks that were placed on the database by the execution of your SQL statements will be released immediately. The syntax for the close() method is as follows:

```
connection.close();
```

execute()

The execute() method of the Statement object will execute the passed SQL statement against the database using the JDBC driver. The execute() method is used primarily when a SQL statement will return multiple result sets. This occurs mainly in stored procedures where the stored procedure will return different selection results.

To illustrate the need to use the execute() method, suppose you have a stored procedure called pResults that returns a selection that contains all rows from tEmployee and tArticle. Because the stored procedure returns more than one result set, you must use the execute() method in place of the executeQuery() method. First, create a string with a call to the stored procedure as follows:

```
String sql = "pResults";
```

Then, create a Statement object and call the execute() method to execute the stored procedure and return the results to the Statement object. The execute() method will return a Boolean true if the first result set is a ResultSet object, and a Boolean false if the first result is an integer result. The syntax for calling the execute() method is as follows:

```
Statement sqlStatement = connection.createStatement();
boolean result = sqlStatement.execute(sql);
```

executeQuery()

The executeQuery() method of the Statement object enables you to send SQL select statements to the database and to receive results from the database. Executing a query, in effect, sends a SQL `select` statement to the database and returns the appropriate results back in a `ResultSet` object. The `executeQuery()` method takes a SQL `select` statement as a parameter and returns a `ResultSet` object that contains all of the records that match the `select` statement's criteria.

In the `QueryExample` class, select all of the employees from the database table tEmployee and display the first name and last name of every employee in a `TextArea` object. The SQL `select` statement to get the first and last names of every employee is as follows:

```
select FirstName, LastName from tEmployee
```

Taking what you have learned about creating a `Connection` and a `Statement` object, execute the preceding SQL statement using the preceding SQL `select` statement. The following is the syntax for this:

```
String sql = "select FirstName, LastName from tEmployee";
ResultSet results = sqlStatement.executeQuery(sql);
```

After you have executed the SQL `select` statement, loop through all rows returned in the results returned by the `ResultSet` object, and display the first and last names in a `TextArea` object. The code for this is as follows:

```
String text = "";
while (results.next()) {
    text += results.getString(1) + " " +
            results.getString(2) + "\n";
}
textArea.setText(text);
```

Notice that a method called `next()` was called for the `ResultSet` object `results`. This method moves the `ResultSet` object to the next record. The `ResultSet` object initially places the record pointer on a blank record preceding the first record. The `next()` method will return a `true` as long as there is a record to go to, and a `false` if there are no more records, meaning that you are at the end of the records.

The full text for the `QueryExample` class is shown in Listing 5.3.

TYPE   **Listing 5.3. The `QueryExample` class.**

```
import java.awt.*;
import java.util.*;
import symjava.sql.*;

public class QueryExample extends Frame {
    public QueryExample () {
        super();
        this.resize(300, 300);
        this.show();
        TextArea textArea = new TextArea(25, 80);
        this.add("Center", textArea);
```

```
    try {
        String driverName = "symantec.itools.db.jdbc.Driver";
        Driver driver = (Driver)Class.forName(driverName).newInstance();
        Properties p = new Properties();
        p.put("user", "dba");
        p.put("password", "sql");

        String dbURL = "jdbc:dbaw://localhost:8889/WATCOM/JDBC/JDBC";
        Connection connection = driver.connect(dbURL, p);

        Statement sqlStatement = connection.createStatement();
        String sql = "select FirstName, LastName from tEmployee";
        ResultSet results = sqlStatement.executeQuery(sql);
        String text = "";
        while (results.next()) {
            text += results.getString(1) + " " +
                    results.getString(2) + "\n";
        }
        textArea.setText(text);
    }
    catch (SQLException e) {}
    catch (Exception e) {}
}

public static void main (String args[]) {
    QueryExample app = new QueryExample();
}
}
```

executeUpdate()

The executeUpdate() method of the Statement object enables you to execute SQL update statements such as delete, insert, and update. The method takes a string containing the SQL update statement and returns an integer that determines how many records were affected by the SQL statement.

In the UpdateExample class, create an application that will change all employees who have the current last name Hobbs to the last name Martin. The following is the SQL statement to execute this:

```
update tEmployee set LastName = 'Martin' where LastName = 'Hobbs'
```

The syntax for calling the executeUpdate() method is very similar to the syntax you use to call the executeQuery() method. To execute the preceding SQL statement, use the following code:

```
String sql =
➡"update tEmployee set LastName = \'Martin\' where LastName = \'Hobbs\'";
int records = sqlStatement.executeUpdate(sql);
```

The records integer will contain the number of records that were affected by the update statement. Therefore, the records variable will contain the total number of employees who have the last name Hobbs. Notice that I used \' in front of and after every string. Like Java, SQL requires that strings be contained in some form of quotation. You must use the escape character because the dbAnywhere driver places an apostrophe (') before and after every SQL statement it sends to the database. If you leave out the escape character before the single quote, then the JDBC driver will interpret it as the end of the SQL command to the database.

The full code for UpdateExample is shown in Listing 5.4.

TYPE   **Listing 5.4. The UpdateExample class.**

```
import java.awt.*;
import java.util.*;
import symjava.sql.*;

public class UpdateExample extends Frame {
    public UpdateExample () {
        super();
        this.resize(300, 300);
        this.show();

        try {
            String driverName = "symantec.itools.db.jdbc.Driver";
            Driver driver = (Driver)Class.forName(driverName).newInstance();
            Properties p = new Properties();
            p.put("user", "dba");
            p.put("password", "sql");

            String dbURL = "jdbc:dbaw://localhost:8889/WATCOM/JDBC/JDBC";
            Connection connection = driver.connect(dbURL, p);
            Statement sqlStatement = connection.createStatement();
            String sql = "update tEmployee set LastName = \'Martin\'" +
                " where LastName = \'Hobbs\'";
            int records = sqlStatement.executeUpdate(sql);
        }
        catch (SQLException e) {}
        catch (Exception e) {}
    }

    public static void main (String args[]) {
        UpdateExample app = new UpdateExample();
    }
}
```

getMoreResults(), getResultSet(), getUpdateCount()

The methods getMoreResults(), getResultSet(), and getUpdateCount() are all related. You use these methods when you are processing SQL statements that return multiple result sets. The most common SQL statement that returns multiple result sets is the stored procedure.

The getMoreResults() method determines whether there still exist result sets or result items that have not been processed. The getMoreResults() method does not return a ResultSet object, but moves the current result in the Statement object to the next result to be processed. The getMoreResults() method will return a Boolean true if the next result set is a ResultSet object and a Boolean false if the next result is an integer from a SQL update statement. The syntax for using the getMoreResults() method is as follows:

```
if (connection.getMoreResults()) {
    ResultSet results = connection.getResultSet();
}
else {
    int updateCount = connection.getUpdateCount();
}
```

In the preceding code segment, you see that when the getMoreResults() method returned a Boolean true, the getResultSet() method was called to retrieve the current result set into a local ResultSet object. The getResultSet() method is used to get the Statement object's current result set and return it as a ResultSet object.

In the preceding code, if the getMoreResults() method returned a Boolean false, then the getUpdateCount() method was called and the return value stored in a local integer. If the getMoreResults() method returns false, then the current result for the Statement object is a SQL update statement and not a SQL query. The getUpdateCount() method returns the integer that is normally returned by the executeUpdate() method. Because the update was carried out in a multiple result statement, you can determine how many records were affected by the current update statement.

setEscapeProcessing()

The setEscapeProcessing() method of the Statement object determines how the actual SQL text is sent to the database. If escape processing is turned on, the default for a newly created Statement object, then all escape commands within strings such as \n, \t, \", and \' will be removed and replaced with the actual character for processing. To turn escape processing off, use the following code:

```
connection.setEscapeProcessing(false);
```

To turn escape processing back on, use the following code:

```
connection.setEscapeProcessing(true);
```

WARNING

Be careful when you turn escape processing off. On some databases, if escape processing is turned off and the SQL statement includes a single or double quote, then the database will interpret that quote as the end of the SQL statement. This can cause problems when applications execute SQL statements.

setMaxRows() **and** getMaxRows()

The setMaxRows() and getMaxRows() methods enable you to set and determine the maximum number of rows that can be returned in a result set. These methods let you limit the amount of data that can be returned by a user's queries. If you have a table that contains one million records, then you might possibly want to limit the number of records that can be returned so that the user cannot execute a statement such as select * from table. Select * is a SQL construct to let the database know that you want all records from the specified table or tables returned in the result set. To set the maximum number of rows that can be returned in a result set to 100, use the following code:

```
connection.setMaxRows(100);
```

To determine the maximum number of rows that can be returned, use the following code:

```
int max = connection.getMaxRows();
```

setQueryTimeout() **and** getQueryTimeout()

You can use the setQueryTimeout() and getQueryTimeout() methods to set and determine the current time-out for query execution. You can change the time-out so that a user will be notified after a certain delay if a problem exists. To set the time-out to unlimited, which will make the statement wait indefinitely for a SQL statement to execute, pass 0 as the parameter to setQueryTimeout(). If getQueryTimeout() returns 0, then the time-out is set to wait indefinitely, which is the default. The code to set and get the query time-out is as follows:

```
// Set the timeout to 10 seconds
connection.setQueryTimeout(10);
// Get the current Query Timeout
int seconds = connection.getQueryTimeout();
```

The DatabaseMetaData Interface

The DatabaseMetaData interface provides many useful functions that contain information about the database and database objects. The DatabaseMetaData interface provides functions that let your JDBC applications determine the primary keys for a table and whether or not the database supports outer joins. You can also use it to get a listing of tables that are available in the database. You cannot declare the interface directly, but must create it by assigning it the value returned by the Connection.getMetaData() function.

  All of the examples for the DatabaseMetaData interface use the JDBC database available on the CD-ROM.

The DatabaseMetaData interface provides many functions to access information concerning the database. Table 5.4 shows some of these methods.

Table 5.4. The DatabaseMetaData methods.

Method Name	Action
getSchemas()	Returns a listing of all the available database schemas within the current database.
getColumns()	Returns a listing of all columns for a specified table.
getExportedKeys()	Returns a listing of all foreign keys that use the specified table's primary key.
getImportedKeys()	Returns a listing of all foreign keys that the specified table is using.
getIndexInfo()	Returns a listing of all index information for the specified table.
getMaxColumnsInSelect()	Returns the number of columns that can be used in a Select statement.
getMaxColumnsInTable()	Returns the number of columns that can be used in a table.
getMaxTablesInSelect()	Returns the maximum number of tables that can be used in a Select statement.
getPrimaryKeys()	Returns a listing of all the columns that comprise the primary key for the specified table.
getProcedures()	Returns a listing of all the stored procedures in the current database.
getTables()	Returns a listing of all of the tables within the current database.
getURL()	Returns the URL of the current database.
getUserName()	Returns the username of the currently connected user.
supportsGroupBy()	Returns a Boolean value informing whether the database supports the Group By statement.
supportsOuterJoins()	Returns a Boolean value informing whether the database supports outer joins.
supportsTransactions()	Returns a Boolean value informing whether the database supports the use of transactions.

5

For more detailed information about the functions provided by the DatabaseMetaData interface, check out the JDBC API documentation.

Creating a `DatabaseMetaData` Object

To create a `DatabaseMetaData` object, you will need to first create a connection to the database:

```
String driverName = "symantec.itools.db.jdbc.Driver";
driver = (Driver)Class.forName(driverName).newInstance();
connection = driver.connect(dbURL, p);
```

After you connect to the database, assign the value returned by the `Connection.getMetaData()` method to a variable of the type `DatabaseMetaData`:

```
DatabaseMetaData db = connection.getMetaData();
```

Because both the connection to the database and the creation of the `DatabaseMetaData` interface throw `SQLException` objects, you must put the code within a `try..catch` block or throw the `SQLException`.

```
try {
..
}
catch (SQLException e) {}
```

Listing 5.5 shows an application that creates a `DatabaseMetaData` object.

Type   **Listing 5.5. Creating a `DatabaseMetaData` object.**

```
import java.awt.*;
import java.util.*;
// To be changed to java.sql in future release
import symjava.sql.*;

public class MetaDataExample extends Frame {
    public MetaDataExample () {
        super();
        this.resize(300, 300);
        Driver driver;
        Connection connection;
        String dbURL = "jdbc:dbaw://localhost:8889/Watcom/JDBC/JDBC";
        Properties p = new Properties();
        p.put("user", "dba");
        p.put("password", "sql");
        try {
            String driverName = "symantec.itools.db.jdbc.Driver";
            driver = (Driver)Class.forName(driverName).newInstance();
            connection = driver.connect(dbURL, p);
            DatabaseMetaData db = connection.getMetaData();
        }
        catch (SQLException e) {}
        catch (Exception e) {}
        this.show ();
    }
    public static void main (String args[]) {
        MetaDataExample app = new MetaDataExample();
    }
}
```

5

getSchemas()

The `DatabaseMetaData.getSchemas()` method returns a listing of all of the available database schemas currently available. The schema is required to retrieve certain information about tables, such as columns and primary keys. The method `getSchemas()` returns a `ResultSet` object that contains one column:

`TABLE_SCHEM` - Column containing name of database schema.

The `ResultSet` object returned can have several records containing all of the schemas in the current database. To access the schemas available, first create a `DatabaseMetaData` object as shown previously, and then create a `ResultSet` object in which to return the value:

```
ResultSet schemas = db.getSchemas();
```

After the `ResultSet` object has been populated, you can loop through the items in the result set and access each schema name by using the get*XXX*() methods of the `ResultSet` object. To access each successive record in the result set, call the `next()` method, as shown in the following code:

```
while (next()) {
    String s = schemas.getString(1);
}
```

Notice that I used the `getString()` method, but instead of passing the column name as a parameter, I passed the column number. Because the `TABLE_SCHEM` column is the first column in the result set, you can use the column number to access the result data.

Listing 5.6 shows the complete code to display the available schemas in the current database.

TYPE **Listing 5.6. The `SchemaExample` class.**

```
import java.awt.*;
import java.util.*;
import symjava.sql.*;

public class SchemaExample extends Frame {
    public SchemaExample () {
        super();
        this.resize(300, 300);

        TextArea t = new TextArea(25,80);
        this.add("Center", t);

        Driver driver;
        Connection connection;
            String dbURL = "jdbc:dbaw://localhost:8889/Watcom/JDBC/JDBC";
            Properties p = new Properties();
            p.put("user", "dba");
        p.put("password", "sql");
        try {
```

continues

Listing 5.6. continued

```
                String driverName = "symantec.itools.db.jdbc.Driver";
            driver = (Driver)Class.forName(driverName).newInstance();
            connection = driver.connect(dbURL, p);
        DatabaseMetaData db = connection.getMetaData();
        ResultSet schemas = db.getSchemas();
        String s = "";
        while (schemas.next()) {
                s += schemas.getString(1);
         }
         t.setText(s);
     }
    catch (SQLException e) {}
    catch (Exception e) {}
    this.show ();
}
public static void main (String args[]) {
    SchemaExample app = new SchemaExample();
}
}
```

getColumns()

The getColumns() method of DatabaseMetaData enables you to get all of the columns for a certain table. This can be useful in situations in which you want to enable the user to select columns to be included in a select statement or to specify criteria for the column to be included in the Where clause. The getColumns() method takes a database catalog, database schema, table, and a column pattern as arguments. The column pattern allows for only columns that match the pattern to be returned in the result set. The method returns a ResultSet object that has the columns described in Table 5.5.

Table 5.5. The getColumns() ResultSet columns.

Column	Description
TABLE_CAT	The table catalog of the current column.
TABLE_SCHEM	The table schema of the current column.
TABLE_NAME	The table name of the current column.
COLUMN_NAME	The name of the current column.
DATA_TYPE	The SQL data type of the column from java.sql.Types.
TYPE_NAME	The data source-dependent type name.
COLUMN_SIZE	The size of the column. Char and Date sizes are the maximum number of characters. Numeric and Decimal report the size as the precision size.
BUFFER_LENGTH	Not used.

Column	Description
DECIMAL_DIGITS	The number of fractional digits.
NUM_PREC_RADIX	Which radix (usually 2 or 10) the column value is reported in.
NULLABLE	Whether the column allows NULL values.
REMARKS	A comment describing the column.
COLUMN_DEF	The default value for the column.
CHAR_OCTET_LENGTH	Used in Char columns to determine the maximum number of bytes the column requires.
ORDINAL_POSITION	The index of the column. Column1 = 1, ColumnN = N.
IS_NULLABLE	Returns NO if the column definitely does not allow NULLs. YES means the column might allow NULLs, and " " means that it cannot be determined.

To get a listing of the columns in the tEmployee table in the JDBC database, use the following syntax:

```
ResultSet columns = db.getColumns("", "DBA", "tEmployee", "");
```

If you compile and run the SchemaExample class described previously, you will notice that the only schema returned is DBA. This is the default schema that SQL Anywhere uses for tables.

You can then get the name of the columns by looping through the records in the ResultSet object columns and getting the value from the COLUMN_NAME column, which is column 4.

```
while (columns.next()) {
    s += columns.getString(4);
}
```

The complete listing for the ColumnExample class is shown in Listing 5.7.

TYPE **Listing 5.7. The `ColumnExample` class.**

```
import java.awt.*;
import java.util.*;
import symjava.sql.*;

public class ColumnExample extends Frame {
    public ColumnExample () {
            super();
            this.resize(300, 300);

            TextArea t = new TextArea(25,80);
        this.add("Center", t);

        Driver driver;
```

continues

Listing 5.7. continued

```
            Connection connection;
                String dbURL = "jdbc:dbaw://localhost:8889/Watcom/JDBC/JDBC";
                Properties p = new Properties();
                p.put("user", "dba");
                p.put("password", "sql");

            try {
                    String driverName = "symantec.itools.db.jdbc.Driver";
                    driver = (Driver)Class.forName(driverName).newInstance();
                  connection = driver.connect(dbURL, p);
                DatabaseMetaData db = connection.getMetaData();
                ResultSet columns = db.getColumns("","DBA","tEmployee","");
                String s = "";
                while (columns.next()) {
                      s += columns.getString(4) + "\n";
                    }
                    t.setText(s);
                }
            catch (SQLException e) {}
            catch (Exception e) {}
            this.show ();
        }
        public static void main (String args[]) {
            ColumnExample app = new ColumnExample();
        }
}
```

The window created by Listing 5.7 is displayed in Figure 5.1. The window displays a listing of all the columns that are in the table tEmployee.

Figure 5.1.

The ColumnExample
application.

getExportedKeys() **and** getImportedKeys()

The two methods getExportedKeys() and getImportedKeys() both return a listing of foreign key information for the specified table. Each method takes a table catalog, table schema, and a table as parameters and returns a ResultSet object containing key information.

getExportedKeys() returns all of the foreign keys that use the primary key of the specified table. In the JDBC database included on the CD-ROM, tEmployee would have an exported key to tEmpAddress because tEmpAddress has a foreign key that uses the primary key of tEmployee, EmpId. Using this function can give you a listing of all child tables that depend on the specified table. Because some databases have referential integrity rules that prevent parent records from being deleted before child records have been deleted, this function can provide a list of tables that would need to have child records deleted before a parent record could be deleted.

getImportedKeys() returns all of the foreign keys that the specified table is using. An imported key implies that the table is a child table of another table. In the JDBC database, tEmpAddress is a child table of tEmployee because it contains a foreign key to the primary key of tEmployee.

The columns returned by the two methods are shown in Table 5.6.

Table 5.6. getImportedKeys(), getExportedKeys() **ResultSet columns.**

Column	Description
PKTABLE_CAT	The table catalog of the table that contains the primary key.
PKTABLE_SCHEM	The table schema of the table that contains the primary key.
PKTABLE_NAME	The table name of the table that contains the primary key.
PKCOLUMN_NAME	The column name of the primary key column.
FKTABLE_CAT	The table catalog of the table that contains the foreign key.
FKTABLE_SCHEM	The table schema of the table that contains the foreign key.
FKTABLE_NAME	The table name of the table that contains the foreign key.
FKCOLUMN_NAME	The column name of the foreign key column.
KEY_SEQ	The sequence number within the current foreign key.
UPDATE_RULE	A string that contains a description of what happens when the primary key is updated. Can be importedKeyNoAction, importedKeySetDefault, importedKeyCascade, importedKeyRestrict, or importedKeySetNull.
DELETE_RULE	A string that contains a description of what happens when the primary key is updated. Can be importedKeyCascade, importedKeyRestrict, or importedKeySetNull.
FK_NAME	The name of the foreign key.
PK_NAME	The name of the primary key.
DEFERRABILITY	Determines whether the evaluation of foreign keys can be deferred until commit.

The syntax for calling the getImportedKeys() and getExportedKeys() methods would be as follows, using the tEmpAddress table for the getImportedKeys() method and the tEmployee table for the getExportedKeys() method. Again, you are specifying the schema name to be DBA and the catalog name to be empty.

```
DatabaseMetaData db = connect.getMetaData();
ResultSet importKeys = db.getImportedKeys("", "DBA", "tEmpAddress");
ResultSet exportKeys = db.getExportedKeys("", "DBA", "tEmployee");
```

getIndexInfo()

The getIndexInfo() method returns a listing of all the indexes that are associated with the specified column. The getIndexInfo() method takes five parameters: a catalog, a schema, a table, a Boolean to determine whether or not to return unique indexes, and a Boolean to determine whether or not to display approximate or accurate results.

There are two main indexes that can be created on tables. The first type of index is a unique index. This type of index specifies that certain columns cannot contain duplicate values. A unique index might be placed on a Social Security column to prevent duplicate Social Security numbers from being entered. The second type of index is an index that is created to increase the speed of a table search. This type of index does not prevent duplicate data, but enables searches on the table to be carried out faster.

To retrieve all indexes on the tEmployee table, the syntax would be as follows:

```
DatabaseMetaData db = connection.getMetaData();
ResultSet index = db.getIndexInfo("", "DBA", "tEmployee", false, false);
```

To retrieve only indexes on tEmployee that are unique, you would code the following:

```
DatabaseMetaData db = connection.getMetaData();
ResultSet index = db.getIndexInfo("", "DBA", "tEmployee", true, false);
```

getMaxColumnsInSelect(), getMaxColumnsInTable(), getMaxTablesInSelect()

The DatabaseMetaData interface provides many different methods to provide information about different aspects of the database. Three of these methods, getMaxColumnsInSelect(), getMaxColumnsInTable(), and getMaxTablesInSelect(), provide information that determines some of the limitations of the database being used. The methods getMaxColumnsInSelect() and getMaxTablesInSelect() are especially useful in that they provide information on the limitations the database places on SQL statements.

If getMaxTablesInSelect() is 16, as it is in Sybase, then you cannot have more then 16 tables in the From clause of any SQL statement. You might be thinking that you would never have a From clause that uses that many tables, but the database also builds SQL statements when items are deleted and updated to ensure that referential integrity is maintained. Therefore, if you create a parent table that has more than 15 child tables, you will not be able to delete a record from that table.

Now create an application that will determine the maximum number of columns and tables that can be used in a select statement and also the maximum number of columns that can be in a table for the current database. All of the preceding functions return an integer that contains the appropriate information. The code for getting the database information is shown in Listing 5.8.

TYPE | **Listing 5.8. The MaxExample class.**

```
import java.awt.*;
import java.util.*;
import symjava.sql.*;

public class MaxExample extends Frame {
    public MaxExample() {
        super();
        this.resize(300, 300);
        this.show();

        TextArea t = new TextArea(25, 80);
        this.add("Center", t);

        String driverName = "symantec.itools.db.jdbc.Driver";
        Driver driver;
        Connection connection;
            String dbURL = jdbc:dbaw://localhost:8889/Watcom/JDBC/JDBC";
        Properties p = new Properties()
        p.put("user", "dba");
        p.put("password", "sql");
        try {
            driver = (Driver)Class.forName(driverName).newInstance();
            connection = driver.connect(dbURL, p);
            DatabaseMetaData db = connection.getMetaData();
            String s = "";
            s += Integer.toString(db.getMaxColumnsInSelect());
            s += Integer.toString(db.getMaxTablesInSelect());
            s += Integer.toString(db.getMaxColumnsInTable());
            t.setText(s);
        }
        catch (SQLException e) {}
        catch (Exception e) {}
    }

    public static void main (String args[]) {
        MaxExample app = new MaxExample();
    }
}
```

5

getPrimaryKeys()

The DatabaseMetaData interface also provides a method to get the primary key columns for a specified table. The getPrimaryKeys() method enables you to display a listing of all columns that are contained in the primary key for the specified table. This can give you the ability to determine whether the user is changing primary key information or if they have specified all primary key columns when they want to update an item. The method returns a ResultSet object that contains the columns listed in Table 5.7.

Table 5.7. The getPrimaryKeys() ResultSet columns.

Column	Description
TABLE_CAT	The table catalog for the current column's table.
TABLE_SCHEM	The table schema for the current column's table.
TABLE_NAME	The name of the table in which the current column is located.
COLUMN_NAME	The name of the current column.
KEY_SEQ	The order of the column within the primary key.
PK_NAME	The name of the primary key in which the column is contained.

getPrimaryKeys() takes the table catalog, table schema, and table name as parameters. It returns a ResultSet object with the columns specified in Table 5.7. To get a listing of the column name contained in the primary key for tEmployee, you would use the following syntax:

```
// Get the DatabaseMetaData interface
DatabaseMetaData db = connection.getMetaData();
// Get the ResultSet containing the primary key information
ResultSet keys = db.getPrimaryKeys("", "DBA", "tEmployee");
```

When the information is returned to the ResultSet object keys, you would loop through all records in the result set and display the values from the COLUMN_NAME column using the following syntax:

```
while (keys.next()) {
    // Get the Column Name from COLUMN_NAME (Column 4)
    String s = keys.getString(4);
}
```

getProcedures() and getTables()

The DatabaseMetaData interface also provides methods to return object listings from the system catalog tables. Some information contained in the system catalogs other than primary and foreign key information is a listing of all tables and stored procedures currently on the system.

The getProcedures() method returns a listing of all stored procedures currently in the database. This information is returned as a ResultSet object that contains information about the stored procedures in the current database. For a description and listing of the columns returned, please look at the JDBC API documentation.

The getTables() method returns a listing of all the tables in the current database. The table information is returned in a ResultSet object with the columns listed in Table 5.8.

Table 5.8. The getTables() ResultSet columns.

Column	Description
TABLE_CAT	The catalog for the current table.
TABLE_SCHEM	The schema for the current table.
TABLE_NAME	The name of the current table.
TABLE_TYPE	The table type of the current table. TABLE_TYPE can be one of the following: TABLE, VIEW, SYSTEM TABLE, GLOBAL TEMPORARY, LOCAL TEMPORARY, ALIAS, SYNONYM.
REMARKS	A comment about the current table.

The getTables() method takes four parameters. They are, in order: Catalog, Schema, Table Pattern, and Table Type. Catalog, Schema, and Table Pattern are the same parameters used in the methods described above. The Table Type parameter is a specified table type or types to return. The parameter can take an array of strings containing any of the table types listed in the TABLE_TYPE definition in Table 5.8. Passing a NULL value for Table Type will return a listing of all tables in the database, regardless of the table type. The syntax for getting table information from the database is as follows:

```
ResultSet tables = db.getTables("", "DBA", "", null);
```

Notice that the standard empty catalog, the DBA schema, was passed an empty string for the table pattern, indicating that you wanted all tables, and a NULL for the table type. This will return a listing of all tables contained in the current database.

To get the table name from the tables object, use the getString() method to get the value stored in column 3, the TABLE_NAME column.

```
String s = tables.getString(3);
```

Listing 5.9 contains an application that displays a listing of all the tables contained in the current database.

5

TYPE | **Listing 5.9. The `TableExample` class.**

```java
import java.awt.*;
import java.util.*;
import symjava.sql.*;

public class TableExample extends Frame {
    public TableExample () {
        super();
        this.resize(300,300);
        this.show();

        TextArea t = new TextArea(25, 80);
        this.add("Center", t);

        String driverName = "symantec.itools.db.jdbc.Driver";
        Driver driver;
        Connection connection;
            String dbURL = jdbc:dbaw://localhost:8889/Watcom/JDBC/JDBC";
        Properties p = new Properties()
        p.put("user", "dba");
        p.put("password", "sql");
        try {
            driver = (Driver)Class.forName(driverName).newInstance();
            connection = driver.connect(dbURL, p);
            DatabaseMetaData db = connection.getMetaData();
            ResultSet tables = db.getTables("", "DBA", "", null);
            String s = "";
            while (tables.next()) {
                s += tables.getString(3) + "\n";
            }
            t.setText(s);
        }
        catch (SQLException e) {}
        catch (Exception e) {}
    }

    public static void main (String args[]) {
        TableExample app = new TableExample();
    }
}
```

The application window displaying all of the columns in the database is pictured in Figure 5.2.

Figure 5.2.

The `TableExample`
application.

getURL()

The getURL() method enables you to determine the URL of the current database. The URL is the location of the database on the Internet or intranet. You can then use this URL to create other connection objects, if needed. Getting the URL requires a simple call to getURL(), which returns a string that contains the URL of the current database. The syntax is as follows:

```
String s = db.getURL();
```

getUserName()

The getUserName() method is very similar to the getURL() method. The getUserName() method returns the username that you are logged on to the database as. This username, like the URL, can be used to create a new connection to the database as well as to display connection information to the user. The syntax for getting the username is as follows:

```
String s = db.getUserName();
```

supportsGroupBy(), supportsOuterJoins(), supportsTransactions()

The DatabaseMetaData interface provides many different methods that describe different features offered by the current database. These methods all take the form of supports*FEATURE*(), where *FEATURE* is the database feature supported. The method will return a Boolean true if the database supports the feature or a Boolean false if the database does not support the feature.

The supportsGroupBy() method returns a Boolean true if the database supports the Group By feature in SQL statements. The Group By feature allows results to be reported in such a way that items are displayed with other items that match criteria specified in the Group By clause. A common example is to display customers grouped by state. This would display all customers from North Carolina with other customers from North Carolina. The syntax for determining whether or not the database supports the Group By feature is as follows:

```
boolean groupBy = db.supportsGroupBy();
```

The supportsOuterJoins() method returns a Boolean true if the database supports the outer joins feature and a Boolean false if the database does not support the outer joins feature of SQL. Outer joins enable information to be displayed regardless of whether related information is available. An example of where an outer join would be used is when you want to display a listing of customers and their telephone numbers. If you perform a normal join, and there is not a telephone record in the database for the customer, then no information will be displayed for the customer. Using an outer join in this situation would display the customer

5

name, but not the customer telephone information. The syntax for determining whether or not the database supports outer joins is as follows:

```
boolean outerJoins = db.supportsOuterJoins();
```

The supportsTransactions() method returns a Boolean true if the database supports transaction processing and a Boolean false if the database does not support transaction processing. Transaction processing enables the database to process requests as a logical unit of work. Transaction processing provides for more robust business logic to be implemented. When you save customer information, you might save the customer's name, and then you save the customer's address. If you can successfully save the name but not the address and the database does not support transaction processing, the name will remain in the database without a valid address. With transaction processing, you can force the database to process the save of the customer's name and address at one time so that the whole process will fail or succeed, and not each individual statement. The syntax for determining whether the database supports transaction processing is as follows:

```
boolean transactions = db.supportsTransactions();
```

Summary

In today's lesson, you learned how to use some of the basic JDBC interfaces. You learned how to create and use the Connection object, how to use the Statement object, and how to use the DatabaseMetaData object.

After you have specified a URL and a properties object containing the database username and password, you can create a Connection object, which will then be used to create Statement objects and the DatabaseMetaData interface, which provides database information.

The Statement object enables you to execute queries that return results in the ResultSet object, as well as execute updates. Update can be either delete, update, or insert. The Statement object provides you with the basic functions available in SQL databases. You created multiple applications that displayed general database information as well as features supported by the database.

Q&A

Q Can I create and use multiple Connection objects to the same database?

A Yes. You can, and should, use multiple Connection objects to the same database. You might have one Connection object that you use to get information from the database that has AutoCommit turned off, whereas another Connection object might be used to update information to the database immediately. The only warning when using multiple Connection objects is that each Connection object requires a separate database connection. Because most databases either allow only a certain number of connections or you must purchase connections, this could limit the number of users who could use the database.

Workshop

The Workshop provides quiz questions to help you solidify your understanding of the material covered and exercises to give you experience in using what you've learned. The answers are provided in Appendix A, "Quiz and Exercise Answers." Try to understand the quiz and exercise answers before you go on to tomorrow's lesson.

Quiz

1. What is the difference between a connection and a statement?
2. Why would you use the execute() method of the Statement object?
3. What is the difference between having AutoCommit on or off?
4. Describe the effect of commit and rollback.
5. Is a Statement object used for static or dynamic SQL statements?
6. What is the difference between executeQuery() and executeUpdate()?
7. How do you create a DatabaseMetaData object?
8. What are the different types of database tables?
9. What is the syntax for getting a list of columns for a table?
10. What is the difference between getExportedKeys() and getImportedKeys()?

5

Exercises

1. Create an application that opens two connections to the database using different usernames.
2. Write a stored procedure that performs an endless loop and call the stored procedure from a thread running in an application. In a separate thread, cancel the execution of the SQL statement.
3. Use the supportsOuterJoins() method to determine whether your database supports outer joins. If the database supports outer joins, return all employees regardless of whether they have an article in tArticle; otherwise, return a listing of all employees who have articles in tArticle.

Day **6**

Prepared Statements and Callable Statements

Today's lesson covers how to use the PreparedStatement and CallableStatement interfaces. These interfaces provide a way for you to use dynamic SQL statements and SQL stored procedures. The PreparedStatement interface enables you to use dynamic SQL statements and also SQL stored procedures that have no OUT parameters. An explanation of OUT parameters is provided later in the lesson, in the "IN Parameters" and "OUT Parameters" sections.

Using stored procedures, you can provide faster and more encapsulated database processing. They provide you with a way to put common SQL commands into a precompiled SQL statement. The database determines the execution path at compile time, not at runtime. This can make complex SQL commands execute faster.

The topics that are covered today include the following:

- [ ] Dynamic SQL statements
- [ ] Stored procedures
- [ ] The PreparedStatement interface
- [ ] The CallableStatement interface

Dynamic SQL Statements

This lesson covers the PreparedStatement interface. Along with being able to execute stored procedures, the PreparedStatement interface enables you to build base SQL statements and supply the parameters later in the application. Using this method, you can form basic SQL statements and supply multiple sets of parameters without having to build a new SQL statement. This can make repetitious SQL statements easier to execute. You could, for example, have a base SQL Insert statement that takes parameters for the column values, specify different parameters to the PreparedStatement interface, and have them executed.

To build a dynamic SQL statement to be used in a PreparedStatement object, use ? as a placeholder for any dynamic parameters that you will use. The question mark will be interpreted by the interface to mean that you will specify the value for the placeholder later within the code. Look at the following examples on how to create dynamic SQL statements for use with the PreparedStatement interface.

The following example executes a SQL Select statement to get the first names for all employees in the tEmployee table. The Select statement takes the last name as a dynamic variable. The following syntax would be used to create this SQL statement:

```
Select FirstName
From tEmployee
Where LastName = ?
```

When you want to execute this Select statement, you specify the last name for which you want to get a listing of values. The value will be inserted into the Select statement in place of ?, and you can then execute the statement normally.

The following example shows how to use dynamic SQL statements to perform an update. Three placeholders are specified to be used in the statement. You will later replace these three placeholders with the appropriate data values to be executed against the database.

```
Update tEmployee
Set FirstName = ?,
LastName = ?,
MiddleInitial = ?
```

This statement updates all records in tEmployee to the specified data values that you specify. You could use this statement to change all values within a table just by changing the three values that you pass. This makes executing a SQL statement that differs only by the data values easier to execute and process in your code.

Stored Procedures

SQL stored procedures are widely used in business applications. It is not uncommon to have more stored procedures than windows in an application. The usefulness of stored procedures is similar to the usefulness of a compiler. Imagine having to write each line of code for an application as you ran the application. With normal SQL statements, you must build them on the fly. With stored procedures, you can build SQL statements before they are used.

Not only do stored procedures enable you to build SQL statements in advance, but they also enable you to combine multiple SQL statements into one process. You can have SQL statements that insert into, delete from, and update the database, all in one stored procedure. This stored procedure can then be called from anywhere within your application, and the SQL statements contained in the procedure will be executed.

Stored procedures, along with allowing multiple SQL statements to be executed, enable you to call other stored procedures. You can call multiple stored procedures from within a stored procedure. This enables you to separate SQL functionality into its component parts. You might be wondering why you would ever need to divide a stored procedure, but some stored procedures contain hundreds of lines of code and call about ten other stored procedures, each as big as the first.

TIP Don't be afraid to separate your SQL processing into multiple stored procedures. You wouldn't think twice about separating your Java code into similar functional methods. Sometimes it is preferable to put SQL statements into child procedures for speed improvements.

Along with being used to group SQL statements for execution purposes, stored procedures are also used to improve the speed of processing SQL statements. Stored procedures are compiled by the database before they are ever executed. Compiling in the SQL database realm means that the database determines the execution plan that will be used when the stored procedure is called. The execution plan is simply the actions the database performs to execute the SQL statements of the stored procedure.

You can also use a stored procedure to create temporary tables to process information. You might have information from multiple tables that needs complex processing before it can be returned to the user. Using a stored procedure, you can copy all of the data into a temporary table and perform your processing on the data contained in the newly created table. This temporary table is only around until the stored procedure that created it is removed from scope. This means that you can create a temporary (or temp) table in a parent procedure, and the child procedures can then access the table.

6

It is also sometimes preferable to use a temporary table to speed up the execution of large table joins. Some databases have a limit to the number of tables that they will index in a multiple table join. Upon execution of a SQL statement that contains joins between multiple tables, the database uses indexes for a certain number of the tables. When the limit on the number of index tables has been reached, the database searches the other tables by using a table scan.

NOTE

> In SQL, a table scan can be a four-letter word. When a SQL statement performs a table scan, it looks at every row contained within a table. Hopefully, on most searches the database uses the index for the table to move around the table quickly. In some instances, the database has to use a table scan, which is more costly in processing power and time.

The following example demonstrates how to create a stored procedure to be used in your application. The stored procedure takes a last name and returns the first name for all employees in tEmployee that have the specified last name. This stored procedure is not very complicated and is very short, but it hopefully will give you an idea of how to create a stored procedure. You first will declare the procedure by using the CREATE keyword. The CREATE keyword is used to create various objects in the database, such as tables, triggers, and stored procedures. The following line contains the procedure declaration:

```
create procedure getEmployees(in LastName char)
```

NOTE

> The syntax provided is for creating stored procedures using the Sybase SQL Anywhere database. For the syntax for your database, refer to the user's manual.

Notice that the keyword PROCEDURE was specified after the CREATE keyword. The PROCEDURE keyword informs the database that you are creating a stored procedure, as opposed to creating a table. After the PROCEDURE keyword comes the name of the stored procedure that you are creating. This procedure is named getEmployees(), because you are getting employee information. The last item specified in the procedure declaration is the argument list. In the argument list, you specify all parameters that will be passed to the stored procedure. Along with the name of the argument, you also must specify whether the argument is an IN or OUT argument, as well as the data type of the argument. The difference between the IN and OUT parameters is discussed later in this section.

For some databases, you must specify the values that the stored procedure will return if it returns values from a SQL Select statement. The following syntax shows how to specify the columns that you will return from a SQL Select statement. Notice that the data type and the column name that will be returning are specified. The syntax for the result information is as follows:

```
result(FirstName varchar(20))
```

As is the case with some other programming languages, you have to specify the beginning and end of the stored procedure using the BEGIN and END keywords. All SQL statements must be placed between the top-level BEGIN and END. You can have other BEGIN..END blocks within the code.

For the getEmployees() stored procedure, use a SQL Select statement to get the first name for all employees who have their last name specified in the LastName argument. The syntax for the Select statement is as follows:

```
select tEmployee.FirstName
from tEmployee
where tEmployee.LastName=LastName
```

As you can see, you used the argument LastName as the criteria for the Where clause of the Select statement. You also selected the FirstName column to be returned. The full code for the getEmployees() stored procedure is shown in Listing 6.1.

TYPE **Listing 6.1. The getEmployees() stored procedure.**

```
CREATE PROCEDURE getEmployees(in LastName char)
result(FirstName varchar(20)) begin
  select tEmployee.FirstName
    from tEmployee
    where tEmployee.LastName=LastName
end
```

The stored procedure just created is only the tip of the iceberg. Stored procedures can be used for much more complex processing than was just performed. Only one SQL Select statement is used in the stored procedure. You might need to have a variety of statements encompassing all types of data processing within a stored procedure. The only tip I can give you about stored procedures is to use them.

IN **Parameters**

When you are passing parameters to a stored procedure, you can pass the parameters as IN parameters. IN parameters enable you to specify any type of information that the procedure can use. In the previous example, you passed the last name of the employee to the procedure as an IN parameter. You can pass multiple parameters to the procedure to provide as much or as little information as the procedure will require. The syntax for specifying an IN parameter is as follows:

```
create procedure getEmployees(in LastName char)
```

OUT **Parameters**

OUT parameters enable the stored procedure to return information to the calling location, using the parameter. In standard programming terms, an OUT parameter is a parameter that is passed by reference. If an IN parameter is changed within a stored procedure, the calling location will not receive the changed parameter. However, if an OUT parameter is changed within a stored procedure, the calling location can access the changed parameter returned by the stored procedure. The syntax for specifying an OUT parameter is as follows:

```
create procedure getEmployees(out LastName char)
```

INOUT **Parameters**

Some databases have what is called an INOUT parameter. This parameter performs the functions of both the IN and OUT parameters. Unlike the OUT parameter, the INOUT parameter can be used to pass information to the procedure, and unlike the IN parameter, the INOUT parameter can return information to the calling location. The syntax for using an INOUT parameter is as follows:

```
create procedure getEmployees(inout LastName char)
```

The PreparedStatement **Interface**

The PreparedStatement interface provides you with a means to execute stored procedures and dynamic SQL statements. You learned the methods for creating dynamic SQL statements and basic stored procedures in the "DynamicSQL Statements" section.

The PreparedStatement interface provides you with various methods for executing SQL statements and procedures, as well as setting the dynamic parameters for these SQL statements. The interface must be assigned using a method call. Unlike normal Java objects, the PreparedStatement interface cannot be created directly—it must be instantiated using a method call of another object. To create a PreparedStatement object, you can call the prepareStatement() method of the Connection object. This method enables you to create the PreparedStatement object that you will be using. The method takes as a parameter a String object that contains the stored procedure syntax of the dynamic SQL statement syntax that you will be using. For example, to create a PreparedStatement object that calls the stored procedure getEmployees(), you would use the following syntax:

```
PreparedStatement prepare = connection.prepareStatement("getEmployees(?)");
```

This code creates a PreparedStatement object that you can use to call the stored procedure getEmployees(). Notice that you specify ? as the parameter for the stored procedure. This indicates that you will specify the IN parameter at a later time.

TIP

You could have specified the parameter for the stored procedure in the passed string. This lesson uses dynamic parameters only to illustrate how to use the PreparedStatement interface.

Along with using the PreparedStatement to execute stored procedures, you can also use the interface to execute dynamic SQL statements. These dynamic statements can be executed many times with varying parameters. This makes multiple statement execution easier to handle and process. To create a PreparedStatement object that contains a dynamic SQL statement to get a listing of employees based on a specified last name, you would use the following syntax:

```
String sql = "select * from tEmployee where LastName = ?";
PreparedStatement prepare = connection.prepareStatement(sql);
```

Notice that you specify ? in place of the last name that the SQL statement will be using. This indicates to the PreparedStatement interface that you will specify the parameter to use for ? at a later time, using the methods provided by the PreparedStatement interface.

The PreparedStatement interface provides various methods for executing different types of SQL statements, as well as methods for handling the insertion and removal of parameters to the SQL statements. Table 6.1 lists all of the methods provided by the PreparedStatement interface. I'll go over a few of the set*XXX*() methods. Most of the methods are similar in functionality to the other methods, so only a few of the methods require a description of their use.

6

Table 6.1. `PreparedStatement` **interface methods.**

Method	Description
clearParameters	Clears all of the parameters currently being used by the SQL statement contained in the interface.
execute	Executes the current SQL statement or stored procedure for the interface.
executeQuery	Executes a SQL statement or procedure that returns a result set.
executeUpdate	Executes a SQL statement that updates the database.
setAsciiStream	Sets the specified parameter to the passed ASCII stream.
setBinaryStream	Sets the specified parameter to the passed Binary stream.
setBoolean	Sets the specified parameter to the passed Boolean value.
setByte	Sets the specified parameter to the passed Byte variable.
setBytes	Sets the specified parameter to the passed Byte array.
setDate	Sets the specified parameter to the passed Date object.
setDouble	Sets the specified parameter to the passed Double value.
setFloat	Sets the specified parameter to the passed Float value.
setInt	Sets the specified parameter to the passed Integer value.
setLong	Sets the specified parameter to the passed Long value.
setNull	Sets the specified parameter to a NULL value.
setNumeric	Sets the specified parameter to a Numeric value.
setObject	Sets the specified parameter to the passed object.
setShort	Sets the specified parameter to the passed Short value.
setString	Sets the specified parameter to the passed String value.
setTime	Sets the specified parameter to the passed Time object.
setTimestamp	Sets the specified parameter to the passed Timestamp value.
setUnicodeStream	Sets the specified parameter to the passed Unicode stream.

clearParameters()

The `clearParameters()` method clears all of the parameters currently being used by the dynamic SQL statement or stored procedure for the `PreparedStatement` object. Clearing the parameters enables you to ensure that all old values have been removed before specifying new parameter values. The syntax for calling the method is as follows:

```
prepare.clearParameters();
```

execute()

The execute() method enables you to execute a SQL statement, usually a stored procedure, that returns more than one result set or performs more than one update statement. Using the methods of the ResultSet object, about which you learn on Day 7, "Result Sets and Metadata," you can move throughout the results and update information returned by the execute() method. The syntax for calling the method is as follows:

```
prepare.execute();
```

executeQuery()

The executeQuery() method is used to execute SQL statements and stored procedures that return a result set. Unlike the execute() method, however, this method returns only a single result set. The syntax for using the method is as follows:

```
ResultSet results = prepare.executeQuery();
```

executeUpdate()

The executeUpdate() method enables you to execute SQL statements and stored procedures that perform only updates to the database. This method will not return a result set, but it will return the number of records that were affected by the executed update statement. The syntax for using this method is as follows:

```
int count = prepare.executeUpdate();
```

setAsciiStream()

The setAsciiStream() method enables you to set parameters that are sent to the database as the LongVarChar data type. The method, like all of the setXXX() methods, takes the parameter for which the data will be used. The parameter order is the order in which the ? appeared in the statement; therefore, the first ? is parameter 1, and so on. The method also takes an InputStream object and the length of the input stream. The syntax for using the setAsciiStream() method is as follows:

```
prepare.setAsciiStream(1, inputStreamObject, length);
```

6

setInt()

One of the more common methods that you will use is the setInt() method. This method takes the parameter that specifies an integer value that will be placed into the SQL statement. The syntax for calling the method is as follows:

```
prepare.setInt(1, 1);
```

This code sets the value to use for the first parameter in the SQL statement to the integer value of 1.

setString()

The setString() method is the method that is likely to be called most often. It takes the parameter that will be specified and a String object. The String object is placed into the SQL statement in place of ?. The syntax for calling the method is as follows:

```
prepare.setString(1, "Java is Cool");
```

This code sets the value to use for the first parameter to the string "Java is Cool". The ? contained in the SQL statement will be replaced with the string specified.

DynamicSQL Application

Now that you have learned the methods that the PreparedStatement interface provides, you will write an application to demonstrate the actual use of the PreparedStatement interface. This application will enable you to get a listing of all employees that have a specified last name.

You'll create an application that contains a TextField object as well as a TextArea object. The TextField object enables you to enter the last name of the employees you want to display, and the TextArea object displays the first names of all the employees who have the specified last name. You'll use a PreparedStatement object to enable you to specify the SQL syntax once and use it several times.

The application builds and displays the frame in the constructor method. It also connects to the database and creates the PreparedStatement object with the SQL statement that you will be using. You will want to display the text field and text area on the created frame. You will need to use a BorderLayout to display the TextField in the North and the TextArea in the center.

The handleEvent() method checks to see whether an event occurred within the TextField component. If an event did occur, the method executes the SQL statement with the specified last name and displays the results in the TextArea component.

Listing 6.2 contains the code for the DynamicSQL application.

Listing 6.2. The DynamicSQL application.

```
import java.awt.*;
import java.util.*;
import symjava.sql.*;

public class DynamicSQL extends Frame {
    Connection connection;
    PreparedStatement prepare;
    TextField lastname;
    TextArea text;

    public DynamicSQL () {
        super();

        try {
            String driverName = "symantec.itools.db.jdbc.Driver";
            Driver driver = (Driver)Class.forName(driverName).newInstance();
            Properties p = new Properties();
            p.put("user", "dba");
            p.put("password", "sql");
            String dbURL = "jdbc:dbaw://localhost:8889/WATCOM/JDBC/JDBC";
            connection = driver.connect(dbURL, p);
            // Create the SQL statement that we will use
            String sql = "select FirstName from tEmployee where LastName = ?";
            prepare = connection.prepareCall(sql);
        }
        catch (SQLException e) {}
        catch (Exception e) {}

        // Add the text components
        lastname = new TextField(25);
        text = new TextArea(20,60);
        this.add("North", lastname);
        this.add("Center", text);

        // Resize window and display
        this.resize(300, 300);
        this.show();
    }

    public boolean handleEvent (Event evt) {
        // If the textfield caused the event, display items
        if (evt.target == lastname) {
            try {
                // Clear the parameters for the current statement
                prepare.clearParameters();
                // Specify the lastname parameter
                prepare.setString(1, lastname.getText());
                // Execute the statement and get the result set
                ResultSet results = prepare.executeQuery();

                String stext = "";
                // Loop through the returned items and display
                while (results.next()) {
                    stext += results.getString(1) + "\n";
```

continues

6

Listing 6.2. continued

```
            }
            // Set the text displayed for the textarea component
            text.setText(stext);
        }
        catch (SQLException e) {}
    }

    return super.handleEvent(evt);
}

public static void main (String args[]) {
    DynamicSQL app = new DynamicSQL();
}
}
```

Figure 6.1 contains the output frame produced by the DynamicSQL class. Notice that I have entered Hobbs in the top TextField component, and the corresponding employees with that last name are displayed in the TextArea component.

Figure 6.1.

The DynamicSQL *application.*

The CallableStatement Interface

The CallableStatement interface enables you to execute stored procedures that have OUT parameters. OUT parameters can best be compared to variables passed by reference in the programming world. These variables do not usually contain any information going into the stored procedure but do contain information after the stored procedure finishes execution. They enable you to get information from the stored procedure, above and beyond the normal result set information that a stored procedure can return.

The CallableStatement interface provides several methods for getting the variable that is passed back from the stored procedure, as well as methods for informing the interface that a parameter is actually an OUT parameter. The CallableStatement object is inherited from PreparedStatement and therefore provides all of the functionality of the PreparedStatement object.

The CallableStatement interface provides the methods listed in Table 6.2.

Table 6.2. CallableStatement **interface methods.**

Method	Description
getBoolean	Returns a Boolean from the specified OUT parameter.
getByte	Returns a byte from the specified OUT parameter.
getBytes	Returns an array of bytes from the specified OUT parameter.
getDate	Returns a Date object from the specified OUT parameter.
getDouble	Returns a Double value from the specified OUT parameter.
getFloat	Returns a Float value from the specified OUT parameter.
getInt	Returns an Integer value from the specified OUT parameter.
getLong	Returns a Long value from the specified OUT parameter.
getNumeric	Returns a Numeric value from the specified OUT parameter.
getObject	Returns a Java Object value from the specified OUT parameter.
getShort	Returns a Short value from the specified OUT parameter.
getString	Returns a String value from the specified OUT parameter.
getTime	Returns a Time object from the specified OUT parameter.
getTimestamp	Returns a Timestamp object from the specified OUT parameter.
registerOutParameter	Registers a specified parameter as a specified data type from the Types class.
wasNull	Returns a TRUE if the last parameter received was NULL.

getBoolean()

The getBoolean() method enables you to get an OUT procedure parameter that is of the Boolean data type. You get the OUT parameter by specifying the index of the parameter. The value that is returned is the value returned by the stored procedure in the specified OUT parameter. The syntax for using the getBoolean() method is as follows:

```
boolean b = call.getBoolean(1);
```

This code returns the first parameter specified in the stored procedure syntax.

getByte()

The getByte() method enables you to get an OUT procedure parameter that is a byte. To get an OUT parameter, you must specify the index of the parameter for which you want to get the value. The syntax for using the getByte() method is as follows:

```
byte b = call.getByte(1);
```

This code returns the first parameter specified in the stored procedure as a byte.

getDate()

The getDate() method enables you to get the value of the returned OUT parameter as a Java Date object. The method takes an integer that identifies the parameter for which you want to get the value. The syntax for the getDate() method is as follows:

```
Date d = call.getDate(1);
```

This code returns the value returned by the stored procedure as a Java Date object.

getObject()

The getObject() method enables you to get a database-specific object as a Java language object. The method can take a variety of parameters, but the most effective way to use the method is to declare the object type using the registerOutParameter() method. You will need to define the object description in Java and then return the value returned by the database into this object. The syntax for using the getObject() method is as follows:

```
JavaObject o = call.getObject(1);
```

This code returns the database object that is returned into the first parameter of the stored procedure into the Java object JavaObject.

registerOutParameter()

The registerOutParameter() method enables you to declare parameters as OUT or INOUT parameters so that they can be accessed by Java when execution of the procedure has finished. When you are calling the registerOutParameter() method, you must specify the parameter index of the parameter that you are declaring to be an OUT or INOUT parameter, as well as the SQL data type of the parameter, using the values in the SQL Types class. The syntax for calling the registerOutParameter() method is as follows:

```
call.registerOutParameter(1, Types.INTEGER);
```

This code registers the first parameter in the stored procedure as an OUT or INOUT parameter and declares it to be of type INTEGER. After execution of the stored procedure has finished, you can access the value returned by the stored procedure by using the getInt() method.

wasNull()

The wasNull() method enables you to determine whether the value returned last by the CallableStatement interface was NULL. After calling one of the getXXX() methods, you can call the wasNull() method to determine whether the value returned was a NULL value. The syntax for using the wasNull() method is as follows:

```
int i = call.getInt(1);
boolean b = call.wasNull();
```

This code gets the value returned by the procedure into the first parameter and then stores whether the returned integer was NULL.

CallableStatement **Example**

The following example demonstrates the use of the CallableStatement interface. TextArea displays the number of records returned by the procedure.

You will create the following stored procedure to execute for this example:

```
create procedure getEmployees(out count integer)
begin
  select count(tEmployee.LastName) into count
    from tEmployee
```

As you can see, the procedure returns the number of records in the table tEmployee. It uses the SELECT..INTO method to return the value into the count parameter.

Listing 6.3 contains the code for the CallableSQL application.

TYPE **Listing 6.3. The** CallableSQL **example.**

```
import java.awt.*;
import java.util.*;
import symjava.sql.*;

public class CallableSQL extends Frame {
        TextArea tarea;
        Connection c;

        public CallableSQL () {
                super();
```

continues

Listing 6.3. continued

```
                    // create a connection to the database
                    try {
                            String driverName = "symantec.itools.db.jdbc.Driver";
                            Driver driver =
                            ➡(Driver)Class.forName(driverName).newInstance();
                            Properties p = new Properties();
                            p.put("user", "dba");
                            p.put("password", "sql");
                            String dbURL =
                            ➡"jdbc:dbaw://localhost:8889/WATCOM/JDBC/JDBC";
c = driver.connect(dbURL, p);
                    }
                    catch (Exception e) {}

                    tarea = new TextArea(20,60);
                    this.add("Center", tarea);

                    this.resize(300,300);
                    this.show();

                    // Create the sql that will be executed
                    String sql = "execute getEmployees ?";

                    try {
                            CallableStatement call = c.prepareCall(sql);

                            // declare an integer value and set it for the
                            // first parameter
                            int i = 0;
                            call.setInt(1, i);

                            // register the first parameter as an integer
                            call.registerOutParameter(1, Types.INTEGER);

                            // execute the stored procedure
                            call.execute();

                            // get the returned count
                            i = call.getInt(1);
                            // display the returned result
                            tarea.setText("There are " + Integer.toString(i) +
                                    " Employees");
                    }
                    catch (SQLException e) {}
            }


            public static void main (String args[]) {
                    CallableSQL app = new CallableSQL();
            }
    }
```

Figure 6.2 contains the window created by the CallableSQL example. Notice that the window shows that there are seven employees in the tEmployee table.

Figure 6.2.

The CallableSQL *example.*

Summary

In today's lesson, you learned how to create and use stored procedures, as well as the JDBC objects for using them. You also learned how to use dynamic SQL statements to simplify the execution of a SQL statement several times.

The PreparedStatement object enables you to call a dynamic SQL statement or a stored procedure and pass the parameters for the statement later, using the provided methods of the PreparedStatement interface.

The CallableStatement interface enables you to call stored procedures that have OUT and INOUT parameters. These parameters are equivalent to reference parameters in other programming languages. The methods provided by the CallableStatement interface let you access the parameters returned by the stored procedure.

Workshop

The Workshop provides quiz questions to help you solidify your understanding of the material covered and exercises to give you experience in using what you've learned. The answers are provided in Appendix A, "Quiz and Exercise Answers." Try to understand the quiz and exercise answers before you go on to tomorrow's lesson.

Quiz

1. What character do you use to indicate a dynamic parameter?
2. List the three different types of parameters that can be passed to a stored procedure.
3. What method is used to create a PreparedStatement object?

4. What method is used to create a `CallableStatement` object?

5. What does the `registerOutParameter()` method do?

6. What does the `wasNull()` method tell you?

7. What are some advantages to using stored procedures?

8. What are some advantages to using dynamic SQL statements?

9. What is an `INOUT` parameter?

10. What is the difference between an `IN` and `OUT` parameter?

Exercises

1. Write a stored procedure that lets you pass a last name to the procedure and get the number of employees who have that last name back as an `OUT` parameter.

2. Create a dynamic SQL statement that deletes items from tEmployee based on the employee's Social Security number.

3. Create a dynamic SQL statement that lets you specify the `FirstName`, `LastName`, `MiddleInitial`, and `SSN` columns through the `setXXX()` methods of the `PreparedStatement` object.

Week 1

Day 7

Result Sets and Metadata

In the last two days, you have learned how to make a connection to the database, create and execute SQL statements, get database information, and use dynamic SQL statements and stored procedures. You have learned mainly how to send SQL statements to the database, but today you will learn how to handle and process the information the database sends back. Today, you will learn about ResultSet objects. You will learn how to use a ResultSet object to access values retrieved from the database, and you also will learn how to use the ResultSetMetaData object to get information on the results returned from the database.

Today's lesson covers the following topics:

- ☐ Getting a ResultSet object
- ☐ The ResultSet object methods
- ☐ Getting the metadata for a ResultSet
- ☐ Using the metadata for a ResultSet

Getting a ResultSet **Object**

The ResultSet object is very similar to a multidimensional array. It contains a finite set of records, or rows, and each record contains a finite set of columns. Each of these columns contains some data, whether it be a character, an integer, or a NULL value. Figure 7.1 displays a visual representation of a ResultSet object. The graph displayed contains five records containing five columns. In each column, there is a piece of data that can be accessed using the methods of the ResultSet object.

Figure 7.1.

Graph displaying a result set.

Data	Data	Data	Data	Data
Data	Data	Data	Data	Data
Data	Data	Data	Data	Data
Data	Data	Data	Data	Data
Data	Data	Data	Data	Data

Rows

Columns

On Day 5, "JDBC Interfaces," you used the DatabaseMetaData methods to determine what tables are contained in the database. This method returned a ResultSet object as the return value. You then looped through this result set and extracted all of the table names for the column containing the information.

The process for getting result information from the database is straightforward. To begin, you'll need to make a connection to the database.

NOTE Today's code examples use the JDBC database that is included on this book's CD-ROM.

The code for making a connection to the database is as follows:

```
Connection connection = driver.connect(dbURL, p);
```

The connection is created by calling the connect() method of the Driver object. The returned connection is a static connection to the database and can be closed only by calling the close() method of the Connection object, or it can be closed when the Connection object loses scope.

After connecting to the database, you will want to create a SQL statement that returns results from the database. For this example, select all of the employees contained in the table tEmployee. However, you only want the first name and last name of the employees to be returned, so the SQL code for this statement is as follows:

```
select FirstName, LastName from tEmployee
```

After you have decided what SQL statement you want to send to the database, the next step is to create a Statement object to execute these SQL statements. You create a Statement object by calling the createStatement() method of the Connection object. The code for this is as follows:

```
Statement sqlStatement = connection.createStatement();
```

Now that you have a Statement object, execute your SQL statement and get the results returned into a ResultSet object. The ResultSet object returned will contain all of the records from the database that match the criteria of the SQL statement. Because your SQL statement has no criteria, the database will return all rows from tEmployee. Also, because you selected only the FirstName and LastName columns in the SQL statement, there will be only two columns in the returned ResultSet object. Here's the code to get the results of the executed SQL statement:

```
String sql = "select FirstName, LastName from tEmployee";
ResultSet employees = sqlStatement.executeQuery(sql);
```

Notice that the executeQuery() method of the Statement object is called. This method executes a SQL query and returns the results into a ResultSet object.

Getting Results

In the previous example, you executed a SQL statement and got results back from the database. However, you got only the ResultSet object from the database; you did not actually view any of the results from the database. To view the results that were returned, you must use the next() and getNNN() methods of the ResultSet object. These methods provide for navigating through the records of the ResultSet object and accessing the data values in the ResultSet object, respectively.

The next() method enables you to move the pointer of the ResultSet object to the next record returned from the database. One badly needed method that is missing from the ResultSet object is a previous() method. After you have called the next() method, there is no functionality built into the ResultSet object to go to the previous record. The next()

method returns a Boolean value that indicates whether a record exists at the current pointer. If there is a valid record at the current pointer, then the method will return a `true`; otherwise, the method will return a `false`.

TIP

> You can call the `getResultSet()` method of the `Statement` object to get the current `ResultSet` object again. You can then loop back through the `ResultSet` to the correct record or row. A more robust solution to this problem is presented on Day 8, "Creating JDBC/SQL Objects." As you've learned, the `next()` method moves the `ResultSet` object's pointer to the next record, but the pointer initially starts at a `NULL` record that precedes the first actual record. This means that you will have to call the `next()` method before you try to access any of the data contained in the result set.

The `getNNN()` methods of the `ResultSet` object enable you to access the data contained in the columns of the object. The `getNNN()` methods are overloaded so that you can pass the column name as it appears in the `select` statement, or the column number, which will be the order it occurred in the `select` statement. The method that you call will return the method's specified data type, so the `getString()` method will return its data in a `String` object.

WARNING

> When you get data from columns using the column name to reference the column, the specified column name has to match exactly how it is indicated in the `select` statement. Therefore, the `FirstName` column must be referenced in the `getString()` method exactly as it was referenced in the SQL `select` statement.

The code to move to the next record and access data within a column is as follows:

```
results.next();
String name =
➥results.getString("FirstName") + " " + results.getString("LastName");
```

This example only retrieves information from the initial record. To get the information for all records, you must make a loop that loops through all records in the `ResultSet` object. To do this, create a `while` loop that calls the `next()` method until it returns `false`. Here's the code for the `while` loop:

```
while (results.next()) {
    String name += results.getString(1) + " " + results.getString(2);
}
```

In the `ResultSetExample`, write an application that loops through all records contained in the table tEmployee and displays them within a `TextArea` object. The code for the `ResultSetExample` is shown in Listing 7.1.

TYPE **Listing 7.1. The `ResultSetExample` class.**

```
import java.awt.*;
import java.util.*;
import symjava.sql.*;

public class ResultSetExample extends Frame {
    public ResultSetExample () {
        super();
        this.resize(300, 300);
        this.show();
        TextArea text = new TextArea(25, 80);
        this.add("Center", text);

        try {
            String driverName = "symantec.itools.db.jdbc.Driver";
            Driver driver = (Driver)Class.forName(driverName).newInstance();
            Properties p = new Properties();
            p.put("user", "dba");
            p.put("password", "sql");
            String dbURL = "jdbc:dbaw://localhost:8889/WATCOM/JDBC/JDBC";
            Connection connection = driver.connect(dbURL, p);
            String sql = "select FirstName, LastName from tEmployee";
            Statement sqlStatement = connection.createStatement();
            ResultSet results = sqlStatement.executeQuery(sql);

            String displayText = "";
            while (results.next()) {
                displayText +=
                ➥results.getString("FirstName") + " " +
                ➥results.getString("LastName");
            }

            text.setText(displayText);
        }
        catch (SQLException e) {}
        catch (Exception e) {}
    }

    public static void main (String args[]) {
        ResultSetExample app = new ResultSetExample();
    }
}
```

The output from the `ResultSetExample` class is displayed in Figure 7.2. Notice that the text area displays the first and last names of all employees whom it found in the tEmployee table. The text area easily could have been a `List` or `Choice` object, allowing the user to choose a valid employee.

Figure 7.2.

The ResultSet
Example *application
window.*

ResultSet **Methods**

The complete list of ResultSet methods appears in Table 7.1.

Table 7.1. The ResultSet **methods.**

Method	Description
clearWarnings	Clears the current warning for the ResultSet object.
close	Closes the current ResultSet object.
findColumn	Returns the column index of the passed column name.
getAsciiStream	Returns the column, passed as a column name or a column index, as a Java InputStream object.
getBignum	Returns the column as a Bignum object.
getBinaryStream	Returns the column, passed as a column name or a column index, as a Java InputStream object.
getBoolean	Returns the column, passed as a column name or a column index, as a Boolean data type.
getByte	Returns the column, passed as a column name or a column index, as a byte.
getBytes	Returns the column, passed as a column name or a column index, as an array of bytes.
getCursorName	Returns a string containing the name of the cursor used by the ResultSet object.
getDate	Returns the column, passed as a column name or a column index, as a Java Date object.
getDouble	Returns the column, passed as a column name or a column index, as a Double data type.

7

Method	Description
getFloat	Returns the column, passed as a column name or a column index, as a Float data type.
getInt	Returns the column, passed as a column name or a column index, as an Integer data type.
getLong	Returns the column, passed as a column name or a column index, as a Long data type.
getMetaData	Returns a ResultSetMetaData object containing information about the current result set.
getObject	Returns the column, passed as a column name or a column index, as a Java object.
getShort	Returns the column, passed as a column name or a column index, as a Short data type.
getString	Returns the column, passed as a column name or a column index, as a Java string.
getTime	Returns the column, passed as a column name or a column index, as a Java Time object.
getTimestamp	Returns the column, passed as a column name or a column index, as a Java Timestamp object.
getUnicodeStream	Returns the column, passed as a column name or a column index, as a Java InputStream object.
getWarnings	Returns the current warning for the ResultSet object as a SQLWarning object.
next	Moves the record pointer to the next valid record in the ResultSet object. Returns true if the next record is valid, false if the next record is not valid.
wasNULL	Returns true if the last column read using a getNNN method had the value of SQL NULL.

getAsciiStream() **and** getUnicodeStream()

Both the getAsciiStream() and getUnicodeStream() methods return an InputStream object containing the data of the column passed. These two methods are used mainly to get data from database columns that are of type LongVarChar. The InputStream object contains all of the information that was contained in the database column as well as standard InputStream methods such as read(), skip(), and mark().

getBinaryStream()

The getBinaryStream() method of the ResultSet object returns the database column data in binary format. This method is used mainly to access data that is stored within database columns of type LongBinary and LongVarBinary. Data typically stored in these types of columns includes audio and video data.

getCursorName()

The getCursorName() method of the ResultSet object returns the name of the current cursor being used by the object. A SQL cursor enables the retrieval of the result set. The cursor name can also be used to delete the current row of the result set. By passing the cursor name to a positioned delete, you can delete the current row of the cursor, which is also the current row in the ResultSet object. This type of procedure can be useful if you are trying to delete a certain item, but don't know the primary key for the item. By looping through the cursor, you can search until you find the record that matches your specifications and then pass the cursor name to a delete statement and have the current record deleted.

As an example, suppose that you want to delete the first item returned by a select statement that gets all of the employees in the tEmployee table. The first item cannot be deleted directly, because this example would not exist if it did. You would execute the SQL query and store the results in a ResultSet object. After calling the next() method to place the cursor position onto the initial record, you would execute the following SQL syntax:

```
delete from tEmployee where current of cursorname
```

In this SQL statement, cursorname would be the name of the cursor that contains the SQL select statement that you executed. The CursorExample class in Listing 7.2 demonstrates the use of the getCursorName() method.

TYPE   **Listing 7.2. The CursorExample class.**

```
import java.awt.*;
import java.util.*;
import symjava.sql.*;

public class CursorExample extends Frame {
    public CursorExample () {
        super();
        this.resize(300, 300);
        this.show();

        try {
            String driverName = "symantec.itools.db.jdbc.Driver";
            Driver driver = (Driver)Class.forName(driverName).newInstance();
            Properties p = new Properties();
            p.put("user", "dba");
            p.put("password", "sql");
```

```
        String dbURL = "jdbc:dbaw://localhost:8889/WATCOM/JDBC/JDBC";
        Connection connection = driver.connect(dbURL, p);
        Statement sqlStatement = connection.createStatement();

        // Create the SQL to get employees
        String sql = "select * from tEmployee";
        // Get the employees
        ResultSet records = sqlStatement.executeQuery(sql);
        // Call the next method to place cursor on initial record
        records.next();
        // Build the string to delete the initial record
        sql = "delete from tEmployee where current of " +
        ➥records.getCursorName();
        sqlStatement.executeUpdate(sql);
    }
    catch (SQLException e) {}
    catch (Exception e) {}
}

public static void main (String args[]) {
    CursorExample app = new CursorExample();
}
}
```

getMetaData()

The getMetaData() method of the ResultSet object returns a ResultSetMetaData object that contains information about the current result set. This information includes the column count and information on the column's data type. The syntax for getting a ResultSetMetaData object is as follows:

```
ResultSetMetaData metaData = resultSetObject.getMetaData();
```

The ResultSetMetaData object is covered in the "The ResultSetMetaData Object" section of today's lesson.

The getObject() Methods

The ResultSet object provides six methods for getting general object data from the database. The getObject() method enables Java developers to get data types other than the type defined in java.sql.Types. This gives developers methods to access object-oriented databases (OODBs), which are making their way into the computing realm.

The ResultSetMetaData Object

The ResultSetMetaData object provides various methods for getting information about the data that was returned into a ResultSet object. These methods provide you with a way to

7

determine such information as the name and type of the column, the table of which a column is a member, and whether a column can accept NULL. These methods let you determine information about the result set columns and provide you with ways to create more robust applications.

The methods available in the ResultSetMetaData object are listed in Table 7.2.

Table 7.2. ResultSetMetaData **interface methods.**

Method	Description
getCatalogName	Returns a string containing the catalog name of the specified column's table.
getColumnCount	Returns an integer containing the number of columns that are in the current ResultSet object.
getColumnDisplaySize	Returns an integer containing the maximum number of characters that the specified column's data requires.
getColumnLabel	Returns a string containing the label that should be used when displaying the column to the user.
getColumnName	Returns a string containing the name of the specified column.
getColumnType	Returns an integer that identifies the type of the specified column. The integer is one of the valid SQL data types listed in java.sql.Types (symjava.sql.Types).
getColumnTypeName	Returns the specified column's type as the current database identifies it.
getPrecision	Returns an integer containing the decimal precision of the specified column.
getScale	Returns an integer containing the decimal scale for the specified column.
getSchemaName	Returns a string containing the database schema for the specified column's table.
getTableName	Returns a string containing the table name of the specified column.
isAutoIncrement	Returns a Boolean value describing whether or not the specified column is an AutoIncrement column.
isCaseSensitive	Returns a Boolean value describing whether or not the case of the specified column is significant.
isCurrency	Returns a Boolean value describing whether or not the specified column identifies a monetary value.

Method	Description
isDefinitelyWritable	Returns a Boolean value describing whether or not the specified column can accept updates.
isNULLable	Returns a Boolean value describing whether or not the specified column can accept SQL NULL.
isReadOnly	Returns a Boolean value describing whether or not the specified column can be updated.
isSearchable	Returns a Boolean value describing whether or not the specified column can be used to determine the criteria of a SQL Select statement.
isSigned	Returns a Boolean value describing whether or not the specified column is a signed data type.
isWritable	Returns a Boolean value describing whether or not the specified column can be updated.

The MetaDataExample class demonstrates how to obtain a ResultSetMetaData object. Listing 7.3 shows the code for the MetaDataExample class.

Listing 7.3. The MetaDataExample class.

```
import java.awt.*;
import java.util.*;
import symjava.sql.*;

public class MetaDataExample extends Frame {
    public MetaDataExample () {
        super();
        this.resize(300, 300);
        this.show();

        try {
            String driverName = "symantec.itools.db.jdbc.Driver";
            Driver driver = (Driver)Class.forName(driverName).newInstance();
            Properties p = new Properties();
            p.put("user", "dba");
            p.put("password", "sql");
            String dbURL = "jdbc:dbaw://localhost:8889/WATCOM/JDBC/JDBC";
            Connection connection = driver.connect(dbURL, p);
            // Specifiy a SQL Statement to get Results
            String sql = "select * from tEmployee";
            Statement sqlStatement = connection.createStatement();
            ResultSet records = sqlStatement.executeQuery(sql);
            // Create a MetaData object by calling
```

continues

Listing 7.3. continued

```
                // the getMetaData method
                ResultSetMetaData meta = records.getMetaData();
        }
        catch (SQLException e) {}
        catch (Exception e) {}
    }

    public static void main (String args[]) {
        MetaDataExample app = new MetaDataExample();
    }
}
```

getCatalogName()

The getCatalogName() method of the ResultSetMetaData object enables you to get the database catalog name for the specified column's table. This catalog name can then be used to get other information from a DatabaseMetaData object, such as primary key information. The getCatalogName() method takes an integer that identifies the column and returns the catalog for that column's table. The syntax for calling the getCatalogName() is as follows:

```
String catalog = records.getCatalogName(1);
```

This code would return the catalog name for the table that contains the first column contained in the result set. Unlike the ResultSet object, however, only the column index can be used to specify a column, not the column name.

getColumnCount()

The getColumnCount() method of the ResultSetMetaData object enables you to determine the number of columns returned in the result set. This is useful when you use a select * statement. Because * indicates that you want all columns returned, there is no way to know how many columns were actually returned. Using the getColumnCount() method, you can determine the exact number of columns that were returned by the SQL query. The ColCountExample class in Listing 7.4 illustrates the use of the getColumnCount() method. The syntax for using the method is as follows:

```
int count = metaData.getColumnCount();
```

The ColCountExample demonstrates how to use the getColumnCount() method to determine the number of columns returned by a SQL query. You will execute a query that selects all information from tEmployee and then determines the number of columns that were returned into the ResultSet object.

Listing 7.4. The `ColCountExample` **class.**

```
import java.awt.*;
import java.util.*;
import symjava.sql.*;

public class ColCountExample extends Frame {
    public ColCountExample () {
        super();
        this.resize(300, 300);
        this.show();

        try {
            String driverName = "symantec.itools.db.jdbc.Driver";
            Driver driver = (Driver)Class.forName(driverName).newInstance();
            Properties p = new Properties();
            p.put("user", "dba");
            p.put("password", "sql");
            String dbURL = "jdbc:dbaw://localhost:8889/WATCOM/JDBC/JDBC";
            Connection connection = driver.connect(dbURL, p);
            // Select all items from tEmployee
            String sql = "select * from tEmployee";
            Statement sqlStatement = connection.createStatement();
            ResultSet records = sqlStatement.executeQuery(sql);
            // Get a meta data object
            ResultSetMetaData metaData = records.getMetaData();
            // Determine the number of columns in result set
            int columns = metaData.getColumnCount();
        }
        catch (SQLException e) {}
        catch (Exception e) {}
    }

    public static void main (String args[]) {
        ColCountExample app = new ColCountExample();
    }
}
```

getColumnName()

The getColumnName() method of the ResultSetMetaData object enables you to get the column name for the specified column index. The getColumnName() method takes the specified column index and returns the column name for that column. The column name returned would match the name specified in a SQL select statement. The syntax for getting the column name is as follows:

```
String colName = metaData.getColumnName();
```

In the ColumnExample class, you will use the ColCountExample class that was created in Listing 7.4 and add a TextArea object. In the text area, you will display a listing of all the columns that were returned by the SQL `select` statement. You will then create a `displayColumns()` method that takes a `ResultSetMetaData` object and displays all of the columns in the specified text area. Listing 7.5 contains the complete code for the `ColumnExample` class.

TYPE **Listing 7.5. The `ColumnExample` class.**

```java
import java.awt.*;
import java.util.*;
import symjava.sql.*;

public class ColumnExample extends Frame {
    public ColumnExample () {
        super();
        this.resize(300, 300);
        this.show();
        // Add the TextArea Object
        TextArea text = new TextArea(25, 80);
        this.add("center", text);

        try {
            String driverName = "symantec.itools.db.jdbc.Driver";
            Driver driver = (Driver)Class.forName(driverName).newInstance();
            Properties p = new Properties();
            p.put("user", "dba");
            p.put("password", "sql");
            String dbURL = "jdbc:dbaw://localhost:8889/WATCOM/JDBC/JDBC";
            Connection connection = driver.connect(dbURL, p);
            String sql = "select * from tEmployee";
            Statement sqlStatement = connection.createStatement();
            ResultSet records = sqlStatement.executeQuery(sql);
            // Get the meta data object
            ResultSetMetaData metaData = records.getMetaData();

            // Call the displayColumns() method
            displayColumns(metaData, text);
        }
        catch (SQLException e) {}
        catch (Exception e) {}
    }

    private void displayColumns (ResultSetMetaData metaData, TextArea text) {
        String s = "";

        try {
            // Get the number of columns in result set
            int count = metaData.getColumnCount();

            // Cycle through columns and get name of each one
```

```
            for (int i = 1; i <= count; i++) {
                s += metaData.getColumnName(i);
            }
        }
        catch (SQLException e) {}

        // Put the text string in the text area
        text.setText(s);
    }

    public static void main (String args[]) {
        ColumnExample app = new ColumnExample();
    }
}
```

getColumnDisplaySize()

The getColumnDisplaySize() method of the ResultSetMetaData object is useful when you are displaying column data on-screen. The method takes a column index as a parameter and returns the maximum width that the column can be in characters. This means that a column that is of type VARCHAR(10) will have a maximum display size of 10 characters, because only 10 characters can be contained in this column. Numerical columns will have varying sizes, based on the maximum numerical value that can be stored in the column. To get the display size for the first column of a result set, you would use the following syntax:

```
int size = metaData.getColumnDisplaySize(1);
```

This code would return the maximum display size for the first column of the result set. With this value, you could then determine how large a text field you would need in order to display all of the available data items contained in this column.

getColumnLabel()

The getColumnLabel() method of the ResultSetMetaData object returns a string that contains the specified column's label. This label indicates what should be displayed as the heading for the column. Some databases allow extra setup of tables to enable you to specify what heading should be displayed for a column. For example, a column might have the name PhoneNbr in the database table, but you want the heading for the column to be Phone Number. Using the getColumnLabel() method, you can determine what, if any, label should be used for the column heading. The following syntax shows how to determine the column label for the first column of the result set:

```
String label = metaData.getColumnLabel(1);
```

7

getColumnType( )

The getColumnType( ) method of the ResultSetMetaData object enables you to determine the column type of the specified column. This column type will be one of the values from the java.sql.Types class (symjava.sql.Types in dbAnywhere). The method returns an integer that contains a value of a type defined in java.sql.Types. Some of the defined types are CHAR, DATE, and NUMERIC. You can use the getColumnType( ) method to determine what type of data a certain column must contain. For example, suppose you want to have a text field that takes in a value for a column and returns all other values from that column that are similar. You could force the user to enter only valid data to search for. Using the getColumnType( ) method, you could determine that a column was a numerical column and then accept only numerical data in the text field. The syntax for getting the column type of the first column of a result set is as follows:

```
int type = metaData.getColumnType(1);
```

getPrecision( )

The getPrecision( ) method of the ResultSetMetaData object enables you to determine the specified column's precision. The *precision* of a column is the number of digits after the decimal that can be used. You can use this method in scientific applications to determine what precision a specified column supports. The syntax for getting the precision is as follows:

```
int precision = metaData.getMetaData(1);
```

getSchemaName( )

The getSchemaName( ) method of the ResultSetMetaData object enables you to get the specified column's table schema name. This schema name is used in the DatabaseMetaData methods to get information about tables, such as primary keys. This can be useful in determining information, such as the primary keys for a table, to ensure that the user is updating its information using the correct columns in the primary key.

getTableName( )

The getTableName( ) method of the ResultSetMetaData object returns a string that contains the table name of the specified column. Because SQL queries can join columns from multiple tables, this method provides a means to determine of which table a column is actually a member. The following example creates a SQL query that selects all information from tEmployee:

```
select * from tEmployee
```

You then get the table name for the first column using the `getTableName()` method. If you are using the JDBC database supplied with this book, then the text area that you are using to display the table name should display the text `tEmployee`. Listing 7.6 contains the full code for the `TableNameExample` class.

TYPE   **Listing 7.6. The `TableNameExample` class.**

```
import java.awt.*;
import java.util.*;
import symjava.sql.*;

public class TableNameExample extends Frame {
    public TableNameExample () {
        super();
        this.resize(300, 300);
        this.show();
        // Create the textarea to display the table name
        TextArea text = new TextArea(25, 80);
        this.add("Center", text);

        try {
            String driverName = "symantec.itools.db.jdbc.Driver";
            Driver driver = (Driver)Class.forName(driverName).newInstance();
            Properties p = new Properties();
            p.put("user", "dba");
            p.put("password", "sql");
            String dbURL = "jdbc:dbaw://localhost:8889/WATCOM/JDBC/JDBC";
            Connection connection = driver.connect(dbURL, p);
            // Select all items from tEmployee
            String sql = "select * from tEmployee";
            Statement sqlStatement = connection.createStatement();
            ResultSet records = sqlStatement.executeQuery(sql);
            ResultSetMetaData metaData = records.getMetaData();
            // Put the table name of the first column
            // into the text area object
            text.setText(metaData.getTableName(1));
        }
        catch (SQLException e) {}
        catch (Exception e) {}
    }

    public static void main (String args[]) {
        TableNameExample app = new TableNameExample();
    }
}
```

7

isAutoIncrement()

The `isAutoIncrement()` method of the `ResultSetMetaData` object enables you to determine whether or not a certain column is an `AutoIncrement` column. An `AutoIncrement` column is a column that automatically assigns itself the next unused value whenever a new record is inserted. Therefore, if you insert the first row in a table with an AutoIncrement column, the column will place a 1 in the column. On most databases, you are not allowed to insert your own values into these columns.

The isAutoIncrement() method returns a Boolean true if the specified column is an AutoIncrement column and a Boolean false if the specified column is not an AutoIncrement column. The syntax for calling the isAutoIncrement() method is as follows:

```
boolean auto = metaData.isAutoIncrement(1);
```

isCaseSensitive()

The isCaseSensitive() method of the ResultSetMetaData object enables you to determine whether the specified column contains case-sensitive data. An example of case-sensitive data is where Java and java would be different data values. A Boolean true returned by the method indicates that the column contains case-sensitive data; a Boolean false indicates that the column does not contain case-sensitive data. The syntax for the method is as follows:

```
boolean sensitive = metaData.isCaseSensitive(1);
```

isCurrency()

The isCurrency() method of the ResultSetMetaData object enables you to determine whether a specified column contains monetary data values. Some databases have a column type that allows only currency data values. The isCurrency() method determines whether the specified column is one of the currency database types. The method returns a Boolean true if the column is a currency column and a Boolean false if the column is not a currency column. The syntax for calling the isCurrency() method is as follows:

```
boolean currency = metaData.isCurrency(1);
```

isNullable()

The isNullable() method of the ResultSetMetaData object enables you to determine whether a specified column can contain SQL NULL values. A SQL NULL value implies that the column does not apply to the current record. For example, most address tables have a column that accepts a second street address. Not all people use this second street address, so the column is usually NULL because the second street address does not apply for some records. The isNullable() method will return an integer containing one of three values. A 0 indicates that the column does not accept NULLs, a 1 indicates that the column can accept NULLs, and a 2 indicates that it is unknown whether the column accepts NULLs. The syntax for calling the isNullable() method is as follows:

```
boolean Null = metaData.isNullable(1);
```

isSigned()

The isSigned() method of the ResultSetMetaData object enables you to determine whether a specified column is a signed or an unsigned numerical type. Signed types include data types such as int, longint, smallint, and so on. Unsigned types include data types such as uint, ulong, ubyte, and so on. The isSigned() method returns a Boolean true if the specified column is a signed numerical column and a Boolean false if the column is not a signed numerical column. The syntax for the method is as follows:

```
boolean signed = metaData.isSigned(1);
```

isDefinitelyWritable(), isReadOnly(), and isWritable()

The three methods isDefinitelyWritable(), isReadOnly(), and isWritable() enable you to determine the update status of a specified column. The three methods return Boolean values that specify whether a column can be updated or is used for display purposes only. The isReadOnly() method returns a Boolean true if the specified column cannot be updated. The difference between the isWritable() and the isDefinitelyWritable() methods is that the latter method returns a Boolean true if an update on the column will succeed, whereas the isWritable() method returns a Boolean true if the specified column's update might succeed. The syntax for all three methods is listed below:

```
boolean readonly = metaData.isReadOnly(1);
boolean writable = metaData.isWritable(1);
boolean definite = metaData.isDefinitelyWritable(1);
```

The IsExample class in Listing 7.7 illustrates the use of all of the isNNN() methods of the ResultSetMetaData object. The class does the usual selection of employees and then displays some statistics for the first column returned by the query. The results are displayed in a TextArea object.

7

TYPE **Listing 7.7. The IsExample class.**

```java
import java.awt.*;
import java.util.*;
import symjava.sql.*;

public class IsExample extends Frame {
    public IsExample () {
        super();
        this.resize(300, 300);
        this.show();
        TextArea text = new TextArea(25, 80);
        this.add("Center", text);

        try {
            String driverName = "symantec.itools.db.jdbc.Driver";
            Driver driver = (Driver)Class.forName(driverName).newInstance();
            Properties p = new Properties();
            p.put("user", "dba");
            p.put("password", "sql");
            String dbURL = "jdbc:dbaw://localhost:8889/WATCOM/JDBC/JDBC";
            Connection connection = driver.connect(dbURL, p);
            String sql = "select * from tEmployee";
            Statement sqlStatement = connection.createStatement();
            ResultSet records = sqlStatement.executeQuery(sql);
            ResultSetMetaData metaData = records.getMetaData();

            // Call method to add items to text area
            displayInfo(metaData, text);
        }
        catch (SQLException e) {}
        catch (Exception e) {}
    }

    private void displayInfo (ResultSetMetaData metaData, TextArea text) {
        String s = "";

        try {
            // Add the column name and table name
            s += "Column Name : " + metaData.getColumnName(1) + "\n";
            s += "Table Name : " + metaData.getTableName(1) + "\n";

            // Add AutoIncrement, CaseSensitive, Currency
            Boolean auto = new Boolean(metaData.isAutoIncrement(1));
            s += "Auto Increment : " + auto.toString() + "\n";
            Boolean caseSense = new Boolean(metaData.isCaseSensitive(1));
            s += "Case Sensitive : " + caseSense.toString() + "\n";
            Boolean currency = new Boolean(metaData.isCurrency(1));
            s += "Currency : " + currency.toString() + "\n";

            // Add NULLable and Signed options
            int nullable = metaData.isNullable(1);
            s += "nullable : " + Integer.toString(nullable) + "\n";
```

7

```
        Boolean signed = new Boolean(metaData.isSigned(1));
        s += "Signed : " + signed.toString() + "\n";

        // Add Definitely, ReadOnly, Writable
        Boolean definite = new Boolean(metaData.isDefinitelyWritable(1));
        s += "Definitely Writable : " + definite.toString() + "\n";
        Boolean readonly = new Boolean(metaData.isReadOnly(1));
        s += "Read Only : " + readonly.toString() + "\n";
        Boolean writable = new Boolean(metaData.isWritable(1));
        s += "Writable : " + writable.toString() + "\n";

        // Set text area to string
        text.setText(s);
        }
    catch (SQLException e) {}

    }

    public static void main (String args[]) {
        IsExample app = new IsExample();
    }
}
```

Figure 7.3 shows the output of Listing 7.7. As you can see, the MetaData object can be very useful in determining the properties of the result set returned by a SQL query.

Figure 7.3.

The output from the
IsExample *class.*

Summary

Today you have learned how to use the ResultSet object to handle results returned by SQL queries. The ResultSet object provides you with a means to traverse the results that are returned, as well as access to data values contained in the result set. One aspect of the ResultSet object that will become useful is the capability to get objects from the result set that are not defined yet. With the introduction of Oracle v8.0, the object-oriented database will enter mainstream computing. The getObject() methods of the ResultSet object allow access to objects within a database that are completely new to the database world.

7

Along with the ResultSet object, you learned how to use the ResultSetMetaData object to find information about the columns contained in the returned results. The ResultSetMetaData object enables you to determine the names of columns dynamically and also to determine certain properties of returned columns, such as whether they can be NULL or updated.

Q&A

Q What if I am using a database type other than the ones that have predefined getXXX() methods? How can I get those data types?

A Using the getObject() methods of the ResultSet object enables you to specify the data type in Java as a class and then retrieve the data type into the Java object.

Q What is the use of the catalog and schema methods?

A The getCatalogName() and getSchemaName() methods enable you to get the column table's catalog and schema, which are used by the DatabaseMetaData methods to retrieve properties for database tables.

Workshop

The Workshop provides quiz questions to help you solidify your understanding of the material covered and exercises to give you experience in using what you've learned. The answers are provided in Appendix A, "Quiz and Exercise Answers." Try to understand the quiz and exercise answers before you go on to tomorrow's lesson.

Quiz

1. In what two ways can you specify a column when you use the getXXX() method?
2. How can you delete a record using the ResultSet object's cursor?
3. On what record is the cursor initially positioned in the ResultSet object?
4. What method moves you to the next record in the result set?
5. Is there any way to move the cursor to the previous record? If so, what is it?
6. What is an AutoIncrement column?
7. How is the column name different from the column label?
8. What is the precision of a column?
9. What does the getColumnDisplaySize() method do?
10. How do you determine whether a column can accept SQL NULL values?

Exercises

1. Write an application that gives the user an option of deleting the current row in the query. Use the `getCursorName()` method to implement the solution.

2. Write an application that enables the user to select a column from the query and view information such as whether the column can accept NULLs, whether the column is an AutoIncrement column, and so on.

7

In Review

In this first week, you learned some of the topics dealing with how to use relational databases and SQL. You also learned how to use most of the objects in the JDBC API. These objects will enable you to create the database components and applications in the following two weeks.

WEEK 2

8

9

10

11

12

13

14

At a Glance

The lessons in Week 2 introduce you to the concept of creating components that use JDBC to provide more functionality than the current objects. You will create objects that will provide you with multiple navigation methods and not the limited navigation methods of the `ResultSet` object. You also will create objects that let you display information from the database with little coding on the user's part. You can use these objects as the basis for more complex data components that you create.

On Day 8, "Creating JDBC/SQL Objects," you create several objects that will give you more flexibility for handling results.

On Day 9, "The Data Interfaces," you are introduced to the interfaces that you will use to create the data components throughout the rest of the week.

On Day 10, "The DataLabel, DataField, and DataArea Components," you create a Label component that provides a hook to a database using JDBC.

On Day 11, "The DataList and DataChoice Components," you create a List component that provides a hook to a database using JDBC.

On Day 12, "The DataCheckbox Component," you create a Checkbox component that provides a hook to a database using JDBC.

On Day 13, "The DataNavigator Component," you create a component that will enable you to control multiple data components.

On Day 14, "The DataPanel Component," you create a Panel component that will provide a hook to a specified database table.

Day 8

Creating JDBC/SQL Objects

In today's lesson, you will create four classes that will enable you to encapsulate the functionality for executing SQL statements. They will enable you to worry about what SQL statement you need to pass, and not how to execute the SQL statement.

You will create a class to implement a SQL Select class. This class will enable you to move forward and backward, as well as access the data values retrieved from the selection statement. You will also implement classes to handle inserting, deleting, and updating the database. These classes will execute the SQL statement passed to the class.

The following topics are covered today:

- ☐ The SQL Select object
- ☐ The SQL Insert object
- ☐ The SQL Delete object
- ☐ The SQL Update object

The SQL `Select` **Object**

The first class that you will create is the SQL `Select` class. This class will enable you to execute a SQL `Select` statement and have the results contained in the object. The object will store all of the data values returned by the selection statement. This will make it easier to pass the entire result set between other components.

You are creating the SQL `Select` object to address some of the shortcomings of the `ResultSet` object. The current `ResultSet` object offers you only a method for moving forward in the result set. You would like to have the capability to move forward and backward as well as being able to access data values anywhere within the current result set.

You will need to create some object variables for the SQL `Select` object. These variables will store the data values and information about these values. You must have an array of `Hashtable` objects to store the data values from the result set. You will use `Hashtable` objects because they enable you to have a dynamic number of items as well as enable you to associate the items with a particular index. Associate each data value with its corresponding record number. The variable declaration for the `Hashtable` array is as follows:

```
Hashtable Records[];
```

Along with using the `Hashtable` array to store the data values from the result set, you need to store information about the number of columns that are contained in the result set. This column count will be used to determine how many `Hashtable` objects you will need in the array. It also will be used to ensure that the user is not trying to get a data value for a column that does not exist. The variable declaration for the column count is as follows:

```
int columns = 0;
```

You will also store two integer values. One of the integer values will be used to determine which record the object is currently on. The other integer variable will be used to indicate the maximum number of records available, or the record count. You use the record count variable to ensure that the user does not try to go beyond the valid number of records. You use the current variable for methods that inform the user of the current record they are on. The variable declarations for the two integer variables are as follows:

```
int current = 0;
```

```
int max = 0;
```

You must store the `Connection` object and the SQL `Select` statement that were passed into the object through the constructor method. These variables will be used strictly for reference throughout the object. Do not use them outside the constructor, but instead store them for use by any other methods that might be added at a later time. The variable declarations for storing the Connection object and the SQL Select statement are as follows:

```
Connection c;
```

```
String sql;
```

Now that you have determined the names of the variables that the object will contain, you can decide what type of methods you would like to implement within your SQL Select object. You will have to implement a constructor method that will take a Connection object, which will give the object a connection to the database, and a SQL Select statement that will be used to populate the object with data.

You also must implement some basic navigation methods. These methods will enable you to move within the component to different locations. Implement next(), previous(), first(), and last() methods. These methods will move the current record position to their respective locations. Also, implement two methods for moving and getting the current record location of the object. The methods, getRow() and setRow(), will enable you to get the current record position and set the current record position, respectively.

You also must implement a method to allow the user to get the data value for a specified row and column position. The data value should be given to the user in a String object, regardless of the original data type. You must do this because implementing an object to allow all data values to remain in their original data types would require more explanation than I can provide in this book. The method getItem() will return a data value for the specified row and column within the object.

You also must provide two methods for getting information about the result set returned by the SQL statement. Enable the user to get the number of columns and the number of records contained within the returned result set. This will let the user determine how big the returned result set is. The two methods are rowCount() and columnCount(). The rowCount() method will return an integer that contains the number of records that were returned in the result set. The columnCount() method will return the number of columns that were returned in the result set.

So, the SQL Select object will implement the following methods:

☐ public Select (Connection c, String sql)

☐ public void next ()

☐ public void previous ()

☐ public void first ()

☐ public void last ()

```
public int getRow ()
public void setRow (int row)
public String getItem (int row, int column)
public int rowCount ()
public int columnCount ()
```

Before you learn to create the various methods contained in the SQL Select object, a brief discussion of the SQL Select statement is needed. The SQL Select statement enables you to select a finite number of records from one or more tables. The SQL Select statement contains three main parts: the Select section, the From section, and the Where section.

The Select section of the SQL Select statement is where you specify which columns from the database tables you would like to have returned. The column or columns specified within the SQL Select statement will be returned within the result set in the order they are listed in the Select section. Therefore, listing FirstName and then LastName in the Select section will return the columns FirstName and LastName, in that order. It is also possible to return information other than column data. You can return a fixed data value, for example. The following Select statement returns the data value "N" for all rows in the table tEmployee:

```
select "N" from tEmployee
```

You also can return column data values that are computed. You could return a data value that contains the computation of a column and a fixed or variable multiplier. This can be useful for getting the tax or total price for items within your database.

The From section of the SQL Select statement determines which tables will be used in the selection statement. The tables specified in the From clause of the SQL statement will be joined together as a Cartesian product. This produces some very large result sets if left as is.

The Where clause of the SQL Select statement is used to limit the results returned from the selection to only those rows that match certain criteria. It is also used to limit the rows that are created when more than one table is joined together in the From clause. Most Where clauses join two or more tables based on the Primary/Foreign key relation. Some tables will contain a primary key that is part of a foreign key in a separate table. The Where clause is also used to limit the rows returned to data matching specific criteria. This criteria can be any matching pattern that you require.

Select()

The constructor for the Select object is responsible for retrieving the data into the object and setting up various object variables needed throughout the object. The constructor method will first assign the passed `Connection` object and SQL string to the object variables that will hold these items. The code for assigning the variables is as follows:

```
this.c = c;
this.sql = sql;
```

After the `Connection` object and SQL statement have been saved to the object variables, you can create a `Statement` object to get the results of the executed SQL statement. Create this `Statement` object and then save the results in a `ResultSet` object. The code for creating the `Statement` object and for getting the results is as follows:

```
Statement sqlStatement = this.c.createStatement();
ResultSet results = sqlStatement.executeQuery(this.sql);
```

After you have the results from the SQL statement, you will need to get a `ResultSetMetaData` object for information needed in the component. To get the `MetaData` object, use the following code:

```
resultsMeta = results.getMetaData();
```

With the `MetaData` object, you can determine the number of columns that are contained in the result set. You need the number of columns in the result set so that you know how big your `Hashtable` array has to be in order to store all of the data values from the result set. You can get the number of columns in the result set by using the following syntax:

```
this.columns = resultsMeta.getColumnCount();
```

After you have determined the number of columns that are contained in the result set, you can create the array of `Hashtables`. This array will be used to store all of the data values from the returned result set. The `Hashtable` array should be created as follows:

```
Records = new Hashtable[columns];
```

Now that you have created the `Hashtable` array to store the data values for the result set, you can begin to add the data values from the result set. Use a `while` loop to call the `next()` method of the `ResultSet` object, and continue moving through the results until you reach the last record.

For each record, use a `for` loop to cycle through each column contained in the result set. For the initial record, you will need to create the appropriate `Hashtable` object to store each column's data. Within the column loop, check the record number, and for the first record, create a `Hashtable` object for the appropriate array position. Because you are looping through the columns with an index starting at `0`, you can create the `Hashtable` object by using the index. The code for creating the `Hashtable` object is as follows:

```
Records[i] = new Hashtable();
```

After you have created the Hashtable objects, you can add the data values to the Hashtable objects in the appropriate positions. Add the data values to their respective Hashtable objects with a key value that indicates the current record of the result set. The syntax for adding the data value is as follows:

```
Records[i].put(new Integer(index), results.getString(i + 1));
```

Looping through all records will store into your Hashtable array all of the data values from the result set. After looping through all records, your index counter variable will have the number of records that were looped through. This value is known as the *record count*. Store this value in the object variable max as follows:

```
max = index;
```

Because you used some of the methods for the symjava.sql.* classes and interfaces, you will need to catch the SQLException. This exception is thrown by most of the interface and class methods for the SQL package. The exception is thrown because a database error can occur on any connection to the database. If the exception occurs, then a problem occurred during the retrieve process. You will want to let the user know of the error, so store a -1 for the record count, indicating that there was an error in retrieving the data. This value will be different if no records are returned. If no records are returned in the result set, then a 0 will be stored for the record count. The syntax for catching the SQLException and assigning a -1 for the record count is as follows:

```
catch (SQLException e) {
  // Error occurred, so return a -1
  max = -1;
}
```

After you have caught the exception thrown by the various SQL methods, you will be finished building your constructor method. The full code for the constructor method is contained in Listing 8.1.

TYPE **Listing 8.1. The Select constructor method.**

```
// Constructor Method
public Select (Connection c, String sql) {
  int index = 0;

  // Assign passed arguments
  this.c = c;
  this.sql = sql;

  try {
  // Create Statement Object and Execute SQL
```

```
Statement sqlStatement = this.c.createStatement();
ResultSet results = sqlStatement.executeQuery(this.sql);

// Get the meta data
ResultSetMetaData resultsMeta = results.getMetaData();
// Get the column count for the result set
this.columns = resultsMeta.getColumnCount();

// Create the array of Hashtable objects
Records = new Hashtable[this.columns];

// Loop through all records
while (results.next()) {
 // Increment the index counter
 index++;

 // Perform a loop to add items for columns
 for (int i = 0;i<columns;i++) {
  // If you are on first record, create Hashtables
  if (index == 1) {
   Records[i] = new Hashtable();
  }
  // Add items
  Records[i].put(new Integer(index), results.getString(i + 1));
  }
 }
 // Store the record count
 max = index;
}
// Catch exception
catch (SQLException e) {
 max = -1;
 }
}
```

next()

The next() method acts similar to the next() method of the ResultSet object. The next()
method moves the current record position to the next valid record in the object. The method
will move to the next record only if a valid record exists. If a valid record does not exist,
meaning that the user is at the last record, then the next() method will not perform any
action.

 NOTE

> As with the ResultSet object, you will need to call the next() method
> initially to place the record pointer on the first record.

You first must check the current record number to ensure that the user does not try to go past the last valid record. Check the current record value against the record count. If the current record is equal to the record count, then you are at the last record, and the next method should not try to move to the next record. If you are not at the last record, the method should move to the next record in the object. The syntax for checking the two values is as follows:

```
if (current == max) {
  return;
}
```

If you are not currently on the last record, you should allow the object to move to the next record. To move the record position, increment the value contained in the current variable. The full code listing for the next() method is contained in Listing 8.2.

TYPE   **Listing 8.2. The next() method.**

```
// Move to next record
public void next () {
  // Check to make sure you are moving to a valid record
  if (current == max) {
   return;
  }

  // Increment record position
  current++;
}
```

previous()

Unlike the ResultSet object, your Select object will contain a method that will enable you to move backward within the returned result set. Not only can you move forward with the next() method, but with the previous() method, you will be able to traverse both directions through the data values.

The previous() method moves to the previous record in the object, provided a valid previous record exists. The method will first check to make sure that a valid row exists previous to the current row. It checks to make sure that the current row is greater than 1. If the current row is 0 or 1, then no row previous to the current row exists, and the method should not try to move the record pointer to this nonexistent row. If the row is any other value other than 0 or 1, then a previous row for the method exists to move to. The syntax for checking for a valid row previous to the current row is as follows:

```
if (current < 2) {
 return;
}
```

8

If a previous row exists, then the method will decrement the value contained in the variable `current`. This variable stores the current record position. Listing 8.3 contains the code for the `previous()` method.

TYPE **Listing 8.3. The `previous()` method.**

```
// Move to previous record
public void previous () {
 // Check for valid row
 if (current < 2) {
  return;
 }

 // Decrement record position
 current--;
}
```

first()

The `first()` method provides the object with a means to move the record position back to the initial record. This method moves to the first record contained in the object. The `first()` method can be useful after the entire result set has been traversed and you want to move the record position back to the initial record so that other functionality can be applied to the values in the result set. Listing 8.4 contains the code for the `first()` method.

TYPE **Listing 8.4. The `first()` method.**

```
// Move to first record in object
public void first () {
 // Set record position to first record
 this.current = 1;
}
```

last()

The `last()` method enables the object to move the record position to the very last record in the result set. This method will set the current record position to the value contained in the record count variable. The last record in the result set is equal to the number of records that were returned in the result set. Listing 8.5 contains the code for the `last()` method.

TYPE | **Listing 8.5. The `last()` method.**

```
// Move to last record in object
public void last () {
// Set record position to last record
 this.current = max;
}
```

getRow()

The `getRow()` method enables the user to get the current record on which the object is positioned. This method returns the value contained in the `current` variable. This variable stores the current record position for the object. This value can then be used to get data values using the `getItem()` method. Listing 8.6 contains the code for the `getRow()` method.

TYPE | **Listing 8.6. The `getRow()` method.**

```
// Get the current row for the object
public int getRow () {
// Return the current record number
 return this.current;
}
```

setRow()

The `setRow()` method enables you to manually set the current row in the object to any valid row. Unlike the previous navigation methods, the `setRow()` method can move to any row within the object in one jump. You can go to any row N as long as the Nth row exists in the object.

The `setRow()` method takes an integer value specifying the row to which to move within the object. The method first checks this row to ensure that the row is valid within the context of the object. The syntax for checking the passed row is as follows:

```
if ((row < 1) || (row > max)) {
 return;
}
```

The preceding code checked to see whether the user passed in a row that was less than 1. The first record is numbered 1, so any specified record below 1 would be a nonexistent row. The method also checks for specified rows that are greater than the value contained in the variable `max`. This variable stores the record count, and because there are no records beyond the last

8

record, the passed row would be invalid. If the specified row falls within this range of records, then the method will change the value of the current record to the specified value. The code for the setRow() method is in Listing 8.7.

TYPE **Listing 8.7. The `setRow()` method.**

```
// Set current row to user specified row
public void setRow (int row) {
 // Check to make sure row is valid
 if ((row < 1) || (row > max)) {
  return;
 }

 // Set current record position to specified row
 this.current = row;
}
```

getItem()

Up until now, you have created methods that have enabled you to move the position of the current record within the object to different locations, fixed and variable. These methods have not, however, enabled you to get at the data values that are contained in the result set for the object. The getItem() method will enable you to get the data values for various record positions within the object.

Unlike the ResultSet object getXXX() methods, the getItem() method enables you to get a data value from any valid position within the current result set. You can be on the last record and get a data value from the first record. This makes finding and displaying data values easier because it is now possible to do all of the data access outside of the ResultSet object. You can get the record count and column count and then get data values in any order required. You could, for example, loop through and get all values from a particular column before moving to the next column.

TIP

You can get values for the current record by specifying the value returned from the getRow() method as the row parameter for the getItem() method.

The method first checks to ensure that both the specified row and column are valid. If either of these values is not valid, then the method will return an empty string back to the user. A valid row will fall between 1 and N, where N is the number of records contained in the component. A valid column will fall between 1 and M, where M is the number of columns contained in the result set. The code for checking both the row and column parameters is as follows:

```
if ((row < 1) || (row > max)) {
 return "";
}
if ((column < 1) || (column > this.columns)) {
 return "";
}
```

After you have determined that both a valid row and column were passed, you can get the appropriate data value and return it to the user. To get the correct data value, you will get the value contained in the Hashtable object that corresponds to the specified column. Because the specified column is based on an initial record of 1, but the Hashtable objects are zero-based, you will need to use the specified column minus one Hashtable object. From this Hashtable, you will want to get the value associated with a specified key. The Hashtable object stores data values with a key that corresponds to the record number of the data value. Listing 8.8 contains the code for the getItem() method.

TYPE   **Listing 8.8. The getItem() method.**

```
// Get a data value for specified row and column
public String getItem (int row, int column) {
 // Check for valid row
 if ((row < 1) || (row > max)) {
  return "";
 }

 // Check for valid column
 if ((column < 1) || (column > this.columns)) {
  return "";
 }

 // Return specified data value
 return (String)Records[column - 1].get(new Integer(row));
}
```

rowCount()

The rowCount() method returns the number of records, or rows, that are contained in the current object. This value is stored in the variable max. This value is set after the retrieve has been completed and all rows are examined and stored. This value will not change through the life of the object. Listing 8.9 contains the code for the rowCount() method.

TYPE   **Listing 8.9. The `rowCount()` method.**

```
// Return the record count for the object
public int rowCount () {
 // Return the value contained in the max variable
 return this.max;
}
```

TIP

> The number of records can help you determine the range of valid rows you can use.

columnCount()

The `columnCount()` method returns the number of columns contained in the result set for the object. The number of columns is stored in the variable `columns`. The column count is used in various methods to check that a specified column is within the valid range of columns for the object. Listing 8.10 contains the code for the `columnCount()` method.

TYPE   **Listing 8.10. The `columnCount()` method.**

```
// Return the number of columns
public int columnCount () {
 // Return the value in the columns variable
 return this.columns;
}
```

Full Code for the `Select` Object

The full text for the `Select` object is in Listing 8.11.

TYPE   **Listing 8.11. The `Select` object.**

```
import java.util.*;
import symjava.sql.*;
public class Select {
 Hashtable Records[];
 int columns = 0;
 int current = 0;
```

continues

Listing 8.11. continued

```
int max = 0;
Connection c;
String sql;

public Select (Connection c, String sql) {
 int index = 0;
 this.c = c;
 this.sql = sql;
 try {
  Statement sqlStatement = this.c.createStatement();
   ResultSet results = sqlStatement.executeQuery(this.sql);
  ResultSetMetaData resultsMeta = results.getMetaData();
  this.columns = resultsMeta.getColumnCount();
  Records = new Hashtable[this.columns];

  while (results.next()) {
   index++;
   for (int i = 0;i<columns;i++) {
    if (index == 1) {
     Records[i] = new Hashtable();
    }
     Records[i].put(new Integer(index), results.getString(i + 1));
   }
  }
  max = index;
 }
 catch (SQLException e) {
  max = -1;
 }
}

public void next () {
 if (current == max) {
  return;
 }
 current++;
}

public void previous () {
 if (current < 2) {
  return;
 }
 current--;
}

public void first () {
 this.current = 1;
}

public void last () {
 this.current = max;
}
```

```
public int getRow () {
 return this.current;
}

public void setRow (int row) {
 if ((row < 1) |¦ (row > max)) {
  return;
 }
 this.current = row;
}

public String getItem (int row, int column) {
 if ((row < 1) |¦ (row > max)) {
  return "";
 }
 if ((column < 1) |¦ (column > this.columns)) {
  return "";
 }
 return (String)Records[column - 1].get(new Integer(row));
}

public int rowCount () {
 return this.max;
}

public int columnCount () {
 return this.columns;
}
}
```

The SQL Insert Object

Today you will also create a SQL Insert object. You will use this object to enable you to execute an Insert statement using a specified Connection object and a SQL statement that contains the Insert statement. The object will be relatively small compared to the SQL Select object you created in the previous section.

The purpose of the Insert object is to enable you to specify the basic components of an Insert statement and have the object handle the execution against the database. The object will have only a constructor method and a method for the user to get the status of the executed SQL statement.

SQL Insert Basics

The SQL Insert statement enables you to insert records into a database table. The Insert statement has two main parts. The first part of the statement contains a listing of the table and optionally the columns into which you want to insert data. Only one table can have rows inserted at one time.

You can specify columns to insert data into, or leave the column list blank. Leaving the column list blank informs the Insert statement that you will specify all data values for the table in the correct order.

TIP
It is always a good idea to manually specify the column list to insert into. If your database table definition changes, then your Insert statement will have a better chance of still working, provided you didn't remove columns or add any NOT NULL columns.

An example for specifying the first section of an Insert statement is as follows:

```
Insert into tEmployee
```

The preceding example does not contain any columns, so the statement will expect all column values to be specified in the correct order. The following example contains the column list of the columns for which you will specify data values:

```
Insert into tEmployee (FirstName, MiddleInitial, LastName, SSN)
```

The preceding example specified four columns for which you would supply data values. In the second section of the Insert statement, you will be expected to supply the values of the four columns.

The second section of the Insert statement is the part of the statement that specifies the values that will be added to the table and columns contained in the first section of the statement. There are two main formats for specifying values to add.

The first format that is used is to specify one record's data values. To do this, you use the reserved word Values. After the Values word, you specify a list of data values contained within a set of parentheses. These values must match exactly the column list that was specified in the first section of the statement. If you mix up data values that have different data types, then the database will return an error when the statement is executed. If the mixed-up values have the same data type, then the statement will execute, but you will end up with unexpected data.

NOTE
SQL is not case-sensitive like Java. The SQL statements can be specified in lower- or uppercase, or a combination of both.

8

An example of specifying one record's worth of values is as follows:

```
Insert into tEmployee (FirstName, MiddleInitial, LastName, SSN)
values ('Ashton', 'C', 'Hobbs', '123456789')
```

This example will insert a record into the tEmployee table with the specified information. This will insert one record, and the statement will have to be changed and repeated to add other data values.

The second format for inserting data is to use a Select statement. You can insert values from another table or tables into a table. The data types of the selected columns must match the columns specified in the first section of the Insert statement. The following is a pseudo-example for using the Select statement within an Insert statement (the table tEmployeeNew does not exist):

```
Insert into tEmployee (FirstName, MiddleInitial, LastName, SSN)
Select tEmployeeNew.FirstName, tEmployeeNew.MiddleInitial,
 tEmployeeNew.LastName, tEmployeeNew.SSN
From tEmployeeNew
```

The preceding example will insert all records from tEmployeeNew into tEmployee. This can be useful when you have temporary tables that store data until it can be processed and copied to a permanent table.

The Insert **Object**

The Insert object will contain a constructor method and status method that will enable the user to obtain the status of the Insert statement. The object will contain one object variable, a Boolean to store the status of the executed Insert statement. The variable declaration for the Boolean variable is as follows:

```
boolean status = false;
```

The Insert **Constructor Method**

The constructor method for the Insert object will take a Connection object and a String object containing the SQL Insert statement as parameters. The method will create a Statement object from the passed Connection object and will then execute the SQL Insert statement passed to the object.

If the Insert statement succeeds, then the object variable status will store a Boolean true. If the Insert statement fails, an exception will occur and a Boolean false will be stored in the Boolean variable. Listing 8.12 contains the code for the Insert object constructor method.

Listing 8.12. The `Insert()` method.

```
// Constructor method
public Insert (Connection c, String sql) {
 try {
  Statement sqlStatement = c.createStatement();
  sqlStatement.executeUpdate(sql);

  // Set status variable to true
  this.status = true;
 }
 catch (SQLException e) {
  // Set status variable to false
  this.status = false;
 }
}
```

getSuccess()

The `getSuccess()` method will return the value contained in the object variable `status`. This variable will contain a `true` value if the SQL `Insert` statement was successful, and a `false` if the `Insert` statement was not successful. The code for the `getSuccess()` method is as follows:

```
// Get status
public boolean getSuccess () {
 return this.status;
}
```

The Full Code for the `Insert` Object

The full code for the `Insert` object is in Listing 8.13.

Listing 8.13. The `Insert` object.

```
import java.util.*;
import symjava.sql.*;

public class Insert {
 boolean status;

 // Constructor method
 public Insert (Connection c, String sql) {
  try {
   Statement sqlStatement = c.createStatement();
   sqlStatement.executeUpdate(sql);

   // Set status variable to true
   this.status = true;
  }
```

```
  catch (SQLException e) {
   // Set status variable to false
   this.status = false;
  }
 }

 public boolean getSuccess () {
  // return status variables
  return this.status;
 }
}
```

The SQL Delete Object

The SQL Delete object enables you to delete items from a database table. You will be able to delete specified items using a preconstructed SQL Delete statement, or enable the Delete object to delete all records from a specified table.

The SQL Delete statement looks very similar to the SQL Select statement. Both statements can have a From and Where clause. The only difference in the statements is that the Delete statement will only take a table name that indicates which table items will be deleted from. This table is necessary only when more than one table is listed in the From clause.

The following example deletes all items from the table, tEmployee. The statement is very compact and can do a lot of damage, so be careful when you use the Delete statement.

```
delete
from tEmployee
```

TIP

Sometimes it is a good idea to turn off AutoCommit when you are performing deletes. If the user changed his mind, then you can roll back the delete and restore the database to its original state.

Basics for the Delete Object

The Delete object will contain two object variables. The first variable will be the Connection object. The Connection object will be specified in one of the constructor methods and will be used to execute the SQL Delete statements. The syntax for the Connection object is as follows:

```
Connection c;
```

The other object variable you will create is a Boolean variable to store the status of the executed SQL Delete statement. The boolean stores a Boolean value indicating the success of the SQL Delete statement. A true value indicates that the statement was successful in updating, and a false indicates that the statement was not successful in updating. The syntax for creating the Boolean variable is as follows:

```
boolean status = false;
```

The Delete object will contain two constructor methods and two executable methods. The two constructors will enable you to specify either the Connection object alone or a Connection object and a String object containing the SQL Delete statement. The first constructor stores the Connection object for use by the deleteAll() method. The deleteAll() method enables the user to pass the name of a table to the Delete object, and the object deletes all records from the specified table. The constructor that takes a SQL Delete statement will execute the statement as is. The final method is the getSuccess() method. This method returns the value of the status Boolean variable, indicating whether the SQL Delete statement was successful.

The Delete(Connection) Method

The basic constructor method will take a Connection object as a parameter. The method will store the passed Connection object in a local variable for use by the deleteAll() method. Listing 8.14 contains the code for the Delete(Connection) method.

TYPE   **Listing 8.14. The Delete(Connection) method.**

```
// Basic Constructor
public Delete (Connection c) {
 // Store passed connection object
 this.c = c;
}
```

The Delete(Connection, String) Method

The second constructor method will take a Connection object as well as a String that will contain a SQL Delete statement. This method will execute the passed SQL statement immediately and store in the Boolean variable whether the statement was successful or not. The code for the constructor method is in Listing 8.15.

TYPE **Listing 8.15. The** `Delete(Connection, String)` **method.**

```
// Constructor to execute SQL Statement
public Delete (Connection c, String sql) {
 try {
  Statement sqlStatement = c.createStatement();
  sqlStatement.executeUpdate(sql);
  // set status to true
  this.status = true;
 }
 catch (SQLException e) {
  this.status = false;
 }
}
```

The `deleteAll()` Method

The `deleteAll()` method will take a `String` object containing the name of a table from which you want to delete all records. The method will construct a SQL `Delete` statement to delete all records from the specified table. The method will use the `Connection` object passed in through the basic constructor. Listing 8.16 contains the code for the `deleteAll()` method.

TYPE **Listing 8.16. The** `deleteAll()` **method.**

```
// Delete all records from specified table
public void deleteAll (String table) {
 String sql;
 sql = "Delete from " + table;

 try {
  Statement sqlStatement = this.c.createStatement();
  sqlStatement.executeUpdate(sql);
  // Set status to true for success
  this.status = true;
 }
 catch (SQLException e) {
  // set status to fail
  this.status = false;
 }
}
```

The `getSuccess()` Method

The `getSuccess()` method performs the same functionality as the `getSuccess()` method for the `Insert` object. It enables you to get the status of the previously executed SQL statement. For a listing of the code, refer to Listing 8.13 for the `Insert` statement `getSuccess()` method.

The Full Code for the Delete Object

Listing 8.17 contains the full code for the Delete object.

TYPE **Listing 8.17. The Delete object.**

```
import symjava.sql.*;
import java.util.*;

public class Delete {
 Connection c;
 boolean status = false;

 public Delete (Connection c) {
  // Store connection object for later use
  this.c = c;
 }
 public Delete (Connection c, String sql) {
  try {
   Statement sqlStatement = c.createStatement();
   sqlStatement.executeUpdate(sql);
   // set status to true
   this.status = true;
  }
  catch (SQLException e) {
   // Set status to false
   this.status = false;
  }
 }

 public void deleteAll (String table) {
 String sql;
 sql = "Delete from " + table;

 try {
  Statement sqlStatement = this.c.createStatement();
  sqlStatement.executeUpdate(sql);
  // Set status to true for success
  this.status = true;
 }
 catch (SQLException e) {
  // set status to fail
  this.status = false;
 }
 }

 public boolean getSuccess () {
  // Get status variable
  return this.status;
 }
}
```

8

The SQL Update **Object**

The SQL Update object provides an easy way for you to execute SQL Update statements. The object enables you to specify a Connection object and a String object containing the SQL Update statement. The object will then execute the statement and store the success of the executed statement for you to retrieve from the object.

The SQL Update statement contains three parts: the Update section, the Set section, and the Where section. The Update section is where you specify the table you will be updating. To update the table tEmployee, you would use the following syntax:

```
update tEmployee
```

The Set section of the Update statement is the section in which you specify which columns will be updated, and the data values that will be placed into the columns. To update the FirstName column of tEmployee to read "Ashton," you would use the following syntax:

```
Set FirstName = 'Ashton'
```

The third and final section of the Update statement enables you to specify which records in the specified table will be updated with the data values from section 2. The Where section looks like any other Where section for the standard SQL statements.

To change the FirstName column to "Ashton" for all records in tEmployee that have the last name "Hobbs," you would use the following Update statement:

```
Update tEmployee
Set FirstName = 'Ashton'
Where LastName = 'Hobbs'
```

The Update object will consist of two methods and one object variable. The one object variable will be a Boolean variable to store the status of the executed SQL Update statement. The constructor method will take a Connection object and a String object containing the SQL Update statement. The constructor method will execute the passed SQL Update statement using the Connection object specified. It then will store the status of the executed SQL Update statement in the Boolean variable.

The second method, getSuccess(), will return the value contained in the object variable. A returned true indicates that the Update statement was successful. A returned false value indicates that the Update statement was not successful.

Listing 8.18 contains the full code for the Update object.

TYPE   **Listing 8.18. The `Update` object.**

```
import symjava.sql.*;
import java.util.*;

public class Update {
 boolean status = false;

 public Update (Connection c, String sql) {
  try {
   Statement sqlStatement = c.createStatement();
   sqlStatement.executeUpdate(sql);

   // set status to true
   this.status = true;
  }
  catch (SQLException e) {
   // Set status to false
   this.status = false;
  }
 }

 public boolean getSuccess () {
  // return status of executed statement
  return this.status;
 }
}
```

Summary

In today's lesson, you learned how to create various SQL objects that can simplify your database applications. These objects have encapsulated the functionality provided by the core SQL statements into easy-to-use objects. The Select object also has provided you with functionality that is not provided through the normal JDBC classes. The Select object gives you the ability to navigate in various directions through the result set. It also enables you to get the number of records that were returned by the executed SQL Select statement.

Hopefully, today's lesson has given you some ideas for creating your own JDBC objects. Use the objects you learned today as examples for creating your own business-specific objects, such as objects that perform cascaded deletes and objects that perform various data checks. Also, you can improve these objects to provide even more functionality than they currently offer.

Workshop

The Workshop provides quiz questions to help you solidify your understanding of the material covered and exercises to give you experience in using what you've learned. The answers are provided in Appendix A, "Quiz and Exercise Answers." Try to understand the quiz and exercise answers before you go on to tomorrow's lesson.

Quiz

1. How many sections does a standard SQL Select statement contain?
2. In a Select statement, what does the From clause specify?
3. What does the setRow() method do?
4. How would you determine which row the Select object is currently on?
5. What is the difference between specifying columns and not specifying columns in the first section of the Insert statement?
6. Why should you always specify columns in an Insert statement?
7. What would be the syntax to delete all records from tMyTable?
8. How would you delete all records from tMyTable using the Delete object?
9. What is specified in the Set section of the SQL Update statement?
10. If getSuccess() returns false, was the execution of the SQL statement successful or not?

Exercises

1. Add functionality to the Select object to enable the user to get the names of the columns in the result set.
2. Add functionality to all SQL objects to allow multiple statements to be executed. Hint: A new method needs to be created to use a Connection object and a new SQL statement.

Day 9

The Data Interfaces

Today's lesson introduces the data component interfaces that you will use for the rest of the week. The interfaces you learn and create in today's lesson will form the basis for creating useful data components that you will be able to utilize in your own applications. The interfaces provide a lot of functionality. There are four main interfaces that provide the functionality of the data components.

The following are the main topics that you will learn today:

- ☐ The data navigation interface methods
- ☐ The data connection interface methods
- ☐ The data update methods
- ☐ The data component methods

Why Use Interfaces?

You might be wondering why I am taking a day to describe the interfaces that you will use in the data components that you will develop throughout the remainder of the week. When you are developing these components, it is possible to run into the following problem: How do you provide common functionality among all of the components and still use the AWT components as ancestors?

When I first decided to create the data components for my personal use, I ran into one of the main problems or differences of Java. I needed to inherit from the AWT components so that I could have the functionality of the AWT provided by Java, but I also wanted to provide common functionality between the components. Because Java does not support multiple inheritance, you will have to rely on the use of interfaces to provide the common methods that you want between the components.

The interfaces that you will create, `DataComponent`, `DataNavigation`, `DataUpdate`, and `DataConnection`, will provide you with a common set of methods, but the methods will have to be implemented in each data component separately. Figure 9.1 displays a diagram of how each of the data components and the interfaces created in this lesson will relate to one another. Your data components will be inherited from the Java AWT components and will implement the appropriate interfaces that the component requires.

Figure 9.1.

An inheritance diagram for data components.

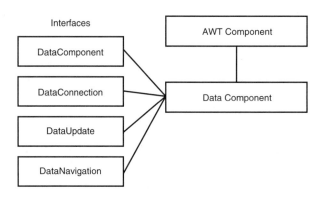

The interfaces are separated into functional groups. I have separated functionality so that if you want to create any further components, you will have to implement only the features that will be required by your users. Multiple interfaces provide for a more object-oriented approach to implementing the functionality you want in your data components. The various interfaces and their methods are described in detail in the following sections.

The `DataConnection` **Interface**

The `DataConnection` interface provides functionality to change the connection for the data component, the SQL for the component, and to provide a method to retrieve information into the component. The `DataConnection` interface could be used alone if all you wanted was a way to hook a Java component to data returned from a database. The code for the `DataConnection` interface is shown in Listing 9.1.

TYPE | **Listing 9.1. The `DataConnection` interface.**

```
import symjava.sql.*;

public interface DataConnection {
 public void setConnection(Connection c);
 public void setConnection(Connection c, boolean noReset);
 public Connection getConnection();
 public void setSQL(String sql);
 public String getSQL();
 public int retrieve();
}
```

The `DataConnection` interface will provide two methods that enable you to set the `Connection` object that will be used by the data component, and also to get the current `Connection` object for the data component. These two methods will enable you to change the `Connection` object that is being used by the data component. The data component will use the supplied `Connection` object in all of the queries and updates that will be performed. You must manually create a `Connection` object outside of the data component and then pass the created `Connection` object, which is connected to a database, to the data component using either the constructor method or the method that enables you to set the `Connection` object for the data component.

The `DataConnection` interface will also provide two methods that will enable you to change the SQL string that is being used to populate the data component and also to get the SQL string that is populating the data component. The data component will use the SQL string that is passed by the developer as the SQL query to populate the component. This SQL string can be changed at any time so that different data can be displayed in the component. This will provide for a more dynamic method of displaying data to the user because he could possibly change the SQL string by clicking on an item in a list and having the data component automatically display the new data based on the user's choice.

The DataConnection interface will provide one other method that will enable you to execute a retrieve. This method will take the current Connection object and execute the current SQL string against the database. The retrieve() method will retrieve all of the data returned by the executed SQL statement into a ResultSet object and copy the data items to an array of Hashtable objects. I am using Hashtable objects because I want the capability to store a dynamic quantity of items, but I also want to be able to reference the data easily. Using the Hashtable object, you can easily store items dynamically and also store them with a particular key. The key value that you will be using throughout the data components is the row or record number. The record numbers will start at 1 and go to the maximum number of rows that are retrieved by the SQL query.

The methods of the DataConnection interface are listed in Table 9.1. Following the table, the methods are described in more detail with a syntactical description of each.

Table 9.1. The DataConnection interface methods.

Method	Description
setConnection()	Provides a means to set or change the current Connection object being used by the data component.
getConnection()	Enables the developer to get the current Connection object being used by the data component.
setSQL()	Provides a means to set or change the current SQL string that is being used by the data component to retrieve results.
getSQL()	Enables the developer to get the current SQL string that is being used to populate the data component.
retrieve()	Executes the current SQL string using the current Connection object and stores the results internally within the data component.

setConnection()

The setConnection() methods provided by the DataConnection interface enable you to set or change the current Connection object being used by the data component. The Connection object is what the data component will use when executing the SQL query that populates the data component and the update methods that update the data component data against the database.

9

There are two different setConnection() methods. The first method takes only a Connection object as a parameter. This method will take the passed Connection object and set it to be the current Connection object. This passed Connection object will then be used on all subsequent queries and updates. This method also resets all of the information contained within the data component. All data values will be cleared as well as the current SQL string. This method acts similarly to how the reset() method works in the data component. As with the reset() method, all items are cleared. However, unlike the reset() method, this setConnection() method will change the current Connection object. The syntax for calling this method is as follows:

```
Connection connection = driver.connect(dbURL, p);
DataComponent.setConnection(connection);
```

The second implementation of the setConnection() method will enable you to change the current Connection object but keep all other items within the data component. This will enable you to change the database connection that the data component is using, but still be able to access the data values and SQL string contained in the data component. Using this method, you could retrieve items from a table using a connection to one database and then change the database connection so that any changes will be applied to a different database. This version of the setConnection() method will take the Connection object just as the first one did, but will also take a Boolean parameter. The Boolean will specify whether you want to keep all items intact or erase them as in the setConnection() method. Passing a Boolean true will force all of the items within the data component to remain, and a Boolean false will clear all of the items within the data component. The syntax for calling this implementation of the setConnection() method is as follows:

```
Connection connection = driver.connect(dbURL, p);
// Don't Clear Items in Data Component
DataComponent.setConnection(connection, true);
// Clear Items in Data Component
DataComponent.setConnection(connection, false);
```

NOTE   If you close the Connection object that is being used by one of the data components, it will make updating and retrieving for those components unavailable.

getConnection()

The getConnection() method of the DataComponent interface provides you, the developer, with a way to get the Connection object being used by the data component. The getConnection() method will take no parameters, but will pass back the current Connection object that it is using. This method will enable you to get a Connection object so that you can use it to set the Connection object of another data component. It could also be used to determine which database the data component is using. Getting the Connection object will enable you to determine the URL and username that the Connection object is currently using. The syntax for calling the getConnection() method is as follows:

```
Connection connection = DataComponent.getConnection();
```

setSQL()

The setSQL() method of the DataConnection interface provides you with a way to specify the SQL statement that the data component should use to populate itself. The SQL string could be passed in one of the constructors that the data component offers; however, it also can be passed outside of the constructor methods. This method also enables you to change the SQL statement being used to populate the data component. For example, you could have the data component change the query to retrieve different information from the database based on the selection chosen by the user.

The setSQL() method will change the SQL string being used to populate the data component, but it will not reset or clear any of the other values being used within the data component. To force the data component to use the newly passed SQL query statement, you will need to explicitly call the retrieve() method. Calling the retrieve() method after you set the new SQL statement will force the data component to be updated with the ResultSet object returned by executing the current SQL query. The syntax for calling the setSQL() method is as follows:

```
String sql = "select * from tEmployee";
// Pass the new SQL statement
DataComponent.setSQL(sql);
// Retrieve the new SQL into the Data Component
DataComponent.retrieve();
```

getSQL()

Much like the getConnection() method, the getSQL() method of the DataConnection interface takes no parameters and returns a string that contains the current SQL statement being used by the data component. The SQL string returned is the SQL string that was passed using either the constructor for the data component or the setSQL() method of the data component. The syntax for calling the getSQL() method is as follows:

```
String sql;
// Get the current SQL string for the Data Component
sql = DataComponent.getSQL();
```

retrieve()

The retrieve() method implemented by the DataConnection interface will populate the data component using the current Connection object and the current SQL string passed into the data component. The retrieve() method will execute the SQL query using the Connection object, and will return the results of the SQL query into a ResultSet object.

After getting the ResultSet objcct, the retrieve() method will determine some basic information for the result set returned, such as the number of columns that are contained in the result set as well as the names of each of the columns. The retrieve() method will then loop through all items in the ResultSet object and copy the data values to Hashtable objects that will be used by the data component. These hash tables will be used to store the data values that are returned by the SQL query.

The retrieve() method will also determine other information such as the maximum number of rows that were returned by the SQL query. The row count will be stored for later use, but it also is returned as the return value for the method. The last thing the retrieve() method does is to call the next() method so that the data component will display the first item in the result set. The syntax for calling the retrieve() method is as follows:

```
int rowCount = DataComponent.retrieve();
```

The DataUpdate Interface

The DataUpdate interface provides functionality to the data components to update any data that was changed by the user. It also provides methods to preview the SQL statement that is being sent to the database. This SQL statement can be previewed, and the execution of the particular SQL statement can be canceled using the methods provided by the DataUpdate interface. The interface also provides methods to change and get the table and columns that will be used to update the database. The code for the DataUpdate interface is shown in Listing 9.2.

TYPE **Listing 9.2. The DataUpdate interface.**

```
import symjava.sql.*;

public interface DataUpdate {
 public final int SELECT = 0;
 public final int INSERT = 1;
 public final int UPDATE = 2;
 public final int DELETE = 3;

 public void setUpdateTable(String table);
 public String getUpdateTable();
```

continues

Listing 9.2. continued

```
public boolean update();
public boolean previewStatement(String sql, int sqlType);
public void setUpdateColumn(String column);
public void setUpdateColumn(int column);
public String[] getUpdateColumn();
}
```

The methods provided by the DataUpdate interface and their descriptions are listed in Table 9.2.

Table 9.2. The DataUpdate methods.

Method	Description
setUpdateTable()	Sets the table to be used when the object executes updates to the database.
getUpdateTable()	Gets the current table that is being used when the object updates data to the database.
update()	Called to update the data contained in the DataComponent against the database.
previewStatement()	Enables you to preview the SQL statements that are being sent to the database. Also allows the SQL statement execution to be canceled.
setUpdateColumn()	Adds a column to the list of columns that will be used when the object updates data.
getUpdateColumn()	Returns a listing of all the columns that will be used when the object updates data to the database.

setUpdateTable()

The setUpdateTable() method will change the table to which the data component will try to update data when the user calls the update() method. To update data against the database, you will need to specify a table to update the data against and the columns that you want to include in the set and where clauses of the update statement.

When you specify a table to update, you are specifying the table that contains the columns that you are updating. There can be only one table updated at one time, so to update different tables, you would need to perform an update to one table and set of columns, and then change the table and columns.

The setUpdateTable() method will take a string that contains a description of the table that you want to update and will not return any value. The syntax for calling the setUpdateTable() method is as follows:

```
String updateTable = "tEmployee";
DataComponent.setUpdateTable(updateTable);
```

getUpdateTable()

The getUpdateTable() method of the DataUpdate interface will return the current table being used for updating. The method will return the table that was specified using the setUpdateTable() method. Using the getUpdateTable() method, you can determine to which table SQL statements are to be applied. This can give you information that you can use to determine who needs access to the database and at what times they need access. The syntax for the getUpdateTable() method is as follows:

```
String updateTable;
updateTable = DataComponent.getUpdateTable();
```

update()

The update() method of the DataUpdate interface takes any data that was changed in the data component and updates the database using the specified update table and update columns. The update() method updates only data that has changed. The method will compare the values in the two arrays of Hashtable objects. It will cycle through all records and if any column information has been changed, the method will perform an update for the record information.

The update() method will determine first whether any data needs to be updated, and then it will construct a SQL statement to execute the updating. The SQL statement will update the specified update table and use the columns specified in the column array. The columns to be updated are specified by the user. After constructing the SQL statement, the update() method will pass the statement to the previewStatement() method. The previewStatement() method will enable you to perform any special processing or business logic before the SQL statement is executed and sent to the database. If the previewStatement() returns a Boolean false, then the update() method will skip execution of the current SQL statement and continue to the next record.

The update() method takes no parameters and returns a Boolean value that determines whether the updates were successful. If the update process was successful, then the method will return a `true` value; otherwise, a `false` will be returned indicating that the update process was not successful. The syntax for calling the `update()` method is as follows:

```
boolean saveSuccessful = DataComponent.update();
```

previewStatement()

The `previewStatement()` method of the `DataUpdate` interface provides you, the developer, with a way to insert your application-specific business logic into the update process for the data component. The `previewStatement()` method is called from the `retrieve()` and the `update()` methods. Its purpose is to enable you to view the SQL statement before it is executed and possibly cancel execution of the SQL statement.

The `previewStatement()` method takes two parameters. The first parameter is the SQL string that is to be executed by the database. The string is built in the calling method and passed to the `previewStatement()` method. The parameter `sql` contains the passed SQL statement. Using this parameter, you can determine what is to be updated before the update occurs. This can give you some added functionality for handling your application-specific business logic. If the SQL statement does not match some criteria contained in your business logic, then you can cancel execution of the SQL statement by returning a `false` value. This will cause the calling method to skip execution of the SQL statement.

The second parameter, `sqlType`, enables you to determine what type of SQL statement is being executed. Currently, only the `SELECT` and `UPDATE` SQL statement types are provided, but with some user-added functionality, the `INSERT` and `DELETE` SQL types can be utilized. The `sqlType` parameter is a predefined integer that determines the type of SQL statement that is to be executed. The `retrieve()` method will pass the `SELECT` constant as the SQL type and the `update()` method will pass the `UPDATE` constant as the SQL type.

The `previewStatement()` method is handled differently than the rest of the data component methods. This method will initially have only a single line of code that returns the Boolean `true` value. For the method to have any effect, you will need to inherit the specific data component you want and add the processing to this method.

setUpdateColumn()

The `setUpdateColumn()` method of the `DataUpdate` interface gives you the ability to specify which column(s) you want included in the `SET` and `WHERE` clauses of the executed SQL statement. The `update()` method will build a SQL statement that contains the specified update columns in the `SET` clause, which updates the data values, and the `WHERE` clause, which determines which records will be updated. The method takes a column, passed as a string or an integer. The method that takes the column as a string will call the `getColumnIndex()`

method to get the index for the specified column and then call the other `setUpdateColumn()` method, passing the column index. The syntax for calling the two methods is as follows:

```
// Pass the Column as a String
DataComponent.setUpdateColumn("FirstName");
// Pass the Column as an Index
DataComponent.setUpdateColumn(1);
```

getUpdateColumn()

The `getUpdateColumn()` method of the `DataUpdate` interface enables you to get an array that contains all of the columns that will be used in an update statement. The columns are returned as an array of `String` objects. The values returned are the values that were passed in when the user used the `setUpdateColumn()` methods. The syntax for calling the `getUpdateColumn()` method is as follows:

```
String columns[];
columns = DataComponent.getUpdateColumn();
```

The `DataComponent` Interface

The `DataComponent` interface provides various methods for accessing data values and for getting information about the columns that make up the data component. You should implement this interface if you want to have access to other data items contained in the data component, other than the displayed column. Listing 9.3 displays the full code for the `DataComponent` interface, and Table 9.3 provides a brief description of all the methods contained in it.

TYPE   **Listing 9.3. The `DataComponent` interface.**

```java
import symjava.sql.*;

public interface DataComponent {
 public int getRow();
 public void setRow(int Row);
 public int rowCount();
 public int columnCount();
 public void reset();
 public String getItem(int row, int column);
 public void setItem(int row, int column, String value);
 public String getColumnName(int index);
 public String getColumnType(int index);
 public String getColumnIndex(String column);
}
```

Table 9.3. `DataComponent` **methods and descriptions.**

Method	Description
getRow()	Gets the current row on which the DataComponent is positioned.
setRow()	Sets the current row for the DataComponent to the passed integer.
rowCount()	Returns an integer that contains the number of records contained in the data component.
columnCount()	Returns an integer that contains the number of columns contained in the data component.
reset()	Clears all information for the data component.
getItem()	Returns the data value for the specified row and column.
setItem()	Sets the data value to the specified value for the specified row and column.
getColumnName()	Returns the column name of the specified column index.
getColumnType()	Returns the column type of the specified column index.
getColumnIndex()	Returns the column index of the specified column name.

getRow()

The getRow() method of the DataComponent interface provides you with a way to determine the current row on which the data component is positioned. The getRow() method will return the current row, or record, that the data component is currently displaying. The row number can be any valid integer between 1 and N, where N is the maximum number of rows that were returned by the SQL statement. You can determine the maximum number of rows by calling the rowCount() method. The syntax for calling the getRow() method is as follows:

```
int row;
row = DataComponent.getRow();
```

setRow()

The setRow() method of the DataComponent interface enables you to change the current row on which the data component is positioned. The setRow() method takes an integer and changes the current row that is displayed to the specified record. The setRow() method can take any valid integer that is between 1 and N, where N is the maximum number of records contained in the data component. The syntax for calling the setRow() method is as follows:

```
// Set the displayed row to be row 10
int newRow = 10;
DataComponent.setRow(newRow)
```

rowCount()

The rowCount() method of the DataComponent interface enables you to determine the number of records or rows that are contained in the data component. The number of records is a fixed variable that is set by the retrieve() method. It is set to the number of rows that are retrieved by the SQL query. The syntax for calling the rowCount() method is as follows:

```
int rowCount;
rowCount = DataComponent.rowCount();
```

columnCount()

The columnCount() method of the DataComponent interface enables you to determine the number of columns that are contained in the data component. The number of columns that are in the data component is different from the number of update columns as specified by the user. The total number of columns is a fixed number that is set by the retrieve() method. The number of columns in the data component exactly matches the number of columns that are returned in the ResultSet object. The syntax for calling the columnCount() method is as follows:

```
int columnCount;
columnCount = DataComponent.columnCount();
```

reset()

The reset() method of the DataComponent interface does just what its name implies; it resets the data component. The reset() method clears the Connection object, the SQL string, and all of the object variables that the data component uses. The reset() method is useful if you want to get the data component back to its original state so that you can perform other processing with the data component. The syntax for calling the reset() method is as follows:

```
DataComponent.reset();
```

getItem()

The getItem() method of the DataComponent interface enables you to get data values from columns and rows other than the currently displayed row and column. The data component displays the first column of the result set; so without the getItem() method, getting the data values for the columns that are not displayed is impossible.

The getItem() method takes an integer specifying a row and an integer specifying the column for which you want to get the data value. For example, if the LastName column is column 2 and you want to get the data value for the current row, you could access the data value by using the following syntax:

```
String dataValue;
int column = 2;
int row = DataComponent.getRow();
dataValue = DataComponent.getItem(row, column);
```

Notice that I used the getRow() method to determine the current row that I was on. I then specified that I wanted to get the data value for the second column of the current row. The getItem() method will always return a String object containing the data value. Due to the time and space limits of this book, it would be impossible to create a full-featured component. I will introduce the basics of creating the component, and you can add any extra functionality that you require. Although all items will be returned as String objects, you can determine the appropriate data type by using the getColumnType() method.

setItem()

The setItem() method of the DataComponent interface enables you to set data values for columns and rows other than the currently displayed record. The setItem() method takes a row, column, and data value as parameters. The row and column parameters specify where you want to put the specified data value. This can enable you to change the value of a column if an event occurs. The following lines of code will change the LastName column, which is column 2, on the current record to be "Hobbs":

```
String newName = "Hobbs";
int row = DataComponent.getRow();
int column = 2;
DataComponent.setItem(row, column, newName);
```

getColumnName()

The getColumnName() method of the DataComponent interface enables you to get the column name based on a column index. The getColumnName() method takes the column index as a parameter and returns the column name for that index value. This method is used internally by the methods of the data component, but can also be used externally. The syntax for calling the method is as follows:

```
// Get the column name for the second column
int column = 2;
String columnName;
columnName = DataComponent.getColumnName(column);
```

getColumnType()

The getColumnType() method of the DataComponent interface enables you to get the column data type of a specified column index. The getColumnType() method takes the passed column index as a parameter and returns the column data type for that index value. The syntax for calling the method is as follows:

```
// Get the column type for the second column
int column = 2;
// Column types based on values in symjava.sql.Types
int columnType;
columnType = DataComponent.getColumnType(column);
```

getColumnIndex()

The getColumnIndex() method of the DataComponent interface enables you to get the column index, or order of the column, from a specified column name. The getColumnIndex() method takes a String object that contains the column name and returns the index of the column. The index of the column is the column's order within the result set. The syntax for calling the method is as follows:

```
// Get Column Index for LastName column
String column = "LastName";
int columnIndex;
columnIndex = DataComponent.getColumnIndex(column);
```

The DataNavigation Interface

The DataNavigation interface provides four methods to move the position of the data component. When the position of the data component is moved, the new data value is displayed in the component. Moving the position involves changing the current record that the data component is displaying.

One of the main problems with the ResultSet object is that it has no easy methods for navigating between records. It provides the next() method, but does not provide any other methods for navigation. The DataNavigation interface and data components plan to solve this shortcoming. The DataNavigation interface provides methods for navigating forward and backward, as well as going to the last record and the first record.

The code for creating the DataNavigation component is shown in Listing 9.4. The methods provided by the DataNavigation interface and their descriptions are listed in Table 9.4.

TYPE   **Listing 9.4. The** `DataNavigation` **interface.**

```
import symjava.sql.*;

public interface DataNavigation {
 public void next();
 public void previous();
 public void first();
 public void last();
}
```

Table 9.4. `DataNavigation` **interface methods.**

Method	Description
`next()`	Moves the record position to the next available record.
`previous()`	Moves the record position to the previous record.
`first()`	Moves the record position to the first record in the data component.
`last()`	Moves the record position to the last record in the data component.

next()

The `next()` method of the `DataNavigation` interface enables you to move the record position in the data component to the next record. The `next()` method will continue to advance through the records until it reaches the last record. When the pointer is at the last record, the `next()` method will not move past the last record.

Along with moving the record position and displaying new data to the user, the `next()` method updates the data value for the currently displayed record. The `next()` method will take the text or data contained in the component and store it in the appropriate `Hashtable` object for the display column. The data value is stored so that when the `update()` method is called, the new data value can be checked against the old data value to determine whether an update is needed.

The syntax for calling the `next()` method is as follows:

```
// Move to next record in data component
DataComponent.next();
```

previous()

The `previous()` method of the `DataNavigation` interface enables you to move the record position in the data component to the previous record. The `previous()` method will continue to backtrack through the records in the data component until it reaches the initial record. When the initial record has been reached, the previous() method will not change the record position.

The previous() method, like the next() method, updates the data value for the current item before moving. The syntax for calling the previous() method is as follows:

```
// Move to previous record in data component
DataComponent.previous();
```

first()

The first() method of the DataNavigation interface enables you to position the record pointer to the initial, or first, record. Calling the first() method will move the currently displayed record to the initial record.

The first() method also updates the data value for the current item before moving to the initial record. The syntax for calling the first() method is as follows:

```
// Move to first record in data component
DataComponent.first();
```

last()

The last() method of the DataNavigation interface enables you to position the record pointer to the last record in the data component. Calling the last() method will move the currently displayed record to the last record in the data component.

The last() method also updates the data value for the current item before moving to the last record. The syntax for calling the last() method is as follows:

```
// Move to last record in data component
DataComponent.last();
```

Summary

Today you learned about the interfaces that you will use to create the data components throughout the rest of Week 2. These interfaces form the basis of the data components. They provide the methods that give the data components most of their functionality. You learned why we chose to use the data interfaces and why we chose to separate the functionality between four different interfaces.

After looking over the four different interfaces that you created, you should have a better understanding of how the data components will work. Hopefully, these interfaces have given you a glimpse of some of the functionality that the data components you will create will give you. It should also encourage you to come up with some other functionality that would be useful in your applications. Using these interfaces as a basis, you can create other methods that provide more power to the data components.

Q&A

Q **Why am I using interfaces instead of just using multiple inheritance?**

A You are using the data interfaces because Java does not support multiple inheritance. The interfaces enable you to guarantee that the data components will all have the same methods available for the user.

Q **Why am I using four interfaces instead of one?**

A We separated the methods between four different interfaces to provide some abstraction. The methods are grouped in their respective interfaces based on their functionality.

Workshop

The Workshop provides quiz questions to help you solidify your understanding of the material covered and exercises to give you experience in using what you've learned. The answers are provided in Appendix A, "Quiz and Exercise Answers." Try to understand the quiz and exercise answers before you go on to tomorrow's lesson.

Quiz

1. What are the four data interfaces that you will be using to build the data components?
2. What is the difference between the two different setConnection() methods?
3. What value does the retrieve() method return?
4. What are the four SQL types that are used in the DataUpdate interface?
5. What is the purpose of the previewStatement() method?
6. What does the reset() method do?
7. What method would you use to set the record position to the fifth record?
8. What value does the getColumnType() method return?
9. List the two ways in which you can move the record position to the initial record.
10. List the two ways in which you can move the record position to the last record.

Exercises

1. Create a new interface, DataModification, that will provide functionality to add new records and delete current records. It should implement the insert() and delete() methods.

2. Add a method in the DataNavigation interface that will enable you to move to any record in the data component. You will code the method in the data component chapters.

3. Add a method in the DataComponent interface that will enable you to change the column being displayed. You will code the method in the data component chapters (Days 10 through 14).

Day 10

The DataLabel, DataField, and DataArea Components

Today's lesson covers the creation of the DataLabel, DataField, and DataArea components. The three components are very similar to create, so you will create the DataField component and learn how to use the methods defined for the DataField component in the DataLabel and DataArea components.

The purpose for creating the data components is to give you an understanding of how JDBC works and how you can use it in real-life situations. Creating the data components this week will expose you to various aspects of JDBC and Java and give you some real programming experience. The components are real-life components and can be used in your day-to-day applications. They provide enough functionality for you to use in real applications, but are simple and short enough to be thoroughly covered in the space limitations of this book.

The topics to be covered today include the following:

- Why you should use data components
- Building the basics of the component
- Constructing the component
- Connecting the component
- Navigating the component
- Updating the component
- Using the component

Why Should You Use Data Components?

You might be wondering why you even should use data components. Using components that provide prebuilt functionality enables you to concentrate on the business logic of your applications and not the building of objects used throughout the application. The data components that you will build will let you provide information from the database with a minimal amount of coding. After you have completed the data components, you can provide components that let your users view data information by coding the minimum amount of information needed. This approach will enable you to concentrate on the business logic of the application and also speed the development of your application.

Building the Basics

The DataField component you create today will be contained in a .java file separated from all other classes. It will be inherited from the TextField component in the AWT package, but it will implement all four of the data interfaces that were described on Day 9, "The Data Interfaces." The component will need to import the following packages for compilation:

```
import java.awt.*;

import java.util.*;

import symjava.sql.*;
```

The purpose of this section is to explain the different object variables that will be used throughout the component. The object variables store various information about the data component. They store any of the following information:

- [ ] The `Connection` object
- [ ] The SQL statement
- [ ] The current record position
- [ ] The maximum number of records
- [ ] The update table
- [ ] The update columns
- [ ] The original data values
- [ ] The user-entered data values
- [ ] The number, names, and types of columns in a result set

10

The `Connection` Object

The first object variable you will create is the `Connection` object variable. This will be used to store the `Connection` object that the component will use for any executions of SQL statements. The `Connection` object will be passed into the component through one of the constructor methods or through the `setConnection()` method. The `Connection` variable will be declared as follows:

```
Connection c;
```

The SQL Statement

The SQL statement that populates the data component will be stored in a `String` object. This object will be passed into the data component through one of the constructors or through the `setSQL()` method. The variable will be declared as follows:

```
String sql;
```

The Current Record Position

You will use an integer variable to store the current record position. The current record position is used to determine which data value is currently being displayed. The current record position can be changed by any of the navigation methods and is initially set to 0. After the retrieve() method has populated the data values from the ResultSet object into the hash tables, it will call the next() method to display the initial record. The variable will be declared as follows:

```
int current = 0;
```

The Maximum Number of Records

The maximum number of records contained in the data component will be stored in an object variable as well. This variable will be used as the return value for the rowCount() method and also will be used to ensure that the user does not try to go past the last record in the data component. This prevents the user from trying to access an item in the hash table that does not exist. The variable declaration is as follows:

```
int max = 0;
```

The Update Table

The update table, the table to which changes will be applied, will be saved in a String object. The update table will be passed in by the user, using the setUpdateTable() method. The update table will store the table to which any changes to data values will be applied. The variable declaration is as follows:

```
String updateTable = "";
```

Update Columns

The columns that are to be updated by the data component will be stored in a hash table. Along with the hash table, there also will be an integer variable that will store the number of columns that are contained in the hash table. A Hashtable object is being used because there needs to be an object that allows a dynamic number of items. The variable declarations for the Hashtable and the integer to store the update column count are as follows:

```
int updateColumnCount = 0;
Hashtable updateColumns;
```

Original Data Values

When the data component retrieves the data from the database, based on the SQL statement for the data component, it stores all of the information in an array of Hashtable objects. The position in the array indicates the column, so that the first Hashtable object will store the information for the first column of the result set. Each `Hashtable` object then stores the data value for each individual record in the result set. The variable declaration is as follows:

```
Hashtable Original[];
```

User-Entered Data Values

Along with the original data values, you will create an array of `Hashtable` objects to store the data values entered by the user. The array will initially be populated with the original data values, but will be changed to any user-updated values. You are keeping two sets of the data values so that you will be able to determine whether the user made any changes, and if any changes were made, you need the original data values to use in the WHERE clause of the SQL update statement. The declaration for the array is as follows:

```
Hashtable Records[];
```

Number, Names, and Types of Columns

The final object variables that will be contained in the data component are the variables that store information about the columns in the result set. The data component will store the names of all of the columns, the types of all columns, and the column count that the result set contains. The column names and types will be stored in arrays that will contain one item for every column. The arrays will be created using the column count obtained during the `retrieve()` method. The column type array will store the column types as they are defined in the `Types` class. Therefore, the array used to store the column types will be an array of integers. The variable declarations are as follows:

```
int columns = 0;
String strColumns[];
int ColumnTypes[];
```

The component also will implement the methods defined in the `DataComponent` interface. These methods provide various services to get information about the component, and also methods to reinitialize the component and manipulate the data values stored in the component. The methods that will be implemented are as follows:

- [ ] `public int getRow()`
- [ ] `public void setRow(int row)`
- [ ] `public int rowCount()`
- [ ] `public int columnCount()`
- [ ] `public void reset()`
- [ ] `public String getItem(int row, int column)`

10

```
☐  public void setItem (int row, int column, String value)
☐  public String getColumnName(int index)
☐  public int getColumnType(int index)
☐  public int getColumnIndex(String column)
```

getRow()

The getRow() method of the component will enable you to determine which record, or row, the data component is currently displaying. The getRow() method will return the value stored in the current object variable. This variable stores the current record position for the component. The code for the method is shown in Listing 10.1.

TYPE | **Listing 10.1. The getRow() method.**

```
// Get the currently displayed row for the component
public int getRow () {
 // Return the current record number
 return this.current;
}
```

setRow(int)

The setRow(int) method enables you to change the currently displayed row in the component to a specified record. The setRow(int) method is different than the next() and previous() methods in that it enables you to specify a specific record that you want to display. The setRow(int) method will move the current record position to the passed record, as long as the record is a valid record within the component.

The setRow(int) method will save the current data value displayed in the component before moving the record position. To do this, it will remove the data value currently stored in the Hashtable object for the current record, and then add the currently displayed text to the Hashtable object for the current item. The code for removing the current item and adding the new item is as follows:

```
// Set value for updated text
Records[0].remove(new Integer(current));
Records[0].put(new Integer(current), this.getText());
```

Listing 10.2 contains the code for the setRow(int) method.

10

Listing 10.2. The `setRow(int)` method.

```
// Set the current row for the component
public void setRow (int Row) {
 // Check to insure that passed row is valid
 if ((Row < 1) || (Row > max)) {
  return;
 }

 // Set value for updated text
 Records[0].remove(new Integer(current));
 Records[0].put(new Integer(current), this.getText());

 // Set the record to be the new row
 this.current = Row;

 // Set the text of the component to new data value
 this.setText((String)Records[0].get(new Integer(current)));
}
```

10

rowCount()

The `rowCount()` method enables you to determine the number of records that are contained in the component. The method's only line of code returns the value contained in the `max` variable. The `max` variable stores the maximum number of records that is contained in the component, which is also the record count. Listing 10.3 contains the code for the `rowCount()` method.

Listing 10.3. The `rowCount()` method.

```
// Return the current record count for the component
public int rowCount () {
 // Return value contained in max variable
 return this.max;
}
```

columnCount()

The `columnCount()` method enables you to determine the number of columns that are currently contained in the component. The number of columns is a fixed number that is determined during the `retrieve()` method. The number of columns in the component exactly matches the number of components that were in the retrieved result set. The number of columns also determines the number of Hashtable objects contained in the original and user-modified arrays. The code for columnCount() is shown in Listing 10.4.

TYPE **Listing 10.4. The `columnCount()` method.**

```
// Return the number of columns contained in the component
public int columnCount () {
 // Return value stored in columns variable
 return this.columns;
}
```

reset()

The reset() method enables you to reinitialize the component. When the reset() method is called, all variables that relate to accessing data in the component are reset. All integer variables are reset to 0, all String objects are reset to the empty string, and the Connection object is reset to null. Listing 10.5 contains the code for the reset() method.

TYPE **Listing 10.5. The `reset()` method.**

```
// Reset the component
public void reset () {
 // Reset the Connection Object
 this.c = null;

 // Reset the SQL statement string and the Update Table
 this.sql = "";
 this.updateTable = "";

 // Reset all of the counter and count variables
 this.current = 0;
 this.max = 0;
 this.columns = 0;
 this.updateColumnCount = 0;
}
```

getItem(int, int)

The purpose of the getItem(int, int) method is to enable you to get data values for the component other than the displayed data value. The component displays the data value for the first column and the current row. To get the data values from the other columns, you will need to use the getItem(int, int) method. The method will first determine whether the passed row and column are valid. If the two parameters are valid, the method will return the data value, based on the row and column specified. If either or both of the passed parameters are not valid, then the method will return an empty string. The code for the getItem(int, int) method is shown in Listing 10.6.

TYPE **Listing 10.6. The** `getItem(int, int)` **method.**

```
// Get a data value for specified row and column
public String getItem (int row, int column) {
 // Check for an invalid row
 if ((row < 1) || (row > max)) {
  return "";
 }

 // Check for an invalid column
 if ((column < 1) || (column > this.columns)) {
  return "";
 }

 // Return the data value for the specified row and column
 return (String)Records[column - 1].get(new Integer(row));
}
```

NOTE

Notice that `column - 1` was used to access the column in the array of `Hashtable` objects. This is because the columns are numbered from 1 to *N*, but the array of hash tables goes from 0 to *N - 1*.

setItem(int, int, String)

The setItem(int, int, String) method enables you to set data values in the component for items other than the currently displayed data item. The method takes the passed data value as a String object and places it into the array of hash tables at the specified position. The method will first check to ensure that the passed row and column are valid. If either or both of the parameters are invalid, then the method will return and nothing will be added to the component. The method will remove the current data value from the specified position in the component before adding the new data value. Listing 10.7 contains the code for the setItem(int, int, String) method.

TYPE **Listing 10.7. The** `setItem(int, int, String)` **method.**

```
// Set item for specified row and column
public void setItem (int row, int column, String value) {
 // Check for invalid row
 if ((row < 1) || (row > max)) {
  return;
 }

 // Check for invalid column
 if ((column < 1) || (column > this.columns)) {
  return;
 }

 // Remove current data value and add new data value
 Records[column].remove(new Integer(row));
 Records[column].put(new Integer(row), value);
}
```

NOTE

All data values are stored as `String` objects. To determine what type of data type the column is, use the `getColumnType()` method.

getColumnName(int)

The `getColumnName()` method takes a specified column index and returns the column name. The index is the order of the column as it was in the SQL statement. Because the array is zero-based, and you number columns from 1, it will return the value stored in the $N-1$ position, where N is the column index specified by the user. If the user specifies an invalid column index, then the method will return the empty string. Listing 10.8 contains the code for the `getColumnName()` method.

TYPE **Listing 10.8. The** `getColumnName()` **method.**

```
// Return the column name for the specified index
public String getColumnName (int index) {
 // Check to make sure that passed column is valid
 if ((index < 1) || (index > this.columns)) {
  return "";
 }

 // Return index-1 item from column array
 return strColumns[index-1];
}
```

getColumnType(int)

The getColumnType(int) method enables you to determine what type of data type the specified column supports. The valid data types are listed in the class symjava.sql.Types. The method takes a column index as a parameter and returns the column type of the specified column as an integer. You can then compare the integer returned to the defined data type values in the Types class. If the user specifies an invalid column index, then +1 will be returned to the user. Listing 10.9 contains the code for the getColumnType(int) method.

TYPE **Listing 10.9. The getColumnType(int) method.**

```
// Return the column type of specified column
public int getColumnType (int index) {
// Check to make sure that passed column is valid
if ((index < 1) || (index > this.columns)) {
  return -1;
}

// Return the column type of the specified column
  return ColumnTypes[index];
}
```

getColumnIndex(String)

The getColumnIndex(String) method provides you with a way to determine the column index, or column order, for a specified column name. The method takes the name of the column as it appears in the SQL Select statement and returns the column index for the column. The column index is used for most of the methods in the component that access data and return information about the column. You could use this method in place of the column parameter and pass the column name to such methods as getItem() and setItem(). As an example, look at the following code:

```
String data = DataComponent.getItem(1, getColumnIndex("FirstName"));
```

The code is using the getItem() method to get a specified data value, but instead of specifying the column index for FirstName, the column name is specified. This can make your code more maintainable, because the column order could change based on the Select statement sent to the data component, but the name of the column does not change. If the user specified a column name that is not contained in the array of columns, then the method will return +1 as the column index. Listing 10.10 contains the full code for the getColumnIndex(String) method.

TYPE　**Listing 10.10. The `getColumnIndex(String)` method.**

```
// Return the column index for specified column name
public int getColumnIndex (String column) {
 int index = -1;

 // Loop through columns in column array
 for (int i = 0;i < this.columns;i++) {
  // Check to see if current item is specified column
  if (column.equals(strColumns[i])) {
   index = i + 1;
   break;
  }
 }

 // Return the column index
 return index;
}
```

Constructing the Component

To provide the most functionality to the component that you can, provide seven different constructor methods for the DataField component. Each of the seven constructors will allow the user to specify different initial values for the component. The seven constructors are

- [ ] `public DataField()`
- [ ] `public DataField (int length);`
- [ ] `public DataField (Connection c);`
- [ ] `public DataField (Connection c, String sql);`
- [ ] `public DataField (int length, Connection c, String sql);`
- [ ] `public DataField (int length, Connection c, String sql, boolean retrieve);`
- [ ] `public DataField (Connection c, String sql, boolean retrieve);`

DataField()

The basic constructor for the component takes no parameters and basically creates the component. The code for the `DataField()` constructor is as follows:

```
// Basic Constructor
public DataField() {
 super();
}
```

10

DataField(int)

The DataField(int) constructor takes an integer indicating the length in characters that you want to size the component to initially. The component will initially be sized to accommodate the number of characters indicated by the length. The code for the DataField(int) constructor is as follows:

```
// Constructor to create DataField with specified length
public DataField (int length) {
 super(length);
}
```

DataField(Connection)

The DataField(Connection) constructor will enable you to specify an initial Connection object to use for the DataComponent. The Connection object passed in will be assigned to the object variable that stores the Connection object. This constructor gives you the ability to pass in the connection to the database without having to call the setConnection() method, thereby eliminating unnecessary lines of code.

Notice that instead of calling super() to create the component, you call this(). Calling the basic constructor method for the component in place of the ancestor constructor enables you to add functionality to the basic constructor at a later time and have it implemented across the various constructor methods that access the basic constructor. The code for the DataField(Connection) method is as follows:

```
// Constructor to assign Connection object
public DataField (Connection c) {
 // Call basic constructor
 this();

 this.c = c;
}
```

DataField(Connection, String)

The DataField(Connection, String) constructor method enables you to specify an initial Connection object and the initial SQL statement that should be used to populate the data component. The two parameters will be stored in the component for use during the retrieve() and update() methods. The constructor calls the DataField(Connection) constructor method, passing the Connection parameter. This reduces the amount of code

needed and makes centralization of business logic available. The code for the
DataField(Connection, String) method is as follows:

```
// Constructor to assign Connection and SQL
public DataField (Connection c, String sql) {
 // Call the basic constructor with connection object
 this(c);

 // Assign SQL to object variable
 this.sql = sql;
}
```

DataField(int, Connection, String)

The DataField(int, Connection, String) constructor method provides a combination of
the DataField(int) and DataField(Connection, String) methods. It enables you to specify
the initial size in characters, along with the initial Connection object and SQL statement. I
made the decision to call the DataField(int) method as the basic constructor, but you could
just as easily change it to call the DataField(Connection, String) constructor, depending on
your application needs. The code for the DataField(int, Connection, String) constructor
is as follows:

```
// Constructor to assign length, Connection, and SQL
public DataField (int length, Connection c, String sql) {
 // Call basic ancestor passing length of component
 this(length);

 // Assign the SQL and the Connection parameters to local variables
 this.c = c;
 this.sql = sql;
}
```

DataField(int, Connection, String, boolean)

The DataField(int, Connection, String, boolean) constructor method provides a way to
specify all possible parameters to the component, as well as forcing the component to
automatically retrieve data into the component once variables have been assigned. This
constructor calls the DataField(int, Connection, String) constructor, passing all of the
arguments to the constructor method.

The constructor method will automatically perform a call to the retrieve() method if the
passed Boolean is true. If false is passed into the method, then the constructor will behave
exactly like the DataField(int, Connection, String) constructor method; otherwise, it will

10

perform the retrieve automatically. This enables you to specify the basic information needed for the component and to have the component ready immediately. The code for the constructor method is as follows:

```
// Constructor to assign size, Connection, SQL, and retrieve
public DataField (int length, Connection c, String sql, boolean retrieve) {
 // Call the basic ancestor passing all needed arguments
 this(length, c, sql);

 // If user passed retrieve = true, then call retrieve method
 if (retrieve) {
  this.retrieve();
 }
}
```

DataField(Connection, String, boolean)

The final constructor method is similar to the constructor that takes all parameters, except that this constructor does not take a default size. The DataField(Connection, String, boolean) constructor method takes only the initial Connection object, SQL statement, and a Boolean value to indicate whether you want to let the constructor perform an automatic retrieve. The code for the constructor method is as follows:

```
// Constructor to assign Connection, SQL, and perform a retrieve
public DataField (Connection c, String sql, boolean retrieve) {
 // Call the basic ancestor passing Connection and SQL
 this(c, sql);

 // If user passed retrieve = true, then call retrieve method
 if (retrieve) {
  this.retrieve();
 }
}
```

Connecting the Component

Now that you have created the variables and methods to handle creating the component, you can create the methods that connect the component to the database and populate the component with data from the database. The DataConnection interface provides six methods that provide services to set and get the Connection object for the component, set and get the SQL statement for the component, and populate the data component with data values. The following are the methods that you will create for the DataConnection interface:

- public void setConnection(Connection c);
- public void setConnection(Connection c, boolean noReset);
- public Connection getConnection();

```
public void setSQL(String sql);
public String getSQL();
public int retrieve();
```

setConnection(Connection)

The setConnection(Connection) method will enable you to specify a new Connection object to be used for retrieving and updating data within the data component. The method takes as a parameter a Connection object. The method will reset the component before assigning the passed Connection object. This will, in effect, reinitialize the component to its original state before assigning the new transaction object. Listing 10.11 contains the code for the setConnection(Connection) method.

TYPE **Listing 10.11. The** setConnection(Connection) **method.**

```
// Reset the component and set the Connection object to passed parameter
public void setConnection (Connection c) {
 // Reset the component
 this.reset();

 // Set Connection object to passed parameter
 this.c = c;
}
```

setConnection(Connection, boolean)

The setConnection(Connection, boolean) method enables you to set the Connection object for the component, but it also allows you to specify whether the component will be reinitialized before the Connection object is set. Depending on the value of the passed Boolean, the method will keep the component's state or reset the component by calling the reset() method. A passed true value will keep the original state, and a passed false value will reset the component. The code for the method is shown in Listing 10.12.

TYPE **Listing 10.12. The** setConnection(Connection, boolean) **method.**

```
// Set the Connection object and reset/noreset the component
public void setConnection (Connection c, boolean noReset) {
 // If noReset = false, then reset the component
 if (!noReset) {
```

10

```
  this.reset();
 }

 // Assign passed Connection object
 this.c = c;
}
```

getConnection()

The getConnection() method enables you to get the Connection object being used by the data component. The method's only line of code is to return the variables storing the current Connection object. The method is in Listing 10.13.

TYPE **Listing 10.13. The getConnection() method.**

```
// Get the current Connection object
public Connection getConnection () {
 // Return the current Connection object
 return this.c;
}
```

setSQL(String)

The setSQL(String) method enables you to specify a new SQL statement to be used by the retrieve() method to populate the data component. The method takes the passed string containing the SQL statement and stores it in an object variable. The SQL statement can then be used by the retrieve() method to populate the component with the result set generated by the passed SQL statement. Listing 10.14 contains the code for the setSQL(String) method.

TYPE **Listing 10.14. The setSQL(String) method.**

```
// Set SQL to populate component
public void setSQL (String sql) {
 // Set object variable to passed SQL
 this.sql = sql;
}
```

getSQL()

The getSQL() method enables you to get the SQL statement currently being used to populate the component. The SQL statement that populates the component is stored in an object variable, and this variable is used as the return value for the getSQL() method. The code for the getSQL() method is shown in Listing 10.15.

TYPE   **Listing 10.15. The getSQL() method.**

```
// Return the SQL statement being used by the component
public String getSQL () {
 // Return value contained in sql variable
 return this.sql;
}
```

retrieve()

The retrieve() method is one of the main methods used by the data component. The retrieve() method is responsible for populating the component with data retrieved by the execution of the component's SQL statement. The retrieve() processing is described in detail later today.

The retrieve() method initially will create a Statement object from the component's current Connection object.

```
sqlStatement = this.c.createStatement();
```

After a Statement object has been created, the method will execute the current SQL statement contained in the object variable, sql. This variable stores a string that contains a SQL SELECT statement that retrieves a result set. This result set is then stored in a ResultSet object such as the following to provide information about the result set returned from the database:

```
results = sqlStatement.executeQuery(this.sql);
```

You will create a ResultSetMetaData object that enables you to get information about the columns in the result set. This ResultSetMetaData object is where you will obtain the column names and types, and the number of columns in the result set to get the column count, which will be used to determine the number of Hashtable objects needed, as well as how big the column names and column type arrays should be.

```
resultsMeta = results.getMetaData();
```

To get the column count, call the `getColumnCount()` method of the `ResultSetMetaData` object.

```
this.columns = resultsMeta.getColumnCount();
```

After you have the number of columns that are in the current result set, create the column name and column type arrays to store the column information.

```
strColumns = new String[columns];
ColumnTypes = new int[columns];
```

After the arrays to store column names and types have been initialized, populate them with the appropriate values. The column names can be retrieved by calling the `getColumnName()` method of the `ResultSetMetaData` object.

```
for (int i = 0;i<columns;i++) {
  strColumns[i] = resultsMeta.getColumnName(i+1);
}
```

NOTE

> Notice that you assign the column i+1 to the i position of the array. This is because arrays are zero-based, but you are storing the columns beginning with 1.

To get the column types for the columns in the result set, use the `getColumnType()` method of the `ResultSetMetaData` object. This method returns an integer that identifies that column type. Store this integer value in your array so that you can access it later.

```
for (int i = 0;i<columns;i++) {
 ColumnTypes[i] = resultsMeta.getColumnType(i+1);
}
```

You will also use the number of columns in the result set to determine the number of `Hashtable` objects that you will need. Because each `Hashtable` object represents a column in the result set, you will need the same number of `Hashtable` objects as you have columns.

```
Records = new Hashtable[this.columns];
Original = new Hashtable[this.columns];
```

Now that you have created all objects to store the information for the component, you can begin the process of getting the data values from the returned result set. To get all of the data values, call the `next()` method of the `ResultSet` object until you have cycled through all records.

For each record that you cycle through, you will loop through all columns that are contained in the result set and add the data values to the Hashtable objects. Although you created an array of the Hashtable objects previously, you will need to make sure that you actually create each individual Hashtable object. You will create the objects one time before you add the values for the first column.

```
Records[i] = new Hashtable();
Original[i] = new Hashtable();
```

After you have created each individual Hashtable object, you can add the current data value for a record to the appropriate Hashtable object. After all items have been added, change the value of the current variable to 0, because this retrieve could be a second retrieve that could make the value of the variable an invalid value. You will also call the next() method of the component so that the first record is displayed in the component. The method will finally return the number of records that were returned in the result set back to the user. The full code for the retrieve() method is in Listing 10.16.

TYPE   **Listing 10.16. The retrieve() method.**

```
// Populate the component
public int retrieve () {
 Statement sqlStatement;
 ResultSet results;
 ResultSetMetaData resultsMeta;
 int index = 0;

 // Determine if user wants to execute retrieve
 //by passing sql to previewStatement
 if (!previewStatement(this.sql, this.SELECT)) {return 0;)

 try {
  // Create a SQL statement
  sqlStatement = this.c.createStatement();

  // Execute the current SQL statement and store results
  results = sqlStatement.executeQuery(this.sql);

  // Get the MetaData for the Result Set
  resultsMeta = results.getMetaData();

  // Get the number of columns in the result set
  columns = resultsMeta.getColumnCount();

  // Create arrays to hold column names and types
  strColumns = new String[columns];
  ColumnTypes = new int[columns];

  // Populate the column names array
  for (int i = 0;i<columns;i++) {
   strColumns[i] = resultsMeta.getColumnName(i+1);
  }
```

```
// Populate the column types array
for (int i = 0;i<columns;i++) {
 strColumns[i] = resultsMeta.getColumnName(i+1);
}

// Create Hashtable arrays to store data values
Records = new Hashtable[columns];
Original = new Hashtable[columns];

// Cycle through all rows and add items to Hashtables
while (results.next()) {
 // Increment the index counter
 index++;

 // Perform a loop to add items for columns
 for (int i = 0;i<columns;i++) {
  // If you are on first record, create Hashtables
  if (index == 1) {
   Records[i] = new Hashtable();
   Original[i] = new Hashtable();
  }

  // Add items
  Records[i].put(new Integer(index), results.getString(i + 1));
  Original[i].put(new Integer(index), results.getString(i + 1));
 }
}

// Store the number of records in the result set
 max = index;
}
catch (SQLException e) {
 // Error occurred, so return a -1
 return -1;
}

// Set the current variable to 0
this.current = 0;

// Call the next() method to display initial value
this.next();

// Return the number of records in the result set
return index;
}
```

Navigating the Component

The DataNavigation interface provides you with four methods to allow navigation within the component. These methods include next(), previous(), first(), and last() and are somewhat self-explanatory. What each of the methods has in common is that they all save the current data value before moving to their respective locations. The current data value is saved in the appropriate position in the Records array. This array holds all of the data that the user has changed or entered. The Original array holds all of the original data values. The following are the methods for the DataNavigation interface:

- ☐ public void next();
- ☐ public void previous();
- ☐ public void first();
- ☐ public void last();

next()

The next() method works similarly to the next() method of the ResultSet object. The method moves the current record position to the next available record in the component. The method first will check to make sure that moving to the next record is valid. If it is not valid to move to the next record, then the method will do nothing. If moving to the next record is valid, then the next() method will save the current data value before moving. It will then move to the next record and display the data value for the first column. Listing 10.17 contains the code for the next() method.

TYPE **Listing 10.17. The next() method.**

```
// Move record position to next available record
public void next () {
 // Check to make sure it is valid to go to next record
 if (current == max) {
  return;
 }

// If this is not the initial display of the component, save current data value
 if (current != 0) {
  // Set data value for current displayed item
  Records[0].remove(new Integer(current));
  Records[0].put(new Integer(current), this.getText());
 }

 // Increment the current counter
 current++;

 // Set the text displayed to the new data value
 this.setText((String)Records[0].get(new Integer(current)));
}
```

10

previous()

The previous() method works similarly to the next() method except that it moves the record position backward instead of forward. The previous() method performs the same processing as the next() method. The code for the previous() method is displayed in Listing 10.18.

TYPE **Listing 10.18. The previous() method.**

```
// Move record position to previous available record
public void previous () {
 // Check to see if previous record is valid
 if (current == 1) {
  return;
 }

 // Set data value for current displayed item
 Records[0].remove(new Integer(current));
 Records[0].put(new Integer(current), this.getText());

 // Decrement the current counter
 current--;

 // Display the new data item
 this.setText((String)Records[0].get(new Integer(current)));
}
```

first() and last()

The first() and last() methods are similar except that the first() method changes the value of the current variable to 1, and the last() method changes the value to the value contained in the variable max. Listing 10.19 contains the code for the first() method. To create the last() method, change the value to which the current variable is set.

TYPE **Listing 10.19. The first() method.**

```
// Move to the first record in the component
public void first () {
 // Set data value for current displayed item
 Records[0].remove(new Integer(current));
 Records[0].put(new Integer(current), this.getText());

 // Decrement the current counter
 current = 1;

 // Display the new data item
 this.setText((String)Records[0].get(new Integer(current)));
}
```

Updating the Component

The DataUpdate interface provides you with some methods that allow the data component to be updated. This enables you to give the user the ability to enter new data and have it saved to the database. The methods contained in the interface enable you to set and get the table that will be updated, as well as get and set the columns to update. The interface provides the following methods:

- ☐ public void setUpdateTable(String table);
- ☐ public String getUpdateTable();
- ☐ public boolean update();
- ☐ public boolean previewStatement(String sql, int sqlType);
- ☐ public void setUpdateColumn(String column);
- ☐ public void setUpdateColumn(int column);
- ☐ public String[] getUpdateColumn();

setUpdateTable()

The setUpdateTable() method enables you to specify the table that will be updated when the user calls the update() method. The table is passed in as a String object and stored in an object variable. When the user calls the update() method, the specified update table is used to build the SQL statements that will be sent to the database. The code for the setUpdateTable() method is as follows:

```
// Set the update table
public void setUpdateTable (String table) {
 this.updateTable = table;
}
```

getUpdateTable()

The getUpdateTable() method allows you to get a string that contains the table against which all updates will be performed. The method takes no parameters and returns only the current value stored in the updateTable variable. The code for the getUpdateTable() method is as follows:

```
// Get the current update table
public String getUpdateTable () {
 return this.updateTable;
}
```

10

update()

The update() method is one of the most important methods in the component. This method is responsible for updating the data contained in the component. The update() component, along with being one of the most important, is also one of the most complicated. The method not only has to determine which records need updating, but it also has to build the update statements and send them to the database. The update() method that you will create for the component is not the best update() method that you could create, but it will do for this example.

First, check to ensure that both an update table and at least one update column have been specified. If either of these items is missing, then the update() method will return a Boolean false, indicating that the update process could not be carried out. There must be at least one update column and an update table before an update statement can be constructed.

After you have determined that the update method can proceed, loop through all records contained within the component. You will need to check every record to determine if there were any changes to that record. You will check only the columns for the record that have been specified as update columns. You will get the data value for the original record and the user data value and compare the two strings. If the two strings are identical, then you will move to the next column or record. If the two strings are not identical, then you will set a Boolean variable to true, indicating that the record has been changed.

After all of the update columns for the current record have been checked, check the value of the Boolean variable that you are using. If the variable contains true, then the record has been changed. If the record has been changed, then you will loop through all of the update columns specified for the component again and build the SQL Update statement. You will have to do the first update column differently than all of the rest. The first column placed in the SQL Update statement will not need an AND in the Where clause, or a comma in the Set clause. Therefore, you will add these items only when the column number is not 1. When you have added or skipped the required SQL separators, you will add the column name to both the Set and Where clauses for the SQL Update statement. The Set clause will contain the data value from the user data values, and the Where clause will contain the data value from the original data values. The original data value is required because that is how you will identify the record in the database you want to alter.

After you have built the SQL Update statement, pass the SQL statement to the previewStatement() method. If the method returns a true, then the update() method will create a Statement object and execute the current SQL statement. If the previewStatement() method returns a false, then the update() method will continue to the next record.

After all of the records have been checked and changed, the update() method will copy the data from the user Hashtable array to the original Hashtable array. You are doing this so that a subsequent update will not try to update the same data. Trying to do so would give unpredictable results, because the records specified in the Where clause would not exist. By copying the user values to the original values after the update, you can ensure that the original data values for your component reflect the data contained in the database.

The code for the update() method can be found in Listing 10.23, later today.

previewStatement()

The previewStatement() method used in the component is a blank method. The method initially contains only a statement to return a true so that the update will proceed normally. You can add your own specific business logic into this method that will prevent certain SQL statements from being executed. If you return a false from this method, then the SQL statement sent to the previewStatement() method will not be executed. The code for the initial previewStatement() method is as follows:

```
// Blank Method
public boolean previewStatement (String sql, int sqlType) {
  // Return a true so that update will occur
  return true;
  }
```

setUpdateColumn()

The two setUpdateColumn() methods perform the same function, but they each accept different values for the column. One method accepts a column index and stores that index in the hash table. The other method determines the appropriate column index and calls the method that takes the index to add it to the hash table of update columns. The code for the setUpdateColumn(String) method is shown in Listing 10.20, and the setUpdateColumn(int) code is shown in Listing 10.21.

TYPE **Listing 10.20. The setUpdateColumn(String) method.**

```
// Add an update column based on the Column Name
public void setUpdateColumn (String column) {
  // Pass the column index to the other method
  this.setUpdateColumn(this.getColumnIndex(column));
  }
```

Listing 10.21. The `setUpdateColumn(int)` **method.**

```
// Add an update column based on the Column Index.
Public void setUpdateColumn (int column) {
 // Make sure that passed column is valid
 if ((column < 1) || (column > this.columns)) {
  return;
 }

 // Check value of updateColumnCount, if 0, then
 // Hashtable will need to be created
 if (updateColumnCount == 0) {
  updateColumns = new Hashtable();
 }

 // Increment the update column counter
 updateColumnCount++;

 // Add the passed column index to the Hashtable
 updateColumns.put(new Integer(updateColumnCount), new Integer(column));
}
```

10

getUpdateColumn()

The `getUpdateColumn()` method enables you to get an array of `String` objects that contain the column names of all of the columns that are to be updated. The array that is returned is built by taking the hash table that contains the column indexes and getting the column name for each index. Listing 10.22 contains the code for the `getUpdateColumn()` method.

Listing 10.22. The `getUpdateColumn()` **method.**

```
// Get a list of columns that will be used in update statements
public String[] getUpdateColumn () {
 String columns[];

 // Create an array big enough for all columns
 columns = new String[updateColumnCount];

 // Add all items from Hashtable to array
 for (int i = 0; i<updateColumnCount; i++) {
  columns[i] = this.getColumnName((
  ➥(Integer)updateColumns.get(new Integer(i + 1))).intValue());
 }

 // Return the string array
 return columns;
}
```

Converting to the DataLabel and DataArea Components

The only changes that would need to be made to convert the DataField component to either a DataLabel or DataArea component would be to change the constructors. The Label and TextArea classes have different constructors than the TextField class, so only the constructor would need to be changed. All other methods would remain the same among the three components.

You could use the DataLabel component for data values that you want displayed to the user, but do not want any editing to be done on. The DataLabel would still provide all of the functionality, but just would prevent direct user editing.

You can use the DataArea component to display database column data of type VARCHAR or LONGVARCHAR. These data types can become very lengthy, and displaying the values in a simple TextField component would limit the amount of data the user could see at once.

The Full Code Listing for the DataField Component

 The full text of the DataField component is shown in Listing 10.23. Due to space limitations, the comments and spacing in the code have been omitted. Please refer to the full code listing on the CD-ROM for the fully commented and properly spaced code listing.

TYPE **Listing 10.23. The DataField component.**

```java
import java.awt.*;
import java.util.*;
import symjava.sql.*;

public class DataField extends TextField implements DataUpdate, DataComponent,
 DataConnection, DataNavigation {
 Connection c;
 String sql;
 int current = 0;
 int max = 0;
 String updateTable = "";
 int updateColumnCount = 0;
 Hashtable updateColumns;
 Hashtable Original[];
 Hashtable Records[];
 int columns = 0;
        String strColumns[];
 int ColumnTypes[];

public DataField() {
 super();
 }
```

```
public DataField (int length) {
 super(length);
}

public DataField (Connection c) {
 // Call basic constructor
 this();
 this.c = c;
}

public DataField (Connection c, String sql) {
 this(c);
 this.sql = sql;
}

public DataField (int length, Connection c, String sql) {
 this(length);
 this.c = c;
 this.sql = sql;
}

public DataField (int length, Connection c, String sql, boolean retrieve) {
 this(length, c, sql);
 if (retrieve) {
  this.retrieve();
 }
}

public DataField (Connection c, String sql, boolean retrieve) {
 this(c, sql);
 if (retrieve) {
  this.retrieve();
 }
}

public void setConnection (Connection c) {
 this.reset();
 this.c = c;
}

public void setConnection (Connection c, boolean noReset) {
 if (!noReset) {
  this.reset();
 }
 this.c = c;
}

public Connection getConnection () {
 return this.c;
}

public void setSQL (String sql) {
```

continues

Listing 10.23. continued

```
 this.sql = sql;
 }

 public String getSQL () {
  return this.sql;
 }

 public int retrieve () {
  Statement sqlStatement;
  ResultSet results;
  ResultSetMetaData resultsMeta;
  int index = 0;
  try {
   sqlStatement = this.c.createStatement();
   results = sqlStatement.executeQuery(this.sql);
   resultsMeta = results.getMetaData();
   columns = resultsMeta.getColumnCount();
   strColumns = new String[columns];
   ColumnTypes = new int[columns];
   for (int i = 0;i<columns;i++) {
    strColumns[i] = resultsMeta.getColumnName(i+1);
   }
   for (int i = 0;i<columns;i++) {
    strColumns[i] = resultsMeta.getColumnName(i+1);
   }
   Records = new Hashtable[columns];
   Original = new Hashtable[columns];
   while (results.next()) {
    index++;
    for (int i = 0;i<columns;i++) {
     if (index == 1) {
      Records[i] = new Hashtable();
      Original[i] = new Hashtable();
     }
     Records[i].put(new Integer(index), results.getString(i + 1));
     Original[i].put(new Integer(index), results.getString(i + 1));
    }
   }
   max = index;
  }
  catch (SQLException e) {
   return -1;
  }
  this.current = 0;
  this.next();
  return index;
 }

 public void next () {
  if (current == max) {
   return;
  }
  if (current != 0) {
   Records[0].remove(new Integer(current));
```

```
  Records[0].put(new Integer(current), this.getText());
 }
 current++;
 this.setText((String)Records[0].get(new Integer(current)));
}

public void previous () {
 if (current == 1) {
  return;
 }
 Records[0].remove(new Integer(current));
 Records[0].put(new Integer(current), this.getText());
 current--;
 this.setText((String)Records[0].get(new Integer(current)));
}

public void first () {
 Records[0].remove(new Integer(current));
 Records[0].put(new Integer(current), this.getText());
 current = 1;
 this.setText((String)Records[0].get(new Integer(current)));
}

public void last () {
 Records[0].remove(new Integer(current));
 Records[0].put(new Integer(current), this.getText());
 current = max;
 this.setText((String)Records[0].get(new Integer(current)));
}

public void setUpdateTable (String table) {
 this.updateTable = table;
}

public String getUpdateTable () {
        return this.updateTable;
}

public boolean update () {
 String sqlBase = "";
 String sqlSet = "";
 String sqlWhere = "";
 Statement sqlStatement;
 boolean changed = false;

 if (updateTable == "") {
  return false;
 }
 if (updateColumnCount == 0) {
  return false;
 }
 sqlBase = "update " + updateTable + "\n";
 sqlSet = "set ";
 sqlWhere = "where ";
```

continues

10

Listing 10.23. continued

```
for (int i=1;i<=max;i++) {
 changed = false;
 for (int j=1;j<=updateColumnCount;j++) {
  int curColumn = ((Integer)updateColumns.get(new Integer(j))).intValue();
  String orgValue = (String)Original[curColumn].get(new Integer(i));
  String userValue = (String)Records[curColumn].get(new Integer(i));
  if (!(orgValue.equals(userValue))) {
   changed = true;
  }
 }
 if (changed) {
  for (int j=1;j<=updateColumnCount;j++) {
   int curColumn = ((Integer)updateColumns.get(new Integer(j))).intValue();
   String colName = getColumnName(curColumn);
   if (j != 1) {
    sqlSet += ", \n" + colName + "= \'";
    sqlWhere += "\nand " + colName + "= \'";
   }
   String userValue = (String)Records[curColumn].get(new Integer(i));
   sqlSet += userValue + "\'\n";
   String orgValue = (String)Original[curColumn].get(new Integer(i));
   ➡sqlWhere += orgValue + "\'\n";
  }
  sqlBase = sqlBase + sqlSet + sqlWhere;
  if (previewStatement(sqlBase,this.UPDATE)) {
   try {
    sqlStatement = this.c.createStatement();
    sqlStatement.executeUpdate(sqlBase);
   }
   catch (Exception e) {
    return false;
   }
  }
  sqlBase = "update " + updateTable + "\n";
  sqlSet = "set ";
  sqlWhere = "where ";
 }
}
this.Original = this.Records;
return true;
}

public boolean previewStatement (String sql, int sqlType) {
 return true;
}

public void setUpdateColumn (String column) {
 this.setUpdateColumn(this.getColumnIndex(column));
}

public void setUpdateColumn (int column) {
 if ((column < 1) || (column > this.columns)) {
  return;
 }
```

```
  if (updateColumnCount == 0) {
   updateColumns = new Hashtable();
  }
  updateColumnCount++;
  updateColumns.put(new Integer(updateColumnCount), new Integer(column));
}

public String[] getUpdateColumn () {
  String columns[];
  columns = new String[updateColumnCount];
  for (int i = 0; i<updateColumnCount; i++) {
                columns[i] = this.getColumnName(((Integer)
                ➥updateColumns.get(new Integer(i + 1))).intValue());
  }
  return columns;
}

public int getRow () {
  return this.current;
}

public void setRow (int Row) {
  if ((Row < 1) ¦¦ (Row > max)) {
   return;
  }
  Records[0].remove(new Integer(current));
  Records[0].put(new Integer(current), this.getText());
  this.current = Row;
  this.setText((String)Records[0].get(new Integer(current)));
}

public int rowCount () {
  return this.max;
}

public int columnCount () {
  return this.columns;
}

public void reset () {
  this.c = null;
  this.sql = "";
  this.updateTable = "";
  this.current = 0;
  this.max = 0;
  this.columns = 0;
  this.updateColumnCount = 0;
}

public String getItem (int row, int column) {
  if ((row < 1) ¦¦ (row > max)) {
   return "";
  }
```

continues

Listing 10.23. continued

```
  if ((column < 1) ¦¦ (column > this.columns)) {
   return "";
  }
  return (String)Records[column - 1].get(new Integer(row));
 }

public void setItem (int row, int column, String value) {
  if ((row < 1) ¦¦ (row > max)) {
   return;
  }
  if ((column < 1) ¦¦ (column > this.columns)) {
   return;
  }
  Records[column].remove(new Integer(row));
  Records[column].put(new Integer(row), value);
 }

public String getColumnName (int index) {
  if ((index < 1) ¦¦ (index > this.columns)) {
   return "";
  }
  return strColumns[index-1];
 }

public int getColumnType (int index) {
  if ((index < 1) ¦¦ (index > this.columns)) {
   return -1;
  }
  return ColumnTypes[index];
 }

public int getColumnIndex (String column) {
  int index = -1;
  for (int i = 0;i < this.columns;i++) {
   if (column.equals(strColumns[i])) {
    index = i + 1;
    break;
   }
  }
  return index;
 }
}
```

Using the Component

Now that you have created the DataField component, create a sample application that will use the component. The application will use the DataField component to retrieve the FirstName column from the sample database. It will then provide buttons to move to the first, previous, next, and last records in the component.

The application will be a frame that measures 300×300 pixels. The constructor for the class will connect to the database and then place the DataField component in the North location. The buttons will be placed on a panel that is set for FlowLayout. The panel will be placed in the South location.

After you have connected to the database and have displayed all of the components on the frame, you will override the `handleEvent()` method to handle the button clicks for your buttons. Each button will call the appropriate data component method when it is clicked. The code for the sample class is shown in Listing 10.24.

TYPE | **Listing 10.24. The `DataExample` class.**

```
import java.awt.*;
import java.util.*;
import symjava.sql.*;

public class DataExample extends Frame {
 Connection c;
 DataField data;

 public DataExample () {
  super();

  // Make a connection to the database
  try {
   String driverName = "symantec.itools.db.jdbc.Driver";
   Driver driver = (Driver)Class.forName(driverName).newInstance();
   Properties p = new Properties();
   p.put("user", "dba");
   p.put("password", "sql");
   String dbURL = "jdbc:dbaw://localhost:8889/WATCOM/JDBC/JDBC";
   c = driver.connect(dbURL, p);

   // Create the DataField component
   // You want to pass the connection object,
   // the SQL statement, and have it retrieve
   String sql = "select FirstName from tEmployee";
   data = new DataField(c, sql, true);

   // Add the component to the window
   this.add("North", data);
  }
  catch (SQLException e) {}
  catch (Exception e) {}

  // Create and add the panel and buttons
  Panel p = new Panel();
  p.setLayout(new FlowLayout());
  p.add(new Button("First"));
  p.add(new Button("Previous"));
```

continues

Listing 10.24. continued

```
p.add(new Button("Next"));
p.add(new Button("Last"));
this.add("South", p);

this.resize(300, 300);
this.show();
}

public boolean handleEvent (Event evt) {
 if ("First".equals(evt.arg)) {
  data.first();
 }
 if ("Previous".equals(evt.arg)) {
  data.previous();
 }
 if ("Next".equals(evt.arg)) {
  data.next();
 }
 if ("Last".equals(evt.arg)) {
  data.last();
 }

 return super.handleEvent(evt);
}

public static void main (String args[]) {
 DataExample app = new DataExample();
}
}
```

The window created by the DataExample class is shown in Figure 10.1. The figure shows the DataField component and the four buttons that you added to the frame.

Figure 10.1.

The DataExample *frame.*

Summary

Today you have used JDBC and Java to create a DataField component that will allow you to seamlessly use the features of database programming without having to manually manage the database processing. The component you created allows full-featured database access to be created with very few lines of code. By encapsulating the database features into the component, you can now concentrate on building applications, and not on building database-processing logic.

In the next four days you will learn how to create other components that use the database. These components will allow you to create list components that display data to the user, and also panel components that allow you to display records of data to users. These components should help you to understand the basics of JDBC, as well as give you some real-world development tasks. These real-world tasks can be more beneficial than any reference guide.

10

Q&A

Q Why were so many constructors created?

A The different constructors were created to give the component more flexibility when it is created. The user has a multitude of ways that he can create the component. He can create the component without specifying any information, he can specify all of the information up front, or he can specify some information. This gives the user more options when developing applications.

Q Why were hash tables used instead of arrays?

A Hash table objects were used in place of arrays because it might be possible in the future to add functionality for deleting and adding records. If this functionality ever comes about, it will be easier to add using hash table objects over arrays, because hash table objects can add and delete records easier than arrays can.

Q Why would I use the `previewStatement()` method?

A The `previewStatement()` method enables you to decide whether a certain SQL statement should be executed. You can look at items within the SQL statement, and if they don't match certain criteria, you can prevent them from being executed against the database.

Workshop

The Workshop provides quiz questions to help you solidify your understanding of the material covered and exercises to give you experience in using what you've learned. The answers are provided in Appendix A, "Quiz and Exercise Answers." Try to understand the quiz and exercise answers before you go on to tomorrow's lesson.

Quiz

1. What constructor gives you the most initial options to specify?
2. What is the difference between the two setConnection() methods?
3. What does the retrieve() method do?
4. Describe what the setRow() method does.
5. What does the getColumnType() method return?
6. What two values are passed to the previewStatement() method?
7. What does returning a false from the previewStatement() do?
8. Name two ways to set the record to the initial record immediately.
9. What does setItem() allow you to do?
10. How do you specify an update table to be tEmployeeAddress?

Exercises

1. Extend the DataExample application to enable users to click an update button to update the component with any new information entered by the user.
2. Add insert() and delete() methods to the component. They can perform immediate inserts and deletes (easier) or wait until the user calls the update() method (more difficult).
3. Inherit the component and add code to the previewStatement() method that will not perform any updates on the column FirstName.

Day **11**

The DataList and DataChoice Components

Today, you learn how to create a DataList component. This component is very similar to the DataField component you created on Day 10, "The DataLabel, DataField, and DataArea Components." The DataList component will contain some of the same functionality, but will be geared to work for the AWT List component. The component will display the current data value, but will also let the user choose from all of the available data values. Using the List component's standard addItem() methods, you will also be able to add your own items for selection by the user.

The lesson today covers how to create the DataList component and also how to use the component. You can also create a DataChoice component, using the methods you create in the DataList component. You need to change only the constructor methods.

The topics covered today include the following:

- Why you should use data components
- Building the basics of the component
- Constructing the component
- Connecting the component
- Navigating the component
- Updating the component
- Using the component

Why Should You Use Data Components?

The DataList component will provide you with a way to let your applications display a selection of choices to the user. Instead of having to type in information, your users will be able to pick an item from a predefined list. This eliminates users having to type in information repeatedly, and also enables you to validate entries easier, because the user can pick a value only from a finite set.

The DataList component gives you an easy way to provide information and an easy way for users to pick information. Some common uses of list boxes include choices for states and titles. Today's lesson teaches you how to create components that you can reuse in your own applications. Creating the components also will give you practice at using Java and JDBC.

Building the Basics

The DataList component will be stored in its own `.java` file, which will enable you to use the component in any application. You will need only to include the compiled class file to use the component in your applications. The DataList component will be inherited from the List component of the AWT package.

The DataList component will use classes from three packages. These three packages contain all of the classes and interfaces that will be used within the component. The code to import these packages is as follows:

```
import java.awt.*;
import java.util.*;
import symjava.sql.*;
```

This section introduces you to the variables that the component will use. Most of the variables to be contained in the DataList component are the same variables that you use in the DataField component. The following variables, which will be contained in the DataList component, are described briefly:

☐ The `Connection` object

☐ The SQL statement

☐ The current record position

☐ The maximum number of records

☐ The update table

☐ The update columns

☐ The original data values

☐ User-entered data values

☐ Number, names, and types of columns in the result set

☐ The value list and count

The `Connection` Object

The `Connection` object provides the component with a link to the database. You pass in the `Connection` object using one of the constructor methods or the `setConnection()` methods. You use the `Connection` object for all the execution of SQL statements against the database.

NOTE

> The `Connection` object must remain connected during the life of the component. If you close the `Connection` object, then the component no longer will be able to connect to the database.

The SQL Statement

Use the SQL statement to populate the component. As with the DataField component, the DataList component will display the first column in the result set. However, unlike the DataField component, the DataList component will give the user the option to select any of the values contained in the first column of the result set. The current data value will be selected, but all of the values will be available for selection.

TIP

> You can display various useful information to the user. Selecting the first name and last name of an employee or customer will display the employee's or customer's full name in the DataList component.

Current Record Position

The current record position determines which record is currently selected. Because all values are displayed, changing the current record will change only the value that is selected in the list. The navigation and row methods will determine the value of the current record and set the value to the item index that corresponds to the data value.

Maximum Number of Records

The maximum number of records will also be saved. Use this value to ensure that the user does not try to display a record that is outside of the range of valid records.

Update Table

Use the update table variable in the update process to build the SQL statements that update the database with new data from the component. You must specify the update table before any update will occur.

Update Columns

The update columns are columns that the update() method will use in the SET and WHERE clauses of any SQL statements that are built and executed. These columns are the columns that will be updated in the database. At least one update column must be specified before any updating will occur.

Original Data Values

The original data values that were retrieved from the database will be stored in an array of Hashtable objects. The original data values are needed to determine whether any changes have been made to the data values by the user.

User-Entered Data Values

The values that users select from the list will be saved in an array of Hashtable objects, separate from the array that stores the original values. When an update occurs, the update() method will check the user-entered data values against the original data values and, if any changes have been made, will send a SQL statement to the database.

Number, Names, and Types of Columns

A lot of information will be stored for the columns in the DataList component. The column names and types and the number of columns will be available for the user to access.

Value List and Count

The DataList component will introduce some new variables that are not in the DataField component. Use these variables to determine what value needs to be selected, based on the current record. The addItem() methods for the DataList component will be overridden so that any new items also will go into the Hashtable object that will contain a copy of all the values displayed in the list. Store them in the same order as the list so that they will have the same index values. Also, use a counter variable to determine the maximum number of values that are currently displayed. The code for creating the variables is as follows:

```
Hashtable values;
int valueCount = 0;
```

The component also will implement the methods defined in the DataComponent interface. These methods provide various services to get information about the component, and also methods to reinitialize the component and manipulate the data values stored in the component. The methods to be implemented are as follows:

- ☐ public int getRow()
- ☐ public void setRow(int row)
- ☐ public int rowCount()
- ☐ public int columnCount()
- ☐ public void reset()
- ☐ public String getItem(int row, int column)
- ☐ public void setItem (int row, int column, String value)
- ☐ public String getColumnName(int index)
- ☐ public int getColumnType(int index)
- ☐ public String getColumnIndex(String column)
- ☐ private int getValueIndex (String value)

getRow()

The getRow() method returns the current record position for the component. The current record position is the record that is currently selected. The record position will change when a call to any of the navigation methods is called.

NOTE

> Initially, the index of the selected item in the list will be the record
> position in the component. If you select different items in the list for
> different records, then the selected item will be different than the
> record position.

setRow(int)

The setRow() method changes the record position for the component. It changes the current record to the value passed by the user. If the user passes an invalid record, then the setRow() method will not change the current record position. The setRow() method also updates the component with the selected item for the current record before changing the record position. The code for the setRow() method is shown in Listing 11.1.

TYPE   **Listing 11.1. The setRow() method.**

```
// Set the current row for the component
public void setRow (int Row) {
    // Check to insure that passed row is valid
    if ((Row < 1) || (Row > max)) {
        return;
    }
    // Set value for updated text
    Records[0].remove(new Integer(current));
    Records[0].put(new Integer(current), this.getSelectedItem());

    // Deselect the currently select item
    this.deselect(this.getSelectedIndex());

    // Set the record to be the new row
    this.current = Row;
    // Set the text of the component to new data value
    String value = "";
    try {
        value = (String)Records[0].get(new Integer(current));
    }
    catch (Exception e) {
        return;
    }
    // Set the new item to index of value
    this.select(this.getValueIndex(value));
}
```

rowCount()

The rowCount() method returns the number of records contained in the component. This method returns the value stored in the max variable. Because the number of records is equal to the maximum record count, the value that is returned is the value of the max variable.

columnCount()

The columnCount() method returns the number of columns that are contained in the component. The number of columns that are contained in the component is equal to the number of columns that were in the result set. The component creates one Hashtable object for each column that is contained in the result set returned from the database. The number of columns contained in the component is stored in an object variable, and it is this value that is returned to the user.

reset()

The reset() method performs the same function as the DataField component, but the DataList component adds an extra variable that has to be reset. The purpose of the reset() method is to give you a way to reinitialize the component so that you can use the component again. The component reverts back to an original state, and you must specify all needed variables again. Listing 11.2 contains the code for the reset() method.

TYPE **Listing 11.2. The reset() method.**

```
// Reset the component
public void reset () {
    // Reset the Connection Object
    this.c = null;
    // Reset the SQL statement string and the Update Table
    this.sql = "";
    this.updateTable = "";
    // Reset all of the counter and count variables
    this.current = 0;
    this.max = 0;
    this.columns = 0;
    this.updateColumnCount = 0;
    this.valueCount = 0;
}
```

getItem()

The getItem() method enables you to access other data values contained in the component other than the displayed value. Because only the data value for the first column is displayed, the getItem() method is the only way to get data values for columns in the component that are not displayed to the user. By passing a row and a column, you can access data values much like accessing items within a grid. The row specifies the x coordinate of the value, and the column specifies the y coordinate of the value.

NOTE

The value returned will always be a String object. Use the getColumnType() method to determine the data type of the column.

setItem()

The setItem() method of the component enables you to set data values in the component other than the displayed data value. The setItem() method takes a row and column position and sets the current data value to the passed string. This method can be used along with the getItem() method to store and access information in the component that does not need to be displayed to the user.

getColumnName()

The getColumnName() method takes a passed column index and returns the column name. All of the column names for the columns in the component are stored in an array within the component. The array is populated by the retrieve() method. The column index passed is the order of the columns within the selection statement.

getColumnType()

The getColumnType() method takes a passed column index and returns an integer that contains the column type. The integer returned is a predefined integer that is defined in the class Types. The Types class contains only definitions for the column types and is not used for any other purpose.

getColumnIndex(String)

The getColumnIndex() method takes a column name and returns a column index. The column name passed must match the column name in the selection statement exactly. Because Java is case sensitive, the column name for which you are looking must exactly match a column name in the selection statement. The index returned is the column's order within the selection statement. You can then use the column index to get data values within the component or get the column type of the specified column.

getValueIndex()

The getValueIndex() method of the component is specific to the DataList component. The method will take a specific string and determine what the index value of the string is. All of the available strings are stored in the Hashtable object values. The method will find the index of the passed string and pass that index back to the user. The user can then take the index value and select or deselect items. If the user passes in an invalid string, then the method will return -1. The code for the getValueIndex() method is shown in Listing 11.3.

TYPE **Listing 11.3. The** getValueIndex() **method.**

```
// Get index for passed string
private int getValueIndex (String value) {
    int index;
    boolean contains;
    // Check to see if the passed value is contained in the Hashtable Object
    try {
        contains = values.contains(value);
    }
    catch (Exception e) {
        return -1;
    }
    // If value is not in Hashtable, return -1
    if (!contains) {
        return -1;
    }
    // Loop through Hashtable until item is found
    for (int i=0; i<=valueCount; i++) {
        String tempValue = values.get(new Integer(i));

        // Check temp against passed
        if (tempValue.equals(value)) {
            return i;
        }
    }
    return -1;
}
```

11

Constructing the Component

The DataList component implements five different constructors. The constructors vary from supplying no information to supplying all information needed to retrieve data into the component. The basic constructor will not perform any action except to create the component. The most complex constructor not only creates the component, but specifies a Connection object and the SQL statement to execute, executes the SQL statement, and populates the component. The five different constructors that you need to create are as follows:

- ☐ public DataList ()
- ☐ public DataList (int length)
- ☐ public DataList (int length, Connection c, String sql)
- ☐ public DataList (Connection c, String sql, boolean retrieve)
- ☐ public DataList (int length, Connection c, String sql, boolean retrieve)

DataList()

The most basic of the constructors is responsible only for creating the component. This constructor method will not do any data-related activities. The component's only function is to create the component for use by the user. The method takes no parameters, and is created using the default size for the List component. Listing 11.4 contains the code for the DataList() constructor method.

TYPE   **Listing 11.4. The DataList() constructor method.**

```
// Basic Constructor
public DataList () {
    super();
}
```

DataList(int)

The DataList(int) constructor goes one step further than the basic constructor and specifies a size for the DataList component. The size indicates how many items will be displayed at one time. Unlike the List component, the DataList component does not allow multiple items to be selected. Multiple selections are prevented because saving the items for multiple selections is very complex. Listing 11.5 contains the code for the DataList(int) method.

TYPE **Listing 11.5. The** `DataList(int)` **method.**

```
// Create the component and specify a size
public DataList (int length) {
    super(length, false);
}
```

DataList(int, Connection, String)

The `DataList(int, Connection, String)` constructor method enables the user of the component not only to specify the size for the component, but also to specify the initial `Connection` object and SQL statement to be used by the component. The `Connection` object is used on all executions of SQL against the database. The specified SQL statement is used to populate the component, and the first column in the SQL selection is displayed in the component. Listing 11.6 contains the code for the `DataList(int, Connection, String)` method.

TYPE **Listing 11.6. The** `DataList(int, Connection, String)` **method.**

```
// Create the component and specify a size, Connection, and SQL
public DataList (int length, Connection c, String sql) {
    // Call the previous ancestor so that it will be
    // easier to maintain
    this(length);
    // Assign the passed Connection object and SQL String
    this.c = c;
    this.sql = sql;
}
```

DataList (Connection, String, boolean)

The `DataList(Connection, String, boolean)` constructor method gives you the ability to specify the `Connection` object and the SQL statement without having to specify an initial size for the component. This constructor enables you to use the default size for the component but still specify the `Connection` object to use for database access and the SQL statement to populate the component. You can also determine whether the component will automatically retrieve data by passing `true` for the Boolean parameter. Listing 11.7 contains the code for the `DataList(Connection, String, boolean)` method.

Listing 11.7. The `DataList(Connection, String, boolean)`
TYPE   method.

```
// Constructor for specifying Connection object and SQL Statement
public DataList (Connection c, String sql, boolean retrieve) {
    this();

    // Assign Connection object and SQL Statement
    this.c = c;
    this.sql = sql;
    // If user passed retrieve = true, then retrieve data
    if (retrieve) {
        this.retrieve();
    }
}
```

DataList(int, Connection, String, boolean)

The `DataList(int, Connection, String, boolean)` constructor method takes the most arguments of any of the constructor methods. This method enables you to specify all required parameters for the component. The method enables you to create the component to a specified size, as determined by the `length` parameter. The constructor will also let you specify the `Connection` object and SQL statement to use to connect and populate the component. The final Boolean parameter enables you to have the component automatically retrieve information, using the `Connection` object and SQL statement. If a Boolean `true` is passed, then the component will issue a retrieve to the database and populate the component. If a Boolean `false` is passed, then the component will not retrieve information from the database automatically. Listing 11.8 contains the code for this constructor method.

Listing 11.8. The `DataList(int, Connection, String, boolean)`
TYPE   method.

```
// Constructor for specifying all arguments
public DataList (int length, Connection c, String sql, boolean retrieve) {
    // Call the constructor to create using
    // length, Connection, and SQL
    this(length, c, sql);
    // If user passed retrieve = true, then retrieve data into component
    if (retrieve) {
        this.retrieve();
    }
}
```

Along with creating the constructor methods for the DataList component, override some of the standard List component methods. You override the methods so that the DataList component will remain up-to-date with the changes the user makes. The methods to override enable you to add items to the list of choices displayed to the user other than the choices provided from the database. This will let you use a combination of items from a database source, but also gives you the flexibility to add your own items for user selection. Override the two addItem() methods that the List component provides.

In addition to the addItem() methods, override the setMultipleSelections() method. This method lets you turn on or off the selection of multiple items. As mentioned previously, allowing multiple selections will not be possible in this component. Because you save the data values of the selected items, allowing multiple selections would make the component more complex than space allows. Therefore, override the component so that it cannot turn on multiple selections.

addItem(String)

Override the addItem(String) method so that the component not only will display the item in the selection list, but will store the item in your values hash table. This lets you use the added items as data values that can be saved to the database. The method will increment the counter for the values hash table, and then add the passed item to the Hashtable object. When the item has been added to the end of the Hashtable object, the method calls the ancestor method to display the item in the component. Listing 11.9 contains the code for the addItem(String) method.

TYPE | **Listing 11.9. The addItem(String) method.**

```
// Override List.addItem(String)
public void addItem (String item) {
    // Increment the counter for the Hashtable
    valueCount++;
    // Add the item to the Hashtable object
    values.put(new Integer(valueCount),item);
    // Call the ancestor method to display item in list
    super.addItem(item);
}
```

addItem(String, int)

Along with the addItem(String) method, override the addItem(String, int) method. The ancestor method enables you to specify where in the list the item should be displayed, but because all of your data values are based on an index in the hash table, disallow the adding of items to a specific location. Override this method and pass only the passed string to the other addItem() method. Listing 11.10 contains the code for the addItem(String, int) method.

TYPE   **Listing 11.10. The** `addItem(String, int)` **method.**

```
// Disallow adding items to specific locations
public void addItem (String item, int index) {
    // Pass item to appropriate method
    this.addItem(item);
}
```

setMultipleSelections()

The `setMultipleSelections()` method enables you to turn the selection of multiple items on and off. Override this method so that multiple selections cannot be turned on. You are not allowing multiple selections in the DataList component, so make sure that the user will not be able to turn the functionality on. Listing 11.11 contains the code for the `setMultipleSelections()` method.

TYPE   **Listing 11.11. The** `setMultipleSelections()` **method.**

```
// Disallow multiple selections
public void setMultipleSelections (boolean v) {
    // Do nothing
}
```

Connecting the Component

The DataList component implements the same functionality as the DataField component for all methods from the `DataConnection` interface, with the exception of the `retrieve()` method. Therefore, due to space limitations, this book briefly goes over the methods in the `DataConnection` interface. If you have any questions about implementing these methods, refer to the DataField chapter (Day 9). The methods' implementations will be identical for the two components.

The `retrieve()` method for the DataList component contains some of the same functionality as the DataField component, but also will be required to do some extra processing for the DataList component. In addition to the functionality provided in the DataField component, the DataList component must display all of the items retrieved from the database into the DataList component. All of the items retrieved into the first column of the result set will be displayed in the component, as well as saved to the Hashtable object `value` for use by the component.

The following methods will be implemented by the DataList component:

- [ ] `public void setConnection(Connection c)`
- [ ] `public void setConnection(Connection c, boolean noReset)`
- [ ] `public Connection getConnection()`
- [ ] `public void setSQL(String sql)`
- [ ] `public String getSQL()`
- [ ] `public int Retrieve()`

setConnection(Connection)

The `setConnection(Connection)` method enables you to specify an initial or a new `Connection` object for the component. The method resets the component by calling the `reset()` method before setting the new `Connection` object. This enables you to clear the settings for the component before specifying the new `Connection` object, which will possibly provide a new connection to the database.

setConnection(Connection, boolean)

The `setConnection(Connection, boolean)` method enables you to specify a new or initial `Connection` object for the component, but also enables you to decide whether the component should be reset. If a Boolean `false` is passed for the Boolean parameter, then the component will be reset. A Boolean `true` will keep the current settings for the component and change only the current `Connection` object.

 TIP

By changing the `Connection` object for a component, you can retrieve data into the component from one database, and then update any changed data to a different database.

getConnection()

The `getConnection()` method enables you to get the current `Connection` object for the component. This can let you determine which database the component is executing its SQL statements against. After you get the `Connection` object, you can get the `DatabaseMetaData` object that will let you determine various settings for the current database that the component is using.

> You also can use the getConnection() method to get a Connection object to use for another data component. This way, all components can use the same connection to the database.

setSQL(String)

The setSQL(String) method enables you to set or change the SQL statement that the component uses to populate itself. The SQL statement specified is executed in the retrieve() method, and the results are used to populate the component.

getSQL()

The getSQL() method provides you with the SQL statement being used by the data component. The SQL statement returned by this method is the SQL statement that is or will be used by the retrieve() method to populate the component.

retrieve()

The retrieve() method for the DataList component performs the same functionality as the method for the DataField component, but adds some extra functionality to handle the display and storage of items. The retrieve() method uses the same code as the DataField retrieve() method, but adds a loop to add all items in the first column of the result set returned to be displayed in the selection list. All of the items are also added to the Hashtable object values. The Hashtable object will store all of the items displayed in the DataList component.

The retrieve() method uses a for loop to loop through all items in the component. Each data value from the first column is added to the selection list and the Hashtable object. The items are added in the order in which they were retrieved, so initially the order of the items in the selection list will be the order of the items in the component.

TIP

> You can have a sorted list by specifying an ORDER BY clause on the SQL statement that populates the component.

The loop goes through all items and passes the value returned by the getItem() method to the addItem() method of the component. The addItem() method used is the method that you created in Listing 11.9. The previous method already has the functionality to add the item to the Hashtable object as well as display it in the selection list. The code for the loop is as follows:

```
for (int i=1; i<=max; i++) {
    this.addItem(this.getItem(i, 1));
}
```

The preceding code loops through all items in the component, from the first record to the last record. It passes the value obtained by calling the getItem() method with the current record and the first column. This will add all items in the first column to be displayed and stored for use in future selecting and deselecting of items. Listing 11.12 contains the full code for the DataList retrieve() method.

TYPE   **Listing 11.12. The retrieve() method.**

```
// Populate the component
public int retrieve () {
    Statement sqlStatement;
    ResultSet results;
    ResultSetMetaData resultsMeta;
    int index = 0;
    // Determine if user wants to execute retrieve
    // by passing sql to previewStatement
    previewStatement(this.sql, this.SELECT);

    try {
        // Create a SQL statement
        sqlStatement = this.c.createStatement();

        // Execute the current SQL statement and store results
        results = sqlStatement.executeQuery(this.sql);
        // Get the MetaData for the Result Set
        resultsMeta = results.getMetaData();
        // Get the number of columns in the result set
        columns = resultsMeta.getColumnCount();
        // Create arrays to hold column names and types
        strColumns = new String[columns];
        ColumnTypes = new int[columns];
        // Populate the column names array
        for (int i = 0;i<columns;i++) {
            strColumns[i] = resultsMeta.getColumnName(i+1);
        }
        // Populate the column types array
        for (int i = 0;i<columns;i++) {
            strColumns[i] = resultsMeta.getColumnName(i+1);
        }

        // Create Hashtable arrays to store data values
        Records = new Hashtable[columns];
```

continues

11

Listing 11.12. continued

```
            Original = new Hashtable[columns];
            // Cycle through all rows and add items to Hashtables
            while (results.next()) {
                // Increment the index counter
                index++;
                // Perform a loop to add items for columns
                for (int i = 0;i<columns;i++) {
                    // If you are on first record, create Hashtables
                    if (index == 1) {
                        Records[i] = new Hashtable();
                        Original[i] = new Hashtable();
                    }
                    // Add items
                    Records[i].put(new Integer(index), results.getString(i + 1));
                    Original[i].put(new Integer(index), results.getString(i + 1));
                }
            }
            // Store the number of records in the result set
            max = index;
        }
        catch (SQLException e) {
            // Error occurred, so return a -1
            return -1;
        }
        // Set the current variable to 0
        this.current = 0;

        // Add the items to the selection list and Hashtable object values
        for (int i=1; i<=max; i++) {
            this.addItem(this.getItem(i, 1));
        }
        // Call the next() method to display initial value
        this.next();
        // Return the number of records in the result set
        return index;
    }
```

Navigating the Component

The DataList component will implement the four methods contained in the DataNavigation interface. These methods provide functionality for moving the record position of the component. The four methods enable you to navigate the records of the component easily. The four methods provided are as follows:

- ☐ public void next()
- ☐ public void previous()
- ☐ public void first()
- ☐ public void last()

All of the methods for the DataList component are different than the methods in the DataField component. This is due to the fact that the DataField uses the `setText()` method to change the displayed value, whereas the DataList changes the currently selected item for each record.

next()

The `next()` method in the DataList component enables you to go to the next available record within the component. It moves the current record position exactly one position forward in the component. Moving the record position will cause a new item to become selected within the selection list.

The `next()` method saves the value of the current record before moving to the next record. The current value is the currently selected item. The user can change the value of the record by selecting a different item in the list.

Listing 11.13 contains the code for the `next()` method.

TYPE | **Listing 11.13. The `next()` method.**

```
// Move to next available row
public void next () {
    // Check to ensure that a valid next row exists
    if (current == max) {
        return;
    }
    // Set value for updated text only if current != 0
    if (current != 0) {
        Records[0].remove(new Integer(current));
        Records[0].put(new Integer(current), this.getSelectedItem());
    }

    // Deselect the currently select item
    this.deselect(this.getSelectedIndex());

    // Set the record to be the new row
    current++;
    // Set the text of the component to new data value
    String value = "";
    try {
        value = (String)Records[0].get(new Integer(current));
    }
    catch (Exception e) {
        return;
    }
    // Set the new item to index of value
    this.select(this.getValueIndex(value));
}
```

11

previous()

The previous() method enables you to go to the previous record in the component, provided a previous record exists. The method moves the current record position back exactly one position. If no previous record exists, then the method will not perform any action. As with the next() method, the previous() method will save the current data value before moving to the previous record. Listing 11.14 contains the code for the previous() method.

TYPE **Listing 11.14. The previous() method.**

```
// Move to previous available row
public void previous () {
    // Check to insure that a valid previous row exists
    if (current == 1) {
        return;
    }
    Records[0].remove(new Integer(current));
    Records[0].put(new Integer(current), this.getSelectedItem());

    // Deselect the currently select item
    this.deselect(this.getSelectedIndex());

    // Set the record to be the new row
    current--;
    // Set the text of the component to new data value
    String value = "";
    try {
        value = (String)Records[0].get(new Integer(current));
    }
    catch (Exception e) {
        return;
    }
    // Set the new item to index of value
    this.select(this.getValueIndex(value));
}
```

first() and last()

The first() and last() methods provide the functionality to move to the first and last record in the component, respectively. These methods provide you with a quick way to move the record position to the common locations of the first record and the last record. The first() method sets the current record position to 1 and the last() method sets the record position to the value contained in the max value. Listing 11.15 contains the code for the first() method. You can implement the last() method by changing the following line:

```
current = 1;
```

to:

```
current = max;
```

As with the other navigation methods, the `first()` and `last()` methods both save the current data value before moving to their respective locations.

TYPE **Listing 11.15. The `first()` method.**

```
// Move to the first record
public void first () {
    // Save the current record
    Records[0].remove(new Integer(current));
    Records[0].put(new Integer(current), this.getSelectedItem());

    // Deselect the currently select item
    this.deselect(this.getSelectedIndex());

    // Set the record to be the new row
    current = 1;
    // Set the text of the component to new data value
    String value = "";
    try {
        value = (String)Records[0].get(new Integer(current));
    }
    catch (Exception e) {
        return;
    }
    // Set the new item to index of value
    this.select(this.getValueIndex(value));
}
```

Updating the Component

The DataList component also implements the methods contained in the `DataUpdate` interface. These methods provide functionality for updating the data values contained in the component. To provide update capabilities, you must specify a table to be updated and the columns for that table that should be used when updating.

NOTE

The columns used for updating should be contained in the table that is being updated. If they are not in the table, then an exception will occur.

The DataList component implements the methods for the DataUpdate interface exactly as they appear in the DataField component. Therefore, the methods are discussed only briefly in this section. Refer to Day 10 for the code and a more complete explanation of the methods.

The methods provided by the DataUpdate interface are as follows:

- ☐ public void setUpdateTable(String table)
- ☐ public String getUpdateTable()
- ☐ public boolean update()
- ☐ public boolean previewStatement(String sql, int sqlType)
- ☐ public void setUpdateColumn(String column)
- ☐ public void setUpdateColumn(int column)
- ☐ public String[] getUpdateColumn()

setUpdateTable()

The setUpdateTable() method provides you with a means to change the table that the component will use when the update() method is called. The method sets the value of the object variable updateTable. This variable is used by the update() method to build a SQL Update statement to execute against the database.

getUpdateTable()

The getUpdateTable() method returns the value stored in the updateTable object variable. This variable is used to update the database in the update() method.

update()

The update() method is responsible for saving any changes the user makes to data contained in the component. These changes are changed in the database, using SQL Update statements. You construct the statements using the specified update table and update columns. The update table is the table updated within the database, and the columns specified are the columns that will be changed for the specified update table. You also use the specified update columns to determine which data to check in the component. Only columns that will be updated have their values checked for changes. All other columns are ignored by the update() method.

TIP

When you specify columns to update, specify only the columns in which information will be changed or where the column is needed for uniqueness. If you specify only a name column to be updated and someone's name changes, then all members of the table with a matching name will be changed, as well. Make sure you specify the primary key or an alternative key in the update column list.

previewStatement()

The previewStatement() method gives you the ability to use your application-specific business logic in the updating process. The previewStatement() method is called by the update() method. The DataList component will not put any functional code in the previewStatement() method. The method is available for you to inherit and place your code in. Returning a false will cause the passed SQL statement not to be executed. A returned true will force the SQL statement to be executed by the component.

setUpdateColumn()

There are two setUpdateColumn() methods. Each of the methods stores a passed column in an array of updatable columns, but one takes a String object and the other takes an int identifying the column.

getUpdateColumn()

The getUpdateColumn() method enables you to get a string array of all of the columns that will be updated by the update() method. The columns are returned to the user as an array of String objects.

Converting to the DataChoice Components

Because the List and Choice objects are very similar in functionality, you can easily change the code for the DataList component to become a DataChoice component. Only the constructor methods need to be changed to implement a DataChoice component.

11

Full Code Listing for the DataList Component

 Listing 11.16 contains the full code for the DataList component. The comments have been removed due to space limitations, but I urge you to look at the full code included on the CD-ROM.

TYPE **Listing 11.16. The DataList component.**

```java
import java.awt.*;
import java.util.*;
import symjava.sql.*;
public class DataList extends List implements DataUpdate, DataComponent,
    DataConnection, DataNavigation {
    Connection c;
    String sql;
    int current = 0;
    int max = 0;
    String updateTable = "";
    int updateColumnCount = 0;
    Hashtable updateColumns;
    Hashtable Original[];
    Hashtable Records[];
    int columns = 0;
        String strColumns[];
    int ColumnTypes[];
    Hashtable values;
    int valueCount = 0;
public DataList () {
    super();
}
public DataList (int length) {
    super(length, false);
}
public DataList (int length, Connection c, String sql) {
    super(length, false);
    this.c = c;
    this.sql = sql;
}
public DataList (Connection c, String sql, boolean retrieve) {
    this.c = c;
    this.sql = sql;
    if (retrieve) {
        this.retrieve();
    }
}
public DataList (int length, Connection c, String sql, boolean retrieve) {
    this(length, c, sql);
    if (retrieve) {
        this.retrieve();
    }
}
```

11

```
public void addItem (String item) {
    valueCount++;
    values.put(new Integer(valueCount),item);
    super.addItem(item);
}
public void addItem (String item, int index) {
    this.addItem(item);
}
public void setMultipleSelections (boolean v) {
}
public void setConnection (Connection c) {
    this.reset();
    this.c = c;
}
public void setConnection (Connection c, boolean noReset) {
    if (!noReset) {
        this.reset();
    }
    this.c = c;
}
public Connection getConnection () {
    return this.c;
}
public void setSQL (String sql) {
    this.sql = sql;
}
public String getSQL () {
    return this.sql;
}
public int retrieve () {
    Statement sqlStatement;
    ResultSet results;
    ResultSetMetaData resultsMeta;
    int index = 0;
    previewStatement(this.sql, this.SELECT);
    try {
        sqlStatement = this.c.createStatement();
        results = sqlStatement.executeQuery(this.sql);
        resultsMeta = results.getMetaData();
        columns = resultsMeta.getColumnCount();
        strColumns = new String[columns];
        ColumnTypes = new int[columns];
        for (int i = 0;i<columns;i++) {
            strColumns[i] = resultsMeta.getColumnName(i+1);
        }
        for (int i = 0;i<columns;i++) {
            strColumns[i] = resultsMeta.getColumnName(i+1);
        }
        Records = new Hashtable[columns];
        Original = new Hashtable[columns];
        while (results.next()) {
            index++;
            for (int i = 0;i<columns;i++) {
                if (index == 1) {
```

continues

Listing 11.16. continued

```
                    Records[i] = new Hashtable();
                    Original[i] = new Hashtable();
                }
                Records[i].put(new Integer(index), results.getString(i + 1));
                Original[i].put(new Integer(index), results.getString(i + 1));
            }
        }
        max = index;
    }
    catch (SQLException e) {
        return -1;
    }
    this.current = 0;
    for (int i=1; i<=max; i++) {
        this.addItem(this.getItem(i, 1));
    }
    this.next();
    return index;
}
public void next () {
    if (current == max) {
        return;
    }
    if (current != 0) {
        Records[0].remove(new Integer(current));
        Records[0].put(new Integer(current), this.getSelectedItem());
    }
    this.deselect(this.getSelectedIndex());
    current++;
    String value = "";
    try {
        value = (String)Records[0].get(new Integer(current));
    }
    catch (Exception e) {
        return;
    }
    this.select(this.getValueIndex(value));
}
public void previous () {
    if (current == 1) {
        return;
    }
    Records[0].remove(new Integer(current));
    Records[0].put(new Integer(current), this.getSelectedItem());
    this.deselect(this.getSelectedIndex());
    current--;
    String value = "";
    try {
        value = (String)Records[0].get(new Integer(current));
    }
    catch (Exception e) {
        return;
    }
    this.select(this.getValueIndex(value));
}
```

```
public void first () {
    Records[0].remove(new Integer(current));
    Records[0].put(new Integer(current), this.getSelectedItem());
    this.deselect(this.getSelectedIndex());
    current = 1;
    String value = "";
    try {
        value = (String)Records[0].get(new Integer(current));
    }
    catch (Exception e) {
        return;
    }
    this.select(this.getValueIndex(value));
}
public void last () {
    Records[0].remove(new Integer(current));
    Records[0].put(new Integer(current), this.getSelectedItem());
    this.deselect(this.getSelectedIndex());
    current = max;
    String value = "";
    try {
        value = (String)Records[0].get(new Integer(current));
    }
    catch (Exception e) {
        return;
    }
    this.select(this.getValueIndex(value));
}
public void setUpdateTable (String table) {
    this.updateTable = table;
}
public String getUpdateTable () {
        return this.updateTable;
}
public boolean update () {
    String sqlBase = "";
    String sqlSet = "";
    String sqlWhere = "";
    Statement sqlStatement;
    boolean changed = false;
    if (updateTable == "") {
        return false;
    }
    if (updateColumnCount == 0) {
        return false;
    }
    sqlBase = "update " + updateTable + "\n";
    sqlSet = "set ";
    sqlWhere = "where ";
    for (int i=1;i<=max;i++) {
        changed = false;
        for (int j=1;j<=updateColumnCount;j++) {
            int curColumn =
            ⮕((Integer)updateColumns.get(new Integer(j))).intValue();
            String orgValue = (String)Original[curColumn].get(new Integer(i));
```

continues

Listing 11.16. continued

```
                String userValue = (String)Records[curColumn].get(new Integer(i));
                if (!(orgValue.equals(userValue))) {
                    changed = true;
                }
            }
        if (changed) {
            for (int j=1;j<=updateColumnCount;j++) {
                int curColumn =
                ➥((Integer)updateColumns.get(new Integer(j))).intValue();
                String colName = getColumnName(curColumn);
                if (j != 1) {
                    sqlSet += ", \n" + colName + "= \'";
                    sqlWhere += "\nand " + colName + "= \'";
                }
                String userValue =
                ➥(String)Records[curColumn].get(new Integer(i));
                sqlSet += userValue + "\'\n";
                String orgValue =
                ➥(String)Original[curColumn].get(new Integer(i));
            sqlWhere += orgValue + "\'\n";
            }
            sqlBase = sqlBase + sqlSet + sqlWhere;
            if (previewStatement(sqlBase,this.UPDATE)) {
                try {
                    sqlStatement = this.c.createStatement();
                    sqlStatement.executeUpdate(sqlBase);
                }
                catch (Exception e) {
                    return false;
                }
            }
            sqlBase = "update " + updateTable + "\n";
            sqlSet = "set ";
            sqlWhere = "where ";
        }
    }
    this.Original = this.Records;
    return true;
}
public boolean previewStatement (String sql, int sqlType) {
    return true;
}
public void setUpdateColumn (String column) {
    this.setUpdateColumn(this.getColumnIndex(column));
}
public void setUpdateColumn (int column) {
    if ((column < 1) || (column > this.columns)) {
        return;
    }
    if (updateColumnCount == 0) {
        updateColumns = new Hashtable();
    }
    updateColumnCount++;
    updateColumns.put(new Integer(updateColumnCount), new Integer(column));
```

```
    }
public String[] getUpdateColumn () {
    String columns[];
    columns = new String[updateColumnCount];
    for (int i = 0; i<updateColumnCount; i++) {
                columns[i] = this.getColumnName(((Integer)
                ➡updateColumns.get(new Integer(i + 1))).intValue());
    }
    return columns;
}
public int getRow () {
    return this.current;
}
public void setRow (int Row) {
    if ((Row < 1) ¦¦ (Row > max)) {
        return;
    }
    Records[0].remove(new Integer(current));
    Records[0].put(new Integer(current), this.getSelectedItem());
    this.deselect(this.getSelectedIndex());
    this.current = Row;
    String value = "";
    try {
        value = (String)Records[0].get(new Integer(current));
    }
    catch (Exception e) {
        return;
    }
    this.select(this.getValueIndex(value));
}
public void reset () {
    this.c = null;
    this.sql = "";
    this.updateTable = "";
    this.current = 0;
    this.max = 0;
    this.columns = 0;
    this.updateColumnCount = 0;
    this.valueCount = 0;
}
public String getItem (int row, int column) {
    if ((row < 1) ¦¦ (row > max)) {
        return "";
    }
    if ((column < 1) ¦¦ (column > this.columns)) {
        return "";
    }
    return (String)Records[column - 1].get(new Integer(row));
}
public void setItem (int row, int column, String value) {
    if ((row < 1) ¦¦ (row > max)) {
        return;
    }
    if ((column < 1) ¦¦ (column > this.columns)) {
        return;
    }
```

continues

Listing 11.16. continued

```
        Records[column].remove(new Integer(row));
        Records[column].put(new Integer(row), value);
    }
    public String getColumnName (int index) {
        if ((index < 1) || (index > this.columns)) {
            return "";
        }
        return strColumns[index-1];
    }
    public int getColumnType (int index) {
        if ((index < 1) || (index > this.columns)) {
            return -1;
        }
        return ColumnTypes[index];
    }
    public int getColumnIndex (String column) {
        int index = -1;
        for (int i = 0;i < this.columns;i++) {
            if (column.equals(strColumns[i])) {
                index = i + 1;
                break;
            }
        }
        return index;
    }
    private int getValueIndex (String value) {
        int index;
        boolean contains;
        try {
            contains = values.contains(value);
        }
        catch (Exception e) {
            return -1;
        }
        if (!contains) {
            return -1;
        }
        for (int i=0; i<=valueCount; i++) {
                String tempValue = (String)values.get(new Integer(i));
            if (tempValue.equals(value)) {
                return i;
            }
        }
            return -1;
    }
    public int columnCount () {
        return this.columns;
    }
    public int rowCount () {
        return this.max;
    }
}
}
```

Using the Component

Now that you have created the component, write a small application to use the component. The application that you will write is very similar to the application written on Day 10. Write an application to display the first names of all employees in the tEmployee table.

Create a frame that will be sized to 300×300. On this Frame object, place the DataList component in the North section of the frame. For the South section of the frame, place a Panel object that contains various Button objects. The layout for the Panel object should be FlowLayout.

After you have placed all of your objects on the frame, override handleEvent() to handle the clicking of those buttons.

Listing 11.17 contains the code for the DataListExample application.

TYPE **Listing 11.17. The DataListExample application.**

```
import java.awt.*;
import java.util.*;
import symjava.sql.*;
public class DataListExample extends Frame {
    DataList list;
    public DataListExample () {
        super();
        Panel p = new Panel();
        p.setLayout(new FlowLayout());
        p.add(new Button("First"));
        p.add(new Button("Previous"));
        p.add(new Button("Next"));
        p.add(new Button("Last"));
        this.add("South", p);
        try {
            String driverName = "symantec.itools.db.jdbc.Driver";
            Driver driver = (Driver)Class.forName(driverName).newInstance();
            Properties prop = new Properties();
            prop.put("user", "dba");
            prop.put("password", "sql");
            String dbURL = "jdbc:dbaw://localhost:8889/WATCOM/JDBC/JDBC";
            Connection connection = driver.connect(dbURL, prop);

            // Pass connection, sql, and true to datalist component
            String sql = "select FirstName from tEmployee";
            list = new DataList(connection, sql, true);
        }
        catch (Exception e) {}
        this.add("North", list);
        this.resize(300, 300);
        this.show();
    }
```

continues

Listing 11.17. continued

```
public boolean handleEvent (Event evt){
    if ("First".equals(evt.arg)) {
        list.first();
    }
    if ("Previous".equals(evt.arg)) {
        list.previous();
    }
    if ("Next".equals(evt.arg)) {
        list.next();
    }
    if ("Last".equals(evt.arg)) {
        list.last();
    }
    return super.handleEvent(evt);
}
public static void main (String args[]) {
    DataListExample app = new DataListExample();
}
}
```

Summary

In today's lesson, you have learned how to make your second data component. This component enables you to display a list of all choices available in the database. This gives the user more options to choose from, and also gives you an easier way to validate the data, because you know all of the valid choices.

As you learned today, the basics of the component stayed the same between the DataList and DataField components. Most of the functionality will remain the same throughout your components—only the constructor methods and display methods will change. This means you can use the basic functionality of the component to create any type of data component.

Workshop

The Workshop provides quiz questions to help you solidify your understanding of the material covered and exercises to give you experience in using what you've learned. The answers are provided in Appendix A, "Quiz and Exercise Answers." Try to understand the quiz and exercise answers before you go on to tomorrow's lesson.

Quiz

1. List all of the constructor methods for the DataList component.
2. How do you have the component retrieve data without calling the `retrieve()` method?
3. What method enables you to change the `Connection` object?
4. How would you change the `Connection` object without resetting the component?
5. How would you get the number of records in the component?
6. What two items must be specified for an update to occur?
7. What does the `previewStatement()` method return and what does it mean?
8. Initially, are the records in the component and the items in the list the same?
9. How can you add new items to the list for display?
10. How can you display the last column in the component? (There are two ways.)

Exercises

1. Add functionality to change the current column being displayed. You can do this by changing the order of the Hashtable objects and columns.
2. Add functionality to delete items in the list. You will need to make sure that the item is deleted from the `values` object.
3. Write an application that uses a DataField component to populate a DataList component. The DataField component should retrieve all items from the database that match the current string in the DataField. Therefore, Ho in the DataField should display all of the entries in the DataList from the database that start with Ho.

Day 12

The DataCheckBox Component

Today's lesson covers the creation of a DataCheckBox. This component will enable two different data values to be displayed in a check box component. The user of the component will specify which data value will be the checked value and which will be the unchecked value. The component will then display information to the user as an on/off value.

This component will make binary information more informative to the user. Any type of data that requires one of two values can be displayed in a check box component. Data that can have two values includes Sex, Married, and so on.

The following topics are covered today:

- [ ] Why you should use data components
- [ ] Building the basics of the component
- [ ] Constructing the component
- [ ] Connecting the component

☐ Navigating the component
☐ Updating the component
☐ Using the component

Why Should You Use Data Components?

The DataCheckBox component, unlike the DataField and DataList components, does not let the user type any new data into the component. The user can change the value only from on or off. This is very useful for columns that require either a "Y" or "N" or other columns that require only one of two values.

Some columns that can be used for the DataCheckBox component include Sex, Married, and other columns such as those that have Active/Inactive status, Yes/No values, True/False values, and so on. The component will check or uncheck itself based on the values specified by the user. The component will provide two methods that will set the on and off data values. The user will call each of the methods and pass a data value that indicates the on and off status of the component. Then, as the user cycles through the records of the component, the component will update the check box based on the new data value.

Building the Basics

The DataCheckBox component will be contained in its own .java file, which will allow it to be used with any of your applications. The component will need to import three packages that provide various classes needed throughout the component. The following code will import the packages needed for the component:

```
import java.awt.*;
import java.util.*;
import symjava.sql.*;
```

The DataCheckBox component will implement all of the data interfaces that were covered on Day 9, "The Data Interfaces." The class declaration for the DataCheckBox component is as follows:

```
public class DataCheckBox extends CheckBox implements DataUpdate,
➡DataComponent, DataConnection, DataNavigation
```

The purpose of this section is to explain the different object variables that you will use throughout the component. The object variables store quite a bit of information about the data component, including any of the following information:

☐ Connection object
☐ SQL statement
☐ Current record position

☐ Maximum number of records
☐ Update table
☐ Update columns
☐ Original data values
☐ User-entered data values
☐ Number, names, and types of columns in the result set
☐ On/off variables

The `Connection` Object

The `Connection` object variable gives the component a physical connection to the database. You can pass the `Connection` object to the component through one of the constructor methods, or through the `setConnection()` methods.

The SQL Statement

The SQL statement variable is a `String` object that contains the SQL `Select` statement that will populate the component. The SQL can be passed in to the component through one of the constructor methods, or through the `setSQL()` method. The first column returned in the result set from the SQL statement is the column used to change the value of the component.

Current Record Position

Store the current record position in an integer variable, `current`. This variable will store the current record that is being displayed in the component. This variable cannot go below 1 or above the maximum number of records contained in the component.

Maximum Number of Records

An integer variable in the component will contain the maximum number of records contained in the component. This variable will be determined by the number of records that the `retrieve()` method cycles through. Use this variable not only to ensure that the user does not try to display a record that does not exist, but also as the return value for the `rowCount()` method.

Update Table

The update table variable will store the table that will be updated with any changed data in the component. The update table can be any valid table within the current database. The update table is passed as a `String` object and is used in the `update()` method to build SQL statements that will be executed against the database.

Update Columns

Along with an update table, the component will store a list of all the columns that will be updated. The update columns will appear in all of the SQL `Update` statements in the `SET` and `WHERE` clauses. They are included in both clauses so that the new data values will take the place of the old data values.

Original Data Values

The original data values from the result set returned by the SQL statement will be stored in an array of `Hashtable` objects. These objects will store the data values for the component. Each `Hashtable` object will represent a column, and the individual rows will be stored in the objects based on the record index. The original data values are retrieved during the `retrieve()` event, but are not changed by the component. They are used to determine whether any information has been changed in the component.

User-Entered Data Values

Along with the original data values, the component will maintain a separate array of `Hashtable` objects to store any user-changed information. These objects will initially be the same as the original `Hashtable` objects, but will be changed with any user-entered or user-specified information.

Number, Names, and Types of Columns

The component also will maintain arrays of the column names and the column types. These arrays will be used to provide the user with various information. Along with the column name and column types arrays, the component also will keep track of the number of columns that was in the result set returned by the component's SQL statement.

On/Off Variables

The component will maintain two `String` objects for use in checking or unchecking the component. The `onCheck` and `offCheck` variables will store the `On` data value and the `Off` data value, respectively. The `onCheck` variable will initially store the value `"Y"`, and the `offCheck` variable will initially store the value `"N"`. The variable declarations are as follows:

```
String onCheck = "Y";
String offCheck = "N";
```

The component will also implement the methods defined in the DataComponent interface. These methods provide various services to get information about the component, and also methods to reinitialize the component and manipulate the data values stored in the component. The methods that will be implemented are as follows:

- public int getRow()

- public void setRow(int row)

- public int rowCount()

- public int columnCount()

- public void reset()

- public String getItem(int row, int column)

- public void setItem (int row, int column, String value)

- public String getColumnName(int index)

- public int getColumnType(int index)

- public String getColumnIndex(String column)

getRow()

The getRow() method returns an integer variable that identifies the current record the component is displaying. It returns the value contained in the current variable.

setRow()

The setRow() method enables you to change the current record position for the component. The method takes an integer value and changes the current record position to the specified value. If the passed value is invalid, then the method will not perform any action.

The method will save the current data value before moving the current record position. The code for the setRow() method is shown in Listing 12.1.

TYPE **Listing 12.1. The setRow() method.**

```
// Change the current record
public void setRow (int Row) {
    // Check to insure that passed row is valid
    if ((Row < 1) || (Row > max)) {
        return;
    }
```

continues

Listing 12.1. continued

```
// Set value for updated entry
Records[0].remove(new Integer(current));
// Check to see which value will be used (on/off)
String value;
if (this.getState()) {
    value = onCheck;
}
else {
    value = offCheck;
}
Records[0].put(new Integer(current), value);
// Set the record to be the new row
this.current = Row;
// Set the state of the component
value = (String)Records[0].get(new Integer(current));
if (value == onCheck) {
    this.setState(true);
}
else {
    this.setState(false);
}
}
```

rowCount()

The rowCount() method enables you to determine the number of records that are contained in the component. The method returns the value stored in the max variable. The max variable contains the number of records that were contained in the result set retrieved from the SQL statement of the component.

columnCount()

The columnCount() method enables you to determine the number of columns that are contained in the component. The method returns the value stored in the columns variable. You populate this variable by getting the column count for the retrieved result set.

reset()

The reset() method enables you to reset all items in the component to their original states. The method resets all of the same variables that the DataField() method does, but also resets the on/off variables used in the component. The code for the reset() method is contained in Listing 12.2.

TYPE **Listing 12.2. The `reset()` method.**

```
public void reset () {
    // Reset the Connection Object
    this.c = null;
    // Reset the SQL statement string and the Update Table
    this.sql = "";
    this.updateTable = "";
    // Reset all of the counter and count variables
    this.current = 0;
    this.max = 0;
    this.columns = 0;
    this.updateColumnCount = 0;
    // reset the on/off variables
    onCheck = "Y";
    offCheck = "N";
}
```

getItem()

The getItem() method enables you to get data values for columns and rows other than the currently displayed data value. The method takes a row and column and returns the data value for the corresponding item. The column identifies which hash table will be used, and the row specifies which data value in the Hashtable object will be returned. If an invalid row or column is passed, then the method will return an empty string.

setItem()

The setItem() method lets you change data values in the component for items other than the currently displayed data value. The method takes a row number, a column number, and a string containing the new value. If an invalid row or column is passed, then the new data value will not be applied.

getColumnName()

The getColumnName() method takes a column index and returns the column name. The column index is the order in which the column appeared in the SQL Select statement. The method returns the appropriate item from the array of column names.

getColumnType()

The getColumnType() method returns an integer that identifies the data type of the specified column. The method takes the column index of the column for which you want to obtain the data type and returns an integer that identifies the data type. The integers for all of the data types are defined in the Types class.

12

getColumnIndex()

The getColumnIndex() method returns the column index for a specified column name. The method takes the column name and returns the column's index. The index is the order in which the column was placed in the SQL Select statement.

Along with the methods of the DataComponent interface, the component also will implement two methods for specifying the on and off data values. These values will be used to determine whether the current data value should force the component to be checked or unchecked. The two methods that you will implement are as follows:

- setOnValue (String value)
- setOffValue (String value)

setOnValue()

The setOnValue() method will take a passed String object and assign it to the object variable onCheck. This passed value will then be used to make the component checked. When the user changes the record position, the component will check the component if the current data value is equal to the value specified in the setOnValue() method. The code for the setOnValue() method is shown in Listing 12.3.

TYPE **Listing 12.3. The setOnValue() method.**

```
// Set the onCheck value
public void setOnValue (String value) {
    this.onCheck = value;
}
```

setOffValue()

The setOffValue() method will take a passed String object and assign it to the object variable offCheck. This passed value will then be used to make the component unchecked. When the user changes the record position, the component will uncheck the component if the current data value is equal to the value specified in the setOffValue() method. The code for the setOffValue() method is shown in Listing 12.4.

TYPE **Listing 12.4. The setOffValue() method.**

```
// Set the offCheck value
public void setOffValue (String value) {
    this.offCheck = value;
}
```

Constructing the Component

The DataCheckBox component will implement various constructor methods to provide the most functionality to the user. The component will implement all of the constructor methods provided for the CheckBox component and also some specialized constructor methods for specifying the Connection object and SQL statement for the component. The following list contains the constructor methods that you will implement:

- ☐ DataCheckBox ()
- ☐ DataCheckBox (String label)
- ☐ DataCheckBox (String label, CheckboxGroup group, boolean)
- ☐ DataCheckBox (Connection c)
- ☐ DataCheckBox (Connection c, String sql, boolean retrieve)
- ☐ DataCheckBox (String label, Connection c, String sql, boolean retrieve)

DataCheckBox()

The DataCheckBox() method is the most basic constructor method. This method's only function is to create the DataCheckBox component. The method creates a basic constructor that takes no parameters. Use this constructor to create the component and not specify any of the initial settings. Listing 12.5 contains the code for the DataCheckBox() method.

TYPE Listing 12.5. The DataCheckBox() method.

```
// Basic Constructor
public DataCheckBox () {
    super();
}
```

DataCheckBox(String)

The DataCheckBox(String) constructor method gives you the ability to specify the label for the check box. The method takes a String object and passes it to the ancestor method to create the component and specify the label for the component. The label is a string of text that describes what the component is being used for. Listing 12.6 contains the code for the DataCheckBox(String) method.

TYPE   **Listing 12.6. The** `DataCheckBox(String)` **method.**

```
// Create component and specify a label
public DataCheckBox (String label) {
    super(label);
}
```

DataCheckBox(String, CheckboxGroup)

The `DataCheckBox(String, CheckboxGroup)` method enables you to create the component and set the label for the component, but it also lets you put the component into a group of check box components to make the component become mutually exclusive, meaning that only one check box component in the group can be checked at one time. Listing 12.7 contains the code for the `DataCheckBox(String, CheckboxGroup)` method.

TYPE   **Listing 12.7. The** `DataCheckBox(String, CheckboxGroup)` **method.**

```
// Constructor to specify label and group
public DataCheckBox(String label, CheckboxGroup group) {
    super(label, group, false);
}
```

DataCheckBox(Connection)

The `DataCheckBox(Connection)` method enables you to create the component and specify an initial `Connection` object to use. The specified `Connection` object will be used for all transactions against the database. No label was specified for the component, so only a check box would be displayed. Use the `setLabel()` method of the CheckBox component to set or change the label of the component. Listing 12.8 contains the code for the `DataCheckBox(Connection)` method.

TYPE   **Listing 12.8. The** `DataCheckBox(Connection)` **method.**

```
// Create component and assign a Connection object
public DataCheckBox (Connection c) {
    // Call basic constructor
    this();
    // Assign connection object
    this.c = c;
}
```

DataCheckBox(Connection, String, boolean)

The DataCheckBox(Connection, String, boolean) constructor method enables you to specify an initial Connection object as well as an initial SQL Select statement to populate the component. The constructor method also enables you to have the component perform an automatic retrieve. If a true is passed for the Boolean parameter, then the component will retrieve items into the component. Listing 12.9 contains the code for the constructor method.

Listing 12.9. The DataCheckBox(Connection, String, boolean)
TYPE   method.

```
// Assign Connection, SQL, and perform a retrieve
public DataCheckBox (Connection c, String sql, boolean retrieve) {
    // Call ancestor to assign connection
    this(c);
    // Assign SQL Statement
    this.sql = sql;
    // If user passed retrieve = true, then retrieve
    if (retrieve) {
        this.retrieve();
    }
}
```

DataCheckBox(String, Connection, String, boolean)

The final constructor method takes four parameters. It takes a label to be displayed for the component. It also takes the initial Connection object and SQL Select statement. The fourth method is a Boolean value that indicates whether the method should call the retrieve method. The method will call the constructor method that takes just the label in order to make adding new functionality easier and more maintainable. Listing 12.10 contains the code for the method.

Listing 12.10. The DataCheckBox(String, Connection, String,
TYPE   boolean) method.

```
// Specify all initial parameters
public DataCheckBox (String label, Connection c, String sql, boolean retrieve){
    // Call ancestor to create component and specify label
    this(label);
    // Assign Connection and SQL
    this.c = c;
```

continues

Listing 12.10. continued

```
        this.sql = sql;
        // If user passed retrieve = true then retrieve
        if (retrieve) {
            this.retrieve();
        }
    }
}
```

Connecting the Component

The DataCheckBox component will implement all of the functionality provided by the DataConnection interface. The methods from this interface provide the functionality to set or get the Connection object for the component as well as the SQL statement used to populate the component. The interface also implements the retrieve() method, which is essential in populating the component.

The DataCheckBox component implements the functionality of the methods provided by the DataConnection interface exactly as the DataField implements them. Therefore, I will not go into detail or show code for the methods. If you want to see the code, refer to Day 10, "The DataLabel, DataField, and DataArea Components." The methods provided by the DataConnection interface are as follows:

- [ ] public void setConnection(Connection c)
- [ ] public void setConnection(Connection c, boolean noReset)
- [ ] public Connection getConnection()
- [ ] public void setSQL(String sql)
- [ ] public String getSQL()
- [ ] public int Retrieve()

setConnection(Connection)

The setConnection(Connection) method enables you to set or change the Connection object used by the component for all transactions against the database. The Connection object is used in the retrieve() and update() methods to execute SQL statements against the database. This method calls the reset() method to reset all variables in the component before changing the Connection object.

setConnection(Connection, boolean)

The setConnection(Connection, boolean) method provides the same functionality as the other setConnection() method, but this method lets you change the Connection object without resetting the component variables. Passing a Boolean `true` will keep the component the same and change only the `Connection` object. Passing a `false` will cause the method to function like the other `setConnection()` method.

getConnection()

The `getConnection()` method enables you to get the `Connection` object currently being used for the component. The `Connection` object was specified through either one of the constructor methods or one of the `setConnection()` methods.

setSQL()

The `setSQL()` method lets you set or change the SQL `Select` statement used to populate the component. The method takes a string that contains a valid SQL `Select` statement. This statement will be used in the `retrieve()` method to populate the component with the value from the result set retrieved by the execution of the SQL statement. The SQL statement can also be passed in one of the constructor methods.

getSQL()

The `getSQL()` method lets you get the current SQL `Select` statement being used to populate the component. The SQL statement was passed into the component through either a constructor method or the `setSQL()` method.

retrieve()

The `retrieve()` method uses the current SQL `Select` statement and the current `Connection` object to get a result set from the database. The method then takes this returned result set and stores the values from the result set into an array of `Hashtable` objects. These `Hashtable` objects are used to provide data to the component. Along with getting the data to be used in the component, the `retrieve()` method also gets information on the columns in the result set for use by the component and user.

Navigating the Component

The DataCheckBox component also implements the methods provided by the `DataNavigation` interface. This interface provides various functionality for moving the current record position in the component. All of the methods will save the current data value before moving to their appropriate record positions. The methods provided by the DataNavigation interface are as follows:

- [ ] public void next()
- [ ] public void previous()
- [ ] public void first()
- [ ] public void last()

next()

The next() method does just what the name says: It moves the record position to the next available record. The method will save the current data value before moving the record position. This ensures that all user data is saved when the user moves to a different record in the component. The code for the next() method is shown in Listing 12.11.

TYPE **Listing 12.11. The next() method.**

```
public void next () {
    // Check to make sure that a valid next row exists
    if (current == max) {
        return;
    }
    // Set value for updated entry
    Records[0].remove(new Integer(current));
    // Check to see which value will be used (on/off)
    String value;
    if (this.getState()) {
        value = onCheck;
    }
    else {
        value = offCheck;
    }
    Records[0].put(new Integer(current), value);
    // Set the record to the next valid record
    this.current++;
    // Set the state of the component
    value = (String)Records[0].get(new Integer(current));
    if (value == onCheck) {
        this.setState(true);
    }
    else {
        this.setState(false);
    }
}
```

12

previous()

The previous() method moves the record position to the previous record in the component, if one exists. The method first saves the data value for the current record and then moves to the previous record in the component. If no previous record exists in the component, then the method will not perform any action. Listing 12.12 contains the code for the previous() method.

TYPE | **Listing 12.12. The previous() method.**

```
// Move to previous record in component
public void previous () {
    // Check to make sure that a valid next row exists
    if (current == 1) {
        return;
    }
    // Set value for updated entry
    Records[0].remove(new Integer(current));
    // Check to see which value will be used (on/off)
    String value;
    if (this.getState()) {
        value = onCheck;
    }
    else {
        value = offCheck;
    }
    Records[0].put(new Integer(current), value);
    // Set the record to the previous valid record
    this.current--;
    // Set the state of the component
    value = (String)Records[0].get(new Integer(current));
    if (value == onCheck) {
        this.setState(true);
    }
    else {
        this.setState(false);
    }
}
```

12

first() **and** last()

The first() and last() methods move the record position to the first and last records, respectively. They both save the current data value for the record before moving to their appropriate positions. Only the code for the first() method will be shown because then you can implement the last() method by changing one value in the first() method. To change the first() method to the last() record, change the following line:

```
current = 1;
```

to

```
current = max;
```

The first() method sets the record position to 1, and the last() method sets the record position to the value contained in the max variable. Listing 12.13 contains the code for the first() method.

TYPE | **Listing 12.13. The first() method.**

```
// Move to first record in component
public void first () {
    // Set value for updated entry
    Records[0].remove(new Integer(current));
    // Check to see which value will be used (on/off)
    String value;
    if (this.getState()) {
        value = onCheck;
    }
    else {
        value = offCheck;
    }
    Records[0].put(new Integer(current), value);
    // Set the record to the first record
    this.current = 1;
    // Set the state of the component
    value = (String)Records[0].get(new Integer(current));
    if (value == onCheck) {
        this.setState(true);
    }
    else {
        this.setState(false);
    }
}
```

Updating the Component

The final interface that the DataCheckBox component will implement is the DataUpdate interface. This interface provides various methods for updating the data contained in the component to the database. The interface provides methods for specifying which table should be updated as well as which columns from that table should be updated. The methods provided by the DataUpdate interface are as follows:

```
public void setUpdateTable(String table)
public String getUpdateTable()
public boolean update()
public boolean previewStatement(String sql, int sqlType)
public void setUpdateColumn(String column)
public void setUpdateColumn(int column)
public String[] getUpdateColumn()
```

setUpdateTable()

The setUpdateTable() method lets you specify which table the update() method should apply all of its updates against. You must specify an update table in order for the update() method to process. If you don't specify an update table, then the update() method will not update the data.

getUpdateTable()

The getUpdateTable() method complements the setUpdateTable() method. Whereas the setUpdateTable() sets the update table for the component to use, the getUpdateTable() method returns a string that contains the update table being used by the component.

update()

The update() method of the component works exactly as the update() method in the other two components you have built. The method first checks for both an update table and at least one update column. If either of these is missing, then the method will return false because no updating was done. The method will then check the values in the user Hashtable objects against the original Hashtable objects, and if any changes have been made, the method will construct a SQL Update statement. This SQL statement will then be sent to the previewStatement() method. If the method returns true, then the Update statement will be sent to the database; otherwise, the method will continue with the next record.

When the update() method has succeeded in updating all records, the component will assign the values from the user hash tables to the values in the original hash tables. This is so that if any new changes are made, the old changes will not be updated again.

previewStatement()

The previewStatement() method enables you to use your own business logic in the updating process. This method is called from the update() method and is passed the SQL statement

12

to be sent to the database as well as the type of SQL statement that has been passed. You can then process this SQL statement to determine whether you want to allow it to be executed. If you want to stop the SQL statement from being sent to the database, you can return a `false` value. Returning a `true` value will cause the SQL statement to be sent to the database.

setUpdateColumn()

The component implements two `setUpdateColumn()` methods. One takes an integer and the other a `String` object. They both perform the same functionality; they just enable the user to specify the columns he wants to have updated in different ways.

getUpdateColumn()

The `getUpdateColumn()` method returns a `String` array that contains all of the columns that will be used in the update process. These columns are the columns that are checked for changes, and these columns are the ones that will be changed. The array contains all of the column names that will be used by the `update()` method.

Full Code for the DataCheckBox Component

 Listing 12.14 contains the full code for the DataCheckBox component. The code is also available on the included CD-ROM.

Type | **Listing 12.14. The DataCheckBox component.**

```java
import java.awt.*;
import java.util.*;
import symjava.sql.*;
public class DataCheckBox extends Checkbox implements DataUpdate, DataComponent,
    DataConnection, DataNavigation {
    Connection c;
    String sql;
    int current = 0;
    int max = 0;
    String updateTable = "";
    int updateColumnCount = 0;
    Hashtable updateColumns;
    Hashtable Original[];
    Hashtable Records[];
    int columns = 0;
        String strColumns[];
    int ColumnTypes[];
    String onCheck = "Y";
    String offCheck = "N";
public DataCheckBox () {
    super();
```

```
}
public DataCheckBox (String label) {
    super(label);
}
public DataCheckBox(String label, CheckboxGroup group) {
    super(label, group, false);
}
public DataCheckBox (Connection c) {
    this();
    this.c = c;
}
public DataCheckBox (Connection c, String sql, boolean retrieve) {
    this(c);
    this.sql = sql;
    if (retrieve) {
        this.retrieve();
    }
}
public DataCheckBox (String label, Connection c, String sql, boolean retrieve) {
    this(label);
    this.c = c;
    this.sql = sql;
    if (retrieve) {
        this.retrieve();
    }
}
public void setConnection (Connection c) {
    this.reset();
    this.c = c;
}
public void setConnection (Connection c, boolean noReset) {
    if (!noReset) {
        this.reset();
    }
    this.c = c;
}
public Connection getConnection () {
    return this.c;
}
public void setSQL (String sql) {
    this.sql = sql;
}
public String getSQL () {
    return this.sql;
}
public int retrieve () {
    Statement sqlStatement;
    ResultSet results;
    ResultSetMetaData resultsMeta;
    int index = 0;
        if (!previewStatement(this.sql, this.SELECT)) {
        return 0;
    }
    try {
        sqlStatement = this.c.createStatement();
        results = sqlStatement.executeQuery(this.sql);
```

continues

Listing 12.14. continued

```
            resultsMeta = results.getMetaData();
            columns = resultsMeta.getColumnCount();
            strColumns = new String[columns];
            ColumnTypes = new int[columns];
            for (int i = 0;i<columns;i++) {
                strColumns[i] = resultsMeta.getColumnName(i+1);
            }
            for (int i = 0;i<columns;i++) {
                strColumns[i] = resultsMeta.getColumnName(i+1);
            }
            Records = new Hashtable[columns];
            Original = new Hashtable[columns];
            while (results.next()) {
                index++;
                for (int i = 0;i<columns;i++) {
                    if (index == 1) {
                        Records[i] = new Hashtable();
                        Original[i] = new Hashtable();
                    }
                    Records[i].put(new Integer(index), results.getString(i + 1));
                    Original[i].put(new Integer(index), results.getString(i + 1));
                }
            }
            max = index;
        }
        catch (SQLException e) {
            return -1;
        }
        this.current = 0;
        this.next();
        return index;
    }
    public void next () {
        if (current == max) {
            return;
        }
        Records[0].remove(new Integer(current));
        String value;
        if (this.getState()) {
            value = onCheck;
        }
        else {
            value = offCheck;
        }
        Records[0].put(new Integer(current), value);
        this.current++;
        value = (String)Records[0].get(new Integer(current));
        if (value == onCheck) {
            this.setState(true);
        }
        else {
            this.setState(false);
        }
    }
```

```
public void previous () {
    if (current == 1) {
        return;
    }
    Records[0].remove(new Integer(current));
    String value;
    if (this.getState()) {
        value = onCheck;
    }
    else {
        value = offCheck;
    }
    Records[0].put(new Integer(current), value);
    this.current--;
    value = (String)Records[0].get(new Integer(current));
    if (value == onCheck) {
        this.setState(true);
    }
    else {
        this.setState(false);
    }
}
public void first () {
    Records[0].remove(new Integer(current));
    String value;
    if (this.getState()) {
        value = onCheck;
    }
    else {
        value = offCheck;
    }
    Records[0].put(new Integer(current), value);
    this.current = 1;
    value = (String)Records[0].get(new Integer(current));
    if (value == onCheck) {
        this.setState(true);
    }
    else {
        this.setState(false);
    }
}
public void last () {
    Records[0].remove(new Integer(current));
    String value;
    if (this.getState()) {
        value = onCheck;
    }
    else {
        value = offCheck;
    }
    Records[0].put(new Integer(current), value);
    this.current = max;
    value = (String)Records[0].get(new Integer(current));
    if (value == onCheck) {
        this.setState(true);
    }
```

12

continues

Listing 12.14. continued

```
        else {
            this.setState(false);
        }
    }
    public void setUpdateTable (String table) {
        this.updateTable = table;
    }
    public String getUpdateTable () {
            return this.updateTable;
    }
    public boolean update () {
        String sqlBase = "";
        String sqlSet = "";
        String sqlWhere = "";
        Statement sqlStatement;
        boolean changed = false;
        if (updateTable == "") {
            return false;
        }
        if (updateColumnCount == 0) {
            return false;
        }
        sqlBase = "update " + updateTable + "\n";
        sqlSet = "set ";
        sqlWhere = "where ";
        for (int i=1;i<=max;i++) {
            changed = false;
            for (int j=1;j<=updateColumnCount;j++) {
                int curColumn =
                ➥((Integer)updateColumns.get(new Integer(j))).intValue();
                String orgValue = (String)Original[curColumn].get(new Integer(i));
                String userValue = (String)Records[curColumn].get(new Integer(i));
                if (!(orgValue.equals(userValue))) {
                    changed = true;
                }
            }
            if (changed) {
                for (int j=1;j<=updateColumnCount;j++) {
                    int curColumn =
                    ➥((Integer)updateColumns.get(new Integer(j))).intValue();
                    String colName = getColumnName(curColumn);
                    if (j != 1) {
                        sqlSet += ", \n" + colName + "= \'";
                        sqlWhere += "\nand " + colName + "= \'";
                    }
                    String userValue =
                    ➥(String)Records[curColumn].get(new Integer(i));
                    sqlSet += userValue + "\'\n";
                    String orgValue =
                    ➥(String)Original[curColumn].get(new Integer(i));
                    sqlWhere += orgValue + "\'\n";
                }
```

12

```
            sqlBase = sqlBase + sqlSet + sqlWhere;
            if (previewStatement(sqlBase,this.UPDATE)) {
                try {
                    sqlStatement = this.c.createStatement();
                    sqlStatement.executeUpdate(sqlBase);
                }
                catch (Exception e) {
                    return false;
                }
            }
            sqlBase = "update " + updateTable + "\n";
            sqlSet = "set ";
            sqlWhere = "where ";
        }
    }
    this.Original = this.Records;
    return true;
}
public boolean previewStatement (String sql, int sqlType) {
    return true;
}
public void setUpdateColumn (String column) {
    this.setUpdateColumn(this.getColumnIndex(column));
}
public void setUpdateColumn (int column) {
    if ((column < 1) || (column > this.columns)) {
        return;
    }
    if (updateColumnCount == 0) {
        updateColumns = new Hashtable();
    }
    updateColumnCount++;
    updateColumns.put(new Integer(updateColumnCount), new Integer(column));
}
public String[] getUpdateColumn () {
    String columns[];
    columns = new String[updateColumnCount];
    for (int i = 0; i<updateColumnCount; i++) {
            columns[i] = this.getColumnName(((Integer)
        ➡updateColumns.get(new Integer(i + 1))).intValue());
    }
    return columns;
}
public int getRow () {
    return this.current;
}
public void setRow (int Row) {
    if ((Row < 1) || (Row > max)) {
        return;
    }
    Records[0].remove(new Integer(current));
    String value;
    if (this.getState()) {
        value = onCheck;
    }
```

12

continues

Listing 12.14. continued

```
            else {
                value = offCheck;
            }
            Records[0].put(new Integer(current), value);
            this.current = Row;
            value = (String)Records[0].get(new Integer(current));
            if (value == onCheck) {
                this.setState(true);
            }
            else {
                this.setState(false);
            }
    }
    public int rowCount () {
        return this.max;
    }
    public int columnCount () {
        return this.columns;
    }
    public void reset () {
        this.c = null;
        this.sql = "";
        this.updateTable = "";
        this.current = 0;
        this.max = 0;
        this.columns = 0;
        this.updateColumnCount = 0;
        onCheck = "Y";
        offCheck = "N";
    }
    public void setOnValue (String value) {
        this.onCheck = value;
    }
    public void setOffValue (String value) {
        this.offCheck = value;
    public String getItem (int row, int column) {
        if ((row < 1) || (row > max)) {
            return "";
        }
        if ((column < 1) || (column > this.columns)) {
            return "";
        }
        return (String)Records[column - 1].get(new Integer(row));
    }
    public void setItem (int row, int column, String value) {
        if ((row < 1) || (row > max)) {
            return;
        }
        if ((column < 1) || (column > this.columns)) {
            return;
        }
        Records[column].remove(new Integer(row));
        Records[column].put(new Integer(row), value);
```

12

```
        }
    public String getColumnName (int index) {
        if ((index < 1) ¦¦ (index > this.columns)) {
            return "";
        }
        return strColumns[index-1];
    }
    public int getColumnType (int index) {
        if ((index < 1) ¦¦ (index > this.columns)) {
            return -1;
        }
        return ColumnTypes[index];
    }
    public int getColumnIndex (String column) {
        int index = -1;

        for (int i = 0;i < this.columns;i++) {
            if (column.equals(strColumns[i])) {
                index = i + 1;
                break;
            }
        }
        return index;
    }
}
```

Using the Component

Now that you have built your component, write a small application to use the component. In this example, you will create an application that displays the values from a Sex column in a table in the DataCheckBox component.

Create a table in your database called tEmpSex. The table should have the columns EmpId and Sex. Make EmpId an integer column that is a foreign key column from tEmployee.

NOTE To learn how to create new tables and specify foreign keys, see Day 2, "Database Concepts."

Make the Sex column a char column of length 1. This column will contain either an M for Male or an F for Female. After you have created the table, populate the table with the employees from tEmployee and give them a sex designation.

Now that you have created a table with which you can use your component, create the component. The application will create a Frame window sized to 300×300 pixels. Display the component on the top of the frame with four buttons on the bottom. Call the constructor to pass the label to use for the check box, the connection, and the SQL statement, but do not perform an automatic retrieve. First, change the on/off values for the component before you perform a retrieve.

Override the `handleEvent()` method to handle the clicking of the four navigation methods. The code for the CheckBoxExample is shown in Listing 12.15.

TYPE **Listing 12.15. The `CheckBoxExample` application.**

```
import java.awt.*;
import java.util.*;
import symjava.sql.*;
public class CheckBoxExample extends Frame {
    DataCheckBox checkbox;
    public CheckBoxExample () {
        super();
        Panel p = new Panel();
        p.setLayout(new FlowLayout());
        p.add(new Button("First"));
        p.add(new Button("Previous"));
        p.add(new Button("Next"));
        p.add(new Button("Last"));
        this.add("South", p);
        // Create and add the check box component
        checkbox = new DataCheckBox("Sex: Male?");
        // Set the on/off values for the component
        checkbox.setOnValue("M");
        checkbox.setOffValue("F");
        this.add("North", checkbox);
        try {
            String driverName = "symantec.itools.db.jdbc.Driver";
            Driver driver = (Driver)Class.forName(driverName).newInstance();
            Properties prop = new Properties();
            prop.put("user", "dba");
            prop.put("password", "sql");
            String dbURL = "jdbc:dbaw://localhost:8889/WATCOM/JDBC/JDBC";
            Connection connection = driver.connect(dbURL, prop);
            String sql = "select Sex from tEmpSex";
            // Pass connection object and SQL to component
            checkbox.setConnection(connection, true);
            checkbox.setSQL(sql);
        }
        catch (Exception e) {}
        // Retrieve data into component
        checkbox.retrieve();
        // show window
        this.resize(300, 300);
        this.show();
    }
    public boolean handleEvent (Event evt) {
        if ("First".equals(evt.arg)) {
```

```
            checkbox.first();
        }
        if ("Previous".equals(evt.arg)) {
            checkbox.previous();
        }
        if ("Next".equals(evt.arg)) {
            checkbox.next();
        }
        if ("Last".equals(evt.arg)) {
            checkbox.last();
        }
        return super.handleEvent(evt);
    }
    public static void main (String args[]) {
        CheckBoxExample app = new CheckBoxExample();
    }
}
```

Summary

Today's lesson covered the process for creating a data component that uses a check box to display values. This type of component can be useful when you are displaying data that can be one of two values. It makes user selection easier because the user is presented only with the options to turn the component on or off. This type of component makes your application more user-friendly and easier to work with. It also makes validating user data easier because only one of two options is possible.

The component also enables you to display database values to the user in a way that he or she can understand. This can make presenting data to users easier and more understandable.

The component you built today, as well as the components you built on the last two days, are meant to form a basis for future component development. These components provide the basic functionality to use in your applications. For more advanced functionality, you might want to add such things as transaction management, a better update process, and insert and delete options.

Workshop

The Workshop provides quiz questions to help you solidify your understanding of the material covered and exercises to give you experience in using what you've learned. The answers are provided in Appendix A, "Quiz and Exercise Answers." Try to understand the quiz and exercise answers before you go on to tomorrow's lesson.

12

Quiz

1. What are the two variables that indicate on and off for the component?
2. What does the `DataCheckBox(String label)` constructor method do?
3. What does the `setConnection(Connection, boolean)` method do?
4. How can you change the `Connection` object without resetting the other variables in the component?
5. How can you specify the SQL statement for the component?
6. What is the difference between the User and Original Hashtable objects?
7. What method would you call to reset the component?
8. What will happen if you call the `next()` method and no next record exists?
9. What will happen if you call the `update()` method and have not specified an update table?
10. What does the `getColumnType()` method return?

Exercises

1. Write an application using a table of your choice that contains a yes/no switch. Write the application with one check box that will display the value contained in the column.
2. Create a new component from the DataCheckBox that implements both `insert()` and `delete()` methods. For the delete, you should keep the data values stored in an extra `Hashtable` object, or some other object that can keep multiple dynamic objects.
3. After you create the methods in Exercise 2, add a new `update()` method that will save the data. You will need to check to see whether the item has been added for the insert and deleted for the delete. If the item has been added, create a SQL `Insert` statement. If the item was deleted, then create a SQL `Delete` statement.

Day 13

The DataNavigator Component

During the last three days, you have created various components for displaying data from the database. These components have enabled you to retrieve data, display it, and update user-entered data to the database. In today's lesson, you will create a component that will let you manage multiple components through one component.

Today's lesson covers the creation of the DataNavigator component. This component will contain the same methods that are contained in the other data components, but this component will not perform any actions against the database. This component will be responsible only for calling the associated methods for other data components.

The topics covered today include the following:

- ☐ Why you should use data components
- ☐ Building the basics of the component
- ☐ Constructing the component

☐ Connecting the component
☐ Navigating the component
☐ Updating the component
☐ Connecting other components
☐ Using the component

Why Should You Use Data Components?

You might be wondering why you would want to use a component that does not actually perform any database interactivity. The component will enable you to manage easily the database interactions of multiple components placed within your application.

The purpose of the DataNavigator is to hook multiple data components together so that they can be controlled from a central location. The DataNavigator will provide a `Panel` object with four buttons. The buttons will let you move to various positions within all of the components that are connected to the DataNavigator. When a method is called in the DataNavigator, the corresponding method will be called in all data components, with some exceptions that you will learn. This can let you call the `update()` method for the DataNavigator and have it call the `update()` method for all the components on the current window. This can reduce the amount of code needed, as well as make the existing code more maintainable.

Building the Basics

Unlike the other components, the DataNavigator does not contain many object variables, because it does not actually store any data values. The only object variables that are stored for the component include a `Hashtable` array that stores all of the data components connected to the DataNavigator and an integer value that indicates how many components are currently connected.

The DataNavigator will also have a list of predefined integer values that indicate what type of DataComponent the user is passing. They can be used to determine what type of component is being passed, both by the user and by the component. The variable declarations for the DataNavigator are as follows:

```
Hashtable components[] = new Hashtable[2];
int count = 0;
```

The list of predefined component constants is as follows:

```
public final int DATAFIELD = 0;
public final int DATALABEL = 1;
public final int DATAAREA = 2;
```

```
public final int DATALIST = 3;
public final int DATACHOICE = 4;
public final int DATACHECKBOX = 5;
```

The DataNavigator keeps track of the current record number that all of the components should be on. I say *should* because the data components for the DataNavigator could easily have a different number of records, because each component could have a different Select statement. The variable declaration for the current record position is as follows:

```
int current = 0;
```

The component also stores the maximum number of records available in the connected data components. The maximum of the record counts from the connected components will be stored. This means that some components will not respond to the next() or setRow() methods of the DataNavigator, because they might be invalid records. The variable declaration for the record count is as follows:

```
int max = 0;
```

The component contains four buttons for moving the current record position. The component contains buttons to move the record position to the first record, the previous record, the next record, and the last record. Place these buttons on the DataNavigator for the user to click. The DataNavigator will declare these buttons to be object variables so that various methods can be applied to them. The variable declarations for the buttons are as follows:

```
Button first = new Button("First");
Button previous = new Button("Previous");
Button next = new Button("Next");
Button last = new Button("Last");
```

The DataNavigator component also provides four methods that enable you to show or hide the various buttons on the component. All four of the methods take a Boolean value and show the button if the passed Boolean is true, and hide the button if the passed Boolean is false. The four methods are as follows:

- public void showFirst(boolean show)
- public void showPrevious(boolean show)
- public void showNext(boolean show)
- public void showLast(boolean show)

The code for the showFirst() method is shown in Listing 13.1. You can construct the other methods from the showFirst() method by changing the name of the specified Button object.

13

| TYPE | **Listing 13.1. The `showFirst()` method.** |

```
// Show/Hide the first button
public void showFirst (boolean show) {
    if (show) {
        first.show();
    }
    else {
        first.hide();
    }
}
```

The DataNavigator implements one private method. This method is used to determine what type of data component a specified object in the hash table is. The method takes a key value for the `Hashtable` object and returns the type of component to which the key corresponds. Listing 13.2 contains the code for the `getDataType()` method.

| TYPE | **Listing 13.2. The `getDataType()` method.** |

```
// Get the data type of the passed component index
private int getDataType (int index) {
    // Make sure passed component index is valid
    if ((index < 1) || (index > count)) {
        return 0;
    }
    // Return the current index component type
    return ((Integer)components[1].get(new Integer(index))).intValue();
}
```

The DataNavigator does not implement the `DataComponent` interface, because it contains various methods that are specific to getting information on the data values for components. However, it does implement some of the methods from the `DataComponent` interface. The DataNavigator implements the following methods from the `DataComponent` interface:

- ☐ `public int getRow()`
- ☐ `public void setRow(int row)`
- ☐ `public void reset()`

getRow()

The `getRow()` method for the DataNavigator component returns the current record position that the DataNavigator is on. This can be different from the current row that some of the connected components might be on, because they might not contain as many records as some of the other components connected to the DataNavigator. Listing 13.3 contains the code for the getRow() method.

TYPE   **Listing 13.3. The getRow() method.**

```
// Get the current record position
public int getRow () {
    return this.current;
}
```

setRow()

The setRow() method calls the setRow() method for all connected components. It loops through the connected components and calls the setRow() method for all of the connected components. It passes the specified row as the row for all of the components to move to. Listing 13.4 contains the code for the setRow() method.

TYPE   **Listing 13.4. The setRow() method.**

```
// Set row for all connected components
public void setRow (int row) {
    // Make sure row is valid
    if ((row < 1) || (row > max)) {
        return;
    }

    // Set the current row to passed row
    this.current = row;

    // loop through all connected components
    for (int i=1;i<=count;i++) {
        // Get the data type for the current component
        switch (this.getDataType(i)) {
            case DATAFIELD:
                ((DataField)components[0].get(new Integer(i))).setRow(current);
                break;
            case DATALIST:
                ((DataList)components[0].get(new Integer(i))).setRow(current);
                break;
            case DATACHECKBOX:
                ((DataCheckBox)
                ➥components[0].get(new Integer(i))).setRow(current);
                break;
        }
    }
}
```

13

reset()

The reset() method performs the same action as it does on any of the data components. However, in the DataNavigator, the reset() method will reset all of the connected components. Along with resetting all of the connected components, the reset() method will reset all of the variables for the DataNavigator object. Listing 13.5 contains the code for the reset() method.

TYPE | **Listing 13.5. The reset() method.**

```
// Reset the component and all connected components
public void reset () {
    // loop through all connected components and reset
    for (int i=1;i<=count;i++) {
        // Get the data type for the current component
        switch (this.getDataType(i)) {
            case DATAFIELD:
                ((DataField)components[0].get(new Integer(i))).reset();
                break;
            case DATALIST:
                ((DataList)components[0].get(new Integer(i))).reset();
                break;
            case DATACHECKBOX:
                ((DataCheckBox)components[0].get(new Integer(i))).reset();
                break;
        }
    }

    // Reset the object variables
    this.count = 0;
    this.current = 0;
    this.max = 0;
}
```

Constructing the Component

The DataNavigator provides one constructor method, which creates the ancestor Panel object and places in a row all of the buttons on the panel. Give the panel a FlowLayout manager that places the components in the center of the panel. Listing 13.6 contains the code for the constructor method.

TYPE | **Listing 13.6. The DataNavigator() constructor method.**

```
// Constructor for component
public DataNavigator () {
```

13

```
        super();
        // Set layout for Panel
        this.setLayout(new FlowLayout(FlowLayout.CENTER));
        // Add the buttons to the component in order
        this.add(first);
        this.add(previous);
        this.add(next);
        this.add(last);
}
```

Along with the constructor, the component needs to handle the events generated by the different buttons. You handle these actions in the handleEvent() method. In the handleEvent() method, check to see which button was clicked and call the appropriate method, based on the button clicked by the user. The code for the handleEvent() method is shown in Listing 13.7.

TYPE **Listing 13.7. The handleEvent() method.**

```
// Handle events for button clicks
public boolean handleEvent (Event evt) {
    // Check for first button clicked
    if ("First".equals(evt.arg)) {
        this.first();
    }
    // Check for previous button clicked
    if ("Previous".equals(evt.arg)) {
        this.previous();
    }
    // Check for next button clicked
    if ("Next".equals(evt.arg)) {
        this.next();
    }
    // Check for last button clicked
    if ("Last".equals(evt.arg)) {
        this.last();
    }
    // Call ancestor method to handle events
    return super.handleEvent(evt);
}
```

13

Connecting the Component

The component implements various methods from the DataConnection interface, but because you are not using all of the methods, you will not implement the interface, only the methods that you will use. The DataNavigator uses the following methods from the DataConnection interface:

☐   public void setConnection(Connection c)

☐   public void setConnection(Connection c, boolean noReset)

☐   public void setSQL(String sql)

☐   public int retrieve()

setConnection(Connection)

The setConnection(Connection) method calls the same method for all of the connected components. This forces all of the components to use the same Connection object. It also forces a reset of all of the connected components. However, unlike the components connected to the DataNavigator, this method does not reset the variables in the component. The code for the setConnection(Connection) method is shown in Listing 13.8.

TYPE   **Listing 13.8. The** setConnection(Connection) **method.**

```
// Set Connection object for all components after resetting
public void setConnection (Connection c) {
    // loop through all connected components and set Connection
    for (int i=1;i<=count;i++) {
        // Get the data type for the current component
        switch (this.getDataType(i)) {
            case DATAFIELD:
                ((DataField)components[0].get(new Integer(i))).setConnection(c);
                break;
            case DATALIST:
                ((DataList)components[0].get(new Integer(i))).setConnection(c);
                break;
            case DATACHECKBOX:
                ((DataCheckBox)
                ➥components[0].get(new Integer(i))).setConnection(c);
                break;
        }
    }
}
```

setConnection(Connection, boolean)

The setConnection(Connection, boolean) method enables you to change or set the Connection object for all of the connected components, but still keep all the other variables intact for the components. Passing a true for the Boolean parameter will force the Connection object to change without resetting the component. Passing a false for the Boolean parameter will force a resetting of the components before changing the Connection object. Listing 13.9 contains the code for the setConnection(Connection, boolean) method.

13

```
// Set the Connection object and reset/noreset the component
public void setConnection (Connection c, boolean noReset) {
    // If noReset = false, then reset the component
    if (!noReset) {
        this.reset();
    }
    // loop through all connected components and set Connection
    for (int i=1;i<=count;i++) {
        // Get the data type for the current component
        switch (this.getDataType(i)) {
            case DATAFIELD:
                ((DataField)
                ➥components[0].get(new Integer(i))).setConnection(c, true);
                break;
            case DATALIST:
                ((DataList)
                ➥components[0].get(new Integer(i))).setConnection(c, true);
                break;
            case DATACHECKBOX:
                ((DataCheckBox)
                ➥components[0].get(new Integer(i))).setConnection(c, true);
                break;
        }
    }
}
```

setSQL()

The setSQL() method enables you to set the SQL Select statements for all of the connected components to be identical. The method passes the SQL argument to all of the connected components so that they will all have the same SQL Select statement. This can be useful if you want to display the same information in several different ways, for example. Listing 13.10 contains the code for the setSQL() method.

Type **Listing 13.10. The** `setSQL()` **method.**

```
// Set the SQL Statement for all connected components
public void setSQL (String sql) {
    // loop through all connected components and set SQL
    for (int i=1;i<=count;i++) {
        // Get the data type for the current component
        switch (this.getDataType(i)) {
            case DATAFIELD:
                ((DataField)components[0].get(new Integer(i))).setSQL(sql);
```

continues

13

Listing 13.10. continued

```
                break;
            case DATALIST:
                ((DataList)components[0].get(new Integer(i))).setSQL(sql);
                break;
            case DATACHECKBOX:
                ((DataCheckBox)components[0].get(new Integer(i))).setSQL(sql);
                break;
        }
    }
}
```

retrieve()

The retrieve() method for the DataNavigator component calls the retrieve() method for all components that are currently connected to the DataNavigator. You can use the setConnection(), setSQL(), and retrieve() methods in conjunction to set up the components together and then retrieve information into them in conjunction.

Along with retrieving data into all of the connected components, the method stores the values returned from the retrieve() method for the components and saves the maximum value into the max variable for the component. This is used to check for a valid record in methods used throughout the component. Listing 13.11 contains the code for the retrieve() method.

TYPE **Listing 13.11. The retrieve() method.**

```
// Retrieve data into all of the components
public int retrieve () {
    int tempMax = 0;
    // Call the reset method to reset all components before retrieving
    this.reset();
    // loop through all connected components and retrieve data
    for (int i=1;i<=count;i++) {
        // Get the data type for the current component
        switch (this.getDataType(i)) {
            case DATAFIELD:
                tempMax = ((DataField)
                ➥components[0].get(new Integer(i))).retrieve();
                break;
            case DATALIST:
                tempMax = ((DataList)
                ➥components[0].get(new Integer(i))).retrieve();
                break;
            case DATACHECKBOX:
                tempMax = ((DataCheckBox)
                ➥components[0].get(new Integer(i))).retrieve();
                break;
        }
```

13

```
        // If the retrieved record count is greater than current max,
        // assign max the new record count
        if (tempMax > max) {
            max = tempMax;
        }
    }
    // return maximum record count
    return max;
}
```

Navigating the Component

The only interface that the DataNavigator will implement is the `DataNavigation` interface.
Because the DataNavigator implements all of the methods provided by the `DataNavigation`
interface, it is more maintainable to use the interface for the method implementations than
to declare the methods as part of the component. The DataNavigator implements the
following methods, all provided through the `DataNavigation` interface:

- [ ] `public void next()`

- [ ] `public void previous()`

- [ ] `public void first()`

- [ ] `public void last()`

next()

The `next()` method moves the current record position to the next valid record in all of the
components connected to the DataNavigator component. The `next()` method calls the same
method for all connected components, until the maximum valid record for the components
is reached. The `next()` method call for some components might not move the record
position, because there might not be a next valid record. Listing 13.12 contains the code for
the `next()` method.

TYPE   **Listing 13.12. The `next()` method.**

```
// Move to next record in components
public void next () {
    // if we are at last valid record, do nothing
    if (current == max) {
        return;
    }
    // Increment current
    current++;
    // loop through all connected components and move to next record
```

continues

13

Listing 13.12. continued

```
        for (int i=1;i<=count;i++) {
            // Get the data type for the current component
            switch (this.getDataType(i)) {
                case DATAFIELD:
                    ((DataField)components[0].get(new Integer(i))).next();
                    break;
                case DATALIST:
                    ((DataList)components[0].get(new Integer(i))).next();
                    break;
                case DATACHECKBOX:
                    ((DataCheckBox)components[0].get(new Integer(i))).next();
                    break;
            }
        }
}
```

previous()

The previous() method for the DataNavigator component moves to the previous valid record in all connected components. Some connected components might not have a valid previous record and will therefore not move to the previous record. Listing 13.13 contains the code for the previous() method.

TYPE   Listing 13.13. The previous() method.

```
// Move to previous record in connected components
public void previous () {
    // if we are at first valid record, do nothing
    if (current == 1) {
        return;
    }
    // Increment current
    current--;
    // loop through all connected components and move to next record
    for (int i=1;i<=count;i++) {
        // Get the data type for the current component
        switch (this.getDataType(i)) {
            case DATAFIELD:
                ((DataField)components[0].get(new Integer(i))).previous();
                break;
            case DATALIST:
                ((DataList)components[0].get(new Integer(i))).previous();
                break;
            case DATACHECKBOX:
                ((DataCheckBox)components[0].get(new Integer(i))).previous();
                break;
        }
    }
}
```

first() and last()

The first() and last() methods are coded in similar fashion. The only difference is that one moves the record position to the first record and the other moves the record position to the last record. Each method calls the appropriate method for all connected components. Listing 13.14 contains the code for the first() method. You can modify the code to be the last() method by changing which method is called for the components and what value the current variable is set to.

TYPE   **Listing 13.14. The first() method.**

```
// Move to first record
public void first () {
    // Set current to 1
    this.current = 1;
    // loop through all connected components and move to next record
    for (int i=1;i<=count;i++) {
        // Get the data type for the current component
        switch (this.getDataType(i)) {
            case DATAFIELD:
                ((DataField)components[0].get(new Integer(i))).first();
                break;
            case DATALIST:
                ((DataList)components[0].get(new Integer(i))).first();
                break;
            case DATACHECKBOX:
                ((DataCheckBox)components[0].get(new Integer(i))). first();
                break;
        }
    }
}
```

Updating the Component

The DataNavigator implements some of the methods that are contained in the DataUpdate interface. Because it does not use all of the methods from the interface, the DataNavigator does not implement the interface in its class declaration. The DataNavigator implements the methods from the DataUpdate interface that are listed as follows:

- ☐ public void setUpdateTable(String table)
- ☐ public boolean update()
- ☐ public void setUpdateColumn(String column)
- ☐ public void setUpdateColumn(int column)

13

setUpdateTable()

The setUpdateTable() method sets the update table for all of the connected components. The String object passed to the DataNavigator component is then passed on to all of the connected components. This ensures that all connected components will have the same update table for updating data values to the database. Listing 13.15 contains the code for the setUpdateTable() method.

TYPE   **Listing 13.15. The setUpdateTable() method.**

```
// Set update table for all connected components
public void setUpdateTable (String table) {
    // loop through all connected components and set table
    for (int i=1;i<=count;i++) {
        // Get the data type for the current component
        switch (this.getDataType(i)) {
            case DATAFIELD:
                ((DataField)
                ➥components[0].get(new Integer(i))).setUpdateTable(table);
                break;
            case DATALIST:
                ((DataList)
                ➥components[0].get(new Integer(i))).setUpdateTable(table);
                break;
            case DATACHECKBOX:
                ((DataCheckBox)
                ➥components[0].get(new Integer(i))).setUpdateTable(table);
                break;
        }
    }
}
```

update()

The update() method for the DataNavigator calls the update() method for all connected components. This can be useful when you want all of the components contained in a window to be updated at once. This method calls the update() method to update each component that is connected to the DataNavigator. Listing 13.16 contains the code for the update() method.

TYPE   **Listing 13.16. The update() method.**

```
// Update all connected components
public boolean update () {
    // Call update method for all components
```

```
    for (int i=1;i<=count;i++) {
        // Get the data type for the current component
        switch (this.getDataType(i)) {
            case DATAFIELD:
                ((DataField)components[0].get(new Integer(i))).update();
                break;
            case DATALIST:
                ((DataList)components[0].get(new Integer(i))).update();
                break;
            case DATACHECKBOX:
                ((DataCheckBox)components[0].get(new Integer(i))).update();
                break;
        }
    }
    return true;
}
```

setUpdateColumn()

Just like the other data components, the DataNavigator offers two setUpdateColumn()
methods. One method takes a String object as a parameter. This string contains the name
of the column that should be updated. The other method takes an integer that identifies the
column index that should be updated. Listing 13.17 contains the code for the
setUpdateColumn(String) method. The other method is the same except for the argument.

TYPE **Listing 13.17. The setUpdateColumn() method.**

```
// Set update column for all components
public void setUpdateColumn (String column) {
    for (int i=1;i<=count;i++) {
        // Get the data type for the current component
        switch (this.getDataType(i)) {
            case DATAFIELD:
                ((DataField)
                ➥components[0].get(new Integer(i))).setUpdateColumn(column);
                break;
            case DATALIST:
                ((DataList)
                ➥components[0].get(new Integer(i))). setUpdateColumn(column);
                break;
            case DATACHECKBOX:
                ((DataCheckBox)
                ➥components[0].get(new Integer(i))). setUpdateColumn(column);
                break;
        }
    }
}
```

13

Connecting Other Components

In the previous sections you have learned how to call methods for the DataNavigator so that they will be propagated to all of the connected components. However, you have not learned how you will connect the data components to the DataNavigator.

Now create a method called addComponent(). The method will take an argument of type Object and an argument of type integer. The Object argument will contain the component that you want to add to the DataNavigator. The integer argument will contain one of the predefined data component types listed in the DataNavigator.

To pass a DataField component called field1 to be connected to the DataNavigator, you would use the following syntax:

```
datanav.addComponent(field1, datanav.DATAFIELD);
```

Listing 13.18 contains the code for the addComponent() method.

TYPE   **Listing 13.18. The addComponent() method.**

```
// Add a component to the data navigator
public void addComponent (Object component, int type) {
    // Increment the count variable
    count++;
    // If the count = 1, then we need to create the Hashtable objects
    if (count == 1) {
        components[0] = new Hashtable();
        components[1] = new Hashtable();
    }
    // Add the component to the Hashtable object
    components[0].put(new Integer(count), component);
    components[1].put(new Integer(count), new Integer(type));
}
```

Full Code Listing for the DataNavigator Component

The full code listing for the DataNavigator component is shown in Listing 13.19. The listing has been stripped of comments and spacing due to space limitations. For a complete code listing, look for the code on the included CD-ROM.

TYPE   **Listing 13.19. The DataNavigator component.**

```
import java.awt.*;
import java.util.*;
```

```
import symjava.sql.*;
public class DataNavigator extends Panel implements DataNavigation {
    Hashtable components[] = new Hashtable[2];
    int count = 0;
    public final int DATAFIELD = 0;
    public final int DATALABEL = 1;
    public final int DATAAREA = 2;
    public final int DATALIST = 3;
    public final int DATACHOICE = 4;
    public final int DATACHECKBOX = 5;
    int current = 0;
    int max = 0;
    Button first = new Button("First");
    Button previous = new Button("Previous");
    Button next = new Button("Next");
    Button last = new Button("Last");
public void showFirst (boolean show) {
    if (show) {
        first.show();
    }
    else {
        first.hide();
    }
}
public void showPrevious (boolean show) {
    if (show) {
        previous.show();
    }
    else {
        previous.hide();
    }
}
public void showNext (boolean show) {
    if (show) {
        next.show();
    }
    else {
        next.hide();
    }
}
public void showLast (boolean show) {
    if (show) {
        last.show();
    }
    else {
        last.hide();
    }
}
private int getDataType (int index) {
    // Make sure passed component index is valid
    if ((index < 1) || (index > count)) {
        return 0;
    }
    return ((Integer)components[1].get(new Integer(index))).intValue();
}
```

13

continues

Listing 13.19. continued

```
public int getRow () {
    return this.current;
}
public void setRow (int row) {
    if ((row < 1) || (row > max)) {
        return;
    }
    this.current = row;
    for (int i=1;i<=count;i++) {
        switch (this.getDataType(i)) {
            case DATAFIELD:
                ((DataField)components[0].get(new Integer(i))).setRow(current);
                break;
            case DATALIST:
                ((DataList)components[0].get(new Integer(i))).setRow(current);
                break;
            case DATACHECKBOX:
                ((DataCheckBox)
                ➥components[0].get(new Integer(i))).setRow(current);
                break;
        }
    }
}
public void reset () {
    for (int i=1;i<=count;i++) {
        switch (this.getDataType(i)) {
            case DATAFIELD:
                ((DataField)components[0].get(new Integer(i))).reset();
                break;
            case DATALIST:
                ((DataList)components[0].get(new Integer(i))).reset();
                break;
            case DATACHECKBOX:
                ((DataCheckBox)components[0].get(new Integer(i))).reset();
                break;
        }
    }
    this.count = 0;
    this.current = 0;
    this.max = 0;
}
public DataNavigator () {
    super();
    this.setLayout(new FlowLayout(FlowLayout.CENTER));
    this.add(first);
    this.add(previous);
    this.add(next);
    this.add(last);
}
public boolean handleEvent (Event evt) {
    if ("First".equals(evt.arg)) {
        this.first();
    }
    if ("Previous".equals(evt.arg)) {
```

```
                this.previous();
        }
        if ("Next".equals(evt.arg)) {
            this.next();
        }
        if ("Last".equals(evt.arg)) {
            this.last();
        }
        return super.handleEvent(evt);
    }
    public void setConnection (Connection c) {
        for (int i=1;i<=count;i++) {
            switch (this.getDataType(i)) {
                case DATAFIELD:
                    ((DataField)
                    ➥components[0].get(new Integer(i))).setConnection(c);
                    break;
                case DATALIST:
                    ((DataList)components[0].get(new Integer(i))).setConnection(c);
                    break;
                case DATACHECKBOX:
                    ((DataCheckBox)
                    ➥components[0].get(new Integer(i))).setConnection(c);
                    break;
            }
        }
    }
    public void setConnection (Connection c, boolean noReset) {
        if (!noReset) {
            this.reset();
        }
        for (int i=1;i<=count;i++) {
            switch (this.getDataType(i)) {
                case DATAFIELD:
                    ((DataField)
                    ➥components[0].get(new Integer(i))).setConnection(c, true);
                    break;
                case DATALIST:
                    ((DataList)
                    ➥components[0].get(new Integer(i))).setConnection(c, true);
                    break;
                case DATACHECKBOX:
                    ((DataCheckBox)
                    ➥components[0].get(new Integer(i))).setConnection(c, true);
                    break;
            }
        }
    }
    public void setSQL (String sql) {
        for (int i=1;i<=count;i++) {
            switch (this.getDataType(i)) {
                case DATAFIELD:
                    ((DataField)components[0].get(new Integer(i))).setSQL(sql);
                    break;
```

13

continues

Listing 13.19. continued

```
                case DATALIST:
                    ((DataList)components[0].get(new Integer(i))).setSQL(sql);
                    break;
                case DATACHECKBOX:
                    ((DataCheckBox)components[0].get(new Integer(i))).setSQL(sql);
                    break;
            }
        }
    }
    public int retrieve () {
        int tempMax = 0;
        this.reset();
        for (int i=1;i<=count;i++) {
            switch (this.getDataType(i)) {
                case DATAFIELD:
                    tempMax = ((DataField)
                    ➥components[0].get(new Integer(i))).retrieve();
                    break;
                case DATALIST:
                    tempMax = ((DataList)
                    ➥components[0].get(new Integer(i))).retrieve();
                    break;
                case DATACHECKBOX:
                    tempMax = ((DataCheckBox)
                    ➥components[0].get(new Integer(i))).retrieve();
                    break;
            }
            if (tempMax > max) {
                max = tempMax;
            }
        }
        return max;
    }
    public void next () {
        if (current == max) {
            return;
        }
        current++;
        for (int i=1;i<=count;i++) {
            switch (this.getDataType(i)) {
                case DATAFIELD:
                    ((DataField)components[0].get(new Integer(i))).next();
                    break;
                case DATALIST:
                    ((DataList)components[0].get(new Integer(i))).next();
                    break;
                case DATACHECKBOX:
                    ((DataCheckBox)components[0].get(new Integer(i))).next();
                    break;
            }
        }
    }
    public void previous () {
        if (current == 1) {
```

13

```
            return;
        }
        current--;
        for (int i=1;i<=count;i++) {
            switch (this.getDataType(i)) {
                case DATAFIELD:
                    ((DataField)components[0].get(new Integer(i))).previous();
                    break;
                case DATALIST:
                    ((DataList)components[0].get(new Integer(i))).previous();
                    break;
                case DATACHECKBOX:
                    ((DataCheckBox)components[0].get(new Integer(i))).previous();
                    break;
            }
        }
    }
    public void first () {
        this.current = 1;
        for (int i=1;i<=count;i++) {
            switch (this.getDataType(i)) {
                case DATAFIELD:
                    ((DataField)components[0].get(new Integer(i))).first();
                    break;
                case DATALIST:
                    ((DataList)components[0].get(new Integer(i))).first();
                    break;
                case DATACHECKBOX:
                    ((DataCheckBox)components[0].get(new Integer(i))). first();
                    break;
            }
        }
    }
    public void last () {
        this.current = max;
        for (int i=1;i<=count;i++) {
            switch (this.getDataType(i)) {
                case DATAFIELD:
                    ((DataField)components[0].get(new Integer(i))).last();
                    break;
                case DATALIST:
                    ((DataList)components[0].get(new Integer(i))).last();
                    break;
                case DATACHECKBOX:
                    ((DataCheckBox)components[0].get(new Integer(i))). last();
                    break;
            }
        }
    }
    public void setUpdateTable (String table) {
        for (int i=1;i<=count;i++) {
            switch (this.getDataType(i)) {
                case DATAFIELD:
                    ((DataField)
                    ➡components[0].get(new Integer(i))).setUpdateTable(table);
```

continues

Listing 13.19. continued

```
                            break;
                    case DATALIST:
                        ((DataList)
                    ➥components[0].get(new Integer(i))).setUpdateTable(table);
                        break;
                    case DATACHECKBOX:
                        ((DataCheckBox)
                    ➥components[0].get(new Integer(i))).setUpdateTable(table);
                        break;
                }
            }
        }
        public boolean update () {
            for (int i=1;i<=count;i++) {
                switch (this.getDataType(i)) {
                    case DATAFIELD:
                        ((DataField)components[0].get(new Integer(i))).update();
                        break;
                    case DATALIST:
                        ((DataList)components[0].get(new Integer(i))).update();
                        break;
                    case DATACHECKBOX:
                        ((DataCheckBox)components[0].get(new Integer(i))).update();
                        break;
                }
            }
            return true;
        }
        public void setUpdateColumn (String column) {
            for (int i=1;i<=count;i++) {
                switch (this.getDataType(i)) {
                    case DATAFIELD:
                        ((DataField)
                    ➥components[0].get(new Integer(i))).setUpdateColumn(column);
                        break;
                    case DATALIST:
                        ((DataList)
                    ➥components[0].get(new Integer(i))). setUpdateColumn(column);
                        break;
                    case DATACHECKBOX:
                        ((DataCheckBox)
                    ➥components[0].get(new Integer(i))). setUpdateColumn(column);
                        break;
                }
            }
        }
        public void setUpdateColumn (int column) {
            for (int i=1;i<=count;i++) {
                switch (this.getDataType(i)) {
                    case DATAFIELD:
                        ((DataField)
                    ➥components[0].get(new Integer(i))).setUpdateColumn(column);
                        break;
                    case DATALIST:
```

```
                ((DataList)
                ➥components[0].get(new Integer(i))). setUpdateColumn(column);
                break;
            case DATACHECKBOX:
                ((DataCheckBox)
                ➥components[0].get(new Integer(i))). setUpdateColumn(column);
                break;
        }
    }
}
public void addComponent (Object component, int type) {
    count++;
    if (count == 1) {
        components[0] = new Hashtable();
        components[1] = new Hashtable();
    }
    components[0].put(new Integer(count), component);
    components[1].put(new Integer(count), new Integer(type));
}
}
```

Using the Component

Now that you have created the DataNavigator component, use the component to coordinate multiple DataField components. For this example, create a window with the DataNavigator component on the southern part of the frame. The northern part of the frame will contain two DataField components. One of the components will display the FirstName column from tEmployee, and the other will display the LastName column from tEmployee.

Notice that you pass the Connection object and SQL to the DataField components, but you do not retrieve data into the components. You need to let the DataNavigator call the retrieve() method in order to populate itself with the current and max variable values.

Listing 13.20 contains the code for the DataNavExample application.

TYPE **Listing 13.20. The DataNavExample application.**

```
import java.awt.*;
import java.util.*;
import symjava.sql.*;
public class DataNavExample extends Frame {
    DataField firstname;
    DataField lastname;
    DataNavigator datanav;
    public DataNavExample () {
        super();
        datanav = new DataNavigator();
```

continues

Listing 13.20. continued

```
        this.add("South", datanav);

        try {
            String driverName = "symantec.itools.db.jdbc.Driver";
            Driver driver = (Driver)Class.forName(driverName).newInstance();
            Properties p = new Properties();
            p.put("user", "dba");
            p.put("password", "sql");
            String dbURL = "jdbc:dbaw://localhost:8889/WATCOM/JDBC/JDBC";
            Connection connection = driver.connect(dbURL, p);
            String sql = "select FirstName from tEmployee";
            firstname = new DataField(connection, sql, false);
            sql = "select LastName from tEmployee";
            lastname = new DataField(connection, sql, false);
            this.add("North", firstname);
            this.add("Center", lastname);
            datanav.addComponent(firstname, datanav.DATAFIELD);
            datanav.addComponent(lastname, datanav.DATAFIELD);
        }
        catch (SQLException e) {}
        catch (Exception e) {}
    }
    public static void main (String args[]) {
        DataNavExample app = new DataNavExample();
    }
}
```

Summary

In today's lesson, you created a data component that enables you to control other data components. You can use this component as a basis for making your own specific controller components. You could make a component that could move only certain records in components, for example. This type of component helps make implementing your business logic easier than manually keeping track of all the components.

Today you learned how to create a component other than one of the standard AWT components. You created a Panel component with multiple Button objects. This is the basis for creating more advanced data components. You could, for example, create a DataGrid component that would display all of the records from the result set within a grid. You would want to use either a Panel or Canvas object to achieve this.

13

Workshop

The Workshop provides quiz questions to help you solidify your understanding of the material covered and exercises to give you experience in using what you've learned. The answers are provided in Appendix A, "Quiz and Exercise Answers." Try to understand the quiz and exercise answers before you go on to tomorrow's lesson.

Quiz

1. Why doesn't the DataNavigator implement some of the data interfaces?
2. How does the DataNavigator store the connected components?
3. Name the four buttons on the DataNavigator component.
4. How would you hide the Last button?
5. How would you show the Last button?
6. How would you add a component to the DataNavigator?
7. What methods does the DataNavigator implement from the `DataUpdate` interface?
8. What does the `retrieve()` method return?
9. What is stored in the `max` variable?
10. Name some differences between the DataNavigator component and the other data components.

Exercises

1. Add functionality to the DataNavigator component to remove a component, based on a passed index.
2. Add functionality to add DataNavigator components as components of the DataNavigator.

Day 14

The DataPanel Component

Today you will finish creating the data components that you began at the beginning of Week 2. In today's lesson, you will create the DataPanel object, which will enable the user to specify a table name and have all of the data from that table displayed in the panel.

The panel will display all of the column information in Label objects contained on a Panel object. The object will not contain any of the update functionality of the other components because it will not allow the user to edit the data values, only to view them.

The topics that will be covered today include the following:

☐ Why you should use the DataPanel component
☐ Building the basics of the component
☐ Connecting the component
☐ Navigating the component
☐ Using the component

Why Should You Use the DataPanel Component?

The DataPanel component will enable you to display entire ranges of information from a table to the user. Unlike the other data components that only display data from one column, the DataPanel component displays data from all columns within a table.

This gives you, as the developer, a means to display information to the user. Using some of the new features that are promised in the 1.1 release of Java, you could use this component to display data and then allow the user to send the values to a printer for output.

Building the Basics

The basic declaration for the component is as follows:

```
public class DataPanel extends Panel implements DataComponent,
DataConnection, DataNavigation
```

The DataPanel object uses some of the same object variables that are used in the other components, but it also removes and adds some object variables that are needed to allow the component to display information to the user.

The component declares a Connection object variable to store the passed Connection object. This object is used by the retrieve() method of the component to create a Statement object that is used to get results from the database.

```
Connection c;
```

The component also declares a String object variable to be used to store the table name from which the component displays data values. The table name is passed in using the constructor for the DataPanel object.

```
String sql;
```

The object also will maintain two integer variables that will identify the current record being displayed and the maximum number of records that the panel can display. Both of the variables will be initialized to 0.

```
int current = 0;
int max = 0;
```

Use an array of Hashtable objects to store the data values returned by the SQL statement. The size of the array will be determined in the retrieve() method by getting the number of columns in the result set.

```
Hashtable Records[];
```

The DataPanel object will maintain a count of the number of columns in the result set as well as the column names and types. This information will be used for various reasons within the component. The names of the columns will be displayed to the user in the panel.

```
int columns = 0;
String strColumns[];
int ColumnTypes[];
```

The component also will declare two arrays of Label objects that will be used to display information to the user on the DataPanel. The arrays will be the same size as the number of columns in the result set. The description array will contain the labels that will be used to display the column name of each individual column. The data array will be used to display the data values from the result set to the user.

```
Label description[];
Label data[];
```

The constructor for the object will take two parameters that will be used to store information for the object to use later. The constructor will assign the passed Connection object to the local object variable.

```
this.c = c;
```

It then will use the passed table name to create a SQL Select statement that will retrieve all items from the specified table. This SQL statement then will be used by the retrieve() method to populate the result set with all data values from the table.

```
this.sql = "select * from " + table;
```

The constructor then will call the retrieve() method to populate the component with data values from the SQL Select statement built by the constructor.

```
this.retrieve();
```

You can call the constructor by using something similar to the following code:

```
DataPanel d = new DataPanel(connection, "tEmployee");
```

The preceding line of code will display the data contained in the tEmployee table.

Listing 14.1 contains the full code for the DataPanel constructor method.

14

TYPE **Listing 14.1. The DataPanel constructor method.**

```
public DataPanel (Connection c, String table) {
        super();

        // Assign connection object
        this.c = c;

        // Build SQL statement for table
        this.sql = "select * from " + table;

        // call retrieve method
        this.retrieve();
}
```

The component will implement the DataComponent interface, which defines various methods for performing actions and getting information about the component. The interface provides methods to display the current record as well as enabling the user to set the current record being displayed. It also enables the user to get the number of rows and columns in the result set. The methods that are provided through the DataComponent interface are as follows:

- public int getRow()
- public void setRow(int row)
- public int rowCount()
- public int columnCount()
- public void reset()
- public String getItem(int row, int column)
- public void setItem (int row, int column, String value)
- public String getColumnName(int index)
- public int getColumnType(int index)
- public int getColumnIndex(String column)

getRow()

The getRow() method enables the user to get an integer value that contains the current record being displayed by the user. The value is the same as that stored in the object variable current. This method can be used to get the row to pass to the setItem() and getItem() methods.

setRow()

The setRow() method enables you to manually set the row that the component displays to the user. Unlike the navigation methods provided in the component, the setRow() method allows you to set the current row to any valid row in the component.

rowCount()

The `rowCount()` method is a needed record that is not provided in the standard JDBC API. This method returns the number of records that were returned by the database into the result set. This enables you to perform correct loops through the data, using the number of records as the end point for the loop.

columnCount()

The `columnCount()` method enables you to get the number of columns that were returned in the result set. This method gets its value from the `ResultSetMetaData` object. The metadata object returns the number of columns that were returned by the database, and the component stores that value in an object variable. This value is then sent to the user using the `columnCount()` method.

reset()

The `reset()` method enables you to reset the component. Resetting the component will reset all of the values for the object variables to their original state. The number of columns, records, and so on, will all be set to be `0`. This prevents any action from happening until a new SQL statement is specified and the `retrieve()` method is executed again.

getItem()

The `getItem()` method enables you to get a data value for a specific row and column position. The method takes a parameter that indicates a valid row and column and returns the correct data value for the specified position. The data value is retrieved from the array of `Hashtable` objects that is used by the component.

setItem()

The `setItem()` method enables you to change or set the data that the component contains. You can change any of the data values in the component to another value using this method. The method takes a specified row and column and sets the data value for that position to the specified string. Because the component does not allow updates, setting new data values will only change the data the user sees on the panel.

14

getColumnName()

The `getColumnName()` method returns a column's name based on a specified index. The index indicates the placement of the column in the returned result set. If an invalid index is specified, then the method will return an empty string. The value returned is from the object array strColumns.

getColumnType()

The getColumnType() method enables you to get the column's data type. The data type for each column is retrieved and stored in the retrieve() method. The method returns an integer that can be used to identify the data type of the column using the predefined integer constants in the Types object. The value returned is from the object array ColumnTypes.

getColumnIndex()

The getColumnIndex() method enables you to get the placement of a particular column, also known as its index, by specifying its name. You can use this method to obtain the index value of a column to use in the other methods of the component.

Connecting the Component

The DataPanel component will implement the DataConnection interface, so it also will need to implement the methods defined in the DataConnection interface. This interface provides the component with methods for setting and getting the table name being used as well as the Connection object used by the component. The interface also provides the retrieve() method that populates the component with data values.

The component will implement the following methods of the DataConnection interface:

- ☐ public void setConnection(Connection c)
- ☐ public void setConnection(Connection c, boolean noReset)
- ☐ public Connection getConnection()
- ☐ public void setSQL(String sql)
- ☐ public String getSQL()
- ☐ public int retrieve()

setConnection(Connection)

The setConnection() interface will enable you to change the current Connection object being used by the component in the retrieve() method. This method will reset all of the values in the component before setting the new Connection object. Look at the previous data components (DataField, DataList, DataCheckBox) for a listing of the code for the setConnection() method because it uses the exact same code as the other components.

setConnection(Connection, boolean)

The second setConnection() method enables you to determine whether the component will be reset before the new Connection object is assigned. This method performs the same functionality as the other method except that it enables you to use the second parameter to determine whether the component will be reset. For a listing of the code for the setConnection() method, look at the example of the method in the previous days. The method can be found on Day 10, "The DataLabel, DataField, and DataArea Components."

getConnection()

The getConnection() method enables you to get the Connection object being used by the DataPanel component. This provides you with a way to reuse the connection for another component or to execute a SQL statement outside of the component.

setSQL(String)

The setSQL() method enables you to change the table name that will be used by the method to populate data values into the component. The setSQL() method will differ from the other data components in that the method for the DataPanel component will need to add information in front of the passed string before storing it in the component's object variable.

```
this.sql = "select * from " + sql;
```

getSQL()

The getSQL() method will return the current SQL Select statement being used by the component to populate it with data values. The method will not return the table that is being used, but the entire SQL statement that is being used to populate the component.

retrieve()

The retrieve() method will take the SQL statement for the component and, using the specified Connection object, populate the component with data values from the database. The method will retrieve all of the data using the SQL statement and store the values in Hashtable objects that will be used by the component. The retrieve() method will contain most of the same code as the other retrieve() methods in the other components, but it will also add some new code for the Label objects that are used in the object.

This method will create the array of Label objects used by the component to display column information as well as column data. The size of each array will be equal to the number of columns in the returned result set.

14

```
description = new Label[columns];
data = new Label[columns];
```

The method will then set the layout for the Panel object. It will use a grid layout that will enable all of the data values to be displayed on the component. Set the number of rows in the grid to be equal to the number of columns in the result set, and the number of columns in the grid to be equal to 2 so that both the description and the data labels can be displayed.

```
this.setLayout(new GridLayout(columns, 2));
```

The method will then perform a loop to create each of the individual Label objects and will also add the objects to the panel. The loop will first create each description label and set the text of the label to be equal to the column name. It will then add the Label object to the panel.

```
description[i] = new Label();
description[i].setText(strColumns[i]);
this.add(description[i]);
```

The loop will also create the data label and add it to the panel.

```
data[i] = new Label();
this.add(data[i]);
```

Listing 14.2 contains the full code for the retrieve() method.

TYPE **Listing 14.2. The retrieve() method.**

```
// Populate the component
public int retrieve () {
    Statement sqlStatement;
    ResultSet results;
    ResultSetMetaData resultsMeta;
    int index = 0;

    try {
        // Create a SQL statement
        sqlStatement = this.c.createStatement();

        // Execute the current SQL statement and store results
        results = sqlStatement.executeQuery(this.sql);

        // Get the MetaData for the Result Set
        resultsMeta = results.getMetaData();

        // Get the number of columns in the result set
        columns = resultsMeta.getColumnCount();

        // Create arrays to hold column names and types
        strColumns = new String[columns];
        ColumnTypes = new int[columns];

        // Populate the column names array
        for (int i = 0;i<columns;i++) {
            strColumns[i] = resultsMeta.getColumnName(i+1);
        }
```

14

```
                // Create Label objects
                description = new Label[columns];
                data = new Label[columns];

                // Set the layout for the panel to handle all Labels
                this.setLayout(new GridLayout(columns, 2));

                // Go through and create each individual Label object
                for (int i = 0; i < columns; i++) {
                        // Create description label and add to panel
                        description[i] = new Label();
                        description[i].setText(strColumns[i]);
                        this.add(description[i]);

                        // Create data label and add to panel
                        data[i] = new Label();
                        this.add(data[i]);
                }

        // Create Hashtable arrays to store data values
        Records = new Hashtable[columns];

        // Cycle through all rows and add items to Hashtables
        while (results.next()) {
            // Increment the index counter
            index++;

            // Perform a loop to add items for columns
            for (int i = 0;i<columns;i++) {
                // If you are on first record, create Hashtables
                if (index == 1) {
                    Records[i] = new Hashtable();
                }

                // Add items
                Records[i].put(new Integer(index), results.getString(i + 1));
            }
        }

        // Store the number of records in the result set
        max = index;
    }
    catch (SQLException e) {
        // Error occurred, so return a -1
        return -1;
    }

    // Set the current variable to 0
    this.current = 0;

    // Call the next() method to display initial value
    this.next();

    // Return the number of records in the result set
    return index;
}
```

Navigating the Component

Next, implement the DataNavigation interface. This interface provides the methods to navigate through the records of the component. The interface will provide the next() method that is provided by the ResultSet object, and it will also provide you with methods to move to the previous, first, and last records in the returned result set. You will implement the following methods for the DataPanel component:

- ☐ public void next()
- ☐ public void previous()
- ☐ public void first()
- ☐ public void last()

next()

The next() method will move the record position to the next available record if another record exists. The new record's data values will be displayed to the user in the Label objects contained on the panel. Unlike the other data components, no old data values will be saved because the user cannot edit data. The method will use a loop to add data values for each column in the current record. The method will use the getItem() method of the component to get the data value for the specified row and column.

```
data[i].setText(this.getItem(current, i));
```

Listing 14.3 contains the full code for the next() method.

TYPE **Listing 14.3. The next() method.**

```
// Move record position to next available record
public void next () {
    // Check to make sure it is valid to go to next record
    if (current == max) {
        return;
    }

    // Increment the current counter
    current++;

    // Set the text displayed to the new data value
        for (int i = 0; i < columns; i++) {
                data[i].setText(this.getItem(current, i+1));
        }
}
```

previous()

The previous() method provides you with the functionality of moving back in the result set. This functionality is not provided in the ResultSet object. The method will look similar to the next() method in that it will use a loop to add the data values to the panel for the current record. Listing 14.4 contains the full code for the previous() method.

TYPE   **Listing 14.4. The previous() method.**

```
// Move record position to previous available record
public void previous () {
    // Check to see if previous record is valid
    if (current == 1) {
        return;
    }

    // Decrement the current counter
    current--;

    // Display the new data item
    // Set the text displayed to the new data value
        for (int i = 0; i < columns; i++) {
                data[i].setText(this.getItem(current, i+1));
        }
}
```

first() and last()

The first() and last() methods of the component are similar except for the fact that one changes the current record to the first record and the other changes it to the last record. I will cover the first() method and leave the implementation of the last() method to you. The first() method will set the current record to be 1, the first record of the component. It will then use the same loop as the other navigation methods to add the new data values to the Label objects on the component. Listing 14.5 contains the full code for the first() method.

TYPE   **Listing 14.5. The first() method.**

```
// Move to the first record in the component
public void first () {
    // Decrement the current counter
    current = 1;
```

continues

14

Listing 14.5. continued

```
    // Set the text displayed to the new data value
    for (int i = 0; i < columns; i++) {
            data[i].setText(this.getItem(current, i+1));
    }
}
```

Using the Component

Next, create an example that uses the DataPanel component. The example will create a window that displays the DataPanel object with information from the tEmployee table.

The example will use the JavaSoft JDBC-ODBC Bridge. This driver is freely available from JavaSoft and provides you with a way to connect to any ODBC data source. The JDBC-ODBC Bridge is a general database connector. You will need to specify different parameters for different databases. For Sybase SQL Anywhere, you will only need to specify the username and password.

To install the JDBC-ODBC Bridge, available from JavaSoft, place the class files or the archive file provided from JavaSoft into the location referenced in your classpath environment variable. Within DOS-based machines, you can change the classpath variable by using the following syntax:

```
set classpath=<directory>
```

> **NOTE**
>
> The JDBC-ODBC Bridge is freely available from JavaSoft at http://www.javasoft.com.

The constructor for the example will be responsible for displaying the components on the window and creating a connection to the database. This connection will be used by the DataPanel object to populate itself with data from the database.

After creating the ancestor Frame object, the constructor will create a connection to the database using the JavaSoft JDBC-Bridge Driver. The following lines of code will load the Driver object into memory and register it with the DriverManager object:

```
String driverName = "sun.jdbc.odbc.JdbcOdbcDriver";
Class.forName(driverName);
```

After the Driver object has been loaded using the Class object, you can use the DriverManager object to get a connection to the database using the getConnection() method. Pass a URL to the database as well as the username and password to connect to the database. The following line of code will create a connection to the database specified by the URL jdbc:odbc:JDBC:

```
c = DriverManager.getConnection("jdbc:odbc:JDBC", "dba", "sql");
```

After you have the connection to the database, use the created Connection object to pass to the DataPanel object that you will create. Pass a string that contains the name of the table from which you will display items.

```
String sql = "tEmployee");
this.add("North", data);
```

The constructor also will add several Button objects that will be used to demo the component. Create buttons to test the first(), last(), next(), and previous() methods. The buttons will be added to a Panel object that will, in turn, be added to the frame. When all of the components have been added to the frame, resize the frame and show it to the user.

The application also will use the handleEvent() method to handle button clicks by the user. The method will handle each of the four buttons that were added to the frame. When the user clicks each button, the appropriate method will be called for the DataPanel component.

Listing 14.6 contains the full code for the DataExample application.

TYPE   **Listing 14.6. The DataExample application.**

```
import java.awt.*;
import java.util.*;
import java.sql.*;

public class DataExample extends Frame {
    Connection c;
        DataPanel data;

    public DataExample () {
        super();

        // Make a connection to the database
        try {
                String driverName = "sun.jdbc.odbc.JdbcOdbcDriver";
                Class.forName(driverName);
                c = DriverManager.getConnection("jdbc:odbc:JDBC", "dba", "sql");

                        // Create the DataPanel component
                // You want to pass the connection object,
                // the SQL statement, and have it retrieve
                        String sql = "tEmployee";
                        data = new DataPanel(c, sql);
```

continues

14

Listing 14.6. continued

```
            // Add the component to the window
            this.add("North", data);
        }
        catch (SQLException e) {}
               catch (Exception e) {}

        // Create and add the panel and buttons
        Panel p = new Panel();
        p.setLayout(new FlowLayout());
        p.add(new Button("First"));
        p.add(new Button("Previous"));
        p.add(new Button("Next"));
        p.add(new Button("Last"));
        this.add("South", p);

        this.resize(300, 300);
        this.show();
    }

    public boolean handleEvent (Event evt) {
        if ("First".equals(evt.arg)) {
            data.first();
        }
        if ("Previous".equals(evt.arg)) {
            data.previous();
        }
        if ("Next".equals(evt.arg)) {
            data.next();
        }
        if ("Last".equals(evt.arg)) {
            data.last();
        }
        repaint();
        return super.handleEvent(evt);
    }

    public static void main (String args[]) {
        DataExample app = new DataExample();
    }
}
```

Figure 14.1 displays the window created by the DataExample application. Notice that the panel contains all columns from the table and the column names are all listed, describing each data value to the user.

Figure 14.1.

*A sample record
displayed using the
DataPanel
component.*

Summary

Today's lesson has finished up the data components that you started back on Day 9, "The Data Interfaces." I hope this lesson has introduced some new ideas on how to create useful data components. Unlike the other data components, the DataPanel component displays multiple data values. You can change the component to allow the user to edit the data values for every column. This opens up many possibilities for using data components in your applications.

The components that you have created in this book are fully working components, but they are not complete components. The components lack some of the error checking that you should include in real-world components. By adding some additional features and checking for the components, you could easily make them into production components to use in your applications.

Workshop

The Workshop provides quiz questions to help you solidify your understanding of the material covered and exercises to give you experience in using what you've learned. The answers are provided in Appendix A, "Quiz and Exercise Answers." Try to understand the quiz and exercise answers before you go on to tomorrow's lesson.

14

Quiz

1. How is the DataPanel component different from the other components?
2. What method enables you to get the number of records that are in the result set?
3. What is displayed in the description labels on the panel?
4. What does the `retrieve()` method do differently than the other components?
5. What layout does the component use to display the `Label` objects?

Exercises

1. Change the component so that the data labels can be edited. (Note that you will need to make the objects into text fields.)
2. Create a method `setVisible(int, boolean)` that will enable you to determine whether or not certain columns are displayed.

WEEK 2

In Review

The second week introduced you to the idea and the how-to of creating components that can use JDBC to provide easier and more functional access to the data in your databases. The components not only provide information in a more user-friendly way, but also provide the user with more functionality than the standard JDBC components.

WEEK 3

At a Glance

In the final week of this book, you will actually create two applications that will use JDBC. The first application is a knowledge base application that will be built much like a client/server application. The second application will use Java serialization to build an object server that will serve objects to client applications.

On Day 15, "Creating the Knowledge Base Application GUI," you begin the creation of a sample application that accesses the database using JDBC.

On Day 16, "Handling Events in the Knowledge Base," you continue with the Knowledge Base application you begin on Day 15.

On Day 17, "Using the Database in the Knowledge Base," you finish the Knowledge Base application you began on Day 15.

On Day 18, "Creating an Employee Resource Applet," you are introduced to some of the new features available on the Java 1.1 release of the Java Development Kit (JDK).

On Day 19, "Handling Events in the Employee Resource Applet," you begin the construction of a multi-tier application using JDBC.

On Day 20, "Creating the Employee Resource Application Server," you finish the creation of the application you began on Day 19.

On Day 21, "JDBC and the Future," you learn some new topics and learn what the future holds for Java and JDBC.

Day **15**

Creating the Knowledge Base Application GUI

Today, you will create the basis for an application that will enable you to store articles and tips for use by you and others. The application will introduce you to some of the real-world uses of JDBC. It will also give you a chance to work on a real application that uses JDBC. Sometimes, the best experience is use, so today you will use JDBC as much as possible. In the next three days you will build the basics of the application, handle events within the application, and connect the application to the database.

Today's lesson focuses mainly on creating the main window that you will use throughout the rest of the application. You also learn how to create the splash window that the window will use. Today, you learn about the following topics:

- ☐ Basics of the main window
- ☐ Creating the constructor for the window

☐ Creating objects within the main window
☐ Handling events within the main window
☐ Creating the splash screen for the application

Basics of the Main Window

The purpose of the main window will be to provide a short display description of each article and to enable the user to choose an option from a menu. You will give the user options for adding articles, viewing articles, deleting articles, and searching the database for articles that have specified keywords.

The main window will be an object inherited from the Frame class and will contain a list box to display the titles of all the articles within the database. The list box will be populated when the application is created, with the current titles contained within the database. The article titles displayed in the list box will be re-retrieved whenever the user deletes an article, adds an article, or searches for specified articles.

Name the window class jdbc. To provide all of the functionality needed for the application, you will need to import the following packages:

☐ `import java.awt.*;`
☐ `import symjava.sql.*;`
☐ `import java.io.*;`
☐ `import java.util.*;`

For the JDBC class, declare six object variables. These variables will be used throughout the window to access the database and also to display database results. Store the following object variables:

☐ `Driver driver`
☐ `Connection connection`
☐ `Properties p`
☐ `List articles`
☐ `Label knowledgeBase`
☐ `Splash splash`

The Driver variable will store the Driver instance that you create to the database. The Driver variable will enable you to create Connection objects. The Connection object will be your literal connection to the database. You will use this connection to the database to create and execute SQL statements to retrieve results, and also to execute updates against the database.

15

This `Connection` object will be passed to each of the windows that accesses the database. You will use the `Properties` object to make a connection to the database. The object will store the username and password that you are connecting with.

You can make as many connections to the database as you want, but remember that each connection is usually counted as a user by the database. A database that allows 25 users or connections will allow only a few applications to run at once if each application creates several connections to the database.

The `List` variable will be the list box that will contain the titles of all the articles that you will display to the user.

Because this is the main window of the application and will be displayed first, you will need to provide a `main()` method for this class that will create the class for use by the user. The following code will be called when the class is loaded by the Java Virtual Machine and will create the application to be used by the user:

```
public static void main (String args[]) {
    jdbc app = new jdbc();
}
```

Creating the Constructor for the Window

The constructor method for the window will be responsible for creating the basic frame window and creating the components for the window. The constructor also will create and display the splash window to the user while the application is loading and connecting to the database. The splash window diverts attention away from the wait the application is causing the user. This can provide a pseudo speed improvement, because the user thinks that the application is doing something when the splash window displays.

The constructor method also will be responsible for creating and displaying the menu that the application will use. The menu used for the application will contain the options that you will allow the user to choose from. To create the menu, call a method that will handle the creation of the menu for the constructor. This will give you more flexibility in creating the menu because it will make it easier to change.

The constructor will initially call the ancestor constructor method to initialize and create the application. Pass a title to the frame displaying the name of the application. The following line creates the frame window that you are using and gives it the specified title:

```
super("Knowledge Base");
```

After you have created the base application window, you need to create and display the splash window. As mentioned earlier, the splash window notifies the user that the application is working, so he doesn't think that the application is broken while he waits for the main window to come up. Create the splash window, which will automatically display itself:

```
splash = new Splash();
```

Now that you have given the user something to look at, you can begin to set up and create the components for the main window. You first need to create a `Panel` object to display objects within the window. Create a panel and set the layout for the `Panel` object to be FlowLayout. FlowLayout enables you to place items side by side.

```
Panel top = new Panel();
top.setLayout(new FlowLayout(FlowLayout.CENTER));
```

Using this `Panel` object, place a label that indicates what you are displaying to the user. The label should contain the text `Knowledge Base Articles` to indicate to the user that the articles in the list box are representative of the articles contained in the database. Also, set the font for the label to be fairly large, so that it will be clear to the user. After you have created the label, add the label to the `Panel` object you created, and then add the `Panel` object to the frame window, placing it in the top of the frame:

```
knowledgeBase = new Label("Knowledge Base Articles");
 knowledgeBase.setFont(new Font("TimesRoman",Font.PLAIN,24));
 top.add(knowledgeBase);
 this.add("North", top);
```

Next, create the list box that will be used to display the articles that you will get from the database. The list box should be able to display 20 items and should not allow multiple selection. Then add the list box to the bottom of the frame window, using the South position:

```
articles = new List(20, false);
this.add("South", articles);
```

You have finished placing the components on the frame, so now populate those components with data, and call the method to create the menu for the application. First, call the `dbConnect()` method to connect the application to the database. After you have connected to the database, call the `getArticles()` method to populate the list box you just added to the frame window with the articles' titles you retrieve from the database. When the data has been populated into the list box, call `buildMenu()` to create the menu that will be displayed for the frame window. You are building the menu in a method so that you can make any changes to the menu without altering the constructor method.

When you have created all components and inserted data into the list box, you need to close the splash screen that you displayed to the user. When the splash window is closed, you can display the window after resizing it to 300×400 pixels.

The full code for the constructor method is shown in Listing 15.1.

Listing 15.1. The constructor method for the JDBC class.

```
public jdbc ()
{
        // Call ancestor function to set title
        super("Knowledge Base");
        // Open the Splash screen
        splash = new Splash();
        Panel top = new Panel();
        top.setLayout(new FlowLayout(FlowLayout.CENTER));
        knowledgeBase = new Label("Knowledge Base Articles");
        knowledgeBase.setFont(new Font("TimesRoman",Font.PLAIN,24));
        top.add(knowledgeBase);
        this.add("North", top);
        articles = new List(20, false);
        this.add("South", articles);
        // Call function to connect to database
        dbConnect();
        // Call function to populate list
        getArticles();
        // Call function to build menu structure
        buildMenu();
        // Close the splash screen
        splash.hide();
        app.resize(300, 400);
        app.show();
}
```

Creating Objects Within the Main Window

In the preceding constructor method, you used three methods that created a connection, populated the list box for the application, and created the menu to use for the application. You separated functionality into these methods because these methods could possibly require changes in the future. By placing the business logic for the application in these methods, you can change the logic used for the application without changing any of the basics for the application.

dbConnect()

The first method referred to by the constructor method was the dbConnect() method. This is the method that creates the Connection object that will be used throughout all windows in the application to execute SQL statements and get results from the database.

The basic functionality this method provides is to create a connection to the database that can be used throughout the application. You first will want to create the database URL that points to the database that you are using. The syntax to create the URL to use for the database is as follows:

```
String url = "jdbc:dbaw://localhost:8889/WATCOM/JDBC/JDBC";
```

To connect to the database, you also need to create a Properties object and assign it your username and password to use when the application connects to the database. As with most SQL Anywhere databases, the standard username and password are DBA and SQL, respectively.

```
P = new Properties();
p.put("user", "dba");
p.put("password", "sql");
```

Now that you have all the information to connect to the database, create a Driver object, and then use that Driver object to make a connection to the database.

```
String driverName = "symantec.itools.db.jdbc.Driver";
driver = (Driver)Class.forName(driverName).newInstance();
connection = driver.connect(url, p);
```

Because you must put these statements in a try.. block, you need to catch the exception that is thrown by the preceding statements. The statements must be placed in a try..block method, because most of the methods throw exceptions that must be caught. Output the message provided by the Exception object if an exception occurs.

Listing 15.2 contains the full code listing for the dbConnect() method.

TYPE   **Listing 15.2. The dbConnect() method.**

```
public void dbConnect ()
{
        String url = "jdbc:dbaw://localhost:8889/Watcom/JDBC/JDBC";
        p = new Properties();
        p.put("user", "dba");
        p.put("password", "sql");
        // Connect to database
        try {
        String driverName = "symantec.itools.db.jdbc.Driver";
            driver = (Driver)Class.forName(driverName).newInstance();
            connection = driver.connect(url, p);
        }
```

15

```
        catch (Exception e) {
            System.out.println(e.getMessage());
        }
}
```

getArticles()

The second method referred to by the constructor method is the getArticles() method. This method is responsible for getting all of the article titles from the database and displaying them in the list box created for the window.

The first thing that the method will need to do is make sure that there are no items currently in the list box. Because this method can be called several times, you need to clear the articles currently in the list box before you start adding more items.

```
articles.clear();
```

After you have cleared the list box of all items currently in the list box, use a SQL Select statement to get all of the article titles currently in the database. The SQL statement should be as follows:

```
Select tArticle.Title from tArticle
```

After you have stored the SQL Select statement in a String object, create a Statement object using the connection made to the database in the dbConnect() method. Then, execute the SQL statement created previously to get all of the titles for articles currently in the database. The code to create the statement and execute the SQL Select statement is as follows:

```
String sql;
sql = "Select tArticle.Title from tArticle";
sqlStatement = connection.createStatement();
result = sqlStatement.executeQuery(sql);
```

After you have retrieved the result set for the executed SQL statement, display all of the items in the list box. Call the next() method of the ResultSet object to get each of the records returned in the result set. Then, add the first column data value to the list box using the getString() method. Because the next() method returns true as long as a next record exists, use a while loop to continue until the next() method returns a false value.

```
while (result.next()) {
    articles.addItem(result.getString("Title"));
```

After you have retrieved all the results from the result set, close the Statement object so that it will not continue to keep the resources assigned to it. If you do not close the Statement object, then eventually you will not be able to get another handle to execute SQL statements. To close the Statement object, use the following code:

```
sqlStatement.close();
```

Listing 15.3 contains the full code for the getArticles() method.

TYPE **Listing 15.3. The getArticles() method.**

```
public void getArticles ()
{
        // Clear the list before inserting articles
        articles.clear();
        try {
            String sql;
            ResultSet result;
            Statement sqlStatement;
            // Get all of the article titles
            sql = "SELECT tArticle.Title FROM tArticle";
            sqlStatement = connection.createStatement();
            result = sqlStatement.executeQuery(sql);
            while (result.next()) {
                articles.addItem(result.getString("Title"));
            }
            sqlStatement.close();
            // Change text on label
            knowledgeBase.setText("Knowledge Base Articles");
        }
        catch (SQLException e) {
            System.out.println(e.getMessage());
        }
}
```

buildMenu()

The buildMenu() method is responsible for creating all of the menu items from which the user will be able to choose. The menu will contain three main menu options for the user to choose from. The File menu option will enable the user to exit the application. When the user clicks the Exit menu item, the application will close.

The menu will also provide the user with an Article menu option. This menu option will offer the user the ability to add, delete, view, and search the articles in the database. Also, add an option that will enable the user to display all of the articles after she views a selection of articles based on the keyword she entered.

The final menu option will be the Help menu option. It will have one menu item under it that will enable the user to view the About box for the application. The About box displays some basic information about the application. Listing 15.4 contains the code for the `buildMenu()` method.

TYPE **Listing 15.4. The `buildMenu()` method.**

```
void buildMenu ()
{
        MenuBar menubar = new MenuBar();
        // Create the file menu with Exit menu item
        Menu file = new Menu("File");
        file.add(new MenuItem("Exit"));
        menubar.add(file);
        // Create the article menu with
        // Add Article
        // Delete Article
        // View Article
        // and Search Articles
        Menu article = new Menu("Article");
        article.add(new MenuItem("Add Article"));
        article.add(new MenuItem("Delete Article"));
        article.add(new MenuItem("View Article"));
        article.addSeparator();
        article.add(new MenuItem("Search Articles"));
        article.add(new MenuItem("Display all Articles"));
        menubar.add(article);
        // Create help menu with About item
        Menu help = new Menu("Help");
        help.add(new MenuItem("About Knowledge Base"));
        menubar.setHelpMenu(help);
        // Add menu bar to current window
        this.setMenuBar(menubar);
}
```

Handling Events in the Main Window

Now that you have created all of the objects for the window and have populated the list box with data from the database, you need to handle the events generated by the user's actions. Handle all of the actions generated when the user chooses a menu item, and also handle the action when the user double-clicks an article in the list box. When the user double-clicks an article in the list box, assume that he wants to view the full article listing, and call the method to open the window to display the full article.

Each of the menu items should call a method that opens the specific window that each menu option identifies. The Exit menu option will be the only exception, in that it will dispose of the window and then call the `exit()` method to exit the application.

To handle the events, use the Java 1.02 event model and use the `handleEvent()` method to handle all of the event actions. You first want to check the `id` field of the `Event` object. All menu items will generate an `ACTION_EVENT`. You also need to check the `arg` variable of the `Event` object against the actual text of the menu item chosen by the user.

Table 15.1 lists the menu items in the application and the corresponding method that the menu will call when the user chooses it.

Table 15.1. The menu options.

Menu Item	Method Called
Add Article	`addArticle()`
Delete Article	`deleteArticle()`
View Article	`viewArticle()`
Search Articles	`searchArticles()`
About	`displayAbout()`
Display All Articles	`getArticles()`

Also, you must handle the action event generated when the user double-clicks the list box. When the user double-clicks the list box, call the `viewArticle()` method to display the currently selected article.

After all events have been handled, call the ancestor `handleEvent()` method to handle any other system events that need to be handled.

Listing 15.5 contains the full code for the `handleEvent()` method.

TYPE   **Listing 15.5. The `handleEvent()` method.**

```
// Override handleEvent to handle events for the window
   public boolean handleEvent (Event evt)
   {
       // perform different processing based on event id
       switch(evt.id) {
           // Perform processing for action events
           case Event.ACTION_EVENT:
               // Check to see if the item was a menu item
               if (evt.target instanceof MenuItem) {
                   // Perform different processing for each menu item
                   if ("Exit".equals(evt.arg)) {
                       // Hide window
```

```
                    this.dispose();
                    System.exit(0);
                    return true;
                }
                else if ("Add Article".equals(evt.arg)) {
                    // Call function to handle adding an article
                    addArticle();
                    break;
                }
                else if ("Delete Article".equals(evt.arg)) {
                    // Call function to handle deleting an article
                    deleteArticle();
                    break;
                }
                else if ("View Article".equals(evt.arg)) {
                    // Call function to view the current article
                    viewArticle();
                    break;
                }
                else if ("Search Articles".equals(evt.arg)) {
                    // Call function to search articles
                    searchArticles();
                    break;
                }
                else if ("About Knowledge Base".equals(evt.arg)) {
                    // Call function to display about box
                    displayAbout();
                    break;
                }
                else if ("Display all Articles".equals(evt.arg)) {
                    getArticles();
                    break;
                }
            }
            else if (evt.target == articles) {
                // Call function to display article
                viewArticle();
                break;
            }
            break;
        }
        // Call the ancestor function to process any other items
        return super.handleEvent(evt);
    }
```

addArticle()

The addArticle() method is called when the user chooses the Add Article menu option. This method opens the addArticleDialog window, which enables the user to enter information for a new article.

Before you open the Add Article window, you must give the user a signal that the application is performing some action. There will be a short wait time between when the user clicks the Add Article menu option and when the actual window is displayed. To let the user know that her menu choice was selected, display the cursor that identifies to the user that the system is busy. The WAIT_CURSOR is a default cursor defined in the Frame object. The Frame object provides many different types of cursors that you can use to inform the user of the current state of the application through the mouse cursor. Use the setCursor() method of the Frame object to set the cursor to the one that will inform the user that the application is currently processing. The following line of code will change the current cursor for the frame to the WAIT_CURSOR, which is usually an hourglass:

```
this.setCursor(Frame.WAIT_CURSOR);
```

After you have changed the cursor for the application to inform the user that you are processing, you can begin to open the window for her to add an article in. The name of the class that enables this is called addArticleDialog. The constructor of the addArticleDialog dialog box takes a Connection object and a Frame object. You pass these two objects so that the dialog box will be able to use the same connection to the database that the frame uses, as well as to have access to some of the variables and methods contained in the parent window. The constructor for the dialog box should be called as follows:

```
addArticleDialog dialog = new addArticleDialog(connection, this);
```

Now that you have created the dialog box in which the user can enter article information, you need to size the dialog box to the required size and show it to the user. The following two lines of code will resize the window to 600×400 pixels and then show the window to the user:

```
dialog.resize(600, 400);
dialog.show();
```

After you have shown the dialog box to the user, you need to change the cursor back to the default cursor for the application. The following code will change the cursor from its current value to the default cursor used throughout the application:

```
this.setCursor(Frame.DEFAULT_CURSOR);
```

Listing 15.6 contains the full code for the addArticle() method.

TYPE **Listing 15.6. The addArticle() method.**

```
void addArticle ()
{
        this.setCursor(Frame.WAIT_CURSOR);
        // Display add article dialog
        addArticleDialog dialog = new addArticleDialog(connection, this);
```

15

15

```
        dialog.resize(600, 400);
        dialog.show();
        this.setCursor(Frame.DEFAULT_CURSOR);
}
```

deleteArticle()

The deleteArticle() method is called when the user chooses the Delete Article menu option. This method is responsible for opening the dialog box that will ask the user if he wants to delete the item currently selected in the list box of articles.

The first action the method will have to take is to get the item currently selected in the article list box. To get the item that is currently selected, use the getSelectedItem() method of the List object. This will return the item selected as a String object, or a NULL value if no item is currently selected. The code for getting the current article is as follows:

```
String item;
item = articles.getSelectedItem();
```

After the user selects the item, you need to check the value of the item to determine whether a valid item was actually selected. If the value for the item you got previously is NULL, then the user has not selected an article, and you don't want to try to delete anything. Perform an if statement to compare the value to NULL, as follows:

```
if (item == null) {
    return;
}
```

When you have determined that a valid item is selected, you can begin the process of deleting the item. You first want to set the cursor for the application to a wait cursor. This will indicate to the user that his action is being processed. When you have changed the cursor, create the deleteArticleDialog window. This window will ask the user whether he actually wants to delete the selected item. The constructor for the dialog box will take the Connection object for the frame, the selected item, and a reference to the frame itself. After you have created the dialog box, show the dialog box to the user. The following code will create the Delete Article dialog box and show it to the user:

```
deleteArticleDialog dialog = new deleteArticleDialog(connection, item, this);
dialog.show();
```

After you have created and shown the dialog box, you need to reset the cursor for the application back to the default cursor, indicating to the user that processing is completed. Listing 15.7 contains the full code for the deleteArticle() method.

| TYPE | **Listing 15.7. The `deleteArticle()` method.** |

```
void deleteArticle ()
{
        String item;
        // get the currently selected item
        item = articles.getSelectedItem();
        // Check for an invalid item
        if (item == null) {
            // don't do anything
            return;
        }
        this.setCursor(Frame.WAIT_CURSOR);
        // Create dialog to determine if user wants to delete item
        deleteArticleDialog dialog =
        ➥new deleteArticleDialog(connection, item, this);
        dialog.show();
        this.setCursor(Frame.DEFAULT_CURSOR);
}
```

---

viewArticle()

The `viewArticle()` method of the main window is called by the View Article menu option, as well as when the user double-clicks an article within the list box. This window is responsible for getting the selected item and also for opening a window that displays the information to the user.

The method initially must get the selected item within the list box. If the user has not selected any item in the list box to view, then the method will return and not perform any processing. The following code segment will get the item currently selected in the list box and exit if there is no selected item:

```
String item;
item = articles.getSelectedItem();
if (item == null) {
    return;
}
```

If the user has selected an item to view, the method will create the displayArticle window, which displays the contents of the selected article from the database. The constructor for the `displayArticle` object will take the `Connection` object for the main window, the currently selected item, and a reference to the frame window itself. The following code will create the `displayArticle` window. After it is created, the method will *pack* the window. Packing the window makes the window as small as possible but still shows all of the components. When the window has been packed, it will be shown to the user.

15

```
displayArticle dialog = new displayArticle(connection, item, this);
dialog.pack();
dialog.show():
```

The full code for the `viewArticle()` method is shown in Listing 15.8.

TYPE **Listing 15.8. The `viewArticle()` method.**

```
void viewArticle ()
{
        String item;
        // Get the currently selected item
        item = articles.getSelectedItem();
        // Check for an invalid item
        if (item == null) {
            // don't do anything
            return;
        }
        this.setCursor(Frame.WAIT_CURSOR);
        // Display window to display info for selected item
        // Pass the currently selected item and the connection
        // object
        displayArticle dialog = new displayArticle(connection,item,this);
        dialog.pack();
        dialog.show();
        this.setCursor(Frame.DEFAULT_CURSOR);
}
```

searchArticles()

The `searchArticles()` method is called when the user chooses the Search Articles menu option. The only functionality this method performs is to create the window object `searchArticles` and display it to the user. The constructor for the window will take the `Connection` object being used for the main window and a reference to the main window. Listing 15.9 contains the code for the `searchArticles()` method.

TYPE **Listing 15.9. The `searchArticles()` method.**

```
void searchArticles ()
{
        // Add processing to enable list to display only items
        // that are processed using a search
        // Open dialog to enable user to enter keyword to search for
        searchArticles dialog = new searchArticles(connection, this);
        dialog.show();
}
```

displayAbout()

The displayAbout() method is very similar to the searchArticles() method in that it is responsible only for creating and displaying another window. The displayAbout() method is called when the user clicks the About menu option. When you create the About dialog box, resize it to be 350×350, and then call the show() method to display it to the user. Listing 15.10 contains the code for the displayAbout() method.

TYPE   **Listing 15.10. The displayAbout() method.**

```
void displayAbout ()
{
        // Add processing to display an about box
        aboutDialog dialog =
        ➡new aboutDialog(this, "About Knowledge Base", true);
        dialog.resize(350, 350);
        dialog.show();
}
```

displaySearchArticles()

The final method defined in the main window is the displaySearchArticles() method, which is called by the searchArticleDialog window. The method takes a passed string containing a specified keyword, and then displays only items with that keyword in the list box for the main window. The method also changes the label displayed over the list box to indicate that the articles listed are the result of a search. The user will be able to switch back to the complete listing by choosing the menu option to do so.

The method initially should create a Statement object from the Connection object being used by the main window. The Statement object is used to execute the SQL query that will return the articles that match the specified keyword passed to the method. The following line of code creates the Statement object that is used to execute the SQL query:

```
sqlStatement = connection.createStatement();
```

After you have created the Statement object, you need to create a SQL Select statement that will return the articles that match the keyword specified in the passed String object. Create a SQL Select statement using a String object and insert the passed keyword into the String object to be used to retrieve articles that match the specified keyword. The SQL Select statement to be used is coded as follows:

```
sql = "select tArticle.Title " +
    "from tArticle, tKeyword " +
    "where tKeyword.Keyword = '" + keyword + "' " +
    "and tKeyword.ArticleId = tArticle.ArticleId";
```

15

After you have created a SQL `Select` statement that will return the articles matching the specified keyword, you can execute the statement and get the results back into a `ResultSet` object. You can execute the SQL query by calling the `executeQuery()` method of the `Statement` object as follows:

```
results = sqlStatement.executeQuery(sql);
```

Before you can begin adding items to the list box, you need to ensure that all old articles are removed from the list box so that you do not have duplicate articles in the list box. Call the `clear()` method for the `List` object to clear all of the old articles from the list box before you add the new articles.

Use a `while` loop to loop through every record returned into the `ResultSet` object. For every record, add the data contained in the `Title` column as an item for the list box. The following code demonstrates how to loop through the result set and get each value in turn:

```
while (results.next()) {
    articles.addItem(results.getString("Title"));
}
```

After you have populated the list box with all of the articles retrieved into the result set, change the text of the label above the list box to indicate that the articles displayed are articles returned from a search based on a specific keyword. Listing 15.11 contains the full code listing for the `displaySearchArticles()` method.

TYPE **Listing 15.11. The `displaySearchArticles()` method.**

```
public void displaySearchArticles (String keyword)
{
        Statement sqlStatement;
        String sql = "";
        ResultSet results;
        try {
            // create a statement
            sqlStatement = connection.createStatement();
            // build the SQL string
            sql = "select tArticle.Title " +
                "from tArticle, tKeyword " +
                "where tKeyword.Keyword = '" + keyword + "' " +
                "and tKeyword.ArticleId = tArticle.ArticleId";
            // execute the sql query
            results = sqlStatement.executeQuery(sql);
            // Clear the list box
            articles.clear();
            // cycle through the articles and add them to the list box
            while (results.next()) {
                articles.addItem(results.getString("Title"));
            }
            // Close the statement
            sqlStatement.close();
```

continues

Listing 15.11. continued

```
            // Change the text of the label
            knowledgeBase.setText("      Search Articles      ");
        }
        catch (SQLException e) {
            System.out.println(e.getMessage());
        }
    }
}
```

You have now created the first window of the Knowledge Base application. This window is the basis for all of the other windows that you will create. This window is responsible for handling the user's choice of specific actions. It also gives the user a way to add, delete, view, and search the articles contained in your database. Figure 15.1 displays the main window.

Figure 15.1.

The Knowledge Base main window.

Creating the Splash Screen

To trick the user into believing that the application is actually opening faster than it really is, display a splash screen. This screen will be displayed while the main window creates a connection to the database and lays out the components to be displayed.

Displaying the splash window takes more time than not displaying it, but it gives the user the impression that the application is running. This prevents the user from thinking that the application did not respond because nothing happened immediately.

The splash screen used in this example uses the logo for my company, but you can replace it with the logo for your company or any other graphic that you want.

The constructor for the splash screen is responsible for getting the image from the Internet and then displaying the window. You first need to get the current toolkit for the window, using the following code:

```
Toolkit t = this.getToolkit();
```

The Toolkit object provides you with various methods for getting images to be displayed. Next, use the getImage() method for the Toolkit object to store the image to be displayed in the splash screen:

```
Image img = t.getImage("http://www.stepinc.com/images/step.gif");
```

The only other code needed for the splash screen is in the paint() method. This method displays the text and graphics on the screen. You initially draw the image using the drawImage() method:

```
g.drawImage(img, 29, 1, this);
```

After you have drawn the image, draw various lines of text, using the drawString() method. When the paint() method is completed, the splash screen will be shown to the user and the main window will continue processing. Listing 15.12 contains the code for the Splash class.

TYPE **Listing 15.12. The Splash class.**

```
import java.awt.*;
import java.net.*;
import java.util.*;
public class Splash extends Frame {
    Image img;
    Toolkit t;
    public Splash () {
        super("Knowledge Base");
        t = this.getToolkit();
        try {
            URL url = new URL("http://www.stepinc.com/images/step.gif");
            img = t.getImage(url);
        }
        catch (Exception e) {}
        this.resize(315, 300);
        this.show();
    }
    public void paint (Graphics g) {
        g.drawImage(img, 29,1, this);
        Font f = new Font("Times New Roman", Font.BOLD, 36);
        g.setFont(f);
        g.drawString("STEP Knowledge Base", 1, 125);
        Font h = new Font("Times New Roman", Font.PLAIN, 18);
        g.setFont(h);
        g.drawString("STEP Consulting 1996", 45, 150);
    }
}
```

Figure 15.2 displays the splash screen as it appears to the user.

Figure 15.2.

The splash screen.

Summary

In today's lesson, you have created the basis for the Knowledge Base application. You created the main window that the user will need to add articles, delete articles, and view articles. You also created a splash screen that can be used to display a response to the user that the application is working.

Workshop

The Workshop provides quiz questions to help you solidify your understanding of the material covered and exercises to give you experience in using what you've learned. The answers are provided in Appendix A, "Quiz and Exercise Answers." Try to understand the quiz and exercise answers before you go on to tomorrow's lesson.

Quiz

1. Why are you using the same `Connection` object for all windows?
2. What does the `dbConnect()` method do?
3. Why do you clear all articles before adding new items in the `getArticles()` method?
4. Why is it important to always close the `Statement` object after you use it?
5. What event handles all of the user's actions on the window?
6. Why do you change the cursor before displaying a new window?
7. What is the purpose of the `displaySearchArticles()` method?

15

8. Why do you use a splash screen?

9. What method gets the current `Toolkit` object for the component?

10. What method draws an image on the component?

Exercises

1. Change the image and text displayed on the splash screen to reflect your own information.

2. Add a Help menu option to the main window's menu.

Day 16

Handling Events in the Knowledge Base

On Day 15, "Creating the Knowledge Base Application GUI," you created the main window and the splash screen for the application. Today, you will create the About dialog box, as well as the window to add articles to the database. The About dialog box is a very simple window, but the window to add items to the database includes more complex logic.

Today's lesson hopefully will expand your insight into how JDBC applications are created and give you some ideas on how to create your own applications. The two windows concentrate more on using JDBC and business logic than on displaying items in a particular fashion. In your own applications, you can spend more time ensuring that the GUI for your application is more friendly. The topics that are covered today include the following:

- ☐ Creating the About dialog box
- ☐ Creating the Add Article dialog box
- ☐ Constructing the Add Article dialog box
- ☐ Handling events in the Add Article dialog box

Creating the About Dialog Box

The About dialog box is used to display information about the application. You can place any type of information or graphic you want in the About box. Most applications generally describe the company and the author of the application in this box.

The aboutDialog class needs to import the AWT package to provide all of the classes used in the class. You will declare the dialog box to be inherited from the Dialog object. You will also use the constructor for the object, which enables you to make the dialog box a modal dialog box.

The constructor for the aboutDialog class needs to call the ancestor method to create the window and specify some initial values for the dialog box. The following method call creates the dialog box and assigns it the main window as a parent window, gives it the title specified in the constructor method, and passes the Boolean value passed in the modal parameter:

```
super(parent, title, modal);
```

Set the layout for the dialog box to be GridLayout, which lets you place items in the dialog box in a grid format. Also, set the layout so that it contains four rows and one column:

```
this.setLayout(new GridLayout(4,1));
```

After you have set the proper layout for the dialog box, you can place items on the dialog box. Place three Label objects on the dialog box to display information. The three Label objects display the name of the application, the company name, and the developer's name. The following lines of code create the Label objects and place them on the dialog box:

```
this.add(new Label("Java Knowledge Base", Label.CENTER));
this.add(new Label("STEP Consulting 1996", Label.CENTER));
this.add(new Label("Ashton Hobbs", Label.CENTER));
```

For the final row in the layout, add a Panel object on which you can place a button. Create the Panel object and set the layout to be FlowLayout. Then, add the Button object so that it appears in the middle of the panel.

```
Panel p = new Panel();
p.setLayout(new FlowLayout(FlowLayout.CENTER));
close = new Button("Close");
p.add(close);
this.add(p);
```

The full code listing for the constructor method is shown in Listing 16.1.

16

TYPE **Listing 16.1. The `aboutDialog()` constructor method.**

```
public aboutDialog (Frame parent, String title, boolean modal)
{
        super(parent, title, modal);
        this.setLayout(new GridLayout(4,1));
        this.add(new Label("Java Knowledge Base", Label.CENTER));
        this.add(new Label("STEP Consulting 1996", Label.CENTER));
        this.add(new Label("Ashton Hobbs", Label.CENTER));
        Panel p = new Panel();
        p.setLayout(new FlowLayout(FlowLayout.CENTER));
        close = new Button("Close");
        p.add(close);
        this.add(p);
}
```

handleEvent()

The `handleEvent()` method for the About dialog window handles when the user clicks the Close button. The method checks to see whether an `ACTION_EVENT` type occurred and, if so, closes the window. When the window has been hidden using the `hide()` method, it is disposed of with the `dispose()` method. This method releases the memory resources used for the About dialog box. Listing 16.2 contains the code for the `handleEvent()` method.

TYPE **Listing 16.2. The `handleEvent()` method.**

```
public boolean handleEvent (Event evt)
{
        if ((evt.id == Event.ACTION_EVENT) && (evt.target == close)) {
            this.hide();
            this.dispose();
            return true;
        }
        return super.handleEvent(evt);
}
```

Figure 16.1 shows the About dialog box you just created.

Figure 16.1.

The About dialog box.

The Add Article Dialog Box

The Add Article dialog box that you'll create will let the user add an article to the database. The window enables the user to specify the title for the knowledge base article, the keywords that identify the article, the author of the article, the application that the article identifies with, and the actual article text.

The window is broken up into many different panels for displaying information correctly. Because you are not using the GridBagLayout, you need to create the different panels in which to place objects. The GridBagLayout in Java is one of the more advanced layout managers for placing GUI components. The GridBagLayout enables you to place items in a grid, but provides different weights for the components. These panels will contain different layouts to use for placing the components exactly as needed.

The `addArticleDialog` class, which will extend the `Dialog` object, needs to import some of the standard Java packages to provide all of the objects needed throughout the dialog box. The following `import` statements are required to ensure that all needed objects are available for use in the dialog box:

```
import java.awt.*;
import java.util.*;
import java.lang.*;
import symjava.sql.*;
```

NOTE

When Java 1.1 JDK and Symantec release the version of dbAnywhere with the standard Java package name, you will no longer use the `symjava.sql.*` objects (they will be renamed `java.sql.*`).

The dialog box declares some object variables that are used throughout the dialog box. The remainder of this section details the object variables that will be created for the dialog.

The dialog box will declare an object variable of type `Connection` in which to store the `Connection` object passed from the main window. This `Connection` object contains the connection to the database that is used within the dialog box by various methods. The dialog box uses the `Connection` object from the main window, so that it is not required to create its own connection to the database. The following is the declaration for the `Connection` object that is used for the dialog box:

```
Connection connection;
```

Along with the connection, which is obtained from the main window, the dialog box will also declare an object variable that stores a reference to the main window. This variable is used to access methods contained in the main window. The declaration is as follows:

```
JDBC parent;
```

The dialog box also will declare various objects to use to display choices to the user, as well as objects enabling the user to enter information for various items. The dialog box contains a `Choice` object that shows the user a listing of all applications with which the article can be associated. The dialog box also declares another `Choice` object that contains all of the available authors who are also employees who can be associated with the article. Here are the declarations for both objects:

```
Choice resources;
Choice author;
```

The dialog box also uses two `TextField` objects. The first `TextField` object enables the user to enter the title for the article, which is the text that is displayed from the main window. The title should be descriptive of the article's contents. The second `TextField` object allows the user to enter a list of keywords with which the article should be associated. These keywords are used when the user searches for articles within the database.

```
TextField title;
TextField keywords;
```

The final user-editable object is a `TextArea` object that enables the user to enter the article text. The text area is placed at the bottom of the field listing. This example uses a `TextArea` object instead of a `TextField` object to give the user more room to enter an article for the Knowledge Base application.

```
TextArea article;
```

Along with objects that let the user enter data, also create two buttons that give the user choices for saving newly entered data or canceling the added information and returning to the main window.

```
Button addbutton;
Button cancel;
```

The dialog box should also declare two arrays of String objects to be used throughout the dialog box. The first array stores the resource IDs for all of the applications that can be associated with an article. Because the resource ID will be useless to the user, display the description of the resource, or application, and then store the resource ID to be used when the application saves the data. The second array of String objects contains the social security numbers for every employee displayed in the Choice object named author. Because choosing employees by their social security numbers would be very user-unfriendly, display the users' names and store their social security numbers for use when the application saves the article.

```
String resourceid[];
String ssn[];
```

Constructing the Add Article Dialog Box

The constructor for the addArticleDialog class is responsible for displaying all of the objects employed by the user to enter article information, as well as populating the list of resources and employees that the dialog box allows the user to select from.

The first action that the constructor method needs to perform is to call the ancestor constructor method to create the actual dialog box window. Create a dialog box that is modal, so that the user will be forced to finish processing on this window before going back to the main window. The ancestor constructor method is called as follows:

```
super(parentWin, "Add Knowledge Base Article", true);
```

After you have called the ancestor constructor method, you need to assign the passed frame object to the object variable parent. Use the methods from the main window later in the application using this object variable. The variable assignment is performed as follows. (Notice that the assigned parameter is declared to be of type JDBC. This is done so that the frame will be assigned as a JDBC object type).

```
parent = (JDBC)parentWin;
```

Next, assign the passed Connection object to the local object variable you declared. You are storing the connection passed from the main window to be used for the current window because it eliminates the need to create unnecessary connections to the database. The assignment for the Connection object is shown in the following line of code:

```
Connection = connectionObj;
```

To display the components on the dialog box correctly, initially create two Panel objects. One of the panels is in the top of the dialog box, and the other is in the bottom of the dialog box. The top panel contains the fields in which the user can enter data, whereas the bottom panel contains the buttons that let the user decide which action to take.

The top panel employs a GridLayout with four rows and one column to display the edit fields on the dialog box. The Java GridLayout manager enables you to place GUI components within a grid, with each component being displayed at a certain row and column location. Each row of the grid also contains a `Panel` object that has a different layout than the current panel. The syntax for creating the top component and assigning it the specified GridLayout is as follows:

```
top - new Panel();
top.setLayout(new GridLayout(4,1));
```

Before you create the `Panel` objects to contain the edit fields, you need to create the edit fields for the user to enter data. The following statements create all of the fields within which the user will edit data for the article:

```
Title = new TextField(50);
author = new Choice();
resources  = new Choice();
keywords = new TextField(50);
article = new TextArea(15, 50);
```

After you have created the components to add to the dialog box, you can begin assigning the components to the appropriate `Panel` objects. Declare four `Panel` objects and place each of the objects in one of the four locations on the top panel. For each of the four `Panel` objects, assign a FlowLayout type of `LEFT`. This forces all of the components to start at the left side of the panel and add to the right.

The first `Panel` object contains the edit field for the user to enter a title for the article. You first want to add a `Label` object that describes to the user what to enter. Then add the `TextField` object for the user to enter the title. The following code sets the layout for the `Panel` object and also adds the `Label` object and appropriate edit field:

```
p1.setLayout(new FlowLayout(FlowLayout.LEFT));
p1.add(new Label("Article Title : ", Label.RIGHT));
p1.add(title);
```

The second `Panel` object contains the `Choice` object that lets the user select the employee to be associated with this article. The panel will first display a textual `Label` object that identifies the purpose of the `Choice` object. It then adds the `Choice` object that lets the user choose an employee.

```
p2.setLayout(new FlowLayout(FlowLayout.LEFT));
p2.add(new Label("Author : ", Label.RIGHT));
p2.add(author);
```

The third `Panel` object is used to display the `Choice` object to let the user select the resource with which the article will be associated. It also uses a FlowLayout of type `LEFT` so that the `Label` and `Choice` components appear on the left side of the screen.

```
p3.setLayout(new FlowLayout(FlowLayout.LEFT));
p3.add(new Label("Application : ", Label.RIGHT));
p3.add(resources);
```

The fourth and final `Panel` object is used to display the edit field to allow the user to enter a string of keywords with which the article will be associated. The keywords entered are used by the Search Article window to display articles matching a user-entered keyword.

```
p4.setLayout(new FlowLayout(FlowLayout.LEFT));
p4.add(new Label("Keywords : ", Label.RIGHT));
p4.add(keywords);
```

After you have placed all of the components onto their respective panels, you can then add these panels to the top panel. Place the top `Panel` object in the North section of the dialog box. The code to place the edit-level `Panel` objects onto the top-level `Panel` object and then, in turn, place the top-level `Panel` object onto the dialog box is shown here:

```
top.add(p1);
top.add(p2);
top.add(p3);
top.add(p4);
this.add("North", top);
```

In this section, you added four edit fields to the dialog box. If you will remember, you had five edit fields to add to the dialog box. The fifth and final edit component is the TextArea component, in which the user enters the article text. Place this component in the center of the dialog box, using the following syntax:

```
this.add("Center", article);
```

The only thing left to add to your dialog box is the two buttons that give the user actions to take concerning the window. Provide the user with a button that enables him or her to save the data entered into the window and return to the main window. Also, provide the user with a button that enables him or her to cancel the saving of the data to the database and then return to the main window.

The final actions that will be taken by the constructor method are to call the `getResources()` and `getAuthors()` methods of the dialog box. These two methods are responsible for populating the two `Choice` objects used on the dialog box with information from the database.

Listing 16.3 contains the full code for the constructor method for the `addArticleDialog` window.

Listing 16.3. The constructor method for the `addArticleDialog` class.

```
public addArticleDialog (Connection connectionObj, Frame parentWin)
{
        // Call ancestor function to create dialog
        super(parentWin, "Add Knowledge Base Article", true);
        // Assing passed frame to local jdbc var
        parent = (JDBC)parentWin;
        // Assign passed connection object to local connection
        connection = connectionObj;
```

```
    // Build the layout of the dialog
    Panel top, bottom;
    // Put all edits on top panel
    top = new Panel();
    top.setLayout(new GridLayout(4,1));
    // Create edit controls
    title = new TextField(50);
    author = new Choice();
    resources = new Choice();
    keywords = new TextField(50);
    article = new TextArea(15,50);
    // Add edits to panel
    Panel p1, p2, p3, p4;
    p1 = new Panel();
    p2 = new Panel();
    p3 = new Panel();
    p4 = new Panel();

// Add title edit
p1.setLayout(new FlowLayout(FlowLayout.LEFT));
    p1.add(new Label("Article Title : ", Label.RIGHT));
    p1.add(title);

// add author edit
p2.setLayout(new FlowLayout(FlowLayout.LEFT));
    p2.add(new Label("Author : ", Label.RIGHT));
    p2.add(author);

// add resources edit
p3.setLayout(new FlowLayout(FlowLayout.LEFT));
    p3.add(new Label("Application : ", Label.RIGHT));
    p3.add(resources);

// add keywords edit
p4.setLayout(new FlowLayout(FlowLayout.LEFT));
    p4.add(new Label("Keywords : ", Label.RIGHT));
    p4.add(keywords);

top.add(p1);
    top.add(p2);
    top.add(p3);
    top.add(p4);
    this.add("North", top);
    // Add textarea
    this.add("Center", article);
    // Create bottom panel with two buttons
    bottom = new Panel();
    bottom.setLayout(new FlowLayout(FlowLayout.CENTER));
    // Create buttons and add to panel
    addbutton = new Button("Add");
    cancel = new Button("Cancel");
    // Add buttons to panel
    bottom.add(addbutton);
    bottom.add(cancel);
    this.add("South", bottom);
    // Call function to populate resources and authors
    getResources();
    getAuthors();
}
```

16

getResources()

The getResources() method of the dialog box enables the dialog box to display all of the resources from which the user can select by getting the values from the database. This method executes a SQL Select statement that returns the values from the database. The method then adds these items to the Choice object for the user to select from.

The method also constructs an array of the internal ID values retrieved from the database for the specified resources. These IDs are used by the dialog box when the user saves an article. The resource description is matched with its matching ID, and the ID will be saved to the database in place of the description.

The first action that the getResources() method will take is to create a Statement object that can be used to execute SQL queries. It uses the Connection object that was passed from the main window and stored in an object variable by the constructor method for the dialog box.

```
sqlStatement = connection.createStatement();
```

After you have created a Statement object, you can begin to execute the SQL queries against the database to retrieve results. You first should get the number of records that are contained in the table tResource. You use this method to obtain the number of records so that you know the exact size the array of String objects will need to be. You might be wondering why you are using an array of String objects to store integer values from the database. Because you are not actually going to edit the values and are using them only to build another String object to send to the database, it is easier to have the IDs as String objects so that you are not required to make them into String objects when you build the SQL statement. The query to get the number of records contained in the tResource table is as follows:

```
Select Count(*) From tResource
```

After you have created a String object with this SQL statement, you can execute the query and retrieve the results. You'll return the results into a ResultSet object:

```
results = sqlStatement.executeQuery(sql);
```

Because only one record will be retrieved, don't use a while loop to move through the result set; instead, call the next() method once to move to the first record. When you are on the first record of the result set, you'll get the result returned to the column, indicating the record count for the table. Use this value to create the array of String objects that holds resource IDs:

```
results.next();
resourceid = new String[(results.getInt(1))];
```

After you have created the array to hold the resource IDs for your resources, you can begin to execute the SQL query to get the resource information. Use the following SQL Select statement to get the needed information from the database:

16

```
Select resourceid, title, From tResource
```

You can now execute the `select` statement and get the results in a `ResultSet` object. When you have the result set, loop through the records and add the title for the resource to the `Choice` item list while you add the retrieved resource ID to the array of resources.

```
while (results.next()) {
    resources.addItem(results.getString("title"));
    resourceid[index] = results.getString("resourceid");
}
```

Note that the variable `index` is used in the array index. This variable is initially zero and will be incremented after each addition to the array. After you have retrieved all the needed data values, close the `Statement` object to release the resources it uses. You do this so that the `Connection` object does not run out of available handles to use for the execution of SQL statements:

```
sqlStatement.close();
```

Listing 16.4 contains the full code for the `getResources()` method.

TYPE **Listing 16.4. The `getResources()` method.**

```
void getResources()
{
        // Get the resources the user can choose from for the article
        String sql = "";
        Statement sqlStatement;
        ResultSet results;
        int index = 0;
        try {
            // Create a statement object
            sqlStatement = connection.createStatement();
            // First get a count of the resources
            // to create the resourceId array
            sql = "select count(*) from tResource";
            // get the results
            results = sqlStatement.executeQuery(sql);
            // Create the array using retrieved count
            results.next();
            resourceId = new String[results.getInt(1)];
            // Now get the resource ids and titles
            sql = "select resourceid, title from tResource";
            // get the results
            results = sqlStatement.executeQuery(sql);
            // Cycle throught the results
            // Add resourceid to array
            // Add title to resources object
            while (results.next()) {
                // Add resource title to resources object
                resources.addItem(results.getString("title"));
                // Add resource id to array for later use
```

continues

Listing 16.4. continued

```
                resourceId[index] = results.getString("resourceid");
                // increment the index
                index++;
            }
            // Close the sql statement
            sqlStatement.close();
        }
        catch (SQLException e) {
            System.out.println(e.getMessage());
        }
    }
```

getAuthors()

The getAuthors() method performs a similar function as the getResources() method, in that it gets the employees from the database and displays them in the Choice object for the user to pick from. The method also stores the employee IDs for each employee to use when the application adds the new article to the database.

The method initially creates a Statement object to use for executing all of the SQL statements performed in the method. The following statement creates a SQL Statement object for use in executing SQL queries:

```
sqlStatement = connection.createStatement();
```

As with the getResources() method, you'll also want to get the number of records in the tEmployee table so that you know the exact size needed for the array of employee IDs. The SQL Select statement that follows will get the number of employees who are currently in the tEmployee table:

```
Select Count(*) From tEmployee
```

After you have created a String object with the SQL Select statement to get the number of employees, you can execute the query and create the array of String objects based on the returned count of records, as follows:

```
results = sqlStatement.executeQuery(sql);
results.next();
ssn = new String[(results.getInt(1))];
```

When the array is created in the correct size, you can begin to add data from the database to both the Choice object and the array of employee IDs. Use the following statement to retrieve the social security numbers, which you'll use in place of the employee ID, as well as the first name and last name value to display the user's name in the Choice object:

```
Select ssn, firstname, lastname from tEmployee
```

16

Now execute this SQL Select statement and loop through the result set with a while loop. Add a concatenation of the first and last name to the Choice object, and add the social security number to the array of String objects for use in the Insert statement, which is used later in the dialog box.

```
author.addItem(results.getString("firstname") +
➥" " + results.getString("lastname"));
ssn[index] = results.getString("ssn");
```

After you have looped through all records in the result set, close the Statement object so that it releases the resources it uses. This enables the Connection object to retain more handles for use by other Statement objects:

```
sqlStatement.close();
```

The full code for the getAuthors() method is shown in Listing 16.5.

TYPE   **Listing 16.5. The getAuthors() method.**

```
// Get a list of available employees that can be used as authors
void getAuthors ()
{
        String sql = "";
        Statement sqlStatement;
        ResultSet results;
        int index = 0;
        try {
            // Create a statement object
            sqlStatement = connection.createStatement();
            // Get a count of the employees to use to initialize array
            sql = "select count(*) from tEmployee";
            // Execute statement
            results = sqlStatement.executeQuery(sql);
            // Create the array
            results.next();
            ssn = new String[(results.getInt(1))];
            // Get the ssn, lastname and firstname from table
            sql = "select ssn, firstname, lastname from tEmployee";
            // execute statement
            results = sqlStatement.executeQuery(sql);
            // Cycle through result set
            // add ssn to array
            // add concatenated firstname + lastname to authors choice object
            while (results.next()) {
                // Add item to author choice
                author.addItem(results.getString("firstname") +
                ➥ " " + results.getString("lastname"));
                // Add ssn to array
                ssn[index] = results.getString("ssn");
                // increment index counter
                index++;
            }
```

continues

Listing 16.5. continued

```
            // close the statement
            sqlStatement.close();
        }
        catch (SQLException e) {
            System.out.println(e.getMessage());
        }
    }
```

Handling Events in the Add Article Dialog Box

The Add Article dialog box is responsible mainly for handling two main events that occur within the dialog box. The dialog box needs to handle when the user clicks the Cancel button as well as when the user clicks the Add button.

When the user clicks Cancel, the Add Article dialog box hides (closes) the Add Article dialog box and disposes of the resources used by the Add Article dialog box. When the Add Article dialog box has been hidden and the resources used by the Add Article dialog box are released back to the system, the Add Article dialog box returns control to the main window as shown in the following code:

```
this.hide();
this.dispose();
return true;
```

When the user clicks Add, you want the addArticle() method to be called to add the items entered by the user to the database; then the window closes and the resources being used by the window are disposed of. Listing 16.6 contains the full code for the handleEvent() method.

TYPE   **Listing 16.6. The handleEvent() method.**

```
// handle events from buttons addbutton and cancel
public boolean handleEvent (Event evt)
{
        // If user chose cancel button, then exit dialog
        if ((evt.id == Event.ACTION_EVENT) && (evt.target == cancel))        {
            this.hide();
            this.dispose();
            return true;
        }
        else if ((evt.id == Event.ACTION_EVENT) && (evt.target == addbutton)) {
            // Call function to add data to database
```

16

```
            // and then exit
            if (addArticle()) {
                this.hide();
                this.dispose();
                return true;
            }
        }
        return false;
}
```

16

addArticle()

The addArticle() method is responsible for adding the data entered by the user to the database as a new article record. The method takes all of the items entered into the various edit components and sends the data values to the database as values in an Update statement.

The method initially creates a Statement object to use for the SQL update that will be performed. This Statement object is used when the dialog box sends the SQL Update statement to the database with the user-entered data values.

The method then checks the values entered into the title and article edit fields. It also checks to ensure that the user has entered values into these fields. If the user has not entered values, then any Update statement will return an error, because these values are required for the article record. If the user left either of these values out, then the method returns without adding the data to the database. The following code checks to ensure that both a title and the article text are given by the user:

```
if ((this.title.getText() == "") || (this.article.getText() == "")) {
    return false;
}
```

NOTE

You can add some form of message box to inform the user that he or she did not enter the correct information. You can also inform the user of the correct actions to take.

After you have determined that the user has entered values for both the title and article fields, you can begin to gather the other information needed for an update to the database. You'll want to get the social security number for the employee associated with the article. You'll also need to get the item selected in the author Choice object and get the same index item from the array of social security numbers, as follows.

```
ssn = ssn[this.author.getSelectedIndex()];
```

Now store the values for the article title and article text in String objects, so that you can add them to the SQL Update statement to insert into the database. Store the values entered in the title edit field into the variable titleText. The values entered for the article are stored in the articleText variable:

```
String titleText = this.title.getText();
String articleText = this.article.getText();
```

Now that you have all of the items needed to add an article record to the database, you can build the Insert statement to insert items into the database. The Insert statement combines some static text with the values entered by the user. The statement is as follows:

```
sql = "insert into tArticle(SSN, Title, Article, SubmissionDT) " +
"values ('" + ssn + "', '" + titleText + "', '" + articleText + "', '" +
today.toString() + "')";
```

Now that you have built a SQL Insert statement, you can send it to the database. Call the executeUpdate() method to execute this Insert statement against the database. If any errors occur during the insertion, they are caught in the catch section of this method.

After you have added the article record, you'll want to get the article ID that was just used for the data you inserted. This article ID will be used in two other tables for reference. You'll want to use a SQL Select statement to get the article ID, using all of the data values you used in the Insert statement as the criteria in the Where clause of the Select statement.

When you have the article ID, use the ID to insert a record into the table tArticleMentionsApp. This table is used to relate an article to an application. Use the following SQL Insert statement to add a record to the table:

```
sql = "insert into tArticleMentionsApp (ArticleId, ResourceId) " +
"values (" + Integer.toString(articleid) + ", " +
resourceid[resource.getSelectedIndex()] + ")";
```

When you have executed this SQL Insert statement to add a new record to the tArticleMentionsApp table, you'll want to add records to the tKeyword table to relate the keywords entered by the user to the article entered. Use a StringTokenizer object to parse the keywords entered in the keyword edit field into individual words.

To create a new StringTokenizer object, pass the data entered into the keyword's edit field. The StringTokenizer object then parses the passed string into its token parts. Then take these tokens and add each one as a separate record in the tKeyword table:

```
keywords = new StringTokenizer(this.keywords.getText());
```

Use the hasMoreTokens() method to determine whether another token exists for the current tokenizer object. To get each individual token, use the nextToken() method of the tokenizer method, and then take the token and the article ID and insert a new record into tKeyword.

```
while (keywords.hasMoreTokens()) {
    sql = "insert into tKeyword (ArticleId, Keyword) " +
```

```
        "values (" + articleId + ", '" + keywords.nextToken() + "')";
    sqlStatement.executeUpdate(sql);
}
```

When all items have been added to the database, call the getArticles() method of the main window. You call this method so that the article you just inserted will be displayed in the main window for the user to perform actions upon. The following code calls the getArticles() method to update the articles displayed in the main window:

```
parent.getArticles();
```

Listing 16.7 contains the full code for the addArticle() method.

TYPE **Listing 16.7. The addArticle() method.**

```
// Add article to database
boolean addArticle ()
{
        String ssn;
        StringTokenizer keywords;
        Statement sqlStatement;
        String sql = "";
        ResultSet results;
        java.util.Date today = new java.util.Date();
        int articleId;
        // Create a new statement
        try {
            sqlStatement = connection.createStatement();
            // Check that all info has been entered
            if ((this.title.getText() == "") ||
                (this.article.getText() == "")) {
                    // MessageBox msg = new MessageBox("Missing Information",
                    // "All information was not entered.  Cannot insert data");
                    return false;
            }
            // All information has been entered, so insert new record
            // Get SSN for current employee
            ssn = ssn[this.author.getSelectedIndex()];
            // Store the article text and title text in Strings
            // So that any ' can be replaced with \'
            String titleText = this.title.getText();
            String articleText = this.article.getText();
            // build the SQL statement
            sql = "insert into tArticle (SSN, Title, Article, SubmissionDt) " +
                "values ('" + ssn + "', '" +
                titleText + "', '" + articleText + "', '" +
                today.toString() + "')";
            // Execute the sql statement
            sqlStatement.executeUpdate(sql);
            // Now retrieve the article id for the inserted row
            sql = "select ArticleId from tArticle " +
                "where title = '" + title.getText() + "' " +
                "and ssn = '" + ssn + "' " +
```

continues

16

Listing 16.7. continued

```
                                "and article = '" + article.getText() + "'";
                    // get the article id
                    results = sqlStatement.executeQuery(sql);
                    // Get the article id of the item inserted
                    results.next();
                    articleId = results.getInt("ArticleId");
                    // insert items into tArticleMentionsApp
                    sql="insert into tArticleMentionsResource (ArticleId, ResourceId)"+
                            "values (" + Integer.toString(articleId) + ", " +
                                    resourceid[resources.getSelectedIndex()] + ")";
                    // execute the sql statement
                    sqlStatement.executeUpdate(sql);
                    // Add all of the keywords to the database
                    keywords = new StringTokenizer(this.keywords.getText());
                    while (keywords.hasMoreTokens()) {
                        // Insert the current token into the database
                        sql = "insert into tKeyword (ArticleId, Keyword) " +
                            "values (" + articleId +
                            ➥", '" + keywords.nextToken() + "')";
                            // add the keyword
                        sqlStatement.executeUpdate(sql);
                    }
                    // Close the sql statement
                    sqlStatement.close();
                }
                catch (SQLException e) {
                    System.out.println(e.getMessage());
                    return false;
                }
                // Update the available articles on the main page
                parent.getArticles();
                return true;
            }
```

Figure 16.2 displays what the Add Article dialog box will resemble when it is completed and called from the main window.

Figure 16.2.

The Add Article dialog box window.

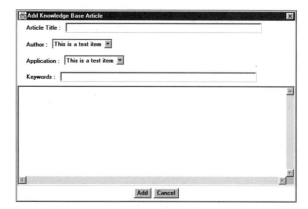

Summary

Today, you expanded the functionality offered by the Knowledge Base application. You added an About dialog box that can be used to display various types of information about the application as well as the author and company of the application.

Today's lesson also showed you how to create a dialog box window that can be used to add article information to the database. It illustrates how to use various components to store information from the database, as well as display information in various formats. The dialog box also illustrates how to use SQL Select and SQL Insert statements against the database, using data entered into standard Java components. Tomorrow's lesson, Day 17, "Using the Database in the Knowledge Base," introduces some of the other dialog boxes used for the Knowledge Base application.

Workshop

The Workshop provides quiz questions to help you solidify your understanding of the material covered and exercises to give you experience in using what you've learned. The answers are provided in Appendix A, "Quiz and Exercise Answers." Try to understand the quiz and exercise answers before you go on to tomorrow's lesson.

Quiz

1. What information does the About dialog box display?
2. Where is the About dialog box called from?
3. What does the Resources Choice object display?
4. What is entered into the article keyword edit field?
5. What two items are checked to ensure that the user has entered values into the Add dialog box?
6. What Java object is used to parse the keywords entered by the user?
7. What does the hasMoreTokens() method tell you?

Exercises

1. Change the Add Article dialog box to use PreparedStatement objects that use dynamic SQL statements that accept parameters.
2. Change the text in the About dialog box to display your name, your company name, and a short description.
3. Create a message box that will be displayed when the user does not enter a title or an article. Let the user know that those items are required.

Week 3

Day 17

Using the Database in the Knowledge Base

Today, you are going to finish the Knowledge Base application by completing the Display Articles, Delete Articles, and Search Articles dialog boxes. So far, you have created a main window that acts as the director for the application. You have also created a splash window that will be displayed before the main window displays. On Day 15, "Creating the Knowledge Base Application GUI," you created an About dialog box that displays information about the application and the Add Article dialog box, which enables the user to add articles to the database.

Today's lesson focuses on showing you how to delete articles from the database as well as how to find various articles by entering a keyword. Today's lesson also shows you how to display an article from the database based on user selection.

The topics covered today include the following:

☐ Displaying an article

☐ Deleting an article

☐ Searching for an article

Displaying an Article

The main window displays the titles for all of the articles in the database. However, if the user wants to view the article text, he or she will need to open a dialog box that displays not only the title for the dialog box, but also the author of the dialog box and the actual article text.

In this section, you'll create the `displayArticle` class. This class enables the user to view the title, author, and text for a chosen article. The dialog box is opened by the main window whenever the user chooses the appropriate menu item, or whenever the user double-clicks on an article in the list box.

The `displayArticle` Constructor

The constructor for the Display Article dialog box is responsible for creating the layout for the dialog box as well as retrieving the data to be displayed in the dialog box. The first thing that the constructor does is call the ancestor constructor and pass the specified items. It passes the specified frame object as well as the title for the dialog box, which is also the title for the article, and a Boolean indicating that the dialog box should be *modal*. Modal dialog boxes force the user to close the window before they perform any other actions in the application. The following code creates the Java `Dialog` object and makes the created dialog a modal dialog:

```
super(parent, item, true);
```

After the ancestor constructor has been called, you'll need to create and lay out the components that are used on the dialog box. You have two panels, top and bottom, that are placed in both the North and South areas of the dialog box. The top `Panel` object contains the author of the article. The bottom `Panel` object contains the OK button that will be used to close the dialog box. Place a `TextArea` object in the center of the dialog box to contain the article text.

The following code segment creates the top `Panel` object and sets the layout for the panel to FlowLayout. You are using FlowLayout to provide a smooth placement of the components in the panel. Next, add the label that contains the author of the article. Because you do not yet know the author, set the text for the label initially to be an empty string.

```
top = new Panel();
top.setLayout(new FlowLayout(FlowLayout.CENTER));
```

17

```
author = new Label("");
top.add(author);
this.add("North", top);
```

The bottom `Panel` object contains the OK button for the dialog box. The panel also uses the FlowLayout method to place components. After you have created the panel and set the layout, create the OK button, place it on the panel, and then place the panel onto the dialog box. The following code adds components to the `bottom` panel and places the panel on the dialog box:

```
bottom = new Panel();
bottom.setLayout(new FlowLayout(FlowLayout.CENTER));
ok = new Button("Ok");
bottom.add(ok);
this.add("South", bottom);
```

In the center of the dialog box, place the article text within a TextArea component. Create the TextArea component with an initial size of 20 rows and 80 columns. Also, call the `setEditable()` method for the TextArea component, passing it a Boolean `false` so that the user is not able to edit any of the text in the component:

```
article = new TextArea(20,80);
article.setEditable(false);
this.add("Center", article);
```

When you have placed the components on the dialog box, you can begin to populate the components with the appropriate data from the database. You need to get the author for the article as well as the article text. First, you need to create a `Statement` object to execute the SQL `Select` statement to get the information for the components:

```
SqlStatement = connection.createStatement();
```

After you create the `Statement` object, you can execute the SQL query to get the results needed for the dialog box. When you have executed the query, call the `next()` method to move the result set to the first record, and then set the article's text and author to the columns retrieved from the result set:

```
article.setText(info.getString("Article"));
author.setText("Author : " + info.getString("FirstName") +
" " + info.getString("LastName"));
```

Listing 17.1 contains the full code for the `displayArticle` dialog constructor.

Listing 17.1. The constructor method for the `displayArticle` class.

TYPE

```
public displayArticle (Connection connection, String item, Frame parent)
{
        // Call the ancestor function
        super(parent, item, true);
```

continues

Listing 17.1. continued

```
String sql = "";
ResultSet info;
Statement sqlStatement;
// Build the layout of the dialog
Panel top, bottom;
// Put a label in top area of the dialog
top = new Panel();
top.setLayout(new FlowLayout(FlowLayout.CENTER));
author = new Label("");
top.add(author);
this.add("North", top);
// Put the button in the bottom portion of the dialog
bottom = new Panel();
bottom.setLayout(new FlowLayout(FlowLayout.CENTER));
ok = new Button("Ok");
bottom.add(ok);
this.add("South", bottom);
// Put the text area in the center
article = new TextArea(20, 80);
article.setEditable(false);
this.add("Center", article);
// Get info from database using a SQL statement
try {
    sqlStatement = connection.createStatement();
    sql = "select tArticle.Article, tEmployee.LastName,
➡tEmployee.FirstName " +
        "from tArticle, tEmployee " +
        "where tArticle.Title = '" + item + "' " +
        "and tArticle.SSN = tEmployee.SSN";
    info = sqlStatement.executeQuery(sql);
    // Call function to put result set on first row
    info.next();
    // Assign the article and the author to appropriate items
    article.setText(info.getString("Article"));
    author.setText("Author : " + info.getString("FirstName") +
    ➡ " " + info.getString("LastName"));
    // Close the SQL Statement
    sqlStatement.close();
}
catch (SQLException e) {
    System.out.println(e.getMessage());
}
}
```

handleEvent()

The handleEvent() method is responsible for handling when the user clicks OK. When the user clicks OK, the method will hide the window and dispose of the resources consumed by the dialog box. Listing 17.2 contains the code for the handleEvent() method.

TYPE   **Listing 17.2. The `handleEvent()` method.**

```
// Override handle event to handle events in the dialog
public boolean handleEvent (Event evt)
    {
        // Handle only the action event for the ok button
        if ((evt.id == Event.ACTION_EVENT) && (evt.target == ok)) {
            // Hide the window
            this.hide();
        }
        // handle the window destroy event
        if (evt.id == Event.WINDOW_DESTROY) {
            // dispose of window instance
            this.dispose();
        }
        return false;
    }
}
```

Figure 17.1 shows the dialog box displayed by the `displayArticle` class.

Figure 17.1.

*The dialog displaying
an article to the user.*

Deleting an Article

The `deleteArticleDialog` class enables the user to delete specified articles from the database. The `deleteArticleDialog` class is called when the user chooses the Delete option from the menu on the main window. The purpose of the dialog box is to ask the users if they are sure that they want to delete the article chosen in the main window. The dialog box contains Yes and No buttons that will enable the user to either delete the specified article or return to the main window without deleting the article.

The constructor method is responsible for displaying the text and buttons on the dialog box and assigning the passed `Connection` object to a local `Connection` object for use in deleting the specified article. The initial line of the constructor method calls the ancestor constructor method to create the dialog box window. Pass the main window as the parent of the dialog box. Also, pass the title for the dialog box and a Boolean `true`, indicating that the dialog box will be modal. The following code creates a modal dialog with the title Delete Article:

```
super(parent, "Delete Article", true);
```

Next, assign the passed Frame window to the object variable that contains a reference to the main window to be used when an article has been deleted. Typecast the passed frame window to be of type `JDBC`, as shown in the following code:

```
parentWin = (JDBC)parent;
```

Next, assign the passed `Connection` object to a local `Connection` object that is used when the user clicks the Yes button to delete an article. Use the same `Connection` object that is used in the main window to prevent unnecessary connections to the database. You can use the same connection to the database for all of the application's queries and updates. The following code stores the passed `Connection` object in a local variable:

```
connectionServer = connection;
```

Next, set the layout for the dialog box to be of type `BorderLayout`. Use this particular layout so that you can place items in the North and South areas of the dialog box.

```
this.setLayout(new BorderLayout());
```

Create two `Panel` objects for placing objects onto the dialog box. The top panel contains the `Label` object that displays the information for the article to be deleted. Use the FlowLayout manager on the panel to lay out components. The following code places components on the top panel:

```
top = new Panel();
top.setLayout(new FlowLayout(FlowLayout.CENTER));
msg = new Label("Delete Article : " + item, Label.CENTER);
top.add(msg);
this.add("North", top);
```

The bottom panel contains the Yes and No buttons for the dialog box. These two buttons are responsible for handling whether or not the user wants to delete the specified item. If the user clicks Yes, then the dialog box should delete the specified article; if the user clicks No, then the dialog box should exit and return execution back to the main window. The following code places components on the `bottom` panel:

```
bottom = new Panel();
bottom.setLayout(new FlowLayout(FlowLayout.CENTER));
yes = new Button("Yes");
no = new Button("No");
bottom.add(yes);
bottom.add(no);
this.add("South", bottom);
```

Listing 17.3 contains the full code for the constructor method used for the Delete Article dialog box.

Listing 17.3. The constructor method for the
TYPE **deleteArticleDialog class.**

```
public deleteArticleDialog (Connection connection, String item, Frame parent)
{
        // Call ancestor function
        super(parent, "Delete Article", true);
        // Assign parent window to local variable
        parentWin = (jdbc)parent;
        // Assign passed connection to local connection object
        connectionServer = connection;
        // Assign item to local string article
        article = item;
        this.setLayout(new BorderLayout());
        // Build the layout for the dialog
        Panel top, bottom;
        // Create top panel and put label on it
        top = new Panel();
        top.setLayout(new FlowLayout(FlowLayout.CENTER));
        msg = new Label("Delete article : " + item, Label.CENTER );
        top.add(msg);
        this.add("North", top);
        // Create bottom panel and put buttons on it
        bottom = new Panel();
        bottom.setLayout(new FlowLayout(FlowLayout.CENTER));
        yes = new Button("Yes");
        no = new Button("No");
        bottom.add(yes);
        bottom.add(no);
        this.add("South", bottom);
        this.resize(350, 100);
}
```

handleEvent() for deleteArticleDialog

The handleEvent() method for the Delete Article dialog box contains code that handles when the user clicks the Yes and No buttons. When the user clicks No, the method hides the window as well as disposes of the resources being used by the window and then returns so that execution returns to the main window. The following code closes and hides the window:

```
this.hide();
this.dispose();
return true;
```

If the user clicks Yes, then the method calls the deleteArticle() method to delete the specified article. When the article has been deleted, the dialog box calls the getArticles() method for the main window to display the updated list of articles. Because an item was deleted, the list that is displayed is out of sync with the database, so you'll need to re-retrieve the current list of articles from the database.

When the article has been deleted and the articles in the main window are in sync with the articles in the database, hide the window and dispose of the resources being used by the dialog box so that execution can return to the main window.

Listing 17.4 contains the full code for the handleEvent() method.

TYPE   **Listing 17.4. The handleEvent() method.**

```
public boolean handleEvent (Event evt)
{
        // Check for when user clicks no button
        if ((evt.id == Event.ACTION_EVENT) && (evt.target == no)) {
            // hide and close window
            this.hide();
            this.dispose();
            return true;
        }
        // Check for when user clicks yes button
        if ((evt.id == Event.ACTION_EVENT) && (evt.target == yes)) {
            // Call function to delete article
            deleteArticle();
            // Call function on parent window to get the articles again
            parentWin.getArticles();
            // hide and close window
            this.hide();
            this.dispose();
            return true;
        }
        return false;
}
```

deleteArticle()

The deleteArticle() method is responsible for deleting the article specified by the user. The method takes the passed article title and deletes all items from the database that reference that article.

The method initially creates a Statement object to perform all of the database updates. This Statement object is created from the Connection object that was specified in the constructor method for the dialog box:

```
sqlStatement = connectionServer.createStatement();
```

When you have created a Statement object, you can begin to execute the SQL Delete statements that delete all items from the database that are related to the article specified to be deleted. First, you must delete items from the table tArticleMentionsResource. You need to delete all items from the child tables of tArticle before you can delete the main record so that orphaned records are not left in the child tables. An *orphan record* is a record that is in a table but does not have a valid parent record to which it refers. Use the following syntax to delete items from tArticleMentionsResource:

```
Delete tArticleMentionsResource
from tArticleMentionsResource, tArticle
where tArticle.Title = <title>
and tArticle.ArticleId = tArticleMentionsResource.ArticleId
```

The <title> in the preceding SQL `Delete` statement is the actual article title that was passed to the dialog box. When you have created this SQL statement for execution, use the created `Statement` object to execute the delete:

```
SqlStatement.executeUpdate(sql);
```

Next, delete all references to the current article that exist in the tKeyword table. You do this to prevent orphaned records in the tKeyword table. The following SQL `Delete` statement deletes items from tKeyword:

```
delete tKeyword
from tKeyword, tArticle,
where tArticle.Title = <title>
and tArticle.ArticleId = tKeyword.ArticleId
```

When these two statements have been executed, delete the main record from tArticle. You can now be sure that all child records have been deleted for the current record, so use the following SQL `Delete` statement to delete the current article from the database:

```
delete from tArticle where Title = <title>
```

After the article has been deleted and the `Statement` object has been closed, releasing the resources used by the object, the method returns execution back to the `handleEvent()` method. Listing 17.5 contains the full code for the `deleteArticle()` method.

TYPE   **Listing 17.5. The `deleteArticle()` method.**

```
void deleteArticle ()
{
      String sql;
      Statement sqlStatement;
      try {
          sqlStatement = connectionServer.createStatement();
          // Delete items from tArticleMentionsResource
          sql = "delete tArticleMentionsResource " +
                "from tArticleMentionsResource, tArticle " +
                "where tArticle.Title = '" + article + "' " + ·
                "and tArticle.ArticleId =
                ➡tArticleMentionsResource.ArticleId";
```

continues

Listing 17.5. continued

```
                        // Execute the statement
                        sqlStatement.executeUpdate(sql);
                        // Delete items from tKeyword with current article
                        sql = "delete tKeyword " +
                                "from tKeyword, tArticle " +
                                "where tArticle.Title = '" + article + "' " +
                                "and tArticle.ArticleId = tKeyword.ArticleId";
                        // Execute the statement
                        sqlStatement.executeUpdate(sql);
                        // Delete item from tArticle
                        sql = "delete from tArticle where Title = '" + article + "' ";
                        // Execute the statement
                        sqlStatement.executeUpdate(sql);
                        // Close the statement
                        sqlStatement.close();
                }
                catch (SQLException e) {
                        System.out.println(e.getMessage());
                }
        }
}
```

Figure 17.2 contains the window displayed by the deleteArticleDialog class.

Figure 17.2.

The Delete Article dialog box.

Searching for an Article

To let the user look through the various articles that have been entered, create a dialog box window that displays all articles that have a keyword matching a user-entered keyword. The dialog box will present the user with an edit field where he or she can enter a keyword. The dialog box will then display all articles that match the entered keyword in the main window.

The constructor for the dialog box is responsible for creating the dialog box's GUI. The method initially calls the ancestor constructor method to create the actual resources used for the dialog box. The dialog box is given the title Search Articles and will be made modal so that the user will be forced to choose an action on the dialog box before returning to the main window. The following code creates a modal dialog box to enable the user to search for various articles:

```
super(parentWin, "Search Articles", true);
```

The method then assigns the passed Frame window and Connection object to local object variables. These variables are used later in the dialog box for various actions taken by the user. The following code stores the passed Frame and Connection objects in local variables:

```
parent = (JDBC)parentWin;
connection = connectionObj;
```

The constructor then resizes the dialog box to a size that will correctly display all of the components on the dialog box. The dialog box will be resized to be 280×175 pixels.

```
this.resize(280, 175);
```

As an example of different ways to place components, the components for this dialog box are placed and reshaped manually, instead of allowing the Java Virtual Machine to determine the placement of the objects. To place objects manually, you need to clear the current Layout Manager being used by the dialog box. The following code sets the layout for the panel to NULL so that the components can be placed manually:

```
this.setLayout(null);
```

After you have cleared the Layout Manager, you can create the components that will be added to the dialog box, adding them as you would normally. When the items have been added, call the reshape() method for each component and manually reshape them on the dialog box to the sizes desired:

```
l.reshape(20, 20, 250, 25);
keyword.reshape(20, 45, 250, 25);
search.reshape(80, 130, 60, 28);
close.reshape(170, 130, 60, 28);
```

Listing 17.6 contains the full code for the constructor method for the Search Articles dialog box.

Listing 17.6. The constructor method for the searchArticles class.

TYPE

```
public searchArticles (Connection connectionObj, Frame parentWin)
{
        // Call ancestor constructor
        super(parentWin, "Search Articles", true);
        // Assign passed frame to local var
        parent = (jdbc)parentWin;
        // Assign passed connection object to local var
        connection = connectionObj;
        // Resize the window to be 280 x 175
        this.resize(280, 175);
        // Set the layout of the window to be null so that
        // we can manually reshape components
        this.setLayout(null);
        // Create the components and add them to dialog
        search = new Button("Search");
        close = new Button("Close");
        keyword = new TextField("", 50);
        Label l = new Label("Enter Keyword to Search For : ");
        // add components to dialog
```

continues

Listing 17.6. continued

```
        this.add(search);
        this.add(close);
        this.add(keyword);
        this.add(l);
        // reshape the components
        l.reshape(20, 20, 250, 25);
        keyword.reshape(20, 45, 250, 25);
        search.reshape(80, 130, 60, 28);
        close.reshape(170, 130, 60, 28);
}
```

`handleEvent()` for the `searchArticles` Dialog

The `handleEvent()` method for the Search Article dialog box contains all of the code to handle user actions on the dialog box. If the user clicks the Close button, then the method will close the window and release the resources being used by the dialog box. If the user clicks the Search button, then the window will call the `displaySearchArticles()` methods for the parent window, close the dialog box, and release all of its resources. Listing 17.7 contains the code for the `handleEvent()` method.

TYPE   **Listing 17.7. The `handleEvent` method.**

```
// handle the search and close buttons
public boolean handleEvent (Event evt)
{
        if ((evt.id == Event.ACTION_EVENT) && (evt.target == search)) {
            // Call function to search for articles and close window
            parent.displaySearchArticles(keyword.getText());
            this.hide();
            return true;
        }
        else if ((evt.id == Event.ACTION_EVENT) && (evt.target == close)) {
            // Close the window
            this.hide();
            return true;
        }
        else if (evt.id == Event.WINDOW_DESTROY) {
            this.dispose();
            return true;
        }
        return super.handleEvent(evt);
}
```

Figure 17.3 shows the window displayed by the `searchArticles` class.

17

Figure 17.3.

The Search Articles dialog box.

Summary

In today's lesson, you created three dialog boxes that are used in various ways to enable the user to handle articles that are stored in the database. You created a dialog box that lets the user view information for a specified article, as well as dialog boxes that let the user delete article information and find articles based on a particular keyword.

Hopefully, today's lesson has given you some ideas about how to begin some of your own Java database applications. The days on creating the Knowledge Base application, Days 15, 16, and 17, are meant to demonstrate how to build a fully functional application using Java and JDBC. In the next three days, you learn how to use the Java 1.1 JDK to build more advanced applications using object servers and n-tier processing.

Workshop

The Workshop provides quiz questions to help you solidify your understanding of the material covered and exercises to give you experience in using what you've learned. The answers are provided in Appendix A, "Quiz and Exercise Answers." Try to understand the quiz and exercise answers before you go on to tomorrow's lesson.

Quiz

1. What must the Layout Manager be set to in order to alter component sizes manually?
2. What is the method used to change the size and placement of a component manually?
3. What is a modal window?
4. If a dialog box is modal, can the user switch between the application window and the dialog box window?
5. What three arguments are passed to the constructor for the `Dialog` class?
6. Why is it always a good idea to close a `Statement` object manually?
7. What is an orphaned record?

8. Why should you always delete child records before deleting the main record?

9. What table contains the keywords that the user entered for the article?

10. What is the method called by the Search Articles dialog box to display the articles in the main window?

Exercises

1. Create a new window that lets the user edit article information. It should let the user change only the article text.

2. Modify the displaySearchArticles() method for the main window so that it allows multiple keyword searching. Use a StringTokenizer to separate the entered text into words.

3. Make the dialog box for searching articles modeless and have it come up at the same time that the main window comes up so that it can search articles and view them directly.

Creating an Employee Resource Applet

Today's lesson covers some new topics related to the new release of Java: Java 1.1. Because the next two lessons introduce some new topics that use some of the Java 1.1 features, today's lesson begins with an introduction to a few of these new features.

There are too many new features to completely cover in one day, so you'll learn some of the new topics that might apply to the application you'll build in the next two days. You learn the following topics today:

☐ Java 1.1 event delegation model
☐ Java 1.1 pop-up menus
☐ Java 1.1 menu shortcuts
☐ Java 1.1 serialization

The Java 1.1 Event Delegation Model

With the introduction of the Java 1.1 JDK, Sun has introduced an entirely new method for handling events in your Java applications. In the previous versions of Java, you handled most events in either the `handleEvent()` or `action()` methods. This restricted you to handling events in the same component as the event occurred. Because true object-oriented programming allows for a separation between GUI and business logic processing, the old model was not well suited for this purpose.

Therefore, Sun has introduced its delegation model for handling events with Java applications and applets. This new model enables event handling to be placed in separate classes or objects other than the GUI, which enables you to create basic event-handling objects that can be associated with any number of AWT components. It also lets you place your business logic completely apart from the GUI design. This separation makes maintaining and changing the business logic easier and does not affect the application's GUI, reducing the items that you need to test because the GUI does not change, only the business logic behind the GUI.

To implement this new delegation model, Sun has introduced various interfaces that you can use to provide you with various event-handling methods. To handle events, you would implement one or more of these interfaces and use their methods to handle the specified events. When you have created the event methods, you need to add the object that contains the event-handling routines to the component that will use these routines.

The interfaces listed in Table 18.1 have been introduced to provide various event-handling routines.

Table 18.1. Sun event interfaces.

Interface	Description
ActionListener	Handles action events
AdjustmentListener	Handles scrolling events
ComponentListener	Handles component events such as hide, show, and so on
FocusListener	Handles focus events for the component
ItemListener	Handles item changes
KeyListener	Handles key operations
MouseListener	Handles mouse actions
MouseMotionListener	Handles mouse movement for the component
WindowListener	Handles window-specific events

18

The following sections cover some often used interfaces. These sections cover the methods offered by the interfaces; they also give descriptions and examples of how to use the interfaces to handle events in your application.

ActionListener

The ActionListener interface provides functionality for handling action events within a component. This interface should be used wherever there was an action() method in your previous applications. This interface handles when the user presses the Enter key in a text field, double-clicks an item within a list box, or clicks a menu item selection.

The ActionListener interface provides one method for handling events. The actionPerformed() method enables you to place code that handles events within a method separated from the rest of the application. The method takes a parameter of type ActionEvent. The ActionEvent provides some methods that let you get information for the component in which the action occurred. The method getActionCommand() returns various information, depending on the component. You can try the method with various components to see what is returned when an action is performed.

The following example demonstrates how to create an application that uses the ActionListener interface. You first want to implement the interface in your application using the following syntax:

```
public class Action extends Frame implements ActionListener
```

NOTE

In this example you are implementing the event handling in the same object as your GUI. You could, however, put the event handling in a separate object and use that object to handle events.

Next, implement the actionPerformed() method to handle events for the components that implement this listener. Your actionPerformed() method uses the getActionCommand() method to output the text entered into a TextField component by the user. When the user presses Enter, the method is called and the current text is output to the system:

```
System.out.println(evt.getActionCommand());
```

Now that you have created a method to handle the events for a TextField, you need to create a TextField and assign the listener to the component. After you have created the component, you can call the addActionListener() to add the current ActionListener object to handle events for the component.

```
TextField t = new TextField();
t.addActionListener(this);
```

Listing 18.1 contains the full code for the Action example.

TYPE   **Listing 18.1. The Action example.**

```java
import java.awt.*;
import java.awt.event.*;

public class Action extends Frame implements ActionListener {

        public Action () {
                super();

                TextField t = new TextField();
                // Add an action listener to handle events for the textfield
                t.addActionListener(this);
                this.add("North", t);

                this.resize(200, 200);
                this.show();

        }


        public void actionPerformed (ActionEvent evt) {
                // output the current text of the texfield
                System.out.println(evt.getActionCommand());
        }

        public static void main (String args[]) {
                Action app = new Action();
        }
}
```

ComponentListener

The ComponentListener interface provides various methods that you can use to handle events
when certain events occur within the component. The interface provides the following four
methods for notification of component events:

☐   componentHidden()

☐   componentMoved()

☐   componentResized()

☐   componentShown()

These methods provide only a notification that the events have occurred within the
component. You cannot stop the component from being hidden—you can only perform
your own processing when the event has occurred.

18

The following example creates a Frame class that implements the ComponentListener interface and outputs information to the system whenever the previously listed events occur. Listing 18.2 contains the code for the Comp example.

TYPE   **Listing 18.2. The Comp example.**

```java
import java.awt.*;
import java.awt.event.*;

public class Comp extends Frame implements ComponentListener {
    public Comp() {
        super();

        // Add the component listener to the Frame
        this.addComponentListener(this);
        this.resize(200, 200);
        this.show();
    }

    public void componentHidden (ComponentEvent evt) {
        System.out.println("Component Hidden");
    }

    public void componentMoved (ComponentEvent evt) {
        System.out.println("Component Moved");
    }

    public void componentResized (ComponentEvent evt) {
        System.out.println("Component resized");
    }

    public void componentShown (ComponentEvent evt) {
        System.out.println("Component Shown");
    }

    public static void main (String args[]) {
        Comp app = new Comp();
    }
}
```

18

KeyListener

The KeyListener interface provides various methods for handling events that occur when the user uses the keyboard. When you implement the KeyListener interface, implement the following three methods:

- keyPressed()
- keyReleased()
- keyTyped()

These methods provide you with a means to handle any typing on the keyboard by the user. Each of these methods takes a parameter of type KeyEvent. The KeyEvent object provides various constants that identify special character keys and also provides some methods that allow you to get the key that was pressed in either its character or integer format. The getKeyChar() method returns the character for the key that the user pressed. The getKeyCode() method gets the integer value for the key that the user pressed.

In the following example, you'll implement the KeyListener interface and output to the system the character that was pressed and its integer value. Use the following line of code in each of the three methods for the KeyListener interface:

```
System.out.println(evt.getKeyChar() + " is " +
➥Integer.toString(evt.getKeyCode()));
```

Listing 18.3 contains the full code for the KeyExample class. The Frame in the KeyExample class implements a KeyListener interface, and the methods in the interface will output the keys to the system output window.

TYPE **Listing 18.3. The KeyExample class.**

```
import java.awt.*;
import java.awt.event.*;

public class KeyExample extends Frame implements KeyListener {

    public KeyExample () {
        super();

        // Add a key listener to the frame
        this.addKeyListener(this);
        this.resize(200,200);
        this.show();
    }

    public void keyPressed (KeyEvent evt) {
        System.out.println(evt.getKeyChar() + " is " +
        ➥Integer.toString(evt.getKeyCode()));
    }

    public void keyTyped (KeyEvent evt) {
        System.out.println(evt.getKeyChar() + " is " +
        ➥Integer.toString(evt.getKeyCode()));
    }

    public void keyReleased (KeyEvent evt) {
        System.out.println(evt.getKeyChar() + " is " +
        ➥Integer.toString(evt.getKeyCode()));
    }

    public static void main (String args[]) {
        KeyExample app = new KeyExample();
    }
}
```

18

MouseListener

The MouseListener interface provides various methods for handling events generated by the user's mouse. The methods provided by this interface are generated when the mouse is used to perform an action such as clicking or entering the boundaries of a component. The interface provides the following methods to handle mouse events within a component:

- mouseClicked()
- mouseEntered()
- mouseExited()
- mousePressed()
- mouseReleased()

Each of these five events takes a parameter of type MouseEvent. The MouseEvent object provides various methods for getting information about the mouse event that occurred. The object provides the getClickCount() method to get the number of times the mouse was clicked. Because you might want to handle single-clicking and double-clicking differently, you can use the getClickCount() method to determine how many times the mouse was clicked.

The getX() and getY() methods enable you to determine the X and Y coordinates of the click relative to the component. The X and Y positions displayed will be the point within the component relative to the extreme top-left of the component.

In the following example, you'll place code in the mouseClicked() method to output the X and Y positions of the mouse click as well as how many times the mouse was clicked. Use the following code to output this information:

```
System.out.println("Mouse clicked " + Integer.toString(evt.getClickCount()) +
" times at " + Integer.toString(evt.getX()) + "," +
➥Integer.toString(evt.getY()));
```

Create a TextField component that uses the MouseListener object, and also send output to the system when the user enters and exits the component. Listing 18.4 contains the full code for the MouseExample class.

Type | **Listing 18.4. The MouseExample class.**

```
import java.awt.*;
import java.awt.event.*;

public class MouseExample extends Frame implements MouseListener {

    public MouseExample () {
        super();
```

continues

Listing 18.4. continued

```
TextField t = new TextField();
    // Add the mouse listener to the text field
    t.addMouseListener(this);
    this.add("North", t);

    this.resize(200, 200);
    this.show();
}

public void mouseClicked (MouseEvent evt) {
    System.out.println("Mouse clicked " +
    ➥Integer.toString(evt.getClickCount()) +
    " times at " + Integer.toString(evt.getX()) +
    ➥"," + Integer.toString(evt.getY()));
}

public void mouseEntered (MouseEvent evt) {
    System.out.println("Mouse Entered");
}

public void mouseExited (MouseEvent evt) {
    System.out.println("Mouse exited");
}

public void mousePressed (MouseEvent evt) {}
public void mouseReleased (MouseEvent evt) {}

public static void main (String args[]) {
    MouseExample app = new MouseExample();
}
}
```

WindowListener

The WindowListener interface provides window-specific event-handling routines. The methods will inform you when special events happen on the window. They do not let you stop the event from happening, but they let you perform your own specific processing when the event occurs. The interface provides the following methods for handling window events:

☐ windowClosed()

☐ windowClosing()

☐ windowDeiconified()

☐ windowIconified()

☐ windowOpened()

All of these methods take a parameter of type WindowEvent. The WindowEvent object provides a method, getWindow(), that returns the window in which the event occurred. Listing 18.5 contains an example of how to use each of the listed window events. The WindowExample class implements the WindowListener interface and outputs various information, depending on the actions performed on the window.

TYPE | **Listing 18.5. The WindowExample class.**

```
import java.awt.*;
import java.awt.event.*;

public class WindowExample extends Frame implements WindowListener {

    public WindowExample () {
        super();

        // Add the window listener
        this.addWindowListener(this);
        this.resize(200, 200);
        this.show();
    }

    public void windowClosed (WindowEvent evt) {
        System.out.println("Window closed");
    }

    public void windowClosing (WindowEvent evt) {
        System.out.println("Window closing");
    }

    public void windowDeiconified (WindowEvent evt) {
        System.out.println("Window deiconfied");
    }

    public void windowIconified (WindowEvent evt) {
        System.out.println("Window iconfied");
    }

    public void windowOpened (WindowEvent evt) {
        System.out.println("Window opened");
    }

    public static void main (String args[]) {
        WindowExample app = new WindowExample();
    }
}
```

18

Pop-Up Menus

With the introduction of Java 1.1, Sun has finally provided developers with a means to display pop-up menus. The PopupMenu component is inherited from the Menu component, so all methods available for the Menu component are available for the PopupMenu component.

To use the PopupMenu component, first create the component as you do other components. The component offers two constructor methods. The first constructor method lets you create the pop-up menu without a title. The second constructor lets you specify a title to be used with the menu.

After you have created the menu, you can add menu items to the component using the add() method. To add a menu item that enables the user to cut information from the current component, use the following syntax:

```
PopupMenu p = new PopupMenu();
p.add(new MenuItem("Cut"));
```

This code describes how to create the component and add menu items to the component. However, this code does not show the component to the user. To show the component to the user, call the show() method provided for the component. This method takes a Component parameter in which to display the menu, as well as the X and Y positions relative to the component that the menu will be displayed in. Listing 18.6 contains the code for the MenuExample class. This class uses the event delegation model (shown earlier in the "The Java 1.1 Event Delegation Model" section) to handle mouse clicks on the Frame object. When the user clicks the window, the menu is displayed at the position he or she clicked.

TYPE   **Listing 18.6. The MenuExample class.**

```
import java.awt.*;
import java.awt.event.*;

public class MenuExample extends Frame implements MouseListener {
    PopupMenu p = new PopupMenu("Example Menu");

    public MenuExample () {
        super();

        // Add the mouse listener
        this.addMouseListener(this);

        // Add items to the Popup menu
        p.add(new MenuItem("Cut"));
        p.add(new MenuItem("Copy"));
        p.add(new MenuItem("Paste"));
        p.addSeparator();
        p.add(new MenuItem("Select All"));
```

18

```
        this.resize(200, 200);
        this.show();
    }

    public void mouseClicked (MouseEvent evt) {
        // show the popup menu at clicked location
        this.add(p);
        p.show(this, evt.getX(), evt.getY());
    }

    public void mousePressed (MouseEvent evt) {}
    public void mouseReleased (MouseEvent evt) {}
    public void mouseEntered (MouseEvent evt) {}
    public void mouseExited (MouseEvent evt) {}

    public static void main (String args[]) {
        MenuExample app = new MenuExample();
    }
}
```

Menu Shortcuts

Sun also has given developers the option to add shortcuts to menu items. Menu shortcuts are standard on most platforms, so Java has provided developers a means to allow quick and easy access to menu items.

To create a menu shortcut, you can create a menu item as you would any other menu item, but also pass it a MenuShortcut object that contains the key that you want to make the shortcut for the menu item. To create a menu item that has a shortcut of A, you would use the following syntax:

```
MenuItem m = new MenuItem("Add Item", new MenuShortcut(65));
```

Because the integer 65 indicates the A key, the shortcut for the menu item is A. Listing 18.7 contains the ShortCutExample that displays a menu with various shortcuts for the menu items. It uses various keys to create the different shortcuts for the menu items.

TYPE **Listing 18.7. The ShortCutExample class.**

```
import java.awt.*;

public class ShortCutExample extends Frame {
    public ShortCutExample () {
        super();

        MenuBar mb = new MenuBar();
        Menu file = new Menu("File");
```

continues

Listing 18.7. continued

```
        file.add(new MenuItem("Add Item", new MenuShortcut(65)));
        file.add(new MenuItem("Save", new MenuShortcut(83)));
        file.add(new MenuItem("Throw Away", new MenuShortcut(84)));
        mb.add(file);
        this.setMenuBar(mb);

        this.resize(200, 200);
        this.show();
    }

    public static void main (String args[]) {
        ShortCutExample app = new ShortCutExample();
    }
}
```

Serialization

Java 1.1 has also introduced a new topic called *serialization*. Serialization enables you to serialize objects using a stream. For example, currently you can save data to a file or send data over a stream such as a network. You can send bytes of data that represent actual data objects such as strings, integers, and so on. However, until now, you could send this only as native data.

With Java 1.1, you can now send entire objects through a stream. This means that you can save actual objects to a file and then reload them exactly as they were. You can also send objects across a stream. Using a stream and serialization, you can now create object servers that store objects and send them to clients when needed. This allows for distributed processing. You can create a client that loads an object, but does not have to have the definition for the object. It can dynamically create the object when it is needed.

Serialization is one of the most important advances introduced with Java 1.1. It enables you to create Java servers that contain various components, allowing clients to be very small because all of the objects are loaded into memory only when they are needed. This enables you to develop very complex applications and also allows for multi-tier applications.

Serialization is accomplished using the new Java objects ObjectInputStream and ObjectOutputStream. These new objects provide the means for transferring objects using a stream. The two classes implement similar methods for reading and writing data. The ObjectInputStream provides various methods for reading in objects and data. It provides a readObject() to read in an object, as well as readString() and readLong() to read in native data types. The ObjectOutputStream provides matching write methods for writing the data to the stream.

The following two-part example demonstrates the use of serialization and saving objects to disk files. This method enables you to save user information and settings exactly. Not only does it save component positions, but it also saves data entered into components. You can use this method of serialization to prevent data loss through hardware failure. You could save a window periodically and, if the computer crashes, you could get the last saved configuration for the window with the data still intact.

The first part of the example creates a window with a list box component. The list box adds two items in the component. After the window has been shown, the application will serialize the window to a file called WINDOW.DAT. This file contains the contents of the serialized window.

To serialize data to a file or stream, you need to create an ObjectOutputStream. To create this object, pass it an OutputStream object. Because you are saving to a file, use the FileOutputStream object to provide you with the required OutputStream. After you have created the ObjectOutputStream, you can use its write methods to write data to the assigned stream. When you have finished writing data, close the OutputStream so that the data is written to the stream. The following code creates the OutputStream and assigns it to the ObjectOutputStream. It then writes the current object to the specified file.

```
FileOutputStream ostream = new FileOutputStream("window.dat");
ObjectOutputStream out = new ObjectOutputStream(ostream);
out.writeObject(this);
ostream.close();
```

Listing 18.8 contains the full code for the Serial class. This is the first part of the file serialization example.

TYPE   **Listing 18.8. The Serial class.**

```
import java.awt.*;
import java.io.*;

public class Serial extends Frame {

        public Serial () {
                super();

                List list = new List();
                list.addItem("Ashton Hobbs");
                list.addItem("Michelle Hobbs");

                // add the gotten object from to frame
                this.add("Center", list);

                this.resize(300, 300);
                this.show();

                try {
                FileOutputStream ostream = new FileOutputStream("window.dat");
```

continues

Listing 18.8. continued

```
                ObjectOutputStream out = new ObjectOutputStream(ostream);
                out.writeObject(this);
                ostream.close();
                }
                catch (Exception e) {}


        }

        public static void main (String args[]) {
                Serial app = new Serial();
        }
}
```

Figure 18.1 contains the window created in this listing. Notice that there are two items in the list box component.

Figure 18.1.

The window created by the Serial *class.*

For the second part of the example, create an application that loads the frame from the file you saved in the previous example and then displays the frame. Use the ObjectInputStream object to load the object from the file and assign it to a Frame object.

The process for getting objects is very similar to writing objects. First, create a FileInputStream. Use the WINDOW.DAT file that you saved in the previous example as the file from which to get the object. Then create an ObjectInputStream and associate it with the input stream created by reading in the specified file. After you have created the ObjectInputStream object, you can begin to read in the objects you saved to the file. Use the readObject() method to read the object you saved to the file. This method returns an object of Object type, but you'll typecast the object to be a Frame component. The following code opens the specified file for reading and then reads the object contained in the file:

```
FileInputStream istream = new FileInputStream("window.dat");
ObjectInputStream in = new ObjectInputStream(istream);
Frame f = (Frame)in.readObject();
istream.close();
```

Listing 18.9 contains the full code for the Serial2 class. This class reads in the data from the WINDOW.DAT file and displays the Frame object stored there.

TYPE **Listing 18.9. The Serial2 class.**

```
import java.awt.*;
import java.io.*;

public class Serial2 {
    public Serial2 () {}

    public static void main (String args[]) {
        try {
            FileInputStream istream = new FileInputStream("window.dat");
            ObjectInputStream in = new ObjectInputStream(istream);
            Frame f = (Frame)in.readObject();
            istream.close();
            f.show();
        }
        catch (Exception e) {}
    }
}
```

Figure 18.2 contains the window displayed by the Serial2 class. Notice that it looks exactly like the window displayed by the Serial class. The serialized object contains not only the actual Frame object that was displayed but also the data that was stored in the list box component.

Figure 18.2.

The window created by using the Serial-ized List object.

Summary

This lesson has introduced you to some of the new functionality available in the new release of Java. The 1.1 release of Java adds some functionality to Java that was lacking in the previous releases. With the addition of a new event-handling model, developers can now separate business logic from component placement. This provides for more robust object-oriented solutions.

18

Some of the new features that are available in the 1.1 release of Java include the new event model, as well as some new functionality for displaying menus to the user. Java 1.1 now has the capability to display pop-up menus to the user. These menus let you provide different functionality for each type of component. Java 1.1 also enables you to create menu shortcuts. These shortcuts enable the user to use key combinations to access menu items quickly.

Java 1.1 has also introduced some brand-new topics such as object serialization. Today's lesson covered serialization, which is the process of sending objects through a stream. This lets developers save objects as files much as they do with data. Serialization opens up new application possibilities, including object servers and advanced property saving.

Workshop

The Workshop provides quiz questions to help you solidify your understanding of the material covered and exercises to give you experience in using what you've learned. The answers are provided in Appendix A, "Quiz and Exercise Answers." Try to understand the quiz and exercise answers before you go on to tomorrow's lesson.

Quiz

1. What interface in Java 1.1 enables you to "listen" for normal mouse events?
2. What method adds an `ActionListener` interface to listen to events for a specified component?
3. What method returns the name of the menu item selected?
4. What method displays a pop-up menu to the user?
5. What is passed to the `show()` method of the `PopupMenu` object?
6. Name the two objects used to allow serialization in Java.
7. What method enables you to write an integer to a stream using the `ObjectOutputStream`?
8. What method enables you to read an object from a stream using the `ObjectInputStream`?
9. What parameter does the `MenuShortcut` constructor take?
10. What does RMI stand for?

18

Exercises

1. Create a frame with two different list boxes. Display different `PopupMenu` objects for each list.

2. Create a frame that lets the user serialize the entire frame at any time. (Use either a `Button` or `MenuItem`.)

18

Day **19**

Handling Events in the Employee Resource Applet

In today's lesson, you'll begin to create another application that uses JDBC. However, this application, unlike the Knowledge Base application, will be able to be run as an applet in a browser (when browsers support the Java 1.1 JDK).

You'll create the Employee Manager application. This application enables users to add, delete, and view employee information from the tEmployee table. This lesson uses some of the new features of Java 1.1, including serialization and the event delegation model.

The following topics are covered in this lesson:

- ☐ The Employee Manager application
- ☐ The Employee Server application

☐ IDList component

☐ `EmployeeMenu`

☐ Server threads

The Employee Manager Application

To illustrate how you can use Java to create multi-tiered applications that can run over an intranet or the Internet, you will build the Employee Manager application. You'll use Java and serialization to create this application. The Employee Manager application contains an object server that is responsible for sending the appropriate objects to the client applications at the correct time.

The client stubs that you'll create for the Employee Manager application are simple stubs that let the client have a small footprint, or space requirement. The client will not contain any business logic directly. The client's only purpose is to enable the user to get objects from the object server.

This approach of using the object server enables the client application to be placed on a user's computer, or the client can be embedded in an HTML page so that it can be loaded as an applet over the Web. Using this approach allows for many different possibilities because the developer does not have to worry about having large client installations. It also enables the developer to have an application that doesn't need to be upgraded on multiple machines. Placing new objects on the object server that serves the client applications enables the developer to upgrade the application without having to install new builds on every user's machine.

For this application, use the JavaSoft JDBC-ODBC Bridge classes. These classes, developed in conjunction with InterSolv, provide a direct way to connect Java to ODBC databases. This product is different from Symantec's dbAnywhere in that it only enables you to connect to a database on the current machine. Whereas dbAnywhere allows a connection to a database over the network, the JDBC-ODBC Bridge requires that the database exists on the same virtual computer.

The Employee Server Application

The main purpose of the Employee Server application is to create the threads that listen for client connections. To facilitate the user being able to connect to the server and get all of the needed objects, the server creates a separate thread for each object. Each thread creates a server socket that listens for client connections. You are doing this to simplify the code needed to perform all of the processing using only one server socket. Using one socket to handle all requests would require the client to pass information that would identify what component it is requesting. By allowing each object to be severed on its own port, you can reduce the amount of code needed to create the application.

The Employee Server application is also responsible for creating a connection to the database. This connection is used by all of the thread objects that require database access. This enables the server to use one database connection to process all of the client requests. This can eliminate the need to have multiple open connections to the database.

The Employee Server also displays a window that simply shows the user that the server is running.

Employee Server Constructor

The Employee Server constructor is the only method contained in the object. The constructor displays a blank window, creates a connection to the database, and initializes all of the thread objects that serve client requests.

The first action the constructor performs is to create the actual Frame object and display it to the user. This gives the user some indication that the server is running and serving requests.

```
super("Employee Server");
this.resize(200, 200);
this.show();
```

After the window has been displayed to the user, the constructor creates a connection to the database. Because you are using a local database, use the JavaSoft JDBC-ODBC Bridge, which enables JDBC calls to be translated into ODBC calls to the database. Initially create the Driver object using the JDBC-ODBC Bridge driver.

```
String driverName = "sun.jdbc.odbc.JdbcOdbcDriver";
Driver driver = (Driver)Class.forName(driverName).newInstance();
```

After the Driver object has been created, you need to create a Properties object that contains the information needed to connect to the database. Set the user parameter to be dba and the password parameter to be sql:

```
Properties p = new Properties();
p.put("user", "dba");
p.put("password", "sql");
```

Now create the URL that connects you to the database. Because you are using a local driver and not dbAnywhere, you need to give only the basic definition. You won't need to specify an IP address or port because the connection is a local connection. Because your datasource is called JDBC, use it at the end of the URL to identify the datasource you're using.

```
String dbURL = "jdbc.odbc.JDBC";
```

Now that all items have been created, you can create a connection to the database using the `Driver` object. Store the connection in an object variable of the server application:

```
c = driver.connect(dbURL, p);
```

When the connection to the database has been created, the constructor method begins to create each of the thread objects that are used to serve objects to the client applications. There are seven different thread objects, one for each operation that can be performed by the client application. All of the thread objects use a class that implements the runnable interface to provide thread operations.

The first thread is responsible for serving the menu bar for the main window. This thread enables the client application to get the current menu that should be displayed on the main window of the client application:

```
GetMenu menuThread = new GetMenu(GETMENU)
Thread t1 = new Thread(menuThread);
t1.start();
```

Notice that the `GetMenu` object is passed a constant named `GETMENU`. All of the constants are located in the `EmpServices` interface. This interface provides the application with constants that identify the port numbers that the different thread objects should listen to. It also is used by the client application to determine which port it should connect to in order to get the various objects needed.

The second thread object is responsible for sending the list object that will be displayed on the client window. This list object contains all of the employee names that are currently in the database. The list will be populated on the server and then sent with all data items to the client. This eliminates the need to have a connection to the database from every client application. The `GetEmployeeList` object handles the sending of the `IDList` object, which contains all of the employees. The constructor for this object takes the port number to use as well as the `Connection` object for the application:

```
GetEmployeeList empThread = new GetEmployeeList(GETEMPLOYEELIST, c);
Thread t2 = new Thread(empThread);
t2.start();
```

The next thread that you create and start is used when the client application requests the Add dialog box. The Add dialog box is sent to the user in its entirety. With the main window, you sent only the menu bar and a list object that the client added to its window. With the dialog boxes in the application, you create the dialog box entirely on the server and then send the full dialog object to the server. This enables you to change the dialog that is sent to the client on the server. It also enables you to remove options at any time.

```
AddDialog addThread = new AddDialog(ADDDIALOG, c);
Thread t3 = new Thread(addThread);
t3.start();
```

Along with the Add dialog box, you also have the Delete dialog box and the View dialog box. The fourth thread sends the Delete dialog box to the client application:

```
DeleteDialog deleteThread = new DeleteDialog(DELETEDIALOG, c);
Thread t4 = new Thread(deleteThread);
t4.start();
```

The View dialog box is served using the fifth thread object. This object enables the user to view information about the employee. You create the dialog box on the server and then send it to the client using serialization.

```
ViewDialog viewThread = new ViewDialog(VIEWDIALOG, c);
Thread t5 = new Thread(viewThread);
t5.start();
```

Along with dialogs and components, you have services in your application that accept actual data values that are used to update the database. There are two objects: one to delete information and one to add information to the employee's table. The sixth thread you create deletes employee information:

```
Delete deleteEmployeeThread = new Delete(DELETE, c);
Thread t6 = new Thread(deleteEmployeeThread);
t6.start();
```

The final thread you create is responsible for accepting new data values to be inserted into the employee's table:

```
Add addEmployeeThread = new Add(ADD, c);
Thread t7 = new Thread(addEmployeeThread);
t7.start();
```

The full code for the `EmpMainServer` class is shown in Listing 19.1. Notice that the main method starts the object server.

19

TYPE   **Listing 19.1. The `EmpMainServer` class.**

```
public class EmpMainServer extends Frame implements EmpServices {
        Connection c;
        Driver driver;
public EmpMainServer () {
                super("Employee Server");
                this.resize(200,200);
                this.show();
                try {
                        String driverName = "sun.jdbc.odbc.JdbcOdbcDriver";
                        Driver driver =
                        ➥(Driver)Class.forName(driverName).newInstance();
                        Properties p = new Properties();
                        p.put("user" ,"dba");
                        p.put("password" , "sql");
                        String dbURL = "jdbc:odbc:JDBC";
```

continues

Listing 19.1. continued

```
                      c = driver.connect(dbURL, p);
          }
          catch (Exception e) {System.out.println("Caught Exception"); }
          // Create the Thread to handle the main menu
          GetMenu menuThread = new GetMenu(GETMENU);
          Thread t1 = new Thread(menuThread);
          t1.start();
          // Create the Thread to handle the Employeee list object
          GetEmployeeList empThread =
          ➥new GetEmployeeList(GETEMPLOYEELIST, c);
          Thread t2 = new Thread(empThread);
          t2.start();
          // Create the Thread to handle the Add Dialog
          AddDialog addThread = new AddDialog(ADDDIALOG,c);
          Thread t3 = new Thread(addThread);
          t3.start();
          // Create the Thread to handle the Delete Dialog
          DeleteDialog deleteThread = new DeleteDialog(DELETEDIALOG,c);
          Thread t4 = new Thread(deleteThread);
          t4.start();
          // Create the Thread to handle the View Dialog
          ViewDialog viewThread = new ViewDialog(VIEWDIALOG,c);
          Thread t5 = new Thread(viewThread);
          t5.start();
          // Create the Thread to handle deleting items from the database
          Delete deleteEmployeeThread = new Delete(DELETE,c);
          Thread t6 = new Thread(deleteEmployeeThread);
          t6.start();
          // Create the Thread to handle adding items to the database
          Add addEmployeeThread = new Add(ADD,c);
          Thread t7 = new Thread(addEmployeeThread);
          t7.start();
     }
     public static void main (String args[]) {
          EmpMainServer app = new EmpMainServer();
     }
}
```

The IDList Component

The IDList component is responsible for displaying all of the employees as well as storing the employee IDs to be used in the various dialog boxes. The IDList is inherited from the normal List component. It also implements the ActionListener interface to provide event handling.

The constructor for the IDList is responsible for adding the employees to the list. Along with adding the employee names to the list to be displayed, the IDList component stores the employee IDs for each employee so that it can pass them to the dialogs. These IDs uniquely identify each employee.

The constructor initially wants to call the ancestor method to create the component. After the component has been created, the component needs to be assigned an `ActionListener` to handle events for the component:

```
this.addActionListener(this);
```

A `Hashtable` object is created to store the IDs for the employees. Each ID is stored with an index that associates it with the item in the list box. The indexes for the items in the list box are identical to the key for the employee IDs in the `Hashtable` object:

```
id = new Hashtable();
```

The component then creates a `Statement` object and SQL statement to retrieve employees into the List component. The SQL `Select` statement retrieves the employee ID column as well as all three of the name columns:

```
Statement sqlStatement = c.createStatement();
String sql = "Select EmpId, FirstName, LastName, MiddleInitial";
```

Next, execute the SQL query and return results into a `ResultSet` object:

```
ResultSet r = sqlStatement.executeQuery(sql);
```

After the results have been retrieved, you cycle through all of the records returned and add each employee name to the List component. First, add the employee ID to the `Hashtable` object and then add the employee's name to the List component:

```
id.put(new Integer(count++), new Integer(r.getInt(1)));
this.addItem(r.getString(2) + " " + r.getString(4) + " " + r.getString(3));
```

After getting all of the results, you need to close the `ResultSet` object and the `Statement` object so that the resources can be released:

```
r.close();
sqlStatement.close();
```

The `getSelectedID()` Method

The `getSelectedID()` method returns the employee ID for the currently selected employee. This method is used by the main menu to get the employee ID to pass to the various dialog boxes. The method returns the value from the `Hashtable` object with the key that matches the currently selected index:

```
Return ((Integer)id.get(new Integer(this.getSelectedIndex()))).intValue();
```

The `actionPerformed()` Method

The `actionPerformed()` method is a blank method that is provided to handle when the user double-clicks on the list. This method is provided through the `ActionListener` interface:

```
public void actionPerformed (ActionEvent evt) {}
```

Listing 19.2 contains the full code for the `IDList` class.

TYPE   **Listing 19.2. The `IDList` class.**

```
public class IDList extends List implements ActionListener {
    Hashtable id;
    int count = 0;
    public IDList (Connection c) {
        // create the list component
        super();
        // handle events using current component
        this.addActionListener(this);
        // create the Hashtable object to use
        id = new Hashtable();
        // populate the list with a collection of employees
        try {
            Statement sqlStatement = c.createStatement();
            String sql =
            ➥"Select EmpId, FirstName, LastName, MiddleInitial from
            ➥tEmployee";
            ResultSet r = sqlStatement.executeQuery(sql);
            while (r.next()) {
                    // Add emp id to Hashtable
                    id.put(new Integer(count++),
                    ➥new Integer(r.getInt(1)));
                    // Add employee name to List
                    this.addItem(r.getString(2) + " " +
                    ➥r.getString(4) + " " + r.getString(3));
            }
            // close the statement and result set objects
            r.close();
            sqlStatement.close();
        }
        catch (Exception e) {}
    }
    public int getSelectedID () {
    // check for a valid index
    if (this.getSelectedIndex() < 0) {
    return -1;
    }

    // return the ID for the currently selected item
            return ((Integer)id.get(new Integer
            ➥ (this.getSelectedIndex())))).intValue();
        }
```

```
public void actionPerformed (ActionEvent e) {
    // don't do anything, provide functionality for use
    // to add event handling
}
}
```

The EmployeeMenu **Class**

The EmployeeMenu class is inherited from the MenuBar class and is used to provide the client with a main menu. The menu adds various items to let the user select application options. The class implements both the ActionListener interface as well as the EmpServices interface. The ActionListener interface provides the class with an actionPerformed() method for handling user clicks on menu items. The EmpServices interface defines the various constants that are used to connect to the object server.

The constructor for the class creates the main menu bar object and adds the menu and menu items. You'll create a File menu object. The File menu contains a menu item that lets the user exit the application. The menu items for the object use the current class as its ActionListener interface:

```
Menu file = new Menu("File");
MenuItem exit = new MenuItem("Exit");
exit.addActionListener(this);
file.add(exit);
this.add(file);
```

The class also creates a Menu object that is used to provide various employee methods. All of the menu items use the current object to provide event handling through the ActionListener interface. The first menu item enables the user to add new employee information:

```
Menu emp = new Menu("Employee");
MenuItem additem = new MenuItem("Add Employee");
additem.addActionListener(this);
emp.add(additem);
```

You'll also create a menu item that lets the user delete the currently selected item:

```
MenuItem deleteitem = new MenuItem("Delete Employee");
deleteitem.addActionListener(this);
emp.add(deleteitem);
```

The final menu item enables the user to view information for the currently selected employee. It opens a dialog box that displays the employee's information:

```
MenuItem viewitem = new MenuItem("View Employee");
viewitem.addActionListener(this);
emp.add(viewitem);
```

19

The final step for the constructor is to add the Employee menu object to the current menu bar:

```
this.add(emp);
```

The `setList()` Method

The `setList()` method sets the specified `List` object to the object variable that is used to store an instance of an `IDList` object. This object is used in the event-handling routines to get the employee ID for passing to the various dialog objects:

```
public void setList (List l) {
    this.list = (IDList)l;
}
```

The `actionPerformed()` Method

The `actionPerformed()` method handles all events that occur on the window that contains the menu. The method handles all of the menu items that are contained on the current menu bar. The method initially calls the `getActionCommand()` method. This method gets a string that identifies the menu that was selected by the user.

You initially check to see whether the menu that was selected was the Exit menu item. If the user chose this menu item, call the `exit()` method. This closes the client application and releases all resources:

```
if (item.equals("Exit")) {
    System.exit(0);
}
```

Next, the method checks to see whether the user chose to add an employee from the menu. If the user chose this option, then the method connects to the object server and gets the Add Employee dialog box to let the user enter a new employee. The method needs to create a `Socket` object that points to the correct host machine and connects to the port that serves the Add dialog box:

```
Socket s = new Socket("localhost", ADDDIALOG);
```

Next, get the `InputStream` object obtained from using the `getInputStream()` method of the socket you just created:

```
InputStream istream = s.getInputStream();
```

Next, create an `ObjectInputStream` object that enables you to get the dialog from the object server:

```
ObjectInputStream in = new ObjectInputStream(istream);
```

After you create the object stream, you can read in the dialog sent from the object server and assign it to a local `Dialog` object. After you have read the passed object into the local `Dialog`, close all of the stream objects and display the dialog box to the user:

```
Dialog d = (Dialog)in.readObject();
istream.close();
s.close();
d.show();
```

Next, the method gets the ID for the currently selected employee. The method calls the `getSelectedID()` method for the current `IDList` object stored by the `MenuBar` object. If no item is currently selected, then the method returns without performing any event handling:

```
if (list.getSelectedID() < 0) {
    return;
}
```

When the user chooses the Delete Employee menu option, then the event creates a new `Socket` object on the object server. It uses the correct host name for the machine and also uses the appropriate port constant from the `EmpServices` interface:

```
Socket s = new Socket("localhost", DELETEDIALOG);
```

The method creates an output stream and outputs the ID for the currently selected employee. The `Dialog` object created depends on the employee ID that is passed. Use an `OutputStream` and an `ObjectOutputStream` object to pass the integer ID to the thread handling the service of the Delete dialog box:

```
OutputStream ostream = s.getOutputStream();
ObjectOutputStream out = new ObjectOutputStream(ostream);
out.writeInt(list.getSelectedID());
ostream.flush();
```

When the method has passed the employee ID, it can begin to receive the Delete dialog that is created for the selected employee ID. Use the `InputStream` and `ObjectInputStream` objects to get the `Dialog` object that is returned from the object server:

```
InputStream istream = s.getInputStream();
ObjectInputStream in = new ObjectInputStream(istream);
Dialog d = (Dialog)in.readObject();
```

When you have retrieved the `Dialog` object returned from the object server, close all objects that need closing and display the returned dialog to the user:

```
ostream.close();
```

```
istream.close();
s.close();
d.show();
```

The final event you need to handle is when the user clicks the View Employee menu option. Like the other menu options, this menu option gets a `Dialog` object from the object server and displays it to the user. This method creates a `Socket` object that connects to the object server on the appropriate machine and the port that serves the view dialog object:

```
Socket s = new Socket("localhost", VIEWDIALOG);
```

Just like the event handling for the delete option, the method passes the currently selected employee ID to the server thread. The View dialog is created based on this ID. When you have written the integer to the server, flush the output stream so that the data is sent to the server immediately:

```
OutputStream ostream = s.getOutputStream();
ObjectOutputStream out = new ObjectOutputStream(ostream);
out.writeInt(list.getSelectedID());
ostream.flush();
```

After the employee ID has been sent to the server thread, you can begin to get the dialog sent back by the object server. Use the `ObjectInputStream` to read in the `Dialog` object:

```
ObjectInputStream in = new ObjectInputStream(istream);
Dialog d = (Dialog)in.readObject();
```

You can then close all of the objects used to send and receive information and show the dialog:

```
ostream.close();
istream.close();
s.close();
d.show();
```

Listing 19.3 contains the full code for the `EmployeeMenu` class.

TYPE   **Listing 19.3. The `EmployeeMenu` class.**

```
public class EmployeeMenu extends MenuBar
➥implements ActionListener, EmpServices {
        IDList list;
        public EmployeeMenu () {
            Menu file = new Menu("File");
            MenuItem exit = new MenuItem("Exit");
            exit.addActionListener(this);
            file.add(exit);
            this.add(file);
            Menu emp = new Menu("Employee");
            MenuItem additem = new MenuItem("Add Employee");
            additem.addActionListener(this);
            emp.add(additem);
            MenuItem deleteitem = new MenuItem("Delete Employee");
```

```
            deleteitem.addActionListener(this);
            emp.add(deleteitem);
            MenuItem viewitem = new MenuItem("View Employee");
            viewitem.addActionListener(this);
            emp.add(viewitem);
            this.add(emp);
    }
    public void setList (IDList l) {
            this.list = (IDList)l;
    }
    public void actionPerformed (ActionEvent evt) {
            // Check for menu items clicked
            String item = evt.getActionCommand();
            if (item.equals("Exit")) {
                    // Exit the application
                    System.exit(0);
            }
            else if (item.equals("Add Employee")) {
                    // Get add dialog from server
                    try {
                        Socket s = new Socket("localhost", ADDDIALOG);
                        InputStream istream = s.getInputStream();
                        ObjectInputStream in =
                        ➥new ObjectInputStream(istream);
                        addEmployeeDialog d =
                        ➥ (addEmployeeDialog)in.readObject();
                        // close stream and socket
                        istream.close();
                        s.close();
                        // display window
                        d.show();

            EmpMain parent = (EmpMain)this.getParent();
            parent.getListBox(false);
            parent.repaint();
                    }
                    catch (Exception e) {}
            }
            // If no item is selected, then no other action can be performed
            if (list.getSelectedID() < 0) {
                    return;
            }
            if (item.equals("Delete Employee")) {
                    // Pass selected id to get delete dialog
                    try {
                        Socket s =
                        ➥new Socket("localhost", DELETEDIALOG);
                        OutputStream ostream = s.getOutputStream();
                        ObjectOutputStream out =
                        ➥new ObjectOutputStream(ostream);
                        out.writeInt(list.getSelectedID());
                        ostream.flush();
                        InputStream istream = s.getInputStream();
                        ObjectInputStream in =
                        ➥new ObjectInputStream(istream);
```

continues

Listing 19.3. continued

```
                            deleteEmployeeDialog d =
                            ➥ (deleteEmployeeDialog)in.readObject();
                            // close all objects
                            ostream.close();
                            istream.close();
                            s.close();
                            // display dialog
                            d.show();

                EmpMain parent = (EmpMain)this.getParent();
                parent.getListBox(false);
                parent.repaint();
                        }
                        catch (Exception e) {}
                }
                else if (item.equals("View Employee")) {
                        try {
                            // Send selected id to get view dialog
                            Socket s = new Socket("localhost", VIEWDIALOG);
                            // Send id
                            OutputStream ostream = s.getOutputStream();
                            ObjectOutputStream out =
                            ➥new ObjectOutputStream(ostream);
                            out.writeInt(list.getSelectedID());
                            ostream.flush();
                            // get dialog
                            InputStream istream = s.getInputStream();
                            ObjectInputStream in = new ObjectInputStream(istream);
                            viewEmployeeDialog d =
                            ➥(viewEmployeeDialog)in.readObject();
                            // Close objects
                            ostream.close();
                            istream.close();
                            s.close();
                            // display dialog
                            d.show();
                        }
                        catch (Exception e) {}
                }
            }
        }
    }
```

Server Threads

In the main application, you created seven `Thread` objects to serve the multiple requests to
the object server. You'll now learn the creation of these objects. Each object implements the
`Runnable` interface to provide it with the `run()` method. Each object also accepts, at a
minimum, the port number that the thread should use for connections. Some of the objects
can also take a `Connection` object to be used when the application connects to a database.

The following is a listing of the seven thread objects you'll create:

- [ ] `GetMenu`
- [ ] `GetEmployeeList`
- [ ] `AddDialog`
- [ ] `DeleteDialog`
- [ ] `ViewDialog`
- [ ] `Delete`
- [ ] `Add`

The `GetMenu` Object

The `GetMenu` object is responsible for sending the menu bar to be used on the client's main window. The menu bar sent is the `EmployeeMenu` that was created in the previous sections. The constructor for the `GetMenu` object takes as a parameter the port number to listen to. This port number is used by a `ServerSocket` object to accept connections to the server:

```
public GetMenu (int port) {
    id = port;
}
```

The `GetMenu` object implements the `Runnable` interface, which means that it is required to implement the `run()` method as well. In the `run()` method, place all of the code to accept connections and send the menu object. You initially want to create a `ServerSocket` object that listens on the port specified by the parameter passed to the constructor:

```
ServerSocket server = new ServerSocket(id);
```

After you have created the server object, you'll want to block further code execution until a client has connected. You do this with the `accept()` method of the `ServerSocket` object. This method blocks further execution until a client has connected to the server:

```
Socket s = server.accept();
```

After a client has connected, you want to get the `OutputStream` object from the `Socket` object and use it to create a new `ObjectOutputStream` object. This object is used to write the menu object to the stream so that the client application can access it and use it:

```
OutputStream ostream = s.getOutputStream();
ObjectOutputStream out = new ObjectOutputStream(ostream);
out.writeObject(new EmployeeMenu());
```

After you have written the object to the stream for the client to access, you can flush the contents of the stream and close both the stream object and the server object:

19

```
        out.flush();
        ostream.close();
        s.close();
```

Listing 19.4 contains the full code for the GetMenu class.

Listing 19.4. The GetMenu class.

```
public class GetMenu implements Runnable {
        int id = 0;
        public GetMenu (int port) {
                id = port;
        }
        public void run () {
                try {
                        ServerSocket server = new ServerSocket(id);
                        while (true) {
                                Socket s = server.accept();
                                OutputStream ostream = s.getOutputStream();
                                ObjectOutputStream out =
                                ➥new ObjectOutputStream(ostream);
                                out.writeObject(new EmployeeMenu());
                                out.flush();
                                ostream.close();
                                s.close();
                        }
                }
                catch (Exception e) {System.out.println(e.getMessage());}
        }
}
```

The GetEmployeeList Object

The GetEmployeeList object serves the IDList component to the client applications. The constructor for the object takes a port number and a Connection object. The port number is used to determine on which port the server should listen for client connections. The Connection object is passed to the IDList constructor so that the component can use it to retrieve employees from the database:

```
public GetEmployeeList (int port, Connection c) {
    id = port;
    this.c = c;
}
```

The object implements the Runnable interface; therefore, it is required to implement the run() method. The run() method handles the creation of the ServerSocket object, which enables connections to the client applications. The ServerSocket object listens on the port number specified in the parameter passed to the constructor object:

```
ServerSocket server = new ServerSocket(id);
```

The method then waits for client connections using the accept() method to block further code execution:

```
Socket s = server.accept();
```

Next, create the IDList object that you'll send back to the client object. Pass the object the Connection object that was passed to the current object in the constructor method:

```
IDList l = new IDList(c);
```

After the list has been created, you can get the OutputStream using the getOutputStream() method for the Socket object and use this stream to create an ObjectOutputStream object. You then use this object to write the list you just created:

```
OutputStream ostream = s.getOutputStream();
ObjectOutputStream out = new ObjectOutputStream(ostream);
out.writeObject(l);
```

After you have written the object to the stream for the client application to access, you'll need to flush the contents of the stream and close all objects that require closing:

```
out.flush();
ostream.close();
s.close();
```

Listing 19.5 contains the full code for the GetEmployeeList object.

TYPE **Listing 19.5. The GetEmployeeList object.**

```
public class GetEmployeeList implements Runnable {
        int id = 0;
        Connection c;
        public GetEmployeeList (int port, Connection c) {
                id = port;
                this.c = c;
        }
        public void run () {
                try {
                        ServerSocket server = new ServerSocket(id);
                        while (true) {
                                Socket s = server.accept();
                                IDList l = new IDList(c);
                                OutputStream ostream = s.getOutputStream();
                                ObjectOutputStream out =
                                ➥new ObjectOutputStream(ostream);
                                out.writeObject(l);
                                out.flush();
                                ostream.close();
                                s.close();
                        }
                }
                catch (Exception e) {System.out.println(e.getMessage());}
        }
}
```

19

The `AddDialog` **Object**

The `AddDialog` object handles all client requests for adding employee information. The `Dialog` object is created and stored as another class. This object is only required to wait for client connections; when a client connects, it sends the dialog over the stream to the client.

The constructor for the dialog takes an integer that identifies the port on which the thread should listen for client connections and a `Connection` object that might possibly be used for later purposes. The constructor assigns the passed port identifier to the local variable ID as well as the passed `Connection` object to the local variable c:

```
public AddDialog (int port, Connection c) {
    id = port;
    this.c = c;
}
```

Because the object is implementing the `Runnable` interface, you are required to implement the `run()` method of the interface. This method contains the code that is run as part of the thread. You initially create a `ServerSocket` object to listen on the port specified in the constructor:

```
ServerSocket server = new ServerSocket(id);
```

After the server has been created, you start a continuous loop that waits for client connections. When a client connects, use the `accept()` method to quit code blocking and to process the client's request:

```
Socket s = server.accept();
```

When the client has connected to the server, get the output stream for the socket and use this output stream to create a new `ObjectOutputStream` object:

```
OutputStream ostream = s.getOutputStream();
ObjectOutputStream out = new ObjectOutputStream(ostream);
```

When the object stream has been created, you can write a new instance of the `addEmployeeDialog` object to the stream for the client to access. When the object has been written to the stream, you need to flush the contents of the object stream and close the output stream and socket object. The `addEmployeeDialog` object is passed a `Frame` object because a `Dialog` object requires a parent frame before it can be created.

```
out.writeObject(new addEmployeeDialog(f));
out.flush();
ostream.close();
s.close();
```

Listing 19.6 contains the full code for the `AddDialog` class.

Listing 19.6. The AddDialog class.

```
public class AddDialog implements Runnable {
        int id = 0;
        Connection c;
        public AddDialog (int port, Connection c) {
                id = port;
                this.c = c;
        }
        public void run () {
        try {
            ServerSocket server = new ServerSocket(id);
            while (true) {
                Socket s = server.accept();

                Frame f = new Frame();

                OutputStream ostream = s.getOutputStream();
                ObjectOutputStream out = new ObjectOutputStream(ostream);
                out.writeObject(new addEmployeeDialog(f));
                out.flush();
                ostream.close();
                s.close();
            }
        }
        catch (Exception e)  {}
    }
}
```

The DeleteDialog Object

The DeleteDialog object is very similar to the AddDialog object in that it returns a prebuilt Dialog object to the user. It does differ, though, in that the DeleteDialog object takes input from the client in the form of the employee ID.

The constructor for the DeleteDialog object looks exactly the same as the constructor for the AddDialog. It takes both the port number and a Connection object:

```
public DeleteDialog (int port, Connection c) {
    id = port;
    this.c = c;
}
```

The object implements the run() method of the Runnable interface. The code contained in this method handles client connections that request the DeleteDialog object. The run() method initially creates a ServerSocket object that listens on the port specified by the integer passed to the constructor:

```
ServerSocket server = new ServerSocket(id);
```

The method then gets the input stream for the current socket being used. The input stream is then used to create the ObjectInputStream object that is used to get the passed employee ID:

```
InputStream istream = s.getInputStream();
ObjectInputStream in = new ObjectInputStream(istream);
int empid = in.readInt();
```

When you have the employee ID, you can pass it to the constructor for the deleteEmployeeDialog class to create a new instance of the dialog:

```
deleteEmployeeDialog d = new deleteEmployeeDialog(f, empid, c);
```

When the dialog has been created, you can get the output stream for the socket and use it to create an object stream that is used to send the dialog back to the client application:

```
OutputStream ostream = s.getOutputStream();
ObjectOutputStream out = new ObjectOutputStream(ostream);
out.writeObject(d);
```

You then flush the contents of the object stream and close the two stream objects and the socket object as well. Listing 19.7 contains the full code for the DeleteDialog object.

TYPE   **Listing 19.7. The DeleteDialog object.**

```
public class DeleteDialog implements Runnable {
        int id = 0;
        Connection c;
        public DeleteDialog (int port, Connection c) {
                id = port;
                this.c = c;
        }
        public void run () {
        try {
            ServerSocket server = new ServerSocket(id);
            while(true) {
                Socket s = server.accept();
                Frame f = new Frame();
                // Get passed employee id
                InputStream istream = s.getInputStream();
                ObjectInputStream in = new ObjectInputStream(istream);
                int empid = in.readInt();

                // Create employee dialog
                deleteEmployeeDialog d = new deleteEmployeeDialog(f, empid, c);
                OutputStream ostream = s.getOutputStream();
                ObjectOutputStream out = new ObjectOutputStream(ostream);
                out.writeObject(d);
                out.flush();

                istream.close();
                ostream.close();
```

19

```
            s.close();
        }
    }
    catch (Exception e) {}
    }
}
```

The ViewDialog Object

The ViewDialog object is responsible for handling the requests for the dialog object to view information for employees. The object handles connections from client applications that request the dialog to view employee information for a specified employee ID.

The constructor for the ViewDialog object performs the same function as the constructors for the other dialog object threads. The constructor stores a passed port and Connection object in local object variables for use in the run() method.

The run() method is implemented because the class implements the Runnable interface. The method initially creates a ServerSocket object that listens on the port specified in the constructor method:

```
ServerSocket server = new ServerSocket(id);
```

Like the DeleteDialog object, this method gets the employee ID passed from the client application and uses this ID to create a new dialog that displays the employee's information. This dialog is then passed back to the client application.

Listing 19.8 contains the full code for the ViewDialog object.

19

TYPE **Listing 19.8. The ViewDialog object.**

```
public class ViewDialog implements Runnable {
        int id = 0;
        Connection c;
        public ViewDialog (int port, Connection c) {
                id = port;
                this.c = c;
        }
        public void run () {
        try {
            ServerSocket server = new ServerSocket(id);
            while (true) {
                Socket s = server.accept();
                Frame f = new Frame();

                // Get passed employee id
                InputStream istream = s.getInputStream();
```

continues

Listing 19.8. continued

```
                    ObjectInputStream in = new ObjectInputStream(istream);
                    int empid = in.readInt();
                    // Create the view dialog
                    viewEmployeeDialog d = new viewEmployeeDialog(f, empid, c);
                    OutputStream ostream = s.getOutputStream();
                    ObjectOutputStream out = new ObjectOutputStream(ostream);
                    out.writeObject(d);
                    out.flush();
                    istream.close();
                    ostream.close();
                    s.close();
                }
            }
        catch (Exception e) {}
        }
    }
```

The Delete Object

The Delete object handles the deletion of employees from the database. The Delete object handles requests from the deleteEmployeeDialog to delete a specified employee from the database.

The constructor for the Delete object looks exactly the same as the constructor for the other objects. It takes an integer identifying a port and a Connection object to use for database access:

```
public Delete (int port, Connection c) {
    id = port;
    this.c = c;
}
```

The run() method contains the code for handling the connections from the client applications. The method creates a ServerSocket object to listen on the port specified by the constructor. This is the port that the client will attempt to connect to when sending the information to delete employees.

```
ServerSocket server = new ServerSocket(id);
```

The method then gets the input stream for the socket and reads in the employee ID that is passed to the server thread. The input stream is used to create a new object stream to enable the method to read the integer value into a local integer:

```
InputStream istream = s.getInputStream();
ObjectInputStream in = new ObjectInputStream(istream);
int empid = in.readInt();
```

19

When you have the employee ID that the client wants to delete, create a SQL statement that deletes the information from the tEmployee table. A `Statement` object is created to execute the SQL `delete` statement.

```
Statement sqlStatement = c.createStatement();
String sql = "delete from tEmployee where empid = " +
            Integer.toString(empid);
sqlStatement.executeUpdate(sql);
sqlStatement.close();
```

Listing 19.9 contains the full code for the `Delete` object.

TYPE **Listing 19.9. The `Delete` object.**

```
public class Delete implements Runnable {
        int id = 0;
        Connection c;
        public Delete (int port, Connection c) {
                id = port;
                this.c = c;
        }
        public void run () {
                try {
                        ServerSocket server = new ServerSocket(id);
                        while (true) {
                                Socket s = server.accept();
                                // Get the passed employee id
                                InputStream istream = s.getInputStream();
                                ObjectInputStream in =
                                ➡new ObjectInputStream(istream);
                                int empid = in.readInt();
                                istream.close();
                                s.close();
                                // delete all records having
                                // the specified employee id
                                Statement sqlStatement = c.createStatement();
                                String sql =
                                ➡"delete from tEmployee where EmpId = " +
                                        Integer.toString(empid);
                                sqlStatement.executeUpdate(sql);
                                sqlStatement.close();
                        }
                }
                catch (Exception e) {System.out.println(e.getMessage());}
        }
}
```

19

The `Add` Object

The `Add` object is used by the `addEmployeeDialog` to add new employees to the database. The object creates a server thread that accepts information from a client application. The information is passed over the socket's stream and is stored in local `String` objects. These strings are then used to create a SQL `Insert` statement that inserts the appropriate items into the database.

The `run()` method for the object handles the client connection and gets the information from the client for the new employee. The method initially creates a `ServerSocket` object to listen on the specified port for client connections:

```
ServerSocket server = new ServerSocket(id);
```

The method then uses the input stream of the socket to create a new object stream to read in values sent by the client application for the new employee. Notice that you need to typecast each of the strings sent by the client application from `Object` to `String` type. Also, you need to read in the strings in the exact order they are written by the client application. All objects retrieved using the `readObject()` method will need to be typecast.

```
InputStream istream = s.getInputStream();
ObjectInputStream in = new ObjectInputStream(istream);
String firstname = (String)in.readObject();
String middleinitial = (String)in.readObject();
String lastname = (String)in.readObject();
String ssn = (String)in.readObject();
```

When all of the information is read in from the client, create a `PreparedStatement` object to insert the data into the database. Create the following SQL `Insert` statement to insert the data into the database:

```
String sql = "insert into tEmployee (FirstName, " +
            "MiddleInitial, LastName, SSN) " +
            "values (?, ?, ?, ?)";
```

The `?` in this string indicates values that you'll set using the `PreparedStatement` object. Create the statement from the `Connection` object stored in the object variable c:

```
PreparedStatement prepare = c.prepareStatement(sql);
prepare.setString(1, firstname);
prepare.setString(2, middleinitial);
prepare.setString(3, lastname);
prepare.setString(4, ssn);
```

When all of the items have been set in the statement, execute the statement and add the new employee to the database:

```
prepare.executeUpdate();
```

Listing 19.10 contains the full code for the `Add` object.

19

TYPE **Listing 19.10. The Add object.**

```
public class Add implements Runnable {
        int id = 0;
        Connection c;
        public Add (int port, Connection c) {
                id = port;
                this.c = c;
        }
        public void run () {
                try {
                        ServerSocket server = new ServerSocket(id);
                        while(true) {
                                Socket s = server.accept();
                                // Get the input stream so as to get all passed
                                // data values
                                InputStream istream = s.getInputStream();
                                ObjectInputStream in =
                                ➥new ObjectInputStream(istream);
                                String firstname = (String)in.readObject();
                                String middleinitial = (String)in.readObject();
                                String lastname = (String)in.readObject();
                                String ssn = (String)in.readObject();
                        String sql = "insert into tEmployee (FirstName, " +
                                "MiddleInitial, LastName, SSN) " +
                                "values (?, ?, ?, ?)";
                        PreparedStatement prepare = c.prepareStatement(sql);
                        prepare.setString(1, firstname);
                        prepare.setString(2, middleinitial);
                        prepare.setString(3, lastname);
                        prepare.setString(4, ssn);
                                // execute sql statement
                                prepare.executeUpdate();
                                // close all objects
                                prepare.close();
                                istream.close();
                                s.close();
                        }
                }
                catch (Exception e) {}
        }
}
```

19

Summary

Today's lesson has introduced you to the basics of creating the Employee Manager application. You have learned various topics, including how to create a basic object server to handle clients that request objects from a centralized server.

In this lesson, you created the object server and all of the objects that are used to handle client connections to the database. You created all of the threads that handle client connections on different ports, and also the list and menu components that are sent to the client to display on the main window.

On Day 20, "Creating the Employee Resource Application Server," you will finish the Employee Manager application by creating the various dialogs that are sent from the object server to the client applications, and you will also create the client application that is used to start the application.

Workshop

The Workshop provides quiz questions to help you solidify your understanding of the material covered and exercises to give you experience in using what you've learned. The answers are provided in Appendix A, "Quiz and Exercise Answers." Try to understand the quiz and exercise answers before you go on to tomorrow's lesson.

Quiz

1. How many thread objects will the object server use for client connections?
2. What is the URL for the database we are using?
3. What method of the IDList component returns the employee ID for the selected item?
4. What object is used to listen for client connections?
5. What method connects a client to a server?
6. What method is used to get the output stream for a socket object?
7. What method is used to read String objects from an object stream?
8. What method clears the contents of an object output stream to ensure that the client receives the data?
9. What is the purpose of the Delete object?
10. What object is used to send the deleteEmployeeDialog to the client?

Exercise

1. Now that you have an idea of how to send and receive information using serialization and sockets, create a small application that will serve various objects from an object server to client machines. The application should enable a user to get Java objects that are already created on the server.

Day 20

Creating the Employee Resource Application Server

Today, you will finish the Employee application that you started yesterday. Today's lesson focuses on creating the application's dialog boxes that provide the user a way to add, delete, and view employee information. You will also create the client application stub that connects to the object server to get the application components.

All three of the dialogs that you create today will be created on the server side, and the object server will send the dialog objects to the client as requested. The dialog boxes are created entirely on the server and sent to the client as entire dialog boxes. The client application stub gets the components for its window instead of getting an entire Frame object.

Today, you learn the following:

☐ The dialog to delete employee information

☐ The dialog to view employee information

☐ The dialog to add employee information

☐ The client application stub

The Dialog to Delete Employee Information

One of the dialogs that you'll create will let the user delete employee information. The dialog box asks the user for confirmation on whether he or she wants to delete the specified employee. The dialog displays a label showing the name of the employee who was selected in the main window and provides two buttons that let the user delete the employee or let the user cancel deletion of the employee.

The deleteEmployeeDialog class extends the Dialog class and implements the EmpServices and ActionListener interface. You'll implement the EmpServices interface so that the dialog can use the port constants in the interface to connect to the object server thread that will delete a specified employee.

The class also implements the ActionListener interface to handle the events when the user clicks the two buttons contained on the dialog. This interface defines the actionPerformed() method, which enables you to handle the events for the buttons:

```
public class deleteEmployeeDialog extends Dialog implements
    EmpServices, ActionListener
```

The class also declares three object variables that are used to store references to the two Button objects as well as the employee ID. The employee ID is sent to the object server so that the employee can be deleted:

```
Button ok, cancel;
int id;
```

Dialog Constructor

The constructor for the deleteEmployeeDialog is responsible for creating the dialog box and displaying the components on the dialog box. The dialog box gets the information for the information label by connecting to the database and using a passed employee ID to obtain the full name of the employee.

The constructor initially calls the super() method of the Dialog object to create the basic object. You pass the ancestor method the Frame object that was passed to the constructor as well as a string identifying the type of the dialog and a Boolean that indicates that the dialog will be a modal dialog. A *modal dialog* is a dialog that's active for the application and remains active until it is closed:

```
super(parent, "Delete Employee", true);
```

This method then stores the passed employee ID in an object variable. This employee ID is used later in the dialog if the user chooses to delete the selected employee:

```
this.id = id;
```

After the employee ID has been stored for later use, it can be used to get the employee's full name from the database. You'll first create a SQL statement that returns the name of the employee who has the specified employee ID:

```
String sql = "select firstname, lastname from tEmployee " +
             "where empid = ?";
```

The question mark (?) in the string indicates that you'll use the set*XXX*() methods of the PreparedStatement interface to set the value. Create a PreparedStatement object using the Connection object that was passed to the dialog:

```
PreparedStatement prepare = c.prepareStatement(sql);
```

After you have the PreparedStatement object, you can set the value of the employee ID using the setInt() method. Pass the method the value 1, which indicates that the first parameter will be set. Also pass the employee ID that was passed to the dialog.

```
prepare.setInt(1, id);
```

When the statement is ready, you can execute the statement against the database and store the results in a ResultSet object:

```
ResultSet r = prepare.executeQuery();
```

Next, call the next() method of the ResultSet object to move the pointer to the first record in the returned result set. When the record pointer has been moved to the first returned record, create a new Label object with the values from the first name and last name columns of the result set:

```
r.next();
Label l = new Label("Delete Employee - " + r.getString(1) +
    " " + r.getString(2));
```

Then change the font for the newly created Label object to be 18-point Times New Roman. This creates a slightly larger than average description to display to the user:

```
l.setFont(new Font("Times New Roman", Font.PLAIN, 18));
```

20

When all of the information has been retrieved and stored in the Label object, add the label to the North section of the dialog box and close the statement object:

```
this.add("North", 1);
prepare.close();
```

Now that the Label object has been created and added to the dialog, create and add the two buttons to let the user confirm or cancel deletion.

Next, create a new Panel object to place on the dialog. This Panel object will contain the two buttons. You are using this panel to display the buttons centered in the bottom of the window. You could use another layout to place the components, but you are going to use the standard, and simpler, Layout Managers. Set the Layout Manager for the new panel to be the FlowLayout Manager, and use the FlowLayout that gives you a centering layout for components:

```
Panel p = new Panel();
p.setLayout(new FlowLayout(FlowLayout.CENTER));
```

Now, create the buttons and place them on the new panel. You use the current object as the event handler for the buttons, so you need to use the addActionListener() method for both buttons and pass it a reference to the current object. The first button that you'll create is the OK button. This button lets the user confirm deletion of the selected employee.

```
ok = new Button("Ok");
ok.addActionListener(this);
```

The second button is the Cancel button. This button lets the user cancel deletion of the selected employee.

```
cancel = new Button("Cancel");
cancel.addActionListener(this);
```

When you have created the buttons, add them to the panel and then add the panel to the dialog, and size the dialog box to an appropriate size to display all items correctly.

```
p.add(ok);
p.add(cancel);
this.add("South", p);
this.resize(350, 120);
```

Listing 20.1 contains the full code for the constructor of the deleteEmployeeDialog class.

TYPE   **Listing 20.1. The deleteEmployeeDialog class.**

```
public deleteEmployeeDialog (Frame parent, int id, Connection c) {
            super(parent, "Delete Employee", true);

            // store id for use in deleting
            this.id = id;
```

```
                // Get the employees name based on passed id
                try {
                        String sql =
                        ➡"select firstname, lastname from tEmployee " +
                                        "where empid = ?";
                        PreparedStatement prepare = c.prepareStatement(sql);
                        prepare.setInt(1, id);
                        ResultSet r = prepare.executeQuery();
                        r.next();
                        Label l =
new Label("Delete employee - " + r.getString(1) + " " + r.getString(2));
                        l.setFont(new Font("Times New Roman", Font.PLAIN, 18));
                        this.add("North", l);
                        prepare.close();
                }
                catch (Exception e) {}

                Panel p = new Panel();
                p.setLayout(new FlowLayout(FlowLayout.CENTER));

                // Create and layout buttons on window
                ok = new Button("Ok");
                ok.addActionListener(this);
                cancel = new Button("Cancel");
                cancel.addActionListener(this);
                p.add(ok);
                p.add(cancel);
                this.add("South", p);

                this.resize(350, 120);
}
```

The `actionPerformed()` Method

The actionPerformed() method is used when the user clicks any of the buttons on the dialog box. The method is defined in the ActionListener interface and takes a parameter of type ActionEvent.

The method initially gets the value returned by the getActionCommand() method. This method returns a string containing information on the item that generated the action event. In our case, the item will contain the label of the Button object that was clicked:

```
String item = evt.getActionCommand();
```

Now compare the value of the item variable to the labels of the two buttons on the dialog. If the value matches the Cancel button label, hide the dialog and dispose of the resources used by the dialog:

```
if ("Cancel".equals(item)) {
    this.hide();
    this.dispose();
}
```

If the user clicks the OK button, connect to the object server and pass the employee ID that was passed to the dialog. You connect to the object server on the port specified as the DELETE port. This port accepts connections from clients that are trying to delete items from the database. You need to create a Socket object that uses the specified port:

```
Socket s = new Socket("localhost", DELETE);
```

After the connection has been created to the object server, get the output stream for the socket and use it to create a new object stream:

```
OutputStream ostream = s.getOutputStream();
ObjectOutputStream out = new ObjectOutputStream(ostream);
```

Next, use the object stream to write the employee ID to the output stream so that the object server gets the employee ID and deletes the employee from the database. When you have written the employee ID to the object server, flush the contents of the stream and close all of the objects, including the dialog:

```
out.writeInt(id);
out.flush();
ostream.close();
s.close();
this.hide();
this.dispose();
```

Listing 20.2 contains the full code for the actionPerformed() method.

TYPE **Listing 20.2. The actionPerformed() method.**

```
public void actionPerformed (ActionEvent evt) {

        String item = evt.getActionCommand();

        if ("Ok".equals(item)) {
                // Connect to server and pass id to delete
                try {
                        Socket s = new Socket("localhost", DELETE);

                        OutputStream ostream = s.getOutputStream();
                        ObjectOutputStream out =
                        ➥new ObjectOutputStream(ostream);
                        out.writeInt(id);
                        out.flush();
                        ostream.close();
                        s.close();
                        this.hide();
                        this.dispose();
                }
                catch (Exception e) {}
        }

        if ("Cancel".equals(item)) {
```

```
                          this.hide();
                          this.dispose();
                   }
            }
```

The Dialog to View Employee Information

The `viewEmployeeDialog` class creates a dialog box that displays information about a specified employee. The class extends the `Dialog` object and implements the `ActionListener` interface. The `ActionListener` interface defines the `actionPerformed()` method that will handle user actions. The dialog box will actually be created on the server and will be sent to the client using serialization.

The Constructor Method

The constructor for the class creates the dialog and gets the information from the database to place on the dialog. The information is retrieved from the database using the employee ID passed to the dialog. The constructor initially calls the ancestor constructor to create the components. This dialog will be modal, so the third parameter to the ancestor method is a Boolean `true`:

```
super(parent, "View Employee", true);
```

After you create the dialog, make a SQL statement to get the information for a selected employee. The SQL statement you'll use is a dynamic SQL statement. Don't specify the actual employee ID value in the statement; instead, use a placeholder that indicates you'll replace it with a data value at a later time.

```
String sql = "select firstname, lastname, middleinitital, " +
             "ssn from tEmployee where empid = ?";
```

Then create a `PreparedStatement` with this SQL statement. Use the `Connection` object that was passed to the dialog from the object server. This connection to the database is used by all objects contained in the object server:

```
PreparedStatement prepare = c.prepareStatement(sql);
```

Because you created a dynamic SQL statement, you need to set the value for the placeholder that you used in the SQL statement. The `setInt()` method will set the value of a specified parameter to an integer value passed to the method.

```
prepare.setInt(1, id);
```

When you have set the parameter for the employee ID, you can execute the query and store the returned `ResultSet` object in a new instance of `ResultSet`. You'll need to call the `next()`

20

method to move the pointer to the first record in the result set. The dialog will only display the first record returned in the result set. If any duplicates exist, they will not be displayed.

```
ResultSet r = prepare.executeQuery();
r.next();
```

Now that you have a result set from which to get the employee information, you can begin to add the information to the dialog to display to the user. Create a separate Panel object on which to place all of the employee information. This panel uses a GridLayout Manager to enable you to place an information label and then a data label.

```
Panel p1 = new Panel();
p1.setLayout(new GridLayout(4,2));
```

Add all of the data values to this panel, as well as an information label describing what the data value means. Create Label objects to store all of the information. The following two lines of code illustrate how you do this for the data contained in the FirstName column. The other columns are handled similarly.

```
p1.add(new Label("First Name"));
p1.add(new Label(r.getString(1)));
```

When all of the data values have been added, place the entire Panel object in the North section of the dialog box, and then create another Panel object to store the button to close the dialog. This new panel uses a centered FlowLayout Manager.

```
Panel p2 = new Panel();
p2.setLayout(new FlowLayout(FlowLayout.CENTER));
```

The new button enables the user to close the dialog and return to the main window. The button adds the current class as its ActionListener. The actionPerformed() method for the current class handles the user's actions on the button:

```
close = new Button("Close");
close.addActionListener(this);
```

When the second panel has been added to the South part of the dialog, close the statement object to release resources and then resize the dialog box to an appropriate size for the user to view. Listing 20.3 contains the code for the constructor of the viewEmployeeDialog class.

TYPE   **Listing 20.3. The viewEmployeeDialog class.**

```
public viewEmployeeDialog (Frame parent, int id, Connection c) {
            super(parent, "View Employee", true);

        // get employee information based on employee id
        try {
            String sql =
            ➥"select firstname, lastname, middleinitial, " +
                    "ssn from tEmployee where empid = ?";
```

```
                    PreparedStatement prepare = c.prepareStatement(sql);
                    prepare.setInt(1, id);
                    ResultSet r = prepare.executeQuery();
                    r.next();

                    Panel p1 = new Panel();
                    p1.setLayout(new GridLayout(4,2));
                    p1.add(new Label("First Name"));
                    p1.add(new Label(r.getString(1)));
                    p1.add(new Label("Last Name"));
                    p1.add(new Label(r.getString(2)));
                    p1.add(new Label("Middle Initial"));
                    p1.add(new Label(r.getString(3)));
                    p1.add(new Label("Social Security #"));
                    p1.add(new Label(r.getString(4)));
                    this.add("North", p1);

                    close = new Button("Close");
                    close.addActionListener(this);
                    Panel p2 = new Panel();
                    p2.setLayout(new FlowLayout(FlowLayout.CENTER));
                    p2.add(close);
                    this.add("South", p2);

                    prepare.close();
                }
                catch (Exception e) {}

                this.resize(200, 200);
        }
```

The `actionPerformed()` Method

The `actionPerformed()` method handles all of the user's actions on the dialog box. The only action that you'll concern yourself with is when the user clicks the Close button. You call the `getActionCommand()` method of the `ActionEvent` object to get a string that contains the label for the button that was clicked.

```
String item = evt.getActionCommand();
```

If the user clicked the Close button, hide the window using the `hide()` method and then dispose of the window so that the resources are released back to the operating system:

```
if ("Close".equals(item)) {
    this.hide();
    this.dispose();
}
```

Listing 20.4 contains the full code for the `actionPerformed()` method of the `viewEmployeeDialog` class.

20

Listing 20.4. The `actionPerformed()` method.

```
public void actionPerformed (ActionEvent evt) {

        String item = evt.getActionCommand();

        if ("Close".equals(item)) {
                this.hide();
                this.dispose();
        }
}
```

The Dialog to Add Employee Information

The final dialog box that you'll create lets the user add an employee to the database. The dialog displays multiple entry fields to the user for entering information for an employee.

The constructor for the dialog is responsible for laying out the components on the dialog. You'll create two separate panels to use for adding components to the dialog box. The top panel contains all of the entry fields for user entry of employee information. The bottom panel contains two buttons to let the user choose whether to add a new employee or close the dialog without adding a new employee.

The constructor method initially calls the ancestor constructor to create the dialog. Pass the parent object that was passed in the constructor method for the dialog as well as a string that is displayed on the dialog and a Boolean value indicating that you want the dialog to be modal:

```
super(parent, "Add Employee", true);
```

Then create the top panel that will display all of the entry fields for the user. Use a GridLayout for this panel so that all of the description labels will be across from the entry fields:

```
Panel top = new Panel();
top.setLayout(new GridLayout(4, 2));
```

When all of the entry fields and description labels have been added to the top panel, create the bottom panel to display the two buttons to the user. The bottom panel uses a centered FlowLayout to display the buttons to the user.

```
Panel bottom = new Panel();
bottom.setLayout(new FlowLayout(FlowLayout.CENTER));
```

After you create the bottom panel, add the buttons to the panel, and add the current component as the `ActionListener` object for each of the two buttons:

```
add.addActionListener(this);
close.addActionListener(this);
```

Listing 20.5 contains the full code for the constructor method for the `addEmployeeDialog` class.

TYPE **Listing 20.5. The `addEmployeeDialog` constructor method.**

```
public addEmployeeDialog (Frame parent) {

                super(parent, "Add Employee", true);

                // Create a panel to display user fields on
                Panel top = new Panel();
                top.setLayout(new GridLayout(4, 2));

                // Create components and add to Panel
                top.add(new Label("First Name : "));
                top.add(firstName = new TextField(25));
                top.add(new Label("Middle Initial : "));
                top.add(middleInitial = new TextField(4));
                top.add(new Label("Last Name : "));
                top.add(lastName = new TextField(25));
                top.add(new Label("SSN : "));
                top.add(SSN = new TextField(12));
                this.add("North", top);

                // Create panel to display buttons
                Panel bottom = new Panel();
                bottom.setLayout(new FlowLayout(FlowLayout.CENTER));

                // Create buttons and add to panel
                bottom.add(add = new Button("Add"));
                add.addActionListener(this);
                bottom.add(close = new Button("Close"));
                close.addActionListener(this);
                this.add("South", bottom);

                this.resize(200, 200);
}
```

To handle clicks on the buttons by the user, the class implements the `actionPerformed()` method of the `ActionListener` interface. This method receives all action events generated for the two buttons. Action events include the user clicking the button. You first want to get the label of the button that was clicked using the `getActionCommand()` method:

```
String item = evt.getActionCommand();
```

When you have the label for the button that was clicked, you can check it against the two labels for the buttons on the dialog. If the user clicked the Close button, hide the dialog and then dispose of its resources:

```
if ("Close".equals(item)) {
    this.setVisible(false);
    this.dispose();
    return;
}
```

20

If the user clicked the Add button, then you want to call the `addEmployee()` method to add the employee information. When the employee information has been added to the database, close the dialog using the same means as used in the earlier code.

Listing 20.6 contains the full code for the `actionPerformed()` method.

TYPE   **Listing 20.6. The `actionPerformed()` method.**

```
public void actionPerformed (ActionEvent evt) {
          String item = evt.getActionCommand();

          // if user clicked close button, then close window and dispose
          if ("Close".equals(item)) {
                 this.setVisible(false);
                 this.dispose();
                 return;
          }
          // If user clicked Add button, call method to add items
          if ("Add".equals(item)) {
                 // Add employee information
                 addEmployee();

                 this.setVisible(false);
                 this.dispose();
                 return;
          }
}
```

The `addEmployee()` method that I mentioned earlier is responsible for sending the entered data to the object server to be inserted into the database. The method creates a connection to the object server using a `Socket` object. The `Socket` object takes the name of the computer that contains the object server application as well as a port number that identifies which port is listening for clients wanting to add employee information.

```
Socket s = new Socket("localhost", ADD);
```

When a connection has been made to the object server, you can get the output stream for the socket and use it to create a new object stream. You then send the text for all of the components on the screen to the object server to be processed. Use the `writeObject()` method to send the `String` objects returned by the `getText()` methods for all of the entry fields.

Listing 20.7 contains the full code for the `addEmployee()` method.

TYPE   **Listing 20.7. The `addEmployee()` method.**

```
void addEmployee () {
          try {
```

20

```
                    // Create a connection to the object server
                    Socket s = new Socket("localhost", ADD);

                    OutputStream ostream = s.getOutputStream();
                    ObjectOutputStream out =
                    ➥new ObjectOutputStream(ostream);
                    out.writeObject(firstName.getText());
                    out.writeObject(middleInitial.getText());
                    out.writeObject(lastName.getText());
                    out.writeObject(SSN.getText());
                    out.flush();
                    ostream.close();
                    s.close();
            }
            catch (Exception e) {}
    }
}
```

The Client Application Stub

The client application that you'll create to connect to the object server will be a stub
application. The application will not contain any business logic. The only purpose of the
client application is to get the objects for the main window and display them. There is no
event handling in the client application. All event handling is handled in the menu
component that is sent from the object server.

The client application constructor is responsible for getting the menu and list components
from the object server and displaying them. The method initially calls the ancestor method
to create the actual Frame object. It then sizes the frame using the setSize() method. This
method replaces the resize() method used previously. We are using the setSize() method
instead of the resize() method because the Java 1.1 API replaced the resize() method with
the setSize() method.

```
super("Employee Maintenance Application");
this.setSize(300, 300);
```

The method then creates a connection to the object server and gets the MenuBar object that
will be displayed. This MenuBar object is the EmployeeMenu object that was defined in
yesterday's lesson. The menu can contain any number of items and can be changed without
the client application having to be recompiled.

You create a Socket object that connects to the local machine on the port that serves the menu
object. Because the client application implements the EmpServices interface, you can use the
predefined port constants to connect to the object server:

```
Socket s = new Socket("localhost", GETMENU);
```

20

After you create the connection to the object server, you can get the input stream for the connection and use this stream to create an `ObjectInputStream` that will enable you to get the menu object from the object server:

```
InputStream istream = s.getInputStream();
ObjectInputStream pin = new ObjectInputStream(istream);
```

When you have an object stream, you can read the menu object sent from the object server into a local object. You need to typecast the object sent from the object server to the appropriate type:

```
mb = (EmployeeMenu)pin.readObject();
```

The object can then be assigned to the frame, and the stream and socket objects closed to release resources:

```
this.setMenuBar(mb);
istream.close();
s.close();
```

After you get the menu for the frame, call the `getListBox()` method. This method is implemented by the client application to get the list object to be displayed on the client from the object server. You are creating a separate method for getting the list because it will need to be retrieved several times throughout the application. This method takes a Boolean parameter that identifies whether or not the method should remove the current list object before adding the new list. Passing a `false` parameter will remove the current object before adding a new object:

```
getListBox(true);
```

Next, call the `setList()` method for the `EmployeeMenu` object. This method hooks the menu for the client to the list that contains employee data. Hooking the two objects enables the menu to get the needed information based on user selection:

```
mb.setList(employees);
```

When all of the components have been retrieved from the object server and displayed on the client application, you need to show the client frame to the user with the `show()` method:

```
this.show();
```

Listing 20.8 contains the full code for the constructor method for the `EmpMain` class.

TYPE   **Listing 20.8. The `EmpMain` constructor method.**

```
public EmpMain () {
                super("Employee Maintenance Application");

                this.setSize(300,300);
```

```
try {
        Socket s = new Socket("localhost", GETMENU);

        InputStream istream = s.getInputStream();
        ObjectInputStream pin = new ObjectInputStream(istream);
        mb = (EmployeeMenu)pin.readObject();
        this.setMenuBar(mb);
        istream.close();
        s.close();
}
catch (Exception e) {System.out.println
➡ ("Caught Exception "+e.getMessage() );}

// Get the list of employees to display
getListBox(true);

// set the list box to use for the menu bar
mb.setList(employees);

this.show();
}
```

In the constructor method, you referenced the getListBox() method, which gets the
employee list from the object server. This method takes one parameter that determines
whether or not the method will remove the current list component before adding the new
component. If the passed Boolean variable is false, then the method will remove the current
list component before adding the new list component:

```
if (!c) {
    this.remove(employees);
}
```

The method then creates a connection to the object server on the port that serves the IDList
component. Create a Socket object that connects to the local computer on the correct port:

```
Socket s = new Socket("localhost", GETEMPLOYEELIST);
```

After the connection has been created, get the input stream for the socket and use this input
stream to create a new object stream. Then, call the readObject() method for the created
object stream to get the IDList component:

```
employees = (IDList)in.readObject();
```

You then add the component to the client application so that the user is able to view the
employees from the database:

```
this.add("Center", employees);
```

Listing 20.9 contains the full code for the getListBox() method.

20

TYPE **Listing 20.9. The `getListBox()` method.**

```
public void getListBox (boolean c) {
                try {
                        if (!c) {
                                this.remove(employees);
                        }

                        // Refresh the List box
                        Socket s =
                        ➥new Socket("localhost", GETEMPLOYEELIST);
                        InputStream istream = s.getInputStream();
                        ObjectInputStream in =
                        ➥new ObjectInputStream(istream);
                        employees = (IDList)in.readObject();
                        istream.close();
                        s.close();

                        this.add("Center", employees);

                        if (!c) {
                                this.repaint();
                        }
                }
                catch (Exception e) {System.out.println(e.getMessage());}

                repaint();
}
```

Summary

Today's lesson completed the Employee Manager application. The last two days have demonstrated how to create dynamic and small applications. The client class for the application can easily be placed within an HTML page, allowing it to be used over the Internet or an intranet. Using serialization, you were able to create an object server that serves objects to client applications. This approach enables a server to maintain the connection to a database and eliminates the security restrictions placed on Java applets. Because the applet connects back to the original location for the object server, the client application can be an applet that conforms to the current security restrictions on applets.

Using serialization, you can also create complex applications that let the object server handle all business logic, while the client handles only the GUI side of applications.

Workshop

The Workshop provides quiz questions to help you solidify your understanding of the material covered and exercises to give you experience in using what you've learned. The answers are provided in Appendix A, "Quiz and Exercise Answers." Try to understand the quiz and exercise answers before you go on to tomorrow's lesson.

Quiz

1. What Boolean value do you pass to the `Dialog` constructor to indicate that you want a modal dialog?
2. What placeholder do you use in a SQL string?
3. What method links an `ActionListener` interface to a component?
4. What method gets the label of a clicked button?
5. What method makes a window or dialog hidden to the user (besides the `hide()` method)?
6. What two parameters does the `Socket` constructor take?
7. What interface contains the constants for the object server ports that the application uses?
8. What will the `getListBox()` method do if a `false` value is passed to it?
9. What does the `prepareStatement()` method take as a parameter?
10. What method do you use to execute a SQL query using the `PreparedStatement` interface?

Exercise

1. Modify the View Employee dialog box to allow editing of employee information. You will need to add a new server port to allow update information to be sent. You also will need to make the View dialog box editable so that the user can enter new information.

20

Day 21

JDBC and the Future

Today's lesson covers the topics that have been introduced to you in this book. You'll also be introduced to some future topics that are up and coming in the Java and computing worlds. This lesson finishes the book and gives you some insight into what you have learned and where you should go from here.

You learn the following topics today:

- ☐ Database basics
- ☐ Java JDBC API
- ☐ Java 1.1
- ☐ JavaBeans
- ☐ Network computers
- ☐ Java applications
- ☐ Java applets

Database Basics

In this book you have been introduced to some of the basics of relational databases. This book has hopefully given you enough of a base to expand upon. It should not be used as a replacement for the database manuals or other books on database theory, but as a beginning base for those who are new to databases.

This section quickly covers some of the database topics that were introduced in the book.

Select **Statement**

One of the basic uses of databases is to enable users to get a set of results based on a certain criteria of items. The SQL Select statement enables users to construct a query that searches the database for specified data values. These data values can be in one particular table or spread across many tables.

Select statements enable users to retrieve data from the database, but they also enable users to determine which data is returned and how it is returned. Select statements can also include sorting criteria as well as grouping criteria that can return results matching specific aggregate values.

Insert **Statement**

The SQL Insert statement gives users the ability to insert new information into the database. The Insert statement enables the user to specify which table and columns within the table will contain the new information supplied by the user.

Delete **Statement**

The SQL Delete statement gives users the ability to delete information from the database. Users can delete information from a specific table that matches specific criteria, or they can choose to delete all data values contained within a table.

Update **Statement**

The SQL Update statement is used to update information that is currently in the database to new values supplied by the user. The Update statement enables the user to specify which columns take new data values and also which records are to be updated.

DDL

All of the statements listed so far are part of the Data Manipulation Language (DML). SQL also has a Data Definition Language (DDL). Whereas the DML is responsible for manipulating the data in the database, the DDL is responsible for creating the structure of the database. The DDL gives users the ability to create tables, triggers, stored procedures, and other objects.

Tables

In relational databases, information is logically separated into what are referred to as *tables*. Each table contains data that is similar in nature. Tables can contain columns that will actually store the data values. Columns can be of different data types depending on the particular database product.

Some columns can be what are known as *primary key* columns. These columns define each individual record and are unique throughout the table. An example of a primary key column in many databases would be a social security number. No two people should have the same number, so this number can uniquely identify every individual.

Other columns can be *foreign key* columns. Foreign key columns are columns that are part of the primary key in another table. These columns are used to link information contained in two separate tables.

Triggers

Relational databases provide objects that are known as *triggers*. Triggers enable the user to insert business logic into database operations. Triggers can be executed before or after database changes take effect and can perform any type of business logic needed on the changed data. Triggers are often used to handle cascading deletes and inserts.

Stored Procedures

Most databases provide objects that are known as *stored procedures*. These objects are similar to functions or procedures in other programming languages. Stored procedures enable you to group multiple SQL statements and have them execute as a whole. Stored procedures also provide you with some speed increases because the stored procedure is compiled before it is called.

21

Java JDBC API

This book has mainly been an introduction and discussion of the Java JDBC API. The JDBC is Java's method for connecting to database systems. This book has covered most of the JDBC API and used the JDBC to create various data components as well as two applications, each using JDBC in a different way.

This book has introduced you to all of the JDBC interfaces. These interfaces provide the majority of functionality in the JDBC.

CallableStatement **Interface**

The CallableStatement interface enables you to execute SQL stored procedures that return OUT or INOUT parameters. It provides methods for registering parameters as returnable parameters and also provides methods for getting the returned values from the stored procedure.

Connection **Interface**

The Connection interface gives your application a literal connection to the database. It provides various methods for controlling the connection to the database as well as methods for creating various statement objects that can be used to execute SQL statements against the database.

DatabaseMetaData **Interface**

The DatabaseMetaData interface provides the user with a means to get information about the database structure. The interface provides methods for getting information on what features the current database supports. It also provides information on the objects in the database such as the tables, stored procedures, and columns.

Driver **Interface**

The Driver interface is the component that enables you to connect to the database. There are multiple driver interfaces available for almost every type of database product. Each database product requires a separate driver object to handle its specifics. The interface provides the method that enables you to create a connection to the database and to get a Connection object that is used to communicate with the database.

PreparedStatement **Interface**

The PreparedStatement interface enables you to execute dynamic SQL statements and stored procedures. Dynamic SQL statements are statements that do not contain certain criteria, but contain placeholders that can be replaced later by actual data values. The interface provides various methods for setting the parameters for these dynamic statements.

ResultSet **Interface**

The ResultSet interface is the object that is returned by the statement objects when a SQL query statement is executed. The ResultSet interface provides a wrapper for a SQL cursor. The interface can be used to move forward in the cursor and also to access the various data values contained in the cursor.

ResultSetMetaData **Interface**

The ResultSetMetaData interface gives the user extra information about a returned ResultSet object. It provides various methods for getting information about the columns that were returned in the result set. It enables the user to get the number of columns that are in the result set, as well as the name and data type of the columns in the result set.

Statement **Interface**

The Statement interface enables you to execute standard SQL statements and stored procedures. The object can execute any static SQL statement and can execute SQL queries as well as SQL Update statements.

Java 1.1

This book briefly introduced some of the new topics in the new release of Java. The Java 1.1 release provides developers with some new objects and interfaces that enhance the overall use of Java. The Java 1.1 release includes a new event delegation model that provides a better separation of GUI and business logic. Java 1.1 also gives the developer more GUI tools such as pop-up menus and menu shortcuts. Serialization and Remote Method Invocation are also new to the Java 1.1 release. As one of the main topics of this book, the JDBC is another new addition to the Java language.

21

Java 1.1 Event Delegation Model

One of the major complaints developers had about Java was that it was difficult to handle events generated by GUI components. Event handling had to be included in the container object or within the component itself. With the release of Java 1.1, Java now offers developers the ability to create applications that use the new Event Delegation Model. This model enables the developer to place event-handling routines in objects that are separated from the objects that handle placement and creation of GUI objects. This enables developers to separate the implementation of the GUI from the business logic to handle user events. This approach allows for more robust and more object-oriented applications.

Java 1.1 Pop-Up Menus and Menu Shortcuts

Java 1.1 has also introduced some new GUI components that developers can use. The `PopupMenu` component enables developers to create menus that can be displayed to the user when the user performs a specified action such as right-clicking a component. These menus provide component-specific actions and are readily accessible by the user.

Java 1.1 has also introduced the `MenuShortcut` object. This object enables developers to include shortcuts to often-used menu items. These shortcuts enable the user to increase the speed at which he or she uses an application.

Java 1.1 Serialization

The Java 1.1 release has also introduced *object serialization* for use by developers. Serialization enables applications to send complete objects over streams much like data is sent. It allows the creation of object servers and also enables an application to create persistent objects, because an object can be serialized and loaded in its exact state at a later date.

Serialization also opens up the possibility of creating Java object servers. These servers can be used as a middle tier in an n-tier application. The client and server can request and send information to the object server, and the object server can handle all of the requests transparently to both the client and the server.

Java 1.1 has also introduced some other new objects as well as improved the current objects available to developers. I urge you to convert to the Java 1.1 release and use it as the basis for your Java development. As time goes by, Java will keep improving and becoming a viable solution to today's business problems.

21

JavaBeans

Although not included with the Java 1.1 beta 2 release, JavaBeans is one of the new technologies that Java will support. JavaBeans will let developers create reusable objects that can be used by most of the GUI development tools in the Java world, such as Visual Café, J++, and others. JavaBeans will also enable the creation of larger scale applications as well as allowing more RAD development.

Network Computers

Another new and exciting technology that will affect Java developers is the advent of the network computer. These machines are scaled-down computers that act much like the dumb clients did in the mainframe world. Most of these new computers plan to run some form of the Java operating system. These computers will help spread the use of Java in business applications.

With many claiming that millions of these NCs will be sold this year and in the years to come, we can expect to see more and more Java applications emerging. With the emergence of these Java applications, we'll begin to see more and better quality Java components and utilities.

Java Applications

There has been a lot of talk and discussion about Java applets. Java applets enable applications to be executed and delivered using the Internet. However, there is more promise in the future of Java applications. Java is poised to replace some of the 3GL languages currently available. Some have touted Java as the successor to C++ and SmallTalk. I believe that there is room for all three languages, but I do believe that Java will begin to take on a much more serious business outlook. With the ease of use and power of Java, more and more applications will be developed in Java.

Java Applets

Java applets are going to be influential in making more interactive material available to users of the Web. Applets will let users run applications from Web pages. These applications can be full-featured demos of products or simple animation applets. With the capability to be sent anywhere in the world, applets will become important as international advertisements.

21

Summary

I hope that this book has successfully introduced you to some of the basics of creating Java database applications using the Java JDBC. This book should be an introduction to more advanced research into the Java language. It was written to provide you with a foundation from which to start developing real-world Java applications. It has introduced you to some database basics as well as covered the JDBC API. It also demonstrated how to create useful components that use the JDBC. The applications created in the book involve two very different approaches to creating applications in Java. The first application covered a very basic approach whereas the second application used some new technologies to create a client/server application.

WEEK 3

In Review

This week concludes the book by demonstrating how to create two entirely different applications using Java and JDBC. It also introduced you to some of the new topics with the new release of Java. Hopefully, this book has given you enough examples and illustrations for you to begin creating your own applications using Java and JDBC.

15

16

17

18

19

20

21

APPENDIX
A

Quiz and Exercise Answers

Day 1, "Introduction to JDBC"

Quiz Answers

1. What are some of the advantages of using Java?

   You can use garbage collection, it is multiplatform, easy to learn, object-oriented, and has no pointers.

2. What are some of the disadvantages of using Java?

   Limited GUI and no database access.

3. What language(s) does Java resemble?

   C and C++.

4. What is garbage collection in Java?

   Garbage collection removes unused objects from memory.

5. What is the difference between an application and an applet?

   An application is usually run on a local computer, whereas an applet is run using a browser.

6. What does the `Statement` interface enable you to do?

   It enables you to execute static SQL statements.

7. What does the `executeQuery()` method do?

   It executes a SQL `Select` statement and returns a result set.

8. What is stored in a `ResultSet` object?

   The cursor for a SQL `Select` statement.

9. What three exceptions can be thrown in JDBC applications?

   `SQLException`, `SQLWarning`, and `DataTruncation`

10. What methods usually throw the `SQLException` exception?

    All JDBC methods.

Day 2, "Database Concepts"

Quiz Answers

1. What is a primary key?

   A column (or columns) that uniquely identifies each row in a table.

2. What is a foreign key?

   A column (or columns) from one table that is included in the primary key of another table.

3. What is a VarChar column?

   A column data type that uses only the amount of space needed to hold the data value contained within it.

4. What is the difference between decimal and numeric columns?

   Decimal columns enable you to place floating point numbers, but numeric columns enable you to specify how many digits of precision should be used.

5. What three types of parameters can you pass into a stored procedure?

   IN, OUT, and INOUT parameters.

6. When can triggers be executed?

   Before or after execution of SQL statements.

7. What is the difference between row-level and statement-level triggers?

   Row-level triggers are executed once for every row updated; statement-level triggers are executed once for the entire SQL statement.

8. What is Data Definition Language (DDL)?

   DDL enables you to define the characteristics of the database.

9. What is the syntax for dropping a table using DDL?

   DROP TABLE <tablename>

10. What information does the system table contain?

    It contains information about the various objects in the database, tables, columns, and so on.

Exercise Answers

1. Create a stored procedure that takes in an IN parameter value and returns it in an OUT parameter value.

   Create a basic stored procedure that takes two parameters: one an IN and the other an OUT.

2. Create a table named tTempTable that contains two columns: TempId and TempName. Use DDL to create the table. After you have created the table, go into the SQL Central utility and make TempId an AutoIncrement column. When you have finished creating the table, drop the table using DDL.

```
Create Table tTempTable {
TempId    int,
TempName char(20)
}
drop table tTempTable
```

3. Display the system tables for the current database. After the tables are displayed, look at the data contained in the SYSTABLE table.

Use SQL Anywhere to view the system tables for the current database.

Day 3, "Connecting to a Database"

Quiz Answers

1. In what package does dbAnywhere store the JDBC API?

   `symjava.sql`

2. Why is the JDBC API stored in a different package than the proposed package?

   Browsers provide security that will not load `java.*` packages.

3. What method of the `Driver` object will create a connection to the database?

   `connect();`

4. What method will get the properties needed to connect to the database?

   `getPropertyInfo();`

5. What is the login timeout?

   The time the driver will wait for a connection to the database before returning an error.

6. What method can change the logging/tracing stream used by the `DriverManager`?

   `setLogStream();`

7. What does a driver need to support in order to be JDBC-compliant?

   JDBC API.

8. In what system property does the `DriverManager` object look for `Driver` objects?

   `jdbc.drivers`

9. List the three different methods that the `DriverManager` can use to create a connection to the database.

   `getConnection(String), getConnection(String, Properties),`
   `getConnection(String,String,String)`

10. For what type of applications should Sybase SQL Anywhere be used?

    Smaller to mid-size applications having less than 100 users.

Exercise Answers

1. Create a database Login window that prompts the user for all properties required to connect to the database. Use the `getPropertyInfo()` method.

   Create a window that asks the user for a username and password and then determines what other properties are needed using the `getPropertyInfo()` method.

2. Use both the `Driver` object and `DriverManager` object to create connections to the database.

   Use the `Driver.connect()` and `DriverManager.getConnection()` method to create connections to the database.

Day 4, "Database Transactions"

Quiz Answers

1. What is a logical unit of work?

   A statement or a group of statements that performs one general function.

2. What is contained within a transaction log?

   The list of statements executed against the database since the last `commit` or `rollback`.

3. What setting of `AutoCommit` will force a `commit` after every SQL statement?

   `TRUE` (on)

4. Describe the difference between the `commit` and `rollback`.

   `commit` will clear the log and make the settings permanent; `rollback` will clear the log and reset the database to its original state.

5. What does the `CEILING` function do?

   Returns the smallest integer larger than the specified number.

6. What would the `FLOOR` function return if passed 7.4?

   7

7. What does the `SOUNDEX` function do?

   Returns an integer value that represents the string.

8. What does the `TRIM` function do?

   Removes all leading and trailing spaces.

9. What does the DATALENGTH function return?

Returns the size of the column, in bytes, for a table.

10. What does the NOW function return?

Returns the current date and time.

Exercise Answers

1. Write and execute a SQL statement that returns the current date and time.

Use the NOW() method to get the current date and time.

2. Write and execute a SQL statement that displays the last name of all employees and the SOUNDEX value for each name.

Use the SOUNDEX() method to display soundex values for employees:

```
select soundex(lastname) from tEmployee
```

3. Write and execute a SQL statement that displays the DATALENGTH for the last name column.

```
Select DATALENGTH(lastname) from tEmployee
```

Day 5, "JDBC Interfaces"

Quiz Answers

1. What is the difference between a connection and a statement?

A connection is a link to a database; a statement is used to send commands to a database.

2. Why would you use the execute() method of the Statement object?

If the SQL statement returned multiple results.

3. What is the difference between having AutoCommit on or off?

AutoCommit on will commit after every statement; off will force the user to issue commits.

4. Describe the effects of commit and rollback.

commit will clear the log and make changes permanent; rollback will clear the log and reset the database to its original state.

5. Is a `Statement` object used for static or dynamic SQL statements?

It is used for static statements.

6. What is the difference between `ExecuteQuery()` and `ExecuteUpdate()`?

`ExecuteQuery()` will execute a SQL `Select` statement. `ExecuteUpdate()` will execute SQL `Insert`, `Delete`, and `Update` statements.

7. How do you create a `DatabaseMetaData` objcct?

Use the `getMetaData()` method.

8. What are the different types of database tables?

User tables and system tables.

9. What is the syntax for getting a list of columns for a table?

`getColumns()`

10. What is the difference between `getExportedKeys()` and `getImportedKeys()`?

Exported keys are primary keys in a table that are used in other tables, whereas imported keys are columns used in a table that are part of the primary key in another table.

Exercise Answers

1. Create an application that opens two connections to the database using different usernames.

Create a connection to the database, change the username in the properties object, and then make another connection to the database.

2. Write a stored procedure that performs an endless loop and call the stored procedure from a thread running in an application. In a separate thread, cancel the execution of the SQL statement.

Use the `cancel()` method of the `Statement` object in the thread to cancel execution of the stored procedure.

3. Use the `supportsOuterJoins()` method to determine whether your database supports outer joins. If the database supports outer joins, return all employees regardless of whether they have an article in tArticle; otherwise, return a listing of all employees who have articles in tArticle.

Create a SQL statement using an outer join to get information from the database.

Day 6, "Prepared Statements and Callable Statements"

Quiz Answers

1. What character do you use to indicate a dynamic parameter?

   The ? character.

2. What three different types of parameters can be passed to a stored procedure?

   `IN`, `OUT`, and `INOUT`.

3. What method is used to create a `PreparedStatement` object?

   `prepareStatement(String)`

4. What method is used to create a `CallableStatement` object?

   `prepareCall(String)`

5. What does the `registerOutParameter()` method do?

   It labels a parameter as being an `OUT` parameter so that it can be accessed after execution.

6. What does the `wasNull()` method tell you?

   Determines whether the last item read was `NULL`.

7. What are some advantages to using stored procedures?

   Allows for execution of multiple SQL statements, faster processing, and simplified development.

8. What are some advantages to using dynamic SQL statements?

   They execute the same SQL statement with different parameters.

9. What is an `INOUT` parameter?

   A parameter that contains a value going into the procedure but can contain a different value when the procedure is finished.

10. What is the difference between an `IN` and `OUT` parameter?

    `IN` procedures have values going into the procedure; `OUT` parameters have values coming out of the procedure.

Exercise Answers

1. Write a stored procedure that lets you pass a last name to the procedure and get the number of employees who have that last name back as an `OUT` parameter.

The procedure will need to look similar to the following:

```
procedure getCount (varchar emp IN, int count OUT)
select count(*) from tEmployee where LastName = emp
```

2. Create a dynamic SQL statement that deletes items from tEmployee based on the employee's Social Security number.

   The SQL statement should look like this:

   ```
   Delete from tEmployee where SSN = ?
   ```

3. Create a dynamic SQL statement that lets you specify the FirstName, LastName, MiddleInitial, and SSN columns through the setXXX() methods of the PreparedStatement object.

   The SQL statement should look like this:

   ```
   Insert into tEmployee(FirstName, MiddleInitial, LastName, SSN)
   Values (?, ?, ?, ?)
   ```

   You can then use the setString() methods to set each column value.

Day 7, "Result Sets and Metadata"

Quiz Answers

1. In what two ways can you specify a column when you use the getXXX() method?

   By name or by index.

2. How can you delete a record using the ResultSet object's cursor?

   Use getCursorName().

3. On what record is the cursor initially positioned in the ResultSet object?

   The cursor is positioned on a NULL record before the first record.

4. What method moves you to the next record in the result set?

   next()

5. Is there any way to move the cursor to the previous record? If so, what is it?

   No.

6. What is an AutoIncrementing column?

   A column that automatically inserts a new number into the column.

7. How is the column name different from the column label?

   The column name is the name as listed in the table schema; the label is what should be displayed to the user.

8. What is the precision of a column?

The number of digits each data value will contain.

9. What does the `getColumnDisplaySize()` method do?

Gets the number of characters that are needed to display the full column.

10. How do you determine whether a column can accept SQL NULL values?

`isNULLable()`

Exercise Answers

1. Write an application that gives the user an option to delete the current row in the query. Use the `getCursorName()` method to implement the solution.

Use the `getCursorName()` method to get the name of the cursor and pass it as the parameter to a SQL `delete` statement.

2. Write an application that enables the user to select a column from the query and view information such as whether the column can accept NULLs, whether the column is an AutoIncrement column, and so on.

Use the `isNULLable()` method of the `DatabaseMetaData` interface to determine whether a column will allow NULLs.

Day 8, "Creating JDBC/SQL Objects"

Quiz Answers

1. How many sections does a standard SQL `Select` statement contain?
Three.

2. In a `Select` statement, what does the `From` clause specify?
The tables that should be looked through.

3. What does the `setRow()` method do?
Sets the row for the object.

4. How would you determine which row the `Select` object is currently on?
The `getRow()` method.

5. What is the difference between specifying columns and not specifying columns in the first section of the `Insert` statement?

Not specifying columns means that you have to include all column data values in the correct order.

6. Why should you always specify columns in an Insert statement?

   So that you will be insulated from database changes.

7. What would be the syntax to delete all records from tMyTable?

   Delete from tMyTable

8. How would you delete all records from tMyTable using the Delete object?

   Use the deleteAll(String) method.

9. What is specified in the Set section of the SQL Update statement?

   The column that will be updated.

10. If getSuccess() returns false, was the execution of the SQL statement successful or not?

    The execution was not successful.

Exercise Answers

1. Add functionality to the Select object to enable the user to get the names of the columns in the result set.

   Create a getColumnName() method that will get a value from an array that contains the column names. The array should be populated by the retrieve() method with the column names retrieved from the ResultSetMetaData object.

2. Add functionality to all SQL objects to allow multiple statements to be executed. Hint: A new method needs to be created to use a Connection object and a new SQL statement.

   Create a setSQL() method that will set the new SQL statement and then re-retrieve.

Day 9, "The Data Interfaces"

Quiz Answers

1. What are the four data interfaces that you will be using to build the data components?

   DataConnection, DataComponent, DataUpdate, and DataNavigation

2. What is the difference between the two different setConnection() methods?

   One will reset the component, whereas the other gives the user the option to reset the component.

3. What value does the `retrieve()` method return?

    The number of records retrieved.

4. What are the four SQL types that are used in the `DataUpdate` interface?

    `DELETE`, `INSERT`, `UPDATE`, and `SELECT`

5. What is the purpose of the `previewStatement()` method?

    It enables the user to add application-specific business logic.

6. What does the `reset()` method do?

    Clears all settings for the component.

7. What method would you use to set the record position to the fifth record?

    `setRow()`

8. What value does the `getColumnType()` method return?

    An integer that contains a predefined constant identifying the data type.

9. List the two ways in which you can move the record position to the initial record.

    `first()` and `setRow(1)`

10. List the two ways in which you can move the record position to the last record.

    `last()` and `setRow(getRow())`

Exercise Answers

1. Create a new interface `DataModification` that will provide functionality to add new records and delete current records. It should implement the `insert()` and `delete()` methods.

    The interface should declare two methods, `insert()` and `delete()`, and provide for appropriate parameters as needed in your application.

2. Add a method in the `DataNavigation` interface that will enable you to move to any record in the data component. You will code the method in the data component chapters.

    Create a method in `DataNavigation` that will be similar to `setRow()`.

3. Add a method in the `DataComponent` interface that will enable you to change the column being displayed. You will code the method in the data component chapters (Days 9 through 14).

    Add a method that will switch information for two specified columns. Make sure that all information for the columns is switched.

Day 10, "The DataLabel, DataField, and DataArea Components"

Quiz Answers

1. What constructor gives you the most initial options to specify?

   `DataField(length, Connection, sql, boolean)`

2. What is the difference between the two `setConnection()` methods?

   One enables the user to reset the component, whereas the other forces a reset of the component.

3. What does the `retrieve()` method do?

   It retrieves data from the database.

4. Describe what the `setRow()` method does.

   It moves the current record to a specified valid record.

5. What does the `getColumnType()` method return?

   It returns the type of the column specified.

6. What two values are passed to the `previewStatement()` method?

   The SQL statement to be executed and the type of statement.

7. What does returning a `false` from the `previewStatement()` do?

   Cancels the execution of a particular SQL statement.

8. Name two ways to set the record to the initial record immediately.

   `first()` and `setRow(1)`

9. What does `setItem()` enable you to do?

   Set the data value for a particular item.

10. How do you specify an update table to be tEmployeeAddress?

    `setUpdateTable("tEmployeeAddress")`

Exercise Answers

1. Extend the DataExample application to enable users to click an update button to update the component with any new information entered by the user.

   Create a button that will call the `update()` method when executed.

2. Add an insert() and delete() method to the component. They can perform immediate inserts and deletes (easier) or wait until the user calls the update() method (more difficult).

   The insert method should add information to the end of the Hashtable object, and the update() method should be changed to handle extra items. The Delete method should mark the item in the hash table for deletion, and the update() method should recognize the deleted items.

3. Inherit the component and add code to the previewStatement() method so that it will not perform any updates on the column FirstName.

   Inherit the previewStatement() method and return false whenever the SQL statement contains the value FirstName.

Day 11, "The DataList and DataChoice Components"

Quiz Answers

1. List all of the constructor methods for the DataList component.

   DataList(), DataList(int), DataList(int, Connection, string), DataList(int, Connection, String, boolean)

2. How do you have the component retrieve data without calling the retrieve() method?

   Use the DataList(int, Connection, String, boolean) method and pass it a true value.

3. What method enables you to change the Connection object?

   setConnection()

4. How would you change the Connection object without resetting the component?

   setConnection(Connection, false)

5. How would you get the number of records in the component?

   rowCount()

6. What two items must be specified for an update to occur?

   Update the table name and at least one update column.

7. What does the previewStatement() method return and what does it mean?

   It returns a Boolean value indicating whether the SQL statement should be executed.

8. Initially, are the records in the component and the items in the list the same?

    Yes.

9. How can you add new items to the list for display?

    `addItem()`

10. How can you display the last column in the component (there are two ways)?

    `last(), setRow(getRow())`

Exercise Answers

1. Add functionality to change the current column being displayed. You can do this by changing the order of the Hashtable objects and columns.

    Add a method that switches all values for two particular columns. You will also need to change the items displayed and stored to match the new column values.

2. Add functionality to delete items in the list. You will need to make sure that the item is deleted from the `values` object.

    Add a `deleteItem()` that deletes a specified item from the list. You will also need to delete the value from the Hashtable object that stores the displayed values.

3. Write an application that uses a DataField component to populate a DataList component. The DataField component should retrieve all items from the database that match the current string in the DataField. Therefore, `Ho` in the DataField should display all of the entries in the DataList from the database that start with `Ho`.

    The application should use the SQL `Like` command to get all values that are like the entered value.

Day 12, "The DataCheckBox Component"

Quiz Answers

1. What are the two variables that indicate on and off for the component?

    `onCheck` and `offCheck`

2. What does the `DataCheckBox(String label)` constructor method do?

    Create the check box object with a label.

3. What does the `setConnection(Connection, boolean)` method do?

    Changes the `Connection` object and resets or doesn't reset the component depending on the Boolean value.

4. How can you change the `Connection` object without resetting the other variables in the component?

    `setConnection(Connection, false)`

5. How can you specify the SQL statement for the component?

    `setSQL()`

6. What is the difference between the `User` and `Original` Hashtable objects?

    The `Original` object stores the data values retrieved from the database, the `User` object stores values entered by the user.

7. What method would you call to reset the component?

    `reset()`

8. What will happen if you call the `next()` method and no next record exists?

    The component will remain on the current record.

9. What will happen if you call the `update()` method and have not specified an update table?

    The update will not occur.

10. What does the `getColumnType()` method return?

    This method returns the column type as a predefined integer value.

Exercise Answers

1. Write an application using a table of your choice that contains a yes/no switch. Write the application with one check box that will display the value contained in the column.

    Use the sample application created today to create the new application.

2. Create a new component from the DataCheckBox that implements both `insert()` and `delete()` methods. For the delete, you should keep the data values stored in an extra Hashtable object, or some other object that can keep multiple dynamic objects.

    Create new `insert()` and `delete()` functionality that should enable the user to insert and delete items from the component.

3. After you create the methods in Exercise 2, add a new `update()` method that will save the data. You will need to check to see whether the item has been added for the insert and deleted for the delete. If the item has been added, create a SQL `Insert` statement. If the item was deleted, then create a SQL `Delete` statement.

    The update method should be able to handle insertions and deletions of data as specified by the user.

Day 13, "The DataNavigator Component"

Quiz Answers

1. Why doesn't the DataNavigator implement some of the data interfaces?

   Not all of the functionality is required for the component.

2. How does the DataNavigator store the connected components?

   In a hash table of objects.

3. Name the four buttons on the DataNavigator component.

   First, Previous, Next, and Last.

4. How would you hide the Last button?

   ```
   showLast(false);
   ```

5. How would you show the Last button?

   ```
   showLast(true);
   ```

6. How would you add a component to the DataNavigator?

   ```
   addComponent()
   ```

7. What method does the DataNavigator implement from the DataUpdate interface?

   ```
   update()
   ```

8. What does the `retrieve()` method return?

   The maximum number of records retrieved from any component.

9. What is stored in the `max` variable?

   The maximum number of records retrieved from any component.

10. Name some differences between the DataNavigator component and the other data components.

    This component does not directly store any data values.

Exercise Answers

1. Add functionality to the DataNavigator component to remove a component based on a passed index.

   Add a `removeComponent()` method that removes components from the list of components in the object.

2. Add functionality to add DataNavigator components as components of the DataNavigator.

Add a method that will add a DataNavigator component to the list of components.

Day 14, "The DataPanel Component"

Quiz Answers

1. How is the DataPanel component different from the other components?

   It displays more than one column's data values.

2. What method enables you to get the number of records that are in the result set?

   `recordCount()`

3. What is displayed in the description labels on the panel?

   The column name.

4. What does the `retrieve()` method do differently than the other components?

   Adds the `Label` components to the panel.

5. What layout does the component use to display the `Label` objects?

   `GridLayout`

Exercise Answers

1. Change the component so that the data labels can be edited. (Note: You will need to make the objects into text fields.)

   Change the data array from `Label` objects to `TextField` objects, and then in `retrieve()`, create `TextField` objects for display.

2. Create a `setVisible(int, boolean)` method that will enable you to determine whether certain columns are displayed.

   The object you create should implement another array that contains Boolean values for each column. If the value is `false`, then methods to display column data should not display particular columns.

Day 15, "Creating the Knowledge Base Application GUI"

A

Quiz Answers

1. Why are you using the same `Connection` object for all windows?

   So that you don't have to create multiple connections to the database.

2. What does the `dbConnect()` method do?

   It connects the application to the database.

3. Why do you clear all articles before adding new items in the `getArticles()` method?

   So that duplicate articles do not appear in the list.

4. Why is it important to always close the `Statement` object after you use it?

   So that the resources used by the object are released back to the system.

5. What event handles all of the user's actions on the window?

   `handleEvent()`

6. Why do you change the cursor before displaying a new window?

   So that the user has some indication that the process is working.

7. What is the purpose of the `displaySearchArticles()` method?

   To display articles that match a specified keyword.

8. Why do you use a splash screen?

   To give the user something to be occupied with while the application loads.

9. What method gets the current `Toolkit` object for the component?

   `getToolkit()`

10. What method draws an image on the component?

    `drawImage()`

Exercise Answers

1. Change the image and text displayed on the splash screen to reflect your own information.

   Change the image that is retrieved to be your own image.

2. Add a Help menu option to the main window's menu.

Create a new menu that contains the Help menu option.

Day 16, "Handling Events in the Knowledge Base"

Quiz Answers

1. What information does the About dialog box display?

Application and company information.

2. Where is the About dialog box called from?

From the Help menu.

3. What does the `Resources Choice` object display?

The application and/or technologies that an article is associated with.

4. What is entered into the article keyword edit field?

Keywords that will be identified with the article.

5. What two items are checked to ensure that the user has entered values in the Add dialog box?

Article title and article text.

6. What Java object is used to parse the keywords entered by the user?

`StringTokenizer`

7. What does the `hasMoreTokens()` method tell you?

Whether there are more keywords left to process.

Exercise Answers

1. Change the Add Article dialog box to use `PreparedStatement` objects that use dynamic SQL statements that accept parameters.

Change the dialog box to use the `PreparedStatement` object in place of the `Statement` object, and then use the `setXXX()` methods to set the parameters.

2. Change the text in the About dialog box to display your name, company name, and a short description.

Change the text displayed in the About dialog box to personal information.

3. Create a message box that will be displayed when the user does not enter a title or an article. Let the user know that those items are required.

Create a dialog box that will be displayed when the user needs to display a line of text to the user.

Day 17, "Using the Database in the Knowledge Base"

Quiz Answers

1. What must the Layout Manager be set to in order to alter component sizes manually?

   NULL

2. What is the method used to change the size and placement of a component manually?

   reshape()

3. What is a modal window?

   A window that is active until it is closed.

4. If a dialog box is modal, can the user switch between the application window and the dialog box window?

   No.

5. What three arguments are passed to the constructor for the Dialog class?

   Parent frame, a title, and a Boolean value indicating modal state.

6. Why is it always a good idea to close a Statement object manually?

   To free resources that are used by an object.

7. What is an orphaned record?

   A record that is left in the database but has no parent information.

8. Why should you always delete child records before deleting the main record?

   To prevent orphaned records.

9. What table contains the keywords that the user entered for the article?

   tKeyword

10. What is the method called by the Search Articles dialog box to display the articles in the main window?

    displaySearchArticles()

Exercise Answers

1. Create a new window that lets the user edit article information. It should let the user change only the article text.

   Create a dialog box similar to the dialog box that adds information, but display old information and let the user update old information in the database.

2. Modify the `displaySearchArticles()` method for the main window so that it allows multiple keyword searching. Use a `StringTokenizer` to separate the entered text into words.

   Create variable-length SQL statements that allow for multiple keyword searching using the `OR` method.

3. Make the dialog box for searching articles be modeless and have it come up at the same time that the main window comes up so that it can search articles and view them directly.

   Change the Boolean passed to the dialog box to `false` so that the dialog box can be modeless.

Day 18, "Creating an Employee Resource Applet"

Quiz Answers

1. What interface in Java 1.1 enables you to "listen" for normal mouse events?

   `MouseListener`

2. What method adds an `ActionListener` interface to listen to events for a specified component?

   `addActionListener()`

3. What method returns the name of the menu item selected?

   `getActionCommand()`

4. What method displays a pop-up menu to the user?

   `show()`

5. What is passed to the `show()` method of the `PopupMenu` object?

   A container object and the position to display at.

6. Name the two objects used to allow serialization in Java.

   `ObjectOutputStream` and `ObjectInputStream`

7. What method enables you to write an integer to a stream using `ObjectOutputStream`?

   `writeInt()`

8. What method enables you to read an object from a stream using `ObjectInputStream`?

   `readObject()`

9. What parameter does the `MenuShortcut` constructor take?

   An integer value identifying an ASCII character.

10. What does RMI stand for?

    Remote Method Invocation.

Exercise Answers

1. Create a frame with two different list boxes. Display different `PopupMenu` objects for each list.

   Create two lists on a frame and then create two different pop-up menus for the frame. In the `mouseClicked()` method, check for which component generated the event and display the appropriate pop-up menu.

2. Create a frame that lets the user serialize the entire frame at any time. (Use either a `Button` or `MenuItem`.)

   Create a button that will serialize its parent into a local file using `ObjectOutputStream`.

Day 19, "Handling Events in the Employee Resource Applet"

Quiz Answers

1. How many thread objects will the object server use for client connections?

   Seven

2. What is the URL for the database we are using?

   `jdbc:odbc:JDBC`

3. What method of the IDList component returns the employee ID for the selected item?

   `getSelectedID()`

4. What object is used to listen for client connections?

    `ServerSocket`

5. What method connects a client to a server?

    `accept()`

6. What method is used to get the output stream for a socket object?

    `getOutputStream()`

7. What method is used to read `String` objects from an object stream?

    `readObject()`

8. What method clears the contents of an object output stream to ensure that the client receives the data?

    `flush()`

9. What is the purpose of the `Delete` object?

    To delete specified employees from the database.

10. What object is used to send the `deleteEmployeeDialog` to the client?

    `ObjectOutputStream`

Exercise Answer

1. Now that you have an idea of how to send and receive information using serialization and sockets, create a small application that will serve various objects from an object server to client machines. The application could enable a user to get Java objects that are already created on the server.

    Use the sample Employee Application to create your sample application.

Day 20, "Creating the Employee Resource Application Server"

Quiz Answers

1. What Boolean value do you pass to the `Dialog` constructor to indicate that you want a modal dialog?

    `true`

2. What placeholder do you use in a SQL string?

    The question mark (?).

3. What method links an `ActionListener` interface to a component?

   `addActionListener()`

4. What method gets the label of a clicked button?

   `getActionCommand()`

5. What method makes a window or dialog hidden to the user (besides the `hide()` method)?

   `setVisible()`

6. What two parameters does the `Socket` constructor take?

   Host name and port number.

7. What interface contains the constants for the object server ports that the application uses?

   `EmpServices`

8. What will the `getListBox()` method do if a `false` value is passed to it?

   Remove the current list before adding the new list.

9. What does the `prepareStatement()` method take as a parameter?

   A SQL statement string.

10. What method do you use to execute a SQL query using the `PreparedStatement` interface?

    `executeQuery()`

Exercise Answer

1. Modify the View Employee dialog box to allow editing of employee information. You will need to add a new server port to allow update information to be sent. You also will need to make the View dialog box be editable so that the user can enter new information.

   Change the fields in the View dialog to be editable and then create a new server port that will accept the update information and send it to the database.

INDEX

A

A VIACOM SERVICE

The Information SuperLibrary™

Bookstore

Search

What's New

Reference

Software

Newsletter

Company Overviews

Yellow Pages

Internet Starter Kit

HTML Workshop

Win a Free T-Shirt!

Macmillan Computer Publishing

Site Map

Talk to Us

CHECK OUT THE BOOKS IN THIS LIBRARY.

You'll find thousands of shareware files and over 1600 computer books designed for both technowizards and technophobes. You can browse through 700 sample chapters, get the latest news on the Net, and find just about anything using our massive search directories.

All Macmillan Computer Publishing books are available at your local bookstore.

We're open 24-hours a day, 365 days a year.

You don't need a card.

We don't charge fines.

And you can be as **LOUD** as you want.

The Information SuperLibrary

http://www.mcp.com/mcp/ ftp.mcp.com

MACMILLAN COMPUTER PUBLISHING USA

A VIACOM COMPANY

Technical ---- Support:

If you need assistance with the information in this book or with a CD/Disk accompanying the book, please access the Knowledge Base on our Web site at **http://www.superlibrary.com/general/support**. Our most Frequently Asked Questions are answered there. If you do not find the answer to your questions on our Web site, you may contact Macmillan Technical Support **(317) 581-3833** or e-mail us at **support@mcp.com**.

Java 1.1 Unleashed, Second Edition

—Michael Morrison, et al.

Java 1.1 Unleashed, Second Edition is an expanded and updated version of the largest, most comprehensive Java book on the market. It covers Java, Java APIs, JavaOS, just-in-time compilers, and more. The CD-ROM includes sample code, examples from the book, and bonus electronic books.

Price: $49.99 USA/$70.95 CDN   *User level: Intermediate–Advanced*
ISBN: 1-57521-197-1   *1,224 pages*

Tricks of the Java Programming Gurus

—Glenn Vanderburg, et al.

This book is a guide for the experienced Java programmer who wants to take his Java skills beyond simple animations and applets. It shows the reader how to streamline his Java code, how to achieve unique results with undocumented tricks, and how to add advanced level functions to his existing Java programs. Skilled Java professionals show how to improve garbage collection before and after compilation for improved performance. The CD-ROM includes all the source code from the book.

Price: $39.99 USA/$56.95 CDN   *User level: Accomplished–Expert*
ISBN: 1-57521-102-5   *880 pages*

Java Developer's Guide

—Jamie Jaworski & Carie Jardeen

Java is one of the major growth areas for developers on the World Wide Web. It brings with it the ability to download and run small applications called applets from a Web server. *Java Developer's Guide* teaches developers everything they need to know to effectively develop Java applications. This book explores new technology and future trends of Java development. The CD-ROM includes source code from the book and valuable utilities.

Price: $49.99 USA/$67.99 CDN   *User level: Accomplished–Expert*
ISBN: 1-57521-069-x   *768 pages*

Microsoft SQL Server 6.5 Unleashed, Second Edition

—David Solomon, et al.

This comprehensive reference details the steps needed to plan, design, install, administer, and tune large and small databases. In many cases, the readers will use the techniques in this tome to create and manage their own complex environments. Covers programming topics, including SQL, data structures, programming constructs, stored procedures, referential integrity, large table strategies, and more. Includes updates to cover all new features of SQL Server 6.5 including the new transaction processing monitor and Internet/database connectivity through SQL Server's new Web Wizard.

Price: $59.99 USA/$84.95 CDN   *User level: Accomplished–Expert*
ISBN: 0-672-30956-4   *1,272 pages*

Oracle Unleashed

—Various authors

Oracle programmers and developers will quickly learn the basics and advanced topics of Oracle. This book includes in-depth coverage of Oracle tools and utilities, database administration, Designer 2000, and Developer 2000. *Oracle Unleashed* covers every key development tool produced by Oracle and will prove itself as the most definitive study of Oracle Publication Date. The CD-ROM contains Oracle Sampler, source code, object libraries, and sample utilities.

Price: $59.99 USA/$81.95 CDN   *User level: Accomplished–Expert*
ISBN: 0-672-30872-X   *1,404 pages*

Teach Yourself Visual J++ in 21 Days

—Laura Lemay, Patrick Winters, and David Blankenbeckler

Readers will learn how to use Visual J++, Microsoft's Windows version of Java, to design and create Java applets for the World Wide Web. Visual J++ includes many new features to Java including visual resource editing tools, source code control, syntax coloring, visual project management, and integrated bills. All of these tools are covered in detail, giving readers the information they need to write professional Java applets for the Web. Includes information on the Java class libraries and how to use them to create specific applet effects and provides a detailed tutorial for developing applications with the new Java.

Price: $39.99 USA/$56.95 CDN   *User level: Causal–Accomplished*
ISBN: 1-57521-158-0   *592 pages*

Web Programming Unleashed

—Bob Breedlove, et al.

This comprehensive book explores all aspects of the latest technology craze: Internet programming. Programmers will turn to the proven expertise of the *Unleashed* series for accurate, day-and-date information on this hot new programming subject. The CD-ROM includes complete source code for all applications in the book, additional programs with accompanying source code, and several Internet application resource tools.

Price: $49.99 USA/$70.95 CDN   *User level: Accomplished–Expert*
ISBN: 1-57521-117-3   *1,056 pages*

Java Developer's Reference

—Mike Cohn, et al.

This is the informative, resource-packed development package for professional developers. It explains the components of the Java Development Kit (JDK) and the Java programming language. Everything you need to program Java is included within this comprehensive reference, making it the tool developers will turn to over and over again for timely and accurate information on Java and the JDK. The CD-ROM contains source code from the book and powerful utilities.

Price: $59.99 USA/$84.95 CDN   *User level: Accomplished–Expert*
ISBN: 1-57521-129-7   *1,296 pages*

Add to Your Sams.net Library Today
with the Best Books for Internet Technologies

ISBN	Quantity	Description of Item	Unit Cost	Total Cost
1-57521-197-1		Java 1.1 Unleashed, Second Edition (Book/CD-ROM)	$49.99	
1-57521-102-5		Tricks of the Java Programming Gurus (Book/CD-ROM)	$39.99	
1-57521-069-X		Java Developer's Guide (Book/CD-ROM)	$49.99	
0-672-30956-4		Microsoft SQL Server 6.5 Unleashed, Second Edition (Book/CD-ROM)	$59.99	
0-672-30872-X		Oracle Unleashed (Book/CD-ROM)	$59.99	
1-57521-158-0		Teach Yourself Visual J++ in 21 Days (Book/CD-ROM)	$39.99	
1-57521-117-3		Web Programming Unleashed (Book/CD-ROM)	$49.99	
1-57521-129-7		Java Developer's Reference (Book/CD-ROM)	$59.99	
		Shipping and Handling: See information below.		
		TOTAL		

Shipping and Handling: $4.00 for the first book, and $1.75 for each additional book. If you need to have it NOW, we can ship product to you in 24 hours for an additional charge of approximately $18.00, and you will receive your item overnight or in two days. Overseas shipping and handling adds $2.00. Prices subject to change. Call between 9:00 a.m. and 5:00 p.m. EST for availability and pricing information on latest editions.

201 W. 103rd Street, Indianapolis, Indiana 46290

1-800-428-5331 — Orders   1-800-835-3202 — Fax   1-800-858-7674 — Customer Service

Book ISBN 1-57521-123-8

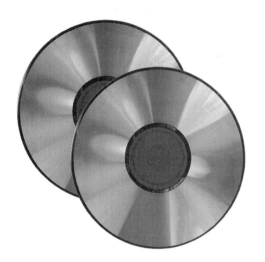

What's on the Disc

The companion CD-ROM contains all of the authors' source code and samples from the book and many third-party software products.

Windows 95 Installation Instructions

1. Insert the CD-ROM into your CD-ROM drive.
2. From the Windows 95 desktop, double-click the My Computer icon.
3. Double-click the icon representing your CD-ROM drive.
4. Double-click the icon titled SETUP.EXE to run the installation program.
5. Installation creates a program group named TY DB PROG JDBC. This group contains icons to browse the CD-ROM.

NOTE

> If Windows 95 is installed on your computer and you have the AutoPlay feature enabled, the SETUP.EXE program starts automatically whenever you insert the disc into your CD-ROM drive.

Windows NT Installation Instructions

1. Insert the CD-ROM into your CD-ROM drive.
2. From File Manager or Program Manager, choose Run from the File menu.
3. Type `<drive>\SETUP.EXE` and press Enter, where `<drive>` corresponds to the drive letter of your CD-ROM. For example, if your CD-ROM is drive D:, type `D:\SETUP.EXE` and press Enter.
4. Installation creates a program named TY DB PROG JDBC. This group contains icons to browse the CD-ROM.